Stairway to *Nirvāṇa*

Stairway to *Nirvāṇa*

A Study of the Twenty *Saṃghas* Based on the Works of Tsong kha pa

James B. Apple

State University of New York Press

Published by
State University of New York Press, Albany

Printed in the United States of America

For information, contact State University of New York Press, Albany, NY
www.sunypress.edu

Production by Dana Foote
Marketing by Anne M. Valentine

Library of Congress Cataloging-in-Publication Data

Apple, James B.
Stairway to nirvana : a study of the twenty samghas based on the works of Tsong kha pa / James B. Apple.
p. cm.
Includes bibliographical references and index.
ISBN 978-0-7914-7375-7 (hardcover : alk. paper)
ISBN 978-0-7914-7376-4 (pbk. : alk. paper)
1. Tson-kha-pa Blo-bzan-grags-pa, 1357–1419. 2. Dge-lugs-pa (Sect)—Doctrines. 3. Abhisamayalankara—Criticism, interpretation, etc. 4. Spiritual life—Mahayana Buddhism. I. Title.

BQ7950.T757A66 2008
294.3'42042—dc22 2007016961

10 9 8 7 6 5 4 3 2 1

CONTENTS

List of Figures and Tables vii

Acknowledgments ix

Abbreviations xi

1 THE TOPIC OF THE TWENTY *SAṂGHAS* 1

Methodological Considerations 4
Tsong kha pa's Hermeneutical Strategy 10
Hermeneutical Strategies in Approaching the Twenty *Saṃghas* 12

2 TSONG KHA PA AND THE *ABHISAMAYĀLAṂKĀRA* COMMENTARIAL TRADITION 21

Indian Predecessors in the *Abhisamayālaṃkāra* Tradition 23
Tsong kha pa's Tibetan Predecessors in the *Abhisamayālaṃkāra* Tradition 31
The *Abhisamayālaṃkāra* and Twenty *Saṃgha*s in Tsong kha pa's Life and Works 36
Summary 46

3 CONTEXTUAL AND DOCTRINAL PRESUMPTIONS 47

Locating the Twenty *Saṃgha*s in the *Abhisamayālaṃkāra* 47
Saṃgha in Early Buddhism and in the *Abhisamayālaṃkāra* 62
Avaivartika-Saṃgha as Refuge in the *Abhisamayālaṃkāra* 65
Path and Yogic Systems of the *Abhisamayālaṃkāra* 66
Cosmological Factors 88
Summary 92

4 ANALYSIS OF THE TWENTY *SAṂGHAS* 93

An Introduction to the Topic from the Root Texts 93
The Allegorical *Saṃgha of Śrāvaka*s 98

5 AN ASSEMBLY OF IRREVERSIBLE *BODHISATTVAS* 149

The Actual *Saṃgha* of *Bodhisattvas* 149
Enumerating *Bodhisattvas* in the *Prajñāpāramitā* 151
Relationship between the Actual *Saṃgha* and the Allegorical *Saṃgha* 171

CONCLUSION 181

Notes 191

Glossary 219

References 237

Index 255

Figures and Tables

Figure 2.1	Tsong kha pa's Lineage of AA Teachings	37
Figure 3.1	Relationship of the Eight Subjects (*padārtha*) of the AA	54
Table 3.1	Ten Factors That Constitute Total Omniscience	57
Table 3.2	Ten Special Instructions for *Bodhisattva*s	61
Table 3.3	Path of Seeing's (*darśanamārga*) Moments of Consciousness	74
Table 3.4	Path Structure Overview	80
Table 3.5	Vehicles (*yāna*) in the *Abhisamayālaṃkāra*	89
Table 3.6	Realms Traveled by Noble Beings on the Path	91
Table 4.1	Terminology Comparison of Indian Buddhist Texts	96
Table 4.2	Stream-enterers	110
Table 4.3	Once-returners	111
Table 4.4	Non-returners	112
Table 4.5	*Arhats*	113
Table 4.6	Tsong kha pa's Division of Distinctive Non-returners (*Anāgāmin*) in the *Śrāvaka Saṃgha* Illustration	126
Figure 4.1	Ten Aspects of the Form Realm Transmigrator	135
Figure 5.1	Twenty *Saṃgha*s According to Ārya Vimuktisena	166
Figure 5.2	Twenty *Saṃgha*s According to Haribhadra and Tsong kha pa	172

ACKNOWLEDGMENTS

Geshe Lhundup Sopa encouraged me to research the topic of the Twenty *Saṃghas* while I was a Buddhist Studies graduate student at the University of Wisconsin–Madison. I can still remember the day many years ago when Geshe Sopa mentioned the word *Abhisamayālaṃkāra* to me. I had never heard of the *Abhisamayālaṃkāra*, nor even the topic of the Twenty *Saṃghas*. Geshe-la has been everything that a true *kalyāṇamitra* could be. Everything I know of Tibetan philosophical language and principles, nuances of *Dge lugs pa Mādhyamika* thought, and of *Mahāyāna* Buddhist soteriology as represented through the *Abhisamayālaṃkāra* I owe to his scholastic guidance. Words cannot relate the many ways in which Geshe-la has benefited my life beyond the life of academic scholarship. I feel truly blessed to have studied under such a learned scholar of the living Tibetan Buddhist scholastic tradition. Any errors in this work, of course, are my sole responsibility.

I would like to thank Dr. John D. Dunne, who served as my dissertation advisor while at University of Wisconsin–Madison when Geshe Sopa retired. John provided much beneficial criticism and advice. A number of tables and figures in chapters 3 and 4 are the result of marathon study sessions under his guidance.

This book is based on a revised version of my doctoral dissertation in Buddhist Studies at the University of Wisconsin–Madison. Material in chapter 1 and chapter 4, including tables and figures, was published in the *Journal of Indian Philosophy* 31 no. 5–6, 2003, pp. 503–592, as "Twenty Varieties of the *Saṃgha* Part 1," by James B. Apple. Material in chapter 5 was published in the *Journal of Indian Philosophy* 32 no. 2–3, 2004, pp. 211–279, as "An Assembly of Irreversible *Bodhisattvas*: Twenty Varieties of the *Saṃgha* Part 2" by James B. Apple. This material has been reproduced with the kind permission of Springer Science and Business Media.

My thanks also go to the multiple universities and colleges in the United States and Canada that furnished me with the resources and the livelihood to focus on the systematic study of Buddhist formations. In particular, I would like to acknowledge the Interdisciplinary Program in Religious Studies at the University of Alberta, directed by

Professor Willi Braun, and the Department of Religious Studies at the University of Alabama, directed by Professor Russell T. McCutcheon, for providing support and funding for computing and copying.

I also want to thank Nancy Ellegate, senior acquisitions editor of State University of New York Press, for her great help and attention in bringing this book to completion. I would like to thank Dana Foote and Kay Butler for their patient and painstaking editing.

I would like to provide a list, in the order that I met them, of the "lineage" of my teachers in the United States, India, and Nepal who have shaped my journey in the understanding of Buddhist and Tibetan cultural formations: Professor Jack Van Horn, Dr. Henopola Gunaratana, Venerable Rahula, Takser Rinpoche Thubtan Jigme Norbu, Geshe Thubtan Thandar, Professor Jan Nattier, Gyurme Kensur Rinpoche Geshe Lobsang Tenzin, Zasep Tulku, Professor Richard Kohn, Professor Dan Martin, Gelek Rinpoche, Geshe Damdul Namgyal, Geshe Lobsang Tenzin Negi, Glenn H. Mullin, Elvin Jones, Geshe Lhundup Sopa, Geshe Sherab Thabkey, Sharpa Tulku, H.H. Dalai Lama Tenzin Gyatso, H.H. Jigdal Dagchen Sakya, C. Robert Pryor, Pema Tenzin, Chos kyi nyi ma Rinpoche, Chobgye Trichen, Lokesh Chandra, and D. S. Ruegg.

I would like to thank my parents, Jeanne Bedwell and James Apple, for their support and advice. Last, but certainly not least, I would like to thank my wife and companion, Shinobu, for all her support and advice throughout the writing of this book.

Abbreviations

AA	*Abhisamayālaṃkāra*
AAĀ	*Abhisamayālaṃkārālokā* of Haribhadra (ed. Wogihara, 1932–1935)
AASPh	*Abhisamayālaṃkārasphuṭārthā* of Haribhadra (ed. Amano, 2000)
AAV	*Abhisamayālaṃkāravṛtti* of Ārya Vimuktisena (ed. Pensa, 1967)
ACIP	Asian Classics Input Project
AK	*Abhidharmakośakārikā* (ed. Gokhale, 1946)
AKBh	*Abhidharmakośabhāṣya* (ed. Pradhan, 1967. Reprint, 1975)
AKV	*Abhidharmakośabhāṣyavyākhyā* (ed. Śāstrī, 1971)
AN	*Aṅguttaranikāya* (ed. Morris and Hardy, 1885–1900)
AS	*Abhidharmasamuccaya* (ed. Pradhan, 1950)
ASBh	*Abhidharmasamuccayabhāṣya* (ed. Tatia, 1976)
Aṣṭa	*Aṣṭasāhasrikāprajñāpāramitāsūtra*
BEFEO	Bulletin de l'Ecole Française d'Extrême-Orient
BHSD	Buddhist Hybrid Sanskrit Dictionary (Edgerton, 1953. Reprint, 1977)
BSOAS	*Bulletin of the School of African & Oriental Studies* (London)
EOB	*Encyclopedia of Buddhism* (G. P. Malalasekara, 1973)
DN	*Dīghanikāya* (Rhys-Davids and Carpenter, Reprint, 1960–1967)
GBBN	*Sgra sbyor bam po gnyis pa* (ed. Ishikawa, 1990)
Golden Garland	*Legs bshad gser phreng* of Tsong kha pa (1970/1977)
IIJ	Indo-Iranian Journal
JAOS	*Journal of the American Oriental Society*
JIABS	*Journal of the International Association for Buddhist Studies*
JIBS	*Indogaku Bukkyō Kenkyū* [Journal of Indian and Buddhist Studies]
JIP	*Journal of Indian Philosophy*

LVP	La Vallèe Poussin's (1923) French translation of AK and AKBh
MHTL	*Materials for a History of Tibetan Literature* (Chandra, 1985)
MN	*Majjhimanikāya* (ed. Trenckner and Chalmers, Reprint, 1960–1964)
MSA	*Mahāyānasūtrālaṃkāra* (ed. Lévi, 1907–1911)
MVP	*Mahāvyutpatti* (1916–1925)
MW	Monier-Williams Sanskrit-English Dictionary (1899)
Pañcaviṃśati	*Pañcaviṃśatisāhasrikāprajñāpāramitāsūtra* (ed. Dutt, 1934)
Pk	Peking edition of the Tibetan Tripiṭaka (ed. Suzuki, 1956–1961)
PP	*Prajñāpāramitā*
PSPh	*Abhisamayālaṃkāraprasphuṭapadā* of Dharmamitra
Pugg	*Puggala-paññatti* (ed. Morris, 1972)
Pugg-A	*Puggala-paññatti-atthakathā* (ed. Landsberg and Davids, 1972)
Rjes gnang	*Dge 'dun nyi shu bsdus pa rjes gnang ba dang zhugs gnas* of Tsong kha pa (1977)
Rnam rgyal	Blo bzang 'phrin las rnam rgyal (1967)
Śgs	*Śūraṃgamasamādhisūtra* (Lamotte 1998)
SN	*Saṃyuttanikāya* (ed. L. Feer, Reprint, 1973–1990)
Stairway	*Blo gsal bgrod pa'i them skas* of Tsong kha pa (1977)
T	*Taishō Shinsū Daizōkyō*
Taipei	Taipei edition of Tibetan Tripiṭaka bka'i 'gyur (ed. Barber, 1991)
Traité	*Le Traité de la Grande Vertu de Sagesse de Nāgārjuna* (Lamotte, 1944–1980)
Vks	*Vimalakīrtinirdeśasūtra* (Lamotte, 1976)
WZKSO	Wiener Zeitschrift für die Kunde süd-und Ostrasiens

1

THE TOPIC OF THE TWENTY *SAṂGHAS*

In Indian and Tibetan Buddhist commentarial literature on the *Prajñāpāramitā (Perfection of Wisdom)*, the "Twenty *Saṃghas*" (Skt. *viṃśatiprabhedasaṃgha*; Tib. *dge 'dun nyi shu*) refers to the stages through which Noble Beings (Skt. *ārya*; Tib. *'phags pa*) may pass in their progress toward *nirvāṇa*[1] through various lifetimes in various cosmological realms. The Twenty Varieties of the *Saṃgha* is a special topic within the Tibetan monastic curriculum and is considered by Indo-Tibetan[2] commentators of the *The Ornament for Clear Realization* (AA; *abhisamayālaṃkāra ≈ mngon par rtogs pa'i rgyan)* tradition to be one of the most difficult topics to comprehend. Its importance as a system reveals not only a soteriological worldview, but also shows the hermenutical and exegetical strategies that Tibetan authors utilize to bring coherence to cryptic, terse verses found in Indian *śāstra*s such as the AA. The Twenty *Saṃgha*s in the AA represents an extension of terminology and doctrinal principles found in the *śrāvaka* vehicle employed as a skillful heuristic device to generate awareness of the *Mahāyāna Saṃgha*. As a typology of ideal figures, the Tibetan exegesis of the Twenty *Saṃghas*, particularly as exhibited by the savant Tsong kha pa (1357–1419), demonstrates a unity in the diversity between the vehicles of *śrāvakas*, *pratyekabuddhas*, and *bodhisattva*s illuminating the ideal of the *saṃgha*.

The subject matter of the "Twenty *Saṃghas*" encompasses a comprehensive list of the stages through which Noble Beings (*ārya*) may pass in their progress toward *nirvāṇa*. This typological list of twenty[3] does not provide a description of any one individual's path to enlightenment; rather, it enumerates all of the *possible* stages through which any given individual might pass, depending upon factors such as that individual's cosmological circumstances and the acuity of his or her faculties. Thus, the Twenty *Saṃghas* presents the defining characteristics of these individuals, providing a complete picture of all possible states on the path to enlightenment. Indian and Tibetan *Mahāyāna*

Buddhist scholars regard this topic as crucially important, and its importance is reflected in the inclusion of the Twenty *Saṃgha*s in the ten topics of special instruction (*avavāda*) mentioned in the body of literature surrounding the AA. The exegetical system of the AA stipulates that *bodhisattvas* must train in these topics of special instruction in order to attain complete omniscience (*sarvākārajñatā*).

Although an extremely complex subject, the topic's title, the "Twenty *Saṃghas*" (*dge 'dun nyi shu*), is well known to Tibetan Buddhists. The topic serves as a *Mahāyāna* Buddhist instruction that centers on one of the three essential components of Tibetan Buddhism: the Buddha, the Dharma, and the *Saṃgha*. In a public discourse on the Stages of the Path (*lam rim*), the Fourteenth Dalai Lama explains the meaning of these "Three Jewels" (Tib. *dkon mchog gsum*; Skt. *triratna*):

> When one meditates on taking refuge in the Three Jewels, one should first generate a recollection of their individual qualities and potencies. . . . [T]aking refuge in the Buddha means that one should meditate on the qualities, wisdoms and powers of a Buddha's body, speech, and mind; refuge in Dharma means that one meditates on all the paths and practices leading to the truth of cessation, or the peace of Nirvāṇa; and refuge in the *Saṃgha* requires an awareness of the twenty types of *Saṃgha*. (Mullin, 1985: 108)

As the distinguished Theravādin Buddhist scholar, Walpola Rahula (1978: 55) has noted, it is important to clearly understand the distinction between what is termed the "spiritual" *saṃgha* and the "institutional" *saṃgha*. The "institutional" *saṃgha* is considered to be the Buddhist community that consists of monks (*bhikṣu*), nuns (*bhikṣuṇī*), and lay followers (*upāsaka*) who follow a code of behavior given in the monastic laws of the *Vinaya*. Custodians of the Dharma, they are the organized, visible, representative body of the *Saṃgha* Jewel and are responsible for its transmission and perpetuation. To understand the "spiritual" *saṃgha* requires an awareness of the twenty types of individuals who are considered to be Noble Beings (*ārya*). Noble Beings are those who have developed a cognitive and meditative understanding of reality (*tattva*) through following the practices of the Buddhist path. The insight gained in this understanding has soteriological[4] value and advances an individual toward *nirvāṇa*. As the renowned Tibetan scholar Geshe Sopa (1985: 156) has mentioned, when an individual attains this level of insight into reality, a stage known as the Noble Path (*āryamārga*), that individual begins to perform all the functions of the *saṃgha* within his or her own person.

The *saṃgha* in this sense refers to the twenty types of Noble Beings who are making progress toward spiritual emancipation. Therefore, Tibetan Buddhists conceive of the *saṃgha* both as an outer object of refuge and as a community of people who follow the values taught by the Buddha, a community to which they can look for guidance and fellowship. Tibetan Buddhists also understand the *saṃgha* to represent "ideal figures as the embodiment and proof of the path" (Buswell and Gimello, 1992: 10). The *saṃgha* in this sense represents those qualities of an ideal figure that provide the structure and worldview in which soteriological results of the path take place. Dreyfus has demonstrated (1997) that the study of the path is the central concept of the Tibetan Buddhist tradition. As Buswell and Gimello (1992: 6) suggest, the path "incorporates, underlies, or presupposes everything else in Buddhism, from the simplest act of charity to the most refined meditative experience and the most rigorous philosophical argument. [It] . . . directs attention . . . to a general pattern of discipline encompassing both the whole life of the individual and corporate life of the whole Buddhist community." Thus, the topic of the Twenty *Saṃgha*s is a soteriological model that is intimately related with the study of the path to *nirvāṇa*.

While soteriologically significant, the objectified, codified, and detailed scholastic descriptions of these ideal figures do not serve as practical guides to Buddhist practice, nor do they provide details of actual spiritual experience. Rather, the topic of the Twenty *Saṃgha*s serves as an archetypal pattern of the worldview in which spiritual liberation is possible for the individual practitioner. What Dreyfus (1997: 62) states for the AA in general, can also be applied to the AA's special topic of the Twenty *Saṃghas*; namely, that it "provides the Tibetan tradition with the framework that makes a narrative of spiritual progress possible and introduces an element of closure without which the commitment required by Buddhist practices cannot be sustained." The topic of the Twenty *Saṃgha*s has this kind of direct soteriological meaning for the Tibetan Buddhist.

The special topic of the Twenty *Saṃgha*s is found in the twenty-third and twenty-fourth verses of the *Abhisamayālaṃkāra*. Sopa (1989: 212) give a brief description of this topic as follows:

> The twenty members of the spiritual community represent a classification of the location and number of lives remaining for practitioners on the way to attaining the fruits of Stream-enterer (*srota-āpanna*,[5] *rgyun du zhugs pa*), Once-returner (*sakṛdāgamin, lan gcig phyir 'ong*), Never-returner (*anāgāmin, phyir mi 'ong*), and *Arhat* (*dgra bcom pa*).

Classification into the one of the four results—Stream-enterer, Once-returner, Non-returner, and *Arhat*—is one of the oldest categorical lists found in the history of Buddhism. The topic is well known to Buddhist Studies, particularly in relation to the Pāli and the Theravādin tradition. The list of four results organizes a sequence of progressive attainments based on moral virtue, meditative cultivation, and cognitive insight through practicing the Noble Eightfold Path (*ārya-aṣṭāṅga-mārga*). In general, a Stream-enterer has fully integrated the stream of the Buddha's teaching (dharma) and is a Noble Being who will never be reborn in a lower cosmological realm as a hell-being, ghost, or animal. A Once-returner will be reborn once more in the desire realm, the ordinary world dominated by sensual gratification. A Never-returner, or Non-returner, will never be born in the desire realm but will attain liberation among the form realm heavens. *Arhat*s have completely overcome karma and mental afflictions (*kleśa*) and are liberated from *saṃsāra*, the unending cycle of birth and death.

Within Tibetan monastic traditions, the Twenty Varieties of the *Saṃgha* is considered a special topic of investigation among the 173 topics addressed in the study of the *Abhisamayālaṃkāra* and the related *Prajñāpāramitā* (*phar phyin*) literature. Within these 173 topics are four that are regarded as distinctive and difficult to comprehend (*rtogs dka' ba*): the teaching concerning dependent origination (*rten 'brel*), the teaching related to the hermeneutics of distinguishing between definitive and interpretable scriptures (*drang nges*) along with the difference between *Madhyamaka* and *Yogācāra* interpretations of the *Prajñāpāramitā sūtra*s, the teachings concerning form and formless realm meditative absorption (*bsam gzugs*), and finally the topic presented *here* concerning the teaching of the Twenty Varieties of the *Saṃgha* (*dge 'dun nyi shu*).

METHODOLOGICAL CONSIDERATIONS

Certainly we could try to interpret the earliest material concerning the Twenty *Saṃgha*s—that is, the root verses of the AA and the prose of the *Pañcaviṃśatiprajñāpāramitāsūtra*—without recourse to any of the Indian commentaries or later Tibetan subcommentaries. However, this type of investigation has already been undertaken in the works of Edward Conze (1954b, 1957). The results of such a study appear, in the light of what the Indo-Tibetan commentarial tradition has to offer, to be superficial and even misleading. Even if Conze's readings of the verses related to the Twenty *Saṃgha*s are historically correct and represent the author of the AA's true intention,[6] we do not gain any insight into the meaning these verses had for the Buddhist scholars of this textual tradition nor the soteriological purpose in understanding them. We aim to present a detailed discussion of the subject matter that addresses these issues by following the interpretation of the AA in the later Tibetan commentaries, specifically the works of Tsong kha pa. We have in mind what Richard Gombrich speaks of when he comments that it "is not . . . that we have to accept the Buddhist tradition uncritically, but that if it interprets texts as coherent, that interpretation deserves the most serious consideration" (Gombrich, 1990: 11). Our approach to the AA by means of the Tibetan commentaries, specifically the work of Tsong kha pa, is similar in manner to the way R. M. L. Gethin has utilized subsequent Pāli commentarial literature in interpreting Buddhist material from the *Nikāyas*.[7] As Gethin states:

> We are concerned . . . to come to grips with what actually interested the minds of those who compiled the literature . . . in the light of what is really known with any certainty about the history of early Buddhist literature, I suggest the burden of proof lies with those who might wish to say that the subsequent tradition has got it fundamentally wrong. However, in order to do so they would first have to demonstrate that they had properly appreciated what the subsequent tradition . . . has to say, and this, the world of Buddhist scholarship is not . . . in a position to do. (Gethin, 1992: 16)

I should clarify here that my approach to understanding and analyzing this material is characterized as "emic" rather than "etic." That is, in my exegesis, I have utilized categories, terms, and structures within the Indo-Tibetan Buddhist intellectual milieu in an effort to "think along"[8] with this tradition of scholarship.

If we were to engage in an "etic" analysis and to approach the material utilizing appropriated conceptual or linguistic apparatuses, our analysis could indeed yield interesting results. For instance, we could appropriate theoretical models from psychology and analyze the ideal figures within the Twenty *Saṃghas* in terms of psychological types or "case histories."[9] Alternatively, amplifying upon Dreyfus's thematic notion that the worldview we are reconstructing is a "narrative of spiritual progress," we could approach the Twenty *Saṃghas* in the light of an appropriation of structuralist literary theory, particularly through the work of Roland Barthes's structural analysis of narratives. Through this appropriation of structuralist theory, our approach to the study of the Twenty *Saṃghas* could be seen as a descriptive structural analysis of a multilayered narrative of Buddhist soteriology.[10]

However, I think that it is imperative to come to terms with the tradition's exegesis on its own terms as a system. As Ruegg (1995: 157) has suggested, an emic analysis "provides as good a foundation as any for generalizing and comparative study, one that will not superimpose from the outside extraneous modes of thinking and interpretative grids." Once we are able to come to terms with a tradition's conceptual system—in this instance the typological analysis of ideal figures found in the Twenty *Saṃghas*—we can then proceed to reflect upon the implications that such a system has in our understanding of that culture.

Why should we, as modern readers, have an interest in scholastic accounts of ideal figures embodied in the Twenty *Saṃghas*? Is this not undue attention placed, according to some scholars, on the "precise views of several obscure monk-scholars on exactly how many *Arhat*s can dance on the tip of the proverbial head of an *Abhidharma* pin"? To follow the trajectories of such sentiments would lead to thinking away rather than thinking through major strands of Buddhist cultural formations.

One way to think about the relevance of ideal figures depicted in the multiple layers of the Twenty *Saṃghas* is by way of analogy to the structure and stages of educational progress in modern institutions of secondary education. The comparison is construed in terms of a generalization of the sociocultural markers of attainment and ideals of cultivated progress reflected between Indo-Tibetan *Mahāyāna* Buddhist cultural systems and North American modern ones. The reader should keep in mind that Indo-Tibetan Buddhist cultural systems are embedded in a worldview where multiple lifetimes, multiple cosmological realms, as well as theories and practices oriented around karma and rebirth are accepted as a given. Needless to say, such cultural formations do not underlie North American institutions.

Nevertheless, in such institutions, there are three degrees of attainment, the BA (Bachelor of Arts), MA (Master of Arts), and the most distinguished attainment—the PhD degree (Doctor of Philosophy). Progress is marked by credits achieved and knowledge gained through courses of study that may terminate in the BA, or the slightly more advanced MA. A student may become inspired to strive for the long, arduous course of study resulting in the eminent PhD degree.

Likewise in the Indo-Tibetan *Mahāyāna* Buddhist path systems of the AA, there are three analogous degrees of attainment—the *Śrāvaka Arhat* (BA), *Pratyekabuddha* (MA), and *Mahāyāna Arhat*, or Buddhahood (PhD). Progress in these degrees is marked by states of knowledge that have been realized and defilements that have been eradicated in relation to the individual's course of study, meditative practice, and insight sustained by a ethos of moral virtue. All of these degrees have multiple stages within them that demarcate progress in attainment. Like academic honors for eminence in scholarship, some stages of attainment are marked by distinction (Tib. *khyad par can*) in their progress.

The first degree of *Śrāvaka Arhat*, like a traditional BA, has four stages marking progress in the course of this degree. There is the novice stage of Stream-enterer, like the collegiate level of freshman. Then the second stage or level of Once-returner is analogous to a sophomore. Next there is the Non-returner, like a junior pertaining to the class below that of senior in American colleges and universities. The final period of time leading up to the attainment of *Arhat* is the course of the collegiate senior. Although not the top or most esteemed achievement, the BA degree is worthy of attainment and has value. Likewise, the state of *Arhat*ship attained by a *Śrāvaka*, from an Indo-Tibetan *Mahāyāna* Buddhist perspective, is a valued attainment although not the most distinguished.

The attainment of *Pratyekabuddha* is comparable to an MA degree, slightly higher than the BA; it may be preceded by the attainment of stages leading to the degree of *Śrāvaka Arhat*. The *Pratyekabuddha* is a solitary individual and achieves the degree in a manner similar to how some modern individuals may achieve the MA—through distance education, without the direct presence of a teacher.

The final degree, and most prestigious, is that of Buddhahood, full and perfectly complete awakening. The individual who undertakes the long, arduous journey to the highest degree is the *bodhisattva*. A *bodhisattva*, like a modern graduate or medical student, masters other degrees and attainments in the course of reaching Buddhahood. *Bodhisattva*s train and acquire multiple skills while self-sacrificing immediate resources toward a higher aim that accomplishes the mutual benefit of themselves and others. As Jan Nattier (2003: 134) notes, the course of a *bodhisattva*'s training is analogous to a "medical school student who devotes herself night and day to solitary study, cutting herself off from family and friends and withdrawing from normal social interactions, but with the ultimate aim of being able to use the skills she is acquiring to accomplish the healing of others." In this self-sacrificing altruistic process, advanced *bodhisattva*s, those who are Noble Beings, gain the ability to help beings and guide them in the course of their attainment. Such *bodhisattva*s are like modern graduate students who teach collegiate-level courses leading to the BA. At advanced levels, Noble Being *bodhisattva*s travel to various cosmological worlds where Buddhas are present, that is, Buddha-fields, to receive advice in furthering their training. The training of an advanced *bodhisattva* is analogous to a resident physician, who trains under the supervision of senior doctors (i.e., Buddhas), until they become fully trained and certified doctors to create their own sphere of influence and practice, that is, a Buddha-field.

Ideal figures in Buddhist discourse represent such analogous cultural values of attainment. A relative explaining around the kitchen table that his child is a "senior" in college, may have listeners who do not fully understand all that is entailed in that classification; nevertheless, parent and listener both know that this position of an "educational aspirant" plays an important part in marking progress and attainment within a North American cultural worldview. Likewise, a classification such as Stream-enterer marks attainment and conveys the values of spiritual progress within a Buddhist cultural worldview.

Along these lines, the guidelines, accounts, and scholastic discourse for achieving the status and attainments exemplified in the ideal figures found in the topic of the Twenty *Saṃgha*s is analogous to academic program guidelines for achieving academic degrees in secondary education. Such academic guidelines provide the ideal structures and sequence for attaining marks of progress toward the desired goal. However, such guidelines do not provide an experiential account of the daily struggles, tribulations, and triumphs of the educational process. Rather, they provide a map of how the educational process is envisioned.

Likewise, the topic of the Twenty *Saṃgha*s in Indo-Tibetan Buddhist cultures serves as a guideline map for marking degrees of progress in the attainment of ideal goals. A map is not territory (Smith, 1978), but rather provides an abstract and reduced representation of the structures of spatial relations between locations. The lack of congruity within the territory covered is a distortion that allows for a map's utility. For instance, a visitor to London who wishes to travel on the London Underground trains, also known as The Tube, gains intelligibility and comprehension with a map. A map of The Tube facilitates the ability to quickly convey needed, accurate information to the traveler through its use of color codes for the various routes, the labeling and depiction of stations for changing trains, and its reduction of the geography of the underground routes from the actual meandering geography of the track. Although geographically inaccurate, maps of the London Underground provide a coherent overview of a complex system. As Jonathan Z. Smith (2004: 59n115) notes, "Maps are structures of transformation, not structures of reproduction." Likewise, the topic of the Twenty *Saṃgha*s is a conceptual map that provides a coherent overview of the complex processes of Buddhist soteriological transformation. The topic of the Twenty *Saṃgha*s embodies the mapping of the temporal and spatial relations and structures through which Buddhist meditative and cognitive processes are envisioned in the transformations from unenlightened states or statuses to enlightened or awakened ones.

Accounts of ideal figures in Buddhist cultures, besides mapping degrees of attainment and stages in Buddhist path systems, also serve as sociological points of reference within Buddhist cultures. As Jan Nattier (2003: 105) has recently noted with regard to Pāli-based Buddhist cultures:

> It is worth recalling that even an unactualized ideal can play a significant role in the life of a community. While few Theravāda Buddhists today, for example, would claim to have met an Arhat (much less to be one), the goal of Arhatship still serves as a point of reference and as an ultimate, if distant, value for members of that tradition.

Accounts of ideal figures, actualized or unactualized, have great purport in the history of Buddhist cultural formations. Mainstream and *Mahāyāna* forms of Buddhism, elite and popular groups, in South, Central, and East Asian forms of Buddhism have been influenced by these markers of progress and the qualities they embody. The ideal figures embodied in the Twenty *Saṃgha*s serve as an indexical reference for attainment throughout Buddhist literature. In the traditional genres of the monastic code of the *Vinaya*, the discourses in the *Nikāya*s, or in the biographic morality tales of the Buddha's previous lives such as the *Divyāvadāna*, all reference such ideal figures as signifiers of Buddhist cultural values of attainment.

In Tibet, as we have noted, the Twenty *Saṃgha*s is a topic of collegiate-level monastic study. The topic is mentioned in public lectures given by Tibetan Buddhist teachers to members of local communities. The Twenty *Saṃgha*s finds a place even at holiday times of periodic commemoration and celebration in Tibetan Buddhist culture. The Great Prayer Festival (*mon lam chen mo*) in Lhasa would witness occasions where monks would have contests to see who could enumerate all the different potential types of ideal figures found from within the Twenty *Saṃgha*s (for example, there can be over twelve thousand different types of Non-returner based on differences of faculty, realization, and cosmological location among others; Geshe Sopa oral communication).

As the world of Buddhist scholarship has neither fully investigated nor completely exposed what the subsequent Tibetan Buddhist tradition has to say about the topic of the Twenty *Saṃgha*s, we will do so by means of Tsong kha pa's commentaries. Related to our concern about investigating what the Tibetan Buddhist tradition has to say concerning the Twenty *Saṃgha*s, at this point I will briefly clarify some interpretative issues related to our endeavor. Principally, I wish to explain the hermeneutical situation and strategy of Tsong kha pa in interpreting the topic of the Twenty *Saṃgha*s, as well as our own hermeneutical situation and strategy in interpreting Tsong kha pa's understanding of the Twenty *Saṃghas*.

TSONG KHA PA'S HERMENEUTICAL STRATEGY

This study of the Twenty *Saṃghas* attempts to reconstruct Tsong kha pa's own intended standpoint with regard to the Twenty *Saṃghas*. The recovery of any author's "intent" is a problematic notion, particularly in relation to subtle nuances of philosophical speculation. The intentions seen in any given author's composition may be shaped by a range of unapparent forces, such as sociopolitical or economic concerns, which allow for an author's intent to be multilayered in nature. In this study of Tsong kha pa's thought on the Twenty *Saṃghas* I have chosen to bracket such unapparent forces and focus rather on the ostensible intention found through a bare-bones reading of the texts. Reading Tsong kha pa's texts in a manner that constructs an ostensible intention may be artificial or fictional in that the actual reality of his alleged intentions may be more complex or comprised of unapparent intentions that may contradict the ostensible. Nevertheless, such a reading of the ostensible intention of Tsong kha pa's understanding of the Twenty *Saṃghas* is justifiable in that it serves as a useful heuristic device that allows us to construct a plausible surface intent of what Tsong kha pa believes himself to be doing. This ostensible intent may not be the one and only real intent of Tsong kha pa's endeavor, but such a reading allows us to bracket a range of potential interpretations that are indefinite as to their plausibility.

Along these lines, the construction of an ostensible intent in regard to our Indian authors is problematic. Most notably, the author of the AA's ostensible intent in regard to the Twenty *Saṃghas* is not clear. As we will see in chapter 4, the AA's verses on the Twenty *Saṃghas* are cryptic and grammatically vague enough to support, outside the context of any commentarial input, almost any interpretative stance that one wishes to posit. Likewise, the recovery of the principal Indian commentators' (Ārya Vimuktisena, ca. sixth century, and Haribhadra, ca. eighth century) interpretative stance on the Twenty *Saṃghas* is also problematic. Their commentaries do provide sufficient evidence to calculate how they arrive at enumerating the Twenty *Saṃghas*, but there are insufficient details to allow us to understand the underlying assumptions of how they arrive at their conclusions. Tsong kha pa's interpretive stance offers a viable commentarial exegesis of the Twenty *Saṃghas*, which may not be *the* objectively correct interpretation (if there can be one), but certainly appears to be an interpretation that is coherent, refined, and well informed. One could say that what I am doing is eliminating certain interpretations, and namely Tsong kha pa's interpretation, from being an unreasonable one based on the evidence we currently have.

In this regard, as Ruegg (1967: 44) has spoken eloquently of scholars within Tibetan culture as representing the "leading forerunners" of those practicing Indology, we can perhaps extend this notion of Tibetan scholarship, in this instance the Buddhist scholarship of Tsong kha pa, as representative of a leading forerunner in Buddhist Theology. Parallel to the developments in late twentieth-century North America Buddhist scholarship of a "Buddhist Theology" (see Jackson and Makransky, 2000), Tibetan scholars like Tsong kha pa are "Buddhist theologians." Innovative in their interpretation and systemization, they see themselves as rationally reconstructing the logical consequences of how Indian *Mahāyāna* Buddhist systems of thought might be expected to evolve. In this context, scholars like Tsong kha pa are specialists in internal history (Tillemans, 1990: 16; 1983: 312). That is, given the key ideas of an Indian Buddhist author, we should see Tsong kha pa as drawing logical conclusions of what could have been said, as opposed to the concern of external history, with its emphasis on what was actually said, or what actually took place.

Tsong kha pa appears to be engaged in two exegetical exercises while interpreting the Twenty *Saṃghas*. First, Tsong kha pa sees himself as properly recovering and presenting the intentions (*dgongs pa*) of the two principal Indian AA commentators, Ārya Vimuktisena and Haribhadra. For Tsong kha pa (*Golden Garland* 1970: 253), although "most Indian and Tibetan scholars have searched out this intention," they have not developed a clear interpretation of these commentators' exegesis. Second, Tsong kha pa sees himself as establishing "his own system" (*rang lugs*) of interpreting the Twenty *Saṃghas* by means of textual Buddhist hermeneutics. This is especially clear in Tsong kha pa's *Stairway* (see below), where he engages in exegesis and analysis of "textual systems" (*gzhung lugs*) in order to arrive at the proper understanding of the defining characteristics (Skt. *lakṣaṇa*; Tib. *mtshan nyid*) of ideal figures.

Tsong kha pa's analysis and exegesis is shaped by traditional Buddhist hermeneutical strategies such as the "Four Reliances"[11] (*rton pa bzhi*, *catuḥpratisaraṇa*): "Rely on the doctrine (*dharma*) and not on the person (*pudgala*); rely on the meaning (*artha*) and not on the word (*vyañjana*); rely on the definitive meaning (*nītārtha*) and not on the interpretable meaning (*neyārtha*); rely on direct realization (*jñāna*) and not on discursive consciousness (*vijñāna*) (*Stairway* 292)." For Tsong kha pa, the scope of this hermeneutical strategy is found in conjunction with an explanation through the proof of scripture (*āgama*) and reasoning (*yukti*).[12] Traditionally, adherence to the doctrine is not dependent on human authority but is based on personal reasoning (*yukti*), on what one has oneself known (*jñāta*), seen (*dṛṣṭa*), and grasped (*vidita*).[13] Tsong kha pa utilizes reasoning to distinguish the proper analysis of the Buddha's scriptures (*rgyal ba'i gsung rab 'pyad pa*) along with the citation of Indian *śāstras* to verify his conclusions. Tsong kha pa's exegetical procedure therefore involves a close reading of the texts, bringing out what he sees as the correct understanding of a word's meaning to substantiate an Indian *śāstra*'s intention (*bstan bcos kyi dgongs pa*).[14]

In this instance, Tsong kha pa walks a fine line between utilizing reasoning in determining proper textual exegesis and paying his respects to Indian Buddhist lineage figures such as Asaṅga, Vasubandhu, Haribhadra, and so on. One of the principal aims on Tsong kha pa's exegetical agenda is to establish a single unified intention between the scholastic systems of Asaṅga and Vasubandhu in constructing a coherent structure to the Twenty *Saṃghas*. At the same time, Tsong kha pa aims to develop a system of interpreting the Twenty *Saṃghas* that can be understood through multiple purviews. In other words, Tsong kha pa's exegesis is such that it produces an awareness of the Twenty *Saṃghas* that is coherent from the perspective of either a *śrāvaka*, *pratyekabuddha*, or *bodhisattva* (*Stairway* 270: *theg pa gsum gyi gang zag rnams kyi mngon rtogs rgyud la bskyes pa'i tshul la sogs pa'i rnam gzhag*).

Thus these aforementioned hermeneutical strategies are present throughout the texts in which Tsong kha pa gives an exegesis on the Twenty *Saṃghas*. In utilizing these strategies, Tsong kha pa sees himself as recovering the authorial intentions of Haribhadra and Ārya Vimuktisena and, in the process, recovering the intention of the AA.

HERMENEUTICAL STRATEGIES IN APPROACHING THE TWENTY *SAṂGHAS*

I should mention at the onset that our endeavor is exegetical[15] in nature. I have attempted to present an interpretation of Tsong kha pa's thought on the Twenty *Saṃghas* through a close reading of the relevant texts, along with an accumulation and ordering of philological, historical, and textual data. In evaluating Tsong kha pa's approach, I have applied my own presuppositions to his intentions based on the historical context of his life when he wrote on the Twenty *Saṃghas*. In this regard, when evaluating the Buddhist scholarship of Tsong kha pa we may be able to posit institutional and sociopolitical concerns, particularly in some of Tsong kha pa's later works written at a more mature stage of his life. However, with regard to the intentions surrounding the topic of the Twenty *Saṃgha*s that were written in his youth (see chapter 2), Tsong kha pa's concerns in this instance are at least in part to establish and develop his scholastic ability in textual hermeneutics. The exegetical strategies and techniques that Tsong kha pa employs in writing on the Twenty *Saṃgha*s in his youth can be seen to be the foundation of the hermeneutic approach that culminates later in his life in his masterpiece of *Mahāyāna* Buddhist hermeneutics, the *Legs bshad snying po* (Thurman, 1984). In this instance of writing on the Twenty *Saṃgha*s, Tsong kha pa's concerns are also in the soteriological implications of his reading. His primary concern is siding with an interpretation that allows for the Twenty *Saṃgha*s to be understood as representing stages of gradual progression toward the liberation from suffering, rather than one that supports sudden, instantaneous progression, or progress that allows for one to "skip over" certain stages. How Tsong kha pa elucidates these concerns in his interpretation of the Twenty *Saṃgha*s will be presented in later chapters and discussed in the conclusion.

Tsong kha pa is important for us in that his decisions regarding the proper interpretation of Indian texts, and in this instance, the interpretation regarding the Twenty *Saṃgha*s in the AA, framed the interpretations for the entire *Dge lugs pa* school that followed after him. His interpretation came to shape Tibetan Buddhist's definitive understanding of one of the three essential components of the Buddhist religion, the *Saṃgha*. In letting Tsong kha pa speak in his own voice, without being obscured "by the lenses of Dge lug pa commentarial scholarship," (Jinpa, 2000: 5) I am trying to recover the interpretation of the "man" and not the subsequent "movement." An understanding of Tsong kha pa's manner of interpretation, rather than the interpretation of him by subsequent commentators, allows us to have insight into the formative processes that lead to what van der Kuijp (1983: 45) suggests was Tsong kha pa's great achievement, the reevaluation of Indian Buddhist *sūtra*s and *śāstra*s resulting in a innovative division and hierarchical arranging of texts of "definitive" and "interpretable" purport.

In this reconstruction and appropriation of a coherent presentation of Tsong kha's system of the Twenty *Saṃgha*s, the comparative elements in our study have the nature of "intra-Buddhist" scholasticism. That is, I will be noting correspondences and comparisons with other Buddhist scholastic accounts of ideal figures. In documenting an overall uniform coherence in the scholastic Buddhist approach to categorical descriptions of ideal figures on the path, I wish to present a system of interpretation of one man who has been greatly influential in the philosophy and practice of Buddhism in Tibet.

In a constructive postmodern[16] approach, one reappropriates or reconstructs traditional worldviews in a critical manner without recourse to a deconstructive, relativistic, or eliminative hermeneutic that grinds down purpose, meaning, and soteriological concerns to the point of nihilism. In other words, we are not interested in totally deconstructing Tsong kha pa's work on the Twenty *Saṃghas* based on minor historical, textual, or hermeneutical problems, if they should happen to appear. The context of our endeavor is to arrive at an overall understanding of the Twenty *Saṃghas* as a coherent system of soteriological thought within Tibetan Buddhism. In this sense our study is diachronically located in fifteenth-century Tibet. The content of the subject matter therefore consists of a synchronic analysis of materials located in this timeframe, although the continuities of the subject matter may reach back to the fifth century and the basis of the system back to the time of the Buddha (Frauwallner, 1995). Thus we avoid a deconstruction that questions the historicity of Indian Buddhist texts attributed to Maitreyanātha, Asaṅga, or Vasubandhu and/or the viability of Tsong kha pa's doctrinal system of the Twenty *Saṃghas* only in relation to Pāli *Nikāya* materials.

In the Twenty *Saṃghas*, there is enough textual evidence to support Tsong kha pa's presentation as being reasonable, but not necessarily *the* one and only correct interpretation of the twenty-third and twenty-fourth verse of the *Abhisamayālaṃkāra's* first chapter. Our approach therefore primarily intends to demonstrate the doctrinal importance of the Twenty *Saṃghas* and their soteriological significance for the Tibetan Buddhists who came to follow Tsong kha pa.

In considering the historical context to Tsong kha pa's understanding and in light of a constructive postmodern approach in interpreting the vast and complex doctrine of the Twenty *Saṃghas*, we have made certain choices in our exegesis, employing a range of interpretative techniques that serve to complement each other in forming our exegetical approach to the Tibetan sources.

Dreyfus refers to the worldview we are reconstructing as a "narrative of spiritual progress." Amplifying this thematic notion, the study of the Twenty *Saṃghas* can be seen as a descriptive analysis of a multilayered narrative of Buddhist soteriology. This descriptive analysis is accentuated by Buddhist soteriological principles as applied to the unified construct of progressing on the path to *nirvāṇa*. Viewed in this manner, the scholastic accounts of ideal figures are similar to a fictional character's soteriological narrative in progressing toward *nirvāṇa*. Drawing upon Indian Buddhist sources, Tsong kha pa provides a metaphor that illustrates our soteriological narrative, the structure of a "stairway" (Tib. *them skas;* Skt. *sopāna*).[17]

In Indo-Tibetan Buddhist cultures, and for Tsong kha pa, a stairway symbolizes the long and gradual step-by-step path to *nirvāṇa*. It serves as a visual metaphor for the ascensional process of mental and bodily transformation, by means of meditative cultivation and analytical insight, that Noble Beings undergo in journeying through numerous lifetimes and various cosmological realms to reach *nirvāṇa*. The stairway metaphor reflects multiple flights of steps in the narrative of this journey.

In this narrative, the central character is a Noble Being (*ārya*) who is progressing toward *nirvāṇa*. Within the narrative, Buddhist scholars demarcate elementary units of content that serve as indices in the progress to *nirvāṇa*. Such indices consist of instances of description that are placed within a hierarchical perspective. In this soteriological narrative, the units of content are the various descriptions of ideal figures such as the Stream-enterer, Once-returner, and so on that comprise the Twenty *Saṃgha*s. These units, the Stream-enterer and others, serve as guidepoints to mark the psychological characteristics, traits, and other parameters that describe the character, in this case a Noble Being (*ārya*), as the narrative toward *nirvāṇa* unfolds. The indices that are comprised of the Stream-enterer and other ideal figures, while being placed in a hierarchical perspective, take on meaning only if they are integrated into a higher level of progression. In addition, this soteriological narrative, as a hierarchy of instances, consists of a discourse distributed into a limited number of classes or combination of narrative units, in this case, the limited number of narrative units that comprise the Twenty *Saṃgha*s.

The soteriological narrative of the Twenty *Saṃgha*s that we document is multilayered and tells two different stories depending upon the perspective that one brings to it. On one level, the indices represent guidepoints in a narrative that describes the story of ideal characters (i.e., *śrāvaka*s) who wish to remove afflictional emotions, abandon the effects that arise from the karmic laws of cause and effect, and attain a state of peace, or *nirvāṇa*, that is the result of the cessation of suffering and rebirth. On another level, the indices within the soteriological narrative represents the story of ideal characters (i.e., *bodhisattva*s) who, while cultivating special wisdom in conjugation with perfecting various virtues such as generosity, patience, energy, along with compassion, voluntarily take on innumerable rebirths in order to attain an inconceivable type of *nirvāṇa* that results in supreme and perfect enlightenment (*anuttarasamyaksaṃbodhi*).

We have also complemented Tsong kha pa's presentation of the Twenty *Saṃgha*s with an intertexualist technique, through documenting in the notes what other Indian Buddhist scholastic traditions say about ideal figures on the path.[18] This enables one to understand the soteriological narrative structure of the Tibetan tradition and also to understand how Indian Buddhist scholastic traditions in general understand the narrative of Buddhist soteriology. In this way, our intertextual approach explicitly reinforces and adds validity to Tsong kha pa's construction of the soteriological narrative within the Twenty *Saṃghas* and implicitly demonstrates the structure of descriptive narrative accounts of ideal figures on the path in Indian Buddhism. Intertextual documentation and verification of Tsong kha pa's Indian Buddhist sources expand our exegetical horizon and allow us to have a more complete understanding of the Indo-Tibetan Buddhist's system of ideal figures' descriptions and the place they have in the narrative of Buddhist soteriology.

In our approach to the Twenty *Saṃghas*, we also employ the decontextualized heuristic device of "scholasticism." José Cabezón (1994) has argued for the usefulness of the notion of scholasticism as a way of understanding Indo-Tibetan thought, and in the volume *Scholasticism*, Cabezón (1998: 4–6) gives a summary of the main principles of scholasticism related to his research on the Indo-Tibetan tradition. His research concludes that scholasticism evinces eight qualities: (1) tradition, (2) a concern with language, (3) proliferativity, (4) completeness, (5) the belief that the universe is epistemologically accessible, (6) a commitment to systematicity, (7) rationalism, and (8) self-reflexivity.

A focus on several of these qualities provides a method to understand and to approach the thought exemplified in the topic of the Twenty *Saṃghas*. In terms of tradition, first and foremost, the Twenty *Saṃghas* is a specialized topic of extended doctrinal discourse located within Tibetan Buddhist scholastic traditions. The Indian Buddhist textual sources, the well-known twenty-one Indian commentaries[19] on the AA, discuss the Twenty *Saṃghas*. However, most of the Indian AA commentators give only fragmentary discussions of the topic, and their remarks are usually given in response to what other Indian commentators have stated. The works of Ārya Vimuktisena and Haribhadra are our earliest textual sources and the most fundamental of the Indian AA commentaries. They serve as the basis for subsequent Indian commentaries and present the most extended discussion of the Twenty *Saṃghas*. However, both of these commentaries end their discussions of the Twenty *Saṃghas* with a rather curious statement: "Here we will not give an extensive discussion; why grind down what is already ground?" (*atra tv asmābhir nopanyastam kiṃ piṣṭaṃ piṃṣma*; AAV, 46.5–6; AAĀ, 36.10–11).

In other words, the subject matter had already been thoroughly "worked out" within the cultural arena of Indian scholasticism. None of the early Indian AA commentators felt obligated to thoroughly discuss a "soteriological narrative" that was already well known in their scholastic arena. Because of this attitude of the early Indian sources and the lack of other early Indian AA source material, a full analysis of the Twenty *Saṃgha*s from just the Indian Sanskrit AA sources alone may not appear as a coherent and complete system.

However, as Ruegg (1981: viii) has commented, "Tibetan scholars developed remarkable philological and interpretative methods that could well justify us in regarding them as Indologists *avant la lettre.*" Therefore, it is our contention that an investigation from the Tibetan scholastic tradition will clearly explain the meaning and significance of the Twenty *Saṃgha*s in the context of Tibetan Buddhism and what the Tibetan tradition sees as the true Indian Buddhist context. The topic of the Twenty *Saṃgha*s in the Tibetan Buddhist scholastic tradition developed in a different manner from that of India. After the AA's reintroduction into Tibet in the eleventh century, each successive generation of Tibetan commentators progressively expanded upon the commentaries of the previous generation. In regard to the Twenty *Saṃgha*s, the Tibetan scholastic tradition of commentarial expansion eventually resulted in subcommentaries that became independent treatises. Among other outcomes, this led to a genre of scholastic literature that focused exclusively on the topic of the Twenty *Saṃgha*s. Our discussion of the Twenty *Saṃgha*s will be derived from this unique genre of scholastic literature found in the Tibetan tradition.

The second quality in Cabezón's list that we can utilize in approaching the Tibetan scholastic articulation of the Twenty *Saṃgha*s is a concern with language, the language of scripture and its commentarial exegesis. The goal of scholastic language is the construction of a complete system through exegetical means. Scholastic language is elliptical, abstract, and has what Paul J. Griffiths has termed "denaturalized discourse." The denaturalized style of language found in scholastic literature leads away from the ambiguity of everyday language and into abstract technical jargon. Scholastic jargon is developed and expanded into an unambiguous artificial lexicon of technical terminology designed to communicate in a highly efficient manner that which everyday language cannot (Griffiths, 1994: 28). We find exactly this type of denaturalized discourse utilized in the Indo-Tibetan exegesis of the Twenty *Saṃgha*s. The list of Twenty *Saṃgha*s itself consists of a denaturalized terminology and a large lexicon of technical jargon developed in the commentarial exegesis to elucidate the list. So for instance, among the Twenty *Saṃgha*s we find the denaturalized term *bhavasyāgraparamo rūparāgahāḥ* (Tib. *srid rtse'i mthar thug 'gro gzugs kyi chags bcom*),[20] utilized to describe the "Non-returner who has reached [by a rebirth or an attainment] the summit of existence and who is freed from all attachment regarding form." It is this type of descriptive terminology and scholastic jargon that the AA and its commentaries employ in presenting the topic of the Twenty *Saṃgha*s.

This concern with language points to the Tibetan scholastic tradition's conviction that technically denaturalized discourse has communicative ability of soteriological value. Specifically, denaturalized discourse has the capability of encoding the spiritual path toward enlightenment through descriptive accounts of an ideal figure. As we have mentioned above, these accounts do not provide personal practical instruction on the nature of spiritual experience. Rather, when the discourse is decoded and internalized by the recipient, it serves as a guidebook to and provides a cultural worldview for a structured narrative of spiritual progress in which soteriologically valid experience is possible. There are many difficulties in finding English renderings for the artificial lexicon of technical terminology utilized by Indian and Tibetan Buddhist scholars for the denaturalized discourse related to ideal figures on the path. This is mainly because the English language has not yet fully developed its own lexicon of terminology to express the subtle nuances found in the description of Buddhist soteriological structures and meditative states.

Confidence in the ability of language to communicate information of soteriological value allows for several other qualities of scholasticism to take place. With this communicative ability, scholasticism develops the tendency for proliferativity, the third quality in Cabezón's list. Analysis of detailed and minute points of scripture and commentary expand into conceptualized ideals, categories, definitions, and divisions. This analysis and proliferativity characterizes the Tibetan commentarial exegesis of the Twenty *Saṃgha*s, with an almost endless analysis of the material into numerous categories, divisions, and subdivisions. Again, the basis of the Twenty *Saṃgha*s is itself a categorical list that provides a typology of individuals who embody twenty phases along the path to *nirvāṇa*. In order to understand and provide the conceptual framework for this soteriological system, each of these Twenty *Saṃgha*s is analyzed, examined, and defined from different categorical perspectives. This methodology of analytical categorization embodies several other tendencies we find in the Tibetan treatment of the Twenty *Saṃgha*s, the scholastic qualities of completeness, epistemological accessibility, and systematicity.

The use of denaturalized discourse in a prolific manner enables the scholiast to believe that the tradition is complete in its presentation—that is, that all major doctrinal points of soteriological value can be expressed with communicative efficiency in a compact manner. This compact and complete presentation of all necessary soteriological doctrinal points is enveloped in systematicity. This is a tendency toward a basic orderliness of presentation that communicates the complex structure of the prolific subject matter. Along with these qualities is the belief that the universe is epistemologically accessible: that the world is knowable. The Tibetan approach to the Twenty *Saṃgha*s adheres to these scholastic qualities in that it holds that the tradition's soteriological typology is complete; namely, that nothing has been left out that is of soteriological value in describing the phases that individuals may progress through to reach *nirvāṇa*.

The aforementioned hermeneutical strategies and exegetical approaches to the Twenty *Saṃgha*s have guided our approach. That is, in the light of a constructive postmodern approach, our endeavor contains elements of historicity, intertextuality, and scholasticism. The scholastic principles that we have briefly enumerated here will be found throughout our study of the Twenty *Saṃgha*s. In our presentation, the scholastic principles of denaturalized discourse, systematicity, and proliferativity will become quickly evident.

Having described the approach through which Tsong kha pa and the scholastic tradition inherited, communicated, described, and analyzed the ideal figures of the path embodied in the Twenty *Saṃgha*s, I would like to outline the sources we will use and the contribution we hope to make. With the above-mentioned scholastic factors in mind we will examine the topic of the Twenty *Saṃgha*s from textual sources of Tsong kha pa blo bzang grags pa (1357–1419). This includes his *Stairway Taken by Those of Lucid Intelligence* (*blo gsal bgrod pa'i them skas* [= *Stairway*]),[21] and sections from his *Golden Garland of Eloquent Sayings* (*legs bshad gser phreng* [=*Golden Garland*]).[22] The *Dge 'dun nyi shu bsdus pa rjes gnang* (= *rjes gnang*),[23] "The Abbreviated Bestowal of the Twenty Varieties of the *Saṃgha*," will be used sparingly since it repeats material from the *Stairway*. The texts of Tsong kha pa that we will employ here explain the twenty varieties of the *Saṃgha* Jewel based on two verses from the first chapter of the AA.

Tsong kha pa's system of the Twenty *Saṃgha*s embodies a worldview in which the path and its results, even if involving the instantaneous abandonment of mental defilements, is a gradual process taking many lifetimes. The path involves continual persistent effort, each stage or result from the beginning up to *nirvāṇa* is not definite unless continual application is made. For Tsong kha pa, the Twenty *Saṃgha*s in the *Abhisamayālaṃkāra* represent an extension of terminology and doctrinal principals found in the *śrāvaka* vehicle of mainstream

Buddhism employed as a skillful heuristic device to generate awareness of the *Mahāyāna saṃgha,* the community of *bodhisattvas* irreversible from the journey to complete Buddhahood. The Twenty *Saṃghas*, in light of Tsong kha pa's interpretation, therefore demonstrates a unity in diversity between the vehicles of *śrāvakas*, *pratyekabuddhas*, and *bodhisattvas* in regard to the ideal of the *saṃgha*. Thus, Tsong kha pa constructs a structural system of *Mahāyāna* scholasticism that presents the Twenty *Saṃghas* coherently from various perspectives, each unit a step upon the stairway to inconceivable and thoroughly complete awakening that results in full omniscient Buddhahood.

2

TSONG KHA PA AND THE *ABHISAMAYĀLAṂKĀRA* COMMENTARIAL TRADITION

Tsong kha pa is famous as an erudite and innovative scholar; his works, the *Stairway* and *Rjes gnang* appear to be the earliest extant Tibetan texts that deal directly with the topic of the Twenty *Saṃghas*. Tsong kha pa occupied a pivotal period in the classical scholastic period of Tibetan Buddhism. That period of time has been described as "the high point of philosophical penetration, exegesis, and systematic hermeneutics, accompanied by the final constitution of the Tibetan religious schools (Ruegg, 1980: 278)." In relation to this period of intense debate and systemization, the scholarship of Tsong kha pa represents a culmination of a long commentarial tradition of the AA. Although Tsong kha pa's compilation and synthesis of the Indo-Tibetan tradition before him may be said to mark a culmination in the history of AA commentarial analysis, his works concerning the Twenty *Saṃghas* marks the beginning of an innovative and new Tibetan systematization of Indian Buddhist doctrine. The work of Tsong kha pa concerning the Twenty *Saṃghas* therefore marks a threshold in Tibetan scholarship between the full assimilation of doctrine concerning the AA and its later definitive systematization.

Our aim in this chapter is to document the scholastic purview that Tsong kha pa inherited from his predecessors and the historical circumstances that were influential in his writing about the Twenty *Saṃghas*. In order to accomplish this, Tsong kha pa's inherited scholastic tradition will be chronicled through utilizing the heuristic device of the "AA lineage tradition." A lineage history provides the Indian and Tibetan scholar with a sense of authenticity and validity to scholastic teachings in that the teachings of a lineage are seen as descending from an original authoritative source in an unbroken transmission. A knowledge of a lineage history provides the Indo-Tibetan Buddhist scholar with explicit and implicit scholastic principles in regard to a particular textual tradition. Explicitly, an Indo-Tibetan scholar gains an understanding of the continuance of the particular teachings and the above-mentioned sense of authenticity. Implicitly the scholar inherits a certain structure and methodology that reflects the scholarship of previous generations. Our presentation will consist of three parts: first we will highlight major AA commentators from India, then sketch the continuance of the AA lineage into Tibet, and finally discuss the relationship of the AA, particularly in regard to the Twenty *Saṃghas*, in Tsong kha pa's life and works.

The first two sections demonstrate that Tsong kha pa inherited a long commentarial tradition that was trans-Himalayan in nature, a tradition that built upon itself and expanded until the time of Tsong kha pa (1357–1419 CE). Specifically, these sections make clear that this trans-Himalayan lineage is "Indo-Tibetan." This is because there is a high degree of continuity between India and Tibet in the tradition that we are discussing here, one in which a root text and its commentarial cycle of literature were directly transmitted from Indian scholars to Tibetan scholars.

Tsong kha pa lived during a unique period of Tibetan Buddhist history for the study of the AA cycle of literature. Ruegg (1980: 278) distinguishes four periods in the development of Buddhism in Tibet: (a) preliminary assimilation (eighth–ninth century), the early propagation (*snga dar*); (b) full assimilation (tenth–fourteenth centuries), during which doctrines were systematized; (c) the classical period (fourteenth–sixteenth centuries); and (d) the scholastic period (sixteenth–twentieth centuries), during which textbooks were systemized in an effort to reach definitive exegesis of previous interpretations. Tsong kha pa matured as a scholar at a pivotal point in the history of Buddhist doctrinal development in Tibet; namely, the cusp between the full assimilation of Indian Buddhism and its systemization. This was a period of Tibetan Buddhist development in which all the major Indian commentaries of the AA had been translated and several generations of indigenous Tibetan AA commentaries had been composed. As such, it was a period where it was possible for the first time to examine all the important AA commentaries in a standardized religious language (*chos skad*) that allowed for new intellectual developments to take place.

The Tibetan scholastic cultural purview that was inherited from India was modeled upon the study, reflection, and exegesis of Indian Buddhist *śāstras* (i.e., *Madhyamakāvatāra*, *Pramāṇavārttika*, *Abhidharmakośa*, etc.) that had been translated primarily during the second wave (*phyi dar*) of scriptural importation into Tibet several hundred years earlier. More specifically, the commentarial lineage that centers around the Indian Buddhist *śāstra* of the AA is known as the lineage of "extensive deeds" (*udārācāraparamparā, rgya chen spyod pa'i brgyud*). This lineage focuses on the soteriological structure of the path and the activities that are necessary to accomplish Buddhahood. The Indian Buddhist scholar Dharmamitra (ca. 800–850 CE) appears to be the first writer to set out this tradition based on the exegesis of the *Prajñāpāramitā sūtras*, for it is Dharmamitra who is possibly the first to make reference to a "profound" (*gambhīra*) and "vast" (*vistara*) tradition of interpreting these *sūtras*.[1]

The "profound" tradition comments on the explicit content of the PP *sūtras* through philosophical analysis and exegesis of emptiness (*śūnyatā*), the profound nature of reality (*tathatā*). The Indo-Tibetan tradition views this lineage as beginning with the *Bodhisattva* Mañjuśrī and as having a foundation in the human realm with the "Six Collections of Reasoning" (*rigs tshogs drug*) of Nāgārjuna (ca. 150–250). This lineage passes down through Buddhapālita (ca. 500), Candrakīrti (ca. 650), and Śāntideva (ca. 695–743).

The "vast" or "extensive" lineage articulates the hidden meaning of the PP *sūtras*, the stages of realization leading to full Buddhahood. It begins with Maitreyanātha and continues on through Asaṅga (ca. fourth century CE), Vasubandhu (ca. fourth to fifth century CE), Ārya Vimuktisena, and so on. This lineage upholds the textual tradition of studying the AA and will be highlighted in the following pages.

Tsong kha pa inherited this tradition, which traces itself back to the fourth or fifth century of the common era in India with the appearance in the human realm of the AA. The lineage is considered to continue unbroken on into Tibet through Tsong kha pa in the fourteenth century and up until the present day. Documenting the Indo-Tibetan lineage tradition of the AA[2] enables us to show the textual sources that influenced Tsong kha pa and the scholastic ideology that existed in his lifetime. Highlighting major figures provides a foundation for examining the influence of the AA in Tsong kha pa's life and the circumstances that lead to his scholastic work on the Twenty *Saṃghas*. While I cannot provide a chronicle of every personage given in the Indian and Tibetan lineage lists, I will chronicle the major commentators who contributed to Tsong kha pa's scholastic purview on the AA with special attention given to the Twenty *Saṃghas*.

Indian Predecessors in the *Abhisamayālaṃkāra* Tradition

The Indian and Tibetan Buddhist lineage history of the AA[3] is considered to begin with the bestowal of the *Prajñāpāramitā sūtras* by Śākyamuni Buddha in Rājagṛha on Mount Gṛdhrakūṭa over twenty-five hundred years ago. The teaching of the PP by the Buddha is regarded by the tradition to have been delivered at Gṛdhrakūṭa simultaneously in five different forms, from the 100,000-verse PP down to the *Heart Sūtra*, varying in length according to the faculty of understanding of the disciples who listened (Bu ston [Obermiller, 1931–1932: 48–49]). Haribhadra, an eighth-century Indian commentator, explicitly states this in his AAĀ (11.27–12.1):

> The *Śatasāhasrikā* was taught to bring benefit to those beings who are devoted to words and delight in an extensive rendition. The *Pañcaviṃśati* was taught, through gathering all the topics together, out of affection for those beings who delight in medium-sized explanation and understand from selective elaboration. The *Aṣṭa* was expounded, through condensing its topics, to produce benefit for beings who are captured by contents, like a slightly opened box, and delight in a brief explanation.

Edward Conze (1978b: 9–33) concludes from his research on the historical formation of the PP literature that four phases of its development can be distinguished:

1. Elaboration of a basic text (ca. 100 BCE to 100 CE), the original impulse;
2. Expansion of the basic text (ca. 100 to 300 CE);
3. Re-statement of doctrine through short *sūtra*s and versified summaries (300–500 CE);
4. Period of Tantric influence (600 to 1200 CE).

As we shall see, the time frame that Conze notes as the "period of Tantric influence" is the period of time in which Indian commentators of the AA flourished. Conze's evaluation of this phase of PP development is therefore misleading. The Indian AA lineage that influenced Tsong kha pa consists of a long tradition of commenting on the versified summary of the PP.

Our immediate concern here is the time period in which the expanded *sūtra* text of the PP (phase 2) was restated in the versified summary of the AA (phase 3). Conze's research (1978b: 17–18) has also shown that the 25,000-verse PP, the 100,000-verse PP, and the 18,000-verse PP are all different versions of one *sūtra*, which he calls the *Large Sūtra on Perfect Wisdom*. Conze notes that any version of the *Large Sūtra* can be related to the 8,000-verse PP, which he believed to be the oldest PP *sūtra* (Conze, 1952: 251–62; 1958: 136–41; 1978b: 9–17). In regard to the Twenty *Saṃghas*, the PP *sūtras* present this subject matter within the instructions regarding the *Saṃgha* Jewel, utilizing the formula "there are *bodhisattvas*, great beings." The *sūtra*s then list the various kinds of *bodhisattvas* from the consideration of differences that arise from the circumstances of their rebirth. The 100,000-verse PP (1914: 266–81) lists up to forty-eight different *bodhisattvas* in this manner, while the 25,000-verse PP (Conze, 1975a: 66–74, Dutt, 1934: 60–72) lists twenty-four different types. The 8000-verse PP does not give this type of list at all, and indeed, Haribhadra must awkwardly fit the instructions on the *saṃgha* into the 8,000-verse PP in his AAĀ (1932: 35–36). The list of twenty-four different types of *bodhisattvas* or Noble Beings (*ārya*) found in the 25,000-verse PP and its recensions corresponds well with the traditional twenty-seven types of personalities, constituted by the eighteen types of *śaikṣa* and nine types of *aśaikṣa*, found in the *Dakṣiṇīyasūtra* (AKV: 566–67), the *Abhidharmasamuccaya* (Pradhan, 88–91), and the *Mahāvyutpatti* (See *Traité*, tome III (1970): 1389–92; see table 4.1, pages 96 and 97).

The 25,000-verse PP *sūtra* exists in two forms: an unrevised and a revised version. The unrevised version of the 25,000-verse PP *sūtra* was translated into Chinese four times. Three of the translations, ones by Mokṣala in 291 CE, Kumārajīva in 403–440 CE, and Hsüan Tsang in 659–663 CE, translate the 25,000-verse PP in its entirety. The revised version of the 25,000-verse PP *sūtra* is extant in Sanskrit and in Tibetan translation. Conze refers to this as the "recast version of the *Pañcaviṃśatisāhasrikāprajñāpāramitāsūtra*," or "the version in 25,000 lines that has been adjusted to conform to the divisions of the *Abhisamayālaṃkāra*." The Sanskrit is based on manuscripts from the eighteenth and nineteenth century, while the Tibetan translation is based on a redaction attributed to Haribhadra. Nancy Lethcoe (1976) has made a comparison of these revised and unrevised recensions of the 25,000-verse PP in order to document the *sūtra*'s relationship to the AA. For our purposes here in regard to the topic of the Twenty *Saṃghas*, Lethcoe's research (1976: 501) indicates that nineteen out of the twenty-four sections that discuss the variety of *bodhisattvas* are present in all of the Chinese translations. This research also indicates that seventeen out of the Twenty *Saṃghas* are listed in all the Chinese translations. This proves that the sections of the 25,000-verse PP *sūtra* that have to do with the variety lists of *bodhisattvas* predates the AA verse summation of the Twenty *Saṃghas*. It also shows that the topic of the Twenty *Saṃghas* is one of the oldest topics brought into the AA, possibly from previous *Abhidharma* sources. A recent work by Makransky (1997: 127–57) has decisively demonstrated that the AA, its earliest commentaries, and most of the later Tibetan commentaries are based on the revised recensions of the 25,000-verse PP *sūtra*, a special revised version of this *sūtra* redacted by Haribhadra, which Makransky refers to as "rP." As we will see below, the tradition also seems to follow this observation in that the hagiographies of the earliest commentators, such as

Ārya Vimuktisena, identify a special relationship between the AA and the 25,000-verse PP *sūtra*.

Origins of the *Abhisamayālaṃkāra*: Maitreyanātha and Asaṅga

At some point in the fourth century CE, a summation of the hidden meaning of the PP *sūtras*, most likely the meaning as expressed in the revised 25,000-verse PP, appeared as the AA. The hidden meaning of the PP, which the AA arranges, concerns the soteriological system of the entire *Mahāyāna* path. The AA expresses this system by either explicitly expressing what is already mentioned in the PP *sūtra* or superimposing a path schema that is foreign to the *sūtra*s and expressed in *Yogācāra* terminology. The text of the AA itself consists of a fusion of buddhalogical teachings found in the *Abhidharma* and PP *sūtra*s and technical terminology found in *Yogācāra* treatises. Along these lines, Makransky (1997) has investigated controversies concerning the *dharmakāya*, one of the most important theories of the AA system, through documenting the theory of *dharmakāya's* historical relationship to *Yogācāra* concepts. Our topic of the Twenty *Saṃgha*s is most likely not a superimposition of *Yogācāra* theory on to the PP *sūtra*s but rather an importation of older *Abhidharma* material into the PP *sūtra*s and versified in the AA. Tsong kha pa will also approach the Twenty *Saṃgha*s as a subject specifically related to the *Abhidharma*. As we will see, his approach will be limited to the textual material that was available to him and the scholastic and historical circumstances in which he was writing.

The Indo-Tibetan tradition ascribes the work of the AA to Maitreyanātha. Some scholars assumed that this is the name of a teacher of the great Indian scholar Asaṅga (ca. fourth century CE), while others believe it was Asaṅga himself who wrote these verses.[4] The legends surrounding Asaṅga, plus the historical and chronological problems associated with his life, cannot be entertained here.[5] The Indo-Tibetan tradition assumes that Maitreyanātha is a celestial *bodhisattva* who is the same being as the future next Buddha (AAĀ 1932: 75.17–22).

This traditional view was inherited in Tibet and explained in great detail by Bu ston rin po che (Obermiller, 1986: 138–39) and Tārānātha (Chattopadhyaya, 1970: 156–60) who both tell of a story that Asaṅga, after meditating for eleven years in solitude, encountered Maitreya at first in the form of a dog and then in his real form as a celestial *bodhisattva*. Asaṅga was then transported through the power of meditative concentration to *Tuṣita* heaven where Maitreya proceeded to instruct him in the *Abhisamayālaṃkāra* and the other four texts that became known to the Tibetans as the five texts of Maitreya (*byams gzhung sde lnga*).[6] In regard to this traditional belief in the relationship between Maitreya and Asaṅga, Tsong kha pa explains that Asaṅga received special instructions (*gdams ngag*) from Maitreya through the meditative concentration of the stream of doctrine (*dharmaśrotas-samādhi*) (*Golden Garland* 1970: 25.3–19).

Tsong kha pa, along with the predecessors of this tradition, assumes that Asaṅga received the AA along with four other texts from Maitreyanātha. In the lineage lists, Asaṅga is praised as "the Noble Being who was prophesied by the Buddha (*rgyal bas lung bstan 'phags pa thogs med zhabs*)." Tsong kha pa (*Golden Garland* 1970: 24–25) indicates predictions concerning Asaṅga from the *Mañjuśrīmūlatantra*, *Madhyamakālaṃkāravṛtti* of Śāntarakṣita, and Atiśa's *Ratnakaraṇḍodghāṭa-nāmamadhyamakopadeśa*. Tsong kha pa also cites Dharmamitra's *Prasphuṭapadā* for the claim that Asaṅga reached the third *bodhisattva* level. In relation to our concern of how Asaṅga fits into the AA lineage tradition, the first and only tangible evidence of Asaṅga's place in this lineage is found in the opening verses of praise in Haribhadra's AAĀ (1932: 1.15–160) and *Sphuṭārthā*.

Haribhadra is the first written source to claim a place for Asaṅga in the AA lineage. The later Tibetan tradition assumed that this homage mentions the name of Asaṅga's commentary. This is mentioned by Bu ston (Obermiller, 1986: 140) while Tsong kha pa (*Golden Garland* 1970: 26) indicates that the authorship of the commentary needs to be investigated. A Tibetan biographer of Tsong kha pa (Rnam rgyal 1967: 147.12) makes the claim that he studied Asaṅga's AA commentary, the so-called *Tattvaviniścaya*. We do have commentaries by Asaṅga to the other four root texts of Maitreya, but the said AA commentary of Asaṅga is not extant. Moreover, neither the works of Ārya Vimuktisena nor those of Haribhadra provide citations from this commentary. However the evidence for the existence of Asaṅga's AA commentary may eventually present itself: the Tibetan tradition certainly maintains the existence of such a commentary.

In regard to the topic of the Twenty *Saṃghas*, Asaṅga plays an essential part for Tsong kha pa. Tsong kha pa utilizes Asaṅga's *Abhidharmasamuccaya* (Rahula, 1971) to document the distinguishing characteristics of the Noble Beings within the Twenty *Saṃghas* and views this text as supplementing the verse summary given in the AA. Tsong kha pa and the Indo-Tibetan tradition find continuance in the lineage through holding that Asaṅga passed the lineage of the AA on to Vasubandhu.

Vasubandhu

Vasubandhu[7] (ca. fourth to fifth century CE) is widely regarded as the younger half-brother of Asaṅga, sons of the same mother but having different fathers. Vasubandhu is praised in the lineage tradition as the "crown ornament of Indian scholars (*'jam gling mkhas pa'i gtsug rgyan dbyig gi gnyen*)."[8] This is likely due to his prolific composition of essential Buddhist texts, most notably the *Abhidharmakośa* and its *Bhāṣya*. Similar to the personage of Asaṅga, Vasubandhu has many mythological stories and historical problems in the documentation of his life that we will not discuss here.[9] The relation of Vasubandhu to the AA lineage is also made by Haribhadra in his AAĀ (1932: 1).

As in the case of Asaṅga, the Tibetan tradition understood Haribhadra's praise to refer to an AA commentary of Vasubandhu. We do not have any extant copy of this purported commentary nor does any subsequent AA commentator utilize any citations from it. Tsong kha pa in his *Golden Garland* (1970: 26ff) argues that the commentary of Vasubandhu's has been confused with a commentary written by Daṃṣṭrasena.[10] Tsong kha pa's biographers claim that he studied the *Paddhati* commentary of Vasubandhu (Rnam rgyal, 1967: 147.12). If there is such a commentary, Tsong kha pa did not utilize it for his study of the Twenty *Saṃghas*. Here, Vasubandhu is still important for Tsong kha pa in regard to the Twenty *Saṃghas* in that Tsong kha pa relies on the *Abhidharmakośa, Bhāṣya,* and its related subcommentaries, to define each of the Noble Beings among the Twenty *Saṃghas*. Vasubandhu is considered to have passed the AA lineage on to Ārya Vimuktisena.

Ārya Vimuktisena

Ārya Vimuktisena (ca. early sixth century CE) is probably the most important figure in the AA lineage. He is the author of the earliest extant commentary on the AA, the *Abhisamayālaṃkāravṛtti* (AAV),[11] which set the standard for all subsequent Indian and Tibetan AA commentaries. The title "Ārya" being an epithet of one who has obtained the path of seeing (*darśanamārga*) in the *bodhisattvas* path, Ārya Vimuktisena is usually praised as being one "who found the middle way."[12] In the lineage tradition he is regarded as being one of the four principal disciples of Ācārya Vasubandhu. The colophon of the AAV in the Nepalese manuscript and also of the Tibetan canon mentions that Ārya Vimuktisena was the nephew of a master named Buddhadāsa, who presided over many *Vihāras* of the *Kaurakulla-Āryasammatīya* school.[13]

Ārya Vimuktisena's commentary served as the basis for all subsequent Indian and Tibetan commentaries. The commentary itself is not that elaborate in that it merely provides brief comments between sections of citations from the 25,000-verse PP. Ārya Vimuktisena correlates each topic of the AA, such as the twenty-two types of *bodhicitta*, to a specific portion of the *sūtra* text. His was the first commentary to establish a textual relationship between the 25,000-verse PP *sūtra* and each topic of the AA. The Tibetan tradition recognizes this as the "pioneering" commentary that correlated the *sūtra* and ornament together (*mdo rgyan sbyar ba'i shing rta'i srol phye*). Ārya Vimuktisena's commentary serves as an important source for identifying a definite correlation between the AA and PP *sūtras*. His commentary provides the basic structure and exegesis that all subsequent commentators were to follow. Tsong kha pa utilizes Ārya Vimuktisena's *Vṛtti* in his own extensive commentary to the AA. The interpretation that Ārya Vimuktisena establishes with regard to the Twenty *Saṃgha*s closely follows the presentation of that given by Vasubandhu in the *Abhidharmakośa* (*Golden Garland* 1970: 260). Ārya Vimuktisena is also the first AA commentator to establish a connection between the *saṃgha* of *bodhisattva*s given in the AA and that presented in the *Avaivartikacakrasūtra*. We will discuss this subject in chapter 5.

Haribhadra

Historically and in the lineage tradition, Haribhadra (c. 730–795; Mano, 1972: 17) is the most important Indian AA commentator after Ārya Vimuktisena. These two commentators are the pillars upon which the Tibetan commentarial tradition of the AA stands. In the Tibetan tradition they are viewed as sharing common philosophical views, grouped as *Yogācāra-Svātantrika-Mādhyamikans* (*rnal 'byor spyod pa'i dbu ma rang rgyud pa*), and their position is referred to as *'Phags seng gi lugs* ("the position of the Ārya and Hari"). Haribhadra is praised in the lineage prayers as the "extensive commentator on the supreme path of *Prajñāpāramitā*" (*lam mchog sher phyin rgyas mdzad*). The tradition relates that Haribhadra survived, while still in his mother's womb, an attack by a lion in which his mother was eaten. Because Haribhadra was not consumed by the lion, he was called "fortunate (*bhadra*) [with regards to the] lion (*hari*)."

Haribhadra composed four works in relation to the PP *sūtra*s and the AA. These four texts are the *Abhisamayālaṃkārālokā* (AAĀ), *Abhisamayālaṃkāraśāstravṛttisphuṭārthā* (AASPh), a recast version of the *Pañcaviṃśati* in eight chapters known as the *Le'u brgyad ma*, and *Subodhinī*. The AAĀ and the AASPh are the most famous of Haribhadra's works and the commentaries most relied upon by the Tibetan commentators. The AAĀ has the unique feature of explaining the *Aṣṭasāhaśrikāprajñāpāramitā* based on the AA. This was the first time such a relationship had been established. The AASPh is not related to any particular *sūtra* but provides a precise and succinct commentary to the AA. We know that Haribhadra was writing during the reign of Dharmapāla (rg. ca. 770–810; Ruegg, 1981: 101), the greatest of the Pāla kings, according to the colophon in the AAĀ (994.15–22): "This fine *pañjikā* which casts light on the truly real was written by me, having lived in this excellent, glorious Trikaṭuka monastery, mine of all good qualities, . . . with the support of the glorious Dharmapāla."

Whatever the surrounding political and educational circumstances at this time may have been, Haribhadra brought a new scholastic agenda to commenting on the AA. Haribhadra's commentaries would set a new standard in the structure and content of AA commentaries that had not significantly changed since Ārya Vimuktisena. His two main commentaries, the AASPh and AAĀ, weave together citations of Buddhist texts from *Abhidharma, Yogācāra*, and *Madhyamaka* sources and utilize Ārya Vimuktisena's *Vṛtti*. He brought out a new controversial interpretation of Dharmakāya (see Makransky, 1997) and applied eighth- and ninth-century *Madhyamaka* philosophical principles, such as the *Madhyamaka* understanding of the two truths, to many of his comments on the AA. Haribhadra also began to apply the Buddhist reasoning and logic originating from Dignāga and Dharmakīrti to epistemological problems that he found in the AA. Haribhadra's preoccupation with bringing the principles of logic and reasoning to the AA is evident in that we find most likely the first Indian Buddhist use of *pramāṇapuruṣa* in the AAĀ (W 1932: 7 and 153).

With regard to the Twenty *Saṃgha*s, Haribhadra's interpretation differs from Ārya Vimuktisena's and his AAĀ and AASPh provide the basis for most Tibetans' understanding of the topic. Tsong kha pa's presentation of both Haribhadra's and Ārya Vimuktisena's enumeration of the Twenty *Saṃgha*s will be discussed in chapter 5.

Other Major Indian Commentators

A major figure in the Indian AA scholastic tradition is the scholar Dharmamitra (fl. 800–850 CE), who is not mentioned in the lineage prayers of either Se ra rje mtsun pa or Rong ston pa (1988: xxi). Dharmamitra was the author of an extremely important subcommentary on Haribhadra's *Sphuṭārthā* called the *Prasphuṭapadā*. Dharmamitra's commentary is meant to clarify Haribhadra's statements in the AASPh rather than to be an independent work on the AA. Dharmamitra's treatise is important because it reveals a form of Indian *Mahāyāna* Buddhism that anticipates many Tibetan Buddhism developments in the eleventh to thirteenth centuries. For instance, besides distinguishing the two modes of interpreting the PP *sūtra*s as given above (i.e., "profound" and "vast"), Dharmamitra substantiates Haribhadra's use of the term *pramāṇapuruṣa* (Pk 5194, p. 90, 66b.4). Dharmamitra also makes reference to Vasubandhu as "the second Buddha"(p. 65, 3b.3), "the seven logical treatises" (*tshad ma'i gzhung rnam pa bdun*) of Dharmakīrti (p. 69, 13a.8), and uses the term *great madhyamaka* (*dbu ma chen po*; p. 93, 73b5). The next step by modern scholarship in the study of the AA should be to translate or provide a major study of this commentary. Dharmamitra is also important for the study of the Twenty *Saṃghas* in that he is utilized by Tibetan scholars for identifying the opinions of Indian scholars from Udeśa, Kong ka na, and Bengal (PSPh, p. 84: 51b2–8) in determining the point on the spiritual path when one becomes "irreversible" (*avaivartika*).

Also outside of the lineage list but utilized by Tsong kha pa in his *Golden Garland*'s discussion of the Twenty *Saṃghas* are the following commentaries: the *Durbodhāloka* of Dharmakīrtiśrī (fl. 925–950 CE), the *Abhisamayālaṃkāravṛttipiṇḍārtha* of Prajñākaramati (ca. 950–1000 CE), the *Śuddhamatī* of Ratnākaraśānti (ca. 1000 CE), and the *Marmakaumudī* and *Munimatālaṃkāra* of Abhayākaragupta (ca. 1100 CE). Each of these commentaries gives fragmentary discussions of the Twenty *Saṃghas* and their remarks are given in response to other Indian commentators. Tsong kha utilizes the essential quotes from these commentaries to explain his system of the Twenty *Saṃghas*. Tsong kha pa's elucidation of the Twenty *Saṃghas* utilizing these commentaries will be presented in chapters 4 and 5.

Tsong kha pa's Tibetan Predecessors in the *Abhisamayālaṃkāra* Tradition

From our brief survey of the major Indian personages in the AA lineage we can see that the two main systems of AA exegesis that the Tibetans would inherit were derived from Ārya Vimuktisena and Haribhadra. Although the Tibetans had translated the root text of the AA and several of its commentaries during the reign of Khri srong lde btsan (ca. 740–798) (Lalou, 1953: 331, texts no. 516, 517) the first indigenous commentary was not composed until Rngog lo tsā ba Blo ldan shes rab (1059–1109 CE).

Rngog lo tsā ba Blo ldan shes rab

Jackson (1994: 372) has referred to Rngog lo as the father of Tibetan scholasticism. The traditions he established in Tibet became the main enduring lineages of not only logic and epistemology and

Svātantrika-Yogācāra-Madhyamaka but also the tradition of the Five Dharmas of Maitreya (*byams chos sde lnga*). Rngog lo may have even brought to Tibet the tradition of studying the five treatises known as the Five Dharmas. Rngog lo was responsible for the distinctly Tibetan tradition of writing long explanations of the AA based on Haribhadra's short commentary, the *Sphuṭārthā*.

One cannot overstate the importance of Rngog blo ldan shes rab in the transmission and establishment of AA studies in Tibet. He translated not only the *Sphuṭārthā*, but also the *Ālokā* of Haribhadra and the *Vṛtti* of Ārya Vimuktisena. Rngog lo also made a revised translation of the AA in collaboration with the Indian *paṇḍita* Go mi 'chi med (Amaragomin). As we have mentioned, Rngog lo composed the first indigenous Tibetan commentaries on the AA. The two principal commentaries Rngog wrote are known as the *ṭīk chung*, or *Lo tsā ba chen po'i bsdus don* (MHTL no. 11471), and the *Lo tsā ba blo ldan shes rab kyi phar phyin ṭīk chen* (MHTL no. 11470). The latter text is not extant and therefore we do not know its contents or its contribution to our present study. However, the *Lo tsā ba chen po'i bsdus don* has been made available recently through the work of Jackson (1993).

Rngog lo's remarks on the Twenty *Saṃgha*s in the *Lo tsā ba chen po'i bsdus don* (1993: 40.6–51.1) are brief and do not present a full scholastic elaboration that one finds in the work of later Tibetan scholiasts. Tsong kha pa in his *Golden Garland* (1970: 264–65) remarks that Rngog incorrectly correlates divisions within the Twenty *Saṃgha*s with stages of *bodhisattva bhūmi*s. Rngog (1993: 41.6ff) does appear to assert this, but we cannot give a full assessment of his comments without his larger commentary. Tsong kha pa was aware of and studied Rngog's commentaries even though he disagreed with his writing on the Twenty *Saṃgha*s.

Gnyal zhig pa 'jam dpal rdo rje

One of the most important Tibetan AA commentators after Rngog lo was Gnyal zhig pa 'jam dpal rdo rje (fl. ca. 1200). Gnyal zhig pa was a student of Zhang g.ye pa byang chub 'bum and composed a commentary on the *Sphuṭārthā* called *Theg chen po la 'jug pa* (MHTL no. 11517). This commentary was recently recovered from communist mainland China in the form of a handwritten manuscript and is preserved at the Library of Tibetan Works and Archives in Dharamsala, India. Two recent articles, Samten (1997) and Sparham (1996), provide details establishing the manuscript as a work of Gnyal zhig pa's and highlight the significance of this text. I have not had access to this important manuscript but based on the above articles we can make some general remarks. Gnyal zhig pa's commentary is five hundred folios long and, based on the first seven folios presented by Sparham (1996: 24–26), contains a minute breakdown of divisions and subdivisions of topical outlines (*sa bcas*). The style and arrangement of this text therefore provides the first literary evidence of the kind of AA exegesis that would dominate the next three hundred years of Tibetan scholasticism: subdivisions of individual AA topics complemented with citations of Indian texts that substantiate minor doctrinal points resulting in expansive encyclopedic volumes of AA commentary. There are five individuals listed in the AA lineage after Gnyal zhig pa that we will not document here: Gzang ring dar tshul, Brtson 'grus rdo rje, Bo dong rin chen, Brtong 'grus seng ge, and Tsad ma'i bu bsod nams mgon. 'Jam skya Nam mkha' dpal (fl. early 1300s) was a great Sa skya pa scholar who is not mentioned in the lineage list and who was influential in the life of Tsong kha pa (see below). He wrote an AA commentary known as the *Phar ṭīk* (MHTL no. 11523) and was a PP teacher of Bu ston rin chen grub.

Bu ston rin chen grub

Bu ston rin chen grub (1290–1364) is well known as a Tibetan historian of Buddhism, formulator of the Tibetan canon, and a great scholar-practitioner of the *Kālācakra Tantra* cycle of teachings. Ruegg (1966) has translated and published a study of his spiritual biography. Bu ston was also a prolific scholar of *Mahāyāna* scholastic works and his AA commentary, the *Lung gi nye ma* (Collected Works, tsha, 1971), provides us with the next evolutionary stage in the development of Tibetan AA commentarial exegesis. Bu ston is said to have used Gnyal zhig's AA commentary when he first came to Zhwa-lu monastery as a young man. As we have mentioned, the template for early Tibetan AA commentary, numerous divisions and encyclopedic expansion, is found in Gnyal zhig's commentary. Bu ston followed this tradition, and in addition, his commentary introduces heuristic techniques not found in earlier extant Tibetan AA commentaries, particularly with regard to the Twenty *Saṃgha*s. The section on the Twenty *Saṃgha*s in Bu ston's commentary is nineteen pages (1971: 243–62). At the beginning of this section we find a distinction in presenting the Twenty *Saṃgha*s between the *allegorical saṃgha* (*mtshon byed dpe*) of *śrāvaka*s and the *actual saṃgha* (*mtshon bya don*) of *bodhisattva*s. Bu ston's commentary is the earliest extant available commentary that mentions such a distinction. The heuristic technique of first presenting the "classic" *śrāvaka saṃgha* as a metaphor for the real *saṃgha* of *bodhisattva*s is followed by every subsequent Tibetan presentation on the Twenty *Saṃgha*s. Bu ston's articulation on the Twenty *Saṃgha*s also utilizes quotations from the *Abhidharmakośa* to give defining characteristics for the individuals within the Twenty *Saṃghas*. These structural factors of exegesis would be utilized and expanded upon by Bu ston's *Prajñāpāramitā* student Nya dbon kun dga' dpal.

Before discussing Nya dbon, we should mention the work on the Twenty *Saṃghas* of Bu ston's contemporary, Dol po pa shes rab rgyal mtshan (1292–1361). Although not mentioned in Tsong kha pa's lineage tradition, Dol po pa gives a brief discussion on the Twenty *Saṃghas* (455ff.) in his AA commentary, the *Rnam bshad mdo'i don bde blag tu rtogs pa* (vol. 6, 1992: 323–882). The presentation gives a general interpretation of the twenty individuals of the *saṃgha* in the confines of strict *Abhidharma* defining characteristics. Dol po pa does not distinguish an *allegorical* from an *actual saṃgha* nor does he cite any Indian *śāstras* other than the AA for his presentation. It is also not clear whether he is following Ārya Vimuktisena or Haribhadra's interpretation on the Twenty *Saṃghas*. Dol po pa's tradition of exegesis on the Twenty *Saṃghas* does not appear to follow the lineage tradition presented by Bu ston and later followed by Tsong kha pa. We mention Dol po pa here because he is cited, along with Bu ston, as one of the two *Prajñāpāramitā* teachers of Nya dbon kun dga' dpal (*Yid kyi mun sel* 1978: 4, Ruegg, 1969: 25, Samten, 1997: 839).

Nya dbon kun dga' dpal

The Sa skya master Nya dbon kun dga' dpal (1285–1379) was one of the greatest *Prajñāpāramitā* commentators of his era. His AA commentary, the *Shad sbyar yid kyi mun sel,* was written at Sa skya in 1371 and represents a reformulation of Bu ston's *Lung gi nye ma*. Nya dbon exemplifies the scholastic trend toward expansion and detailed excursus as his commentary is over four hundred folios printed in two Western-style volumes. His articulation of the Twenty *Saṃghas* (1978: 349–402) gives a detailed analysis of the *allegorical saṃgha* (1978: 349–77) and *actual saṃgha* (1978: 377–402) that is not witnessed in previous commentators. Nya dbon's presentation of the Twenty *Saṃghas* provides the structure and outline that influenced Tsong kha pa's approach to the topic. As one of Tsong kha pa's AA teachers, Nya dbon's commentary on the Twenty *Saṃghas* is the most important extant source we have in that even a brief comparison between the *Yid kyi mun sel* and *Golden Garland* reveals a parallel style of presentation. Nya dbon follows the Twenty *Saṃgha* presentation given in Haribhadra's AAĀ. He provides detailed descriptions of the various Noble Beings among the Twenty *Saṃghas,* documenting the parameters that define their stage in the path substantiated by extensive citations from Indian *śāstras*.

For the *śrāvaka saṃgha*, he cites the *Abhidharmakośa*, its *Bhāṣya*, and the *Vyākhyā* of Yaśomitra. Nya dbon also utilizes the *Abhidharmasamuccaya* and its *Bhāṣya*. Documenting the *bodhisattva saṃgha*, Nya dbon utilizes many of the later Indian AA commentators, such as the commentaries of Dharmakīrtiśrī, Prajñākaramati, and Abhayākaragupta. These are the same Indian sources that Tsong kha pa would utilize in his presentation of the Twenty *Saṃgha*s. However, although Tsong kha pa may have been influenced by Nya dbon's presentation, the doctrinal system of Twenty *Saṃgha*s that Tsong kha pa presents is his own and provides details, particularly with regard to the characteristics of the *śrāvaka arhat*, that are not given in the *Yid kyi mun sel*. Nevertheless, we can say the Nya dbon's commentary is the earliest extant evidence for the foundation of Tsong kha pa's approach to the Twenty *Saṃgha*s.

We note "extant evidence" because the works of the most influential Tibetan AA commentator of all for Tsong kha pa, Red mda' ba gzhon nu blos gros (1349–1412), are not available. As we will see below, Red mda' ba was the greatest influence for Tsong kha pa in writing on the Twenty *Saṃgha*s. It was Red mda' ba's teaching the *Abhidharmakośa* and *Abhidharmasamuccaya* to Tsong kha pa that would give him the textual knowledge to investigate the Twenty *Saṃgha*s.

Recapitulation

A verse summary of the hidden meaning of the *Prajñāpāramitā-sūtra*s emerged as the *Abhisamayālaṃkāra* in the fourth to six centuries of the common era. The later Indian tradition (eighth century) attributed this text to Maitreyanātha. The first chapter's twenty-third and twenty-fourth stanzas of this *śāstra* succinctly presented a paradigm of soteriological typologies known as the Twenty *Saṃgha*s. At an early time in India this verse summary text was correlated with the 25,000-verse PP, which resulted in a standardized revised 25,000-verse PP utilized in conjugation with the AA. The most influential Indian commentators were Ārya Vimuktisena and Haribhadra who presented different systems of interpreting the Twenty *Saṃgha*s. The tradition of commenting on Haribhadra's *Sphuṭārthā* was brought to Tibet by Rngog lo tsā ba in the eleventh century. Rngog lo's work began a tradition of commenting on the AA, which resulted in an enduring lineage of successive generations of more expansive Tibetan commentaries. The tradition of expansive AA commentaries became especially apparent with the *Lung gi nye ma* of Bu ston rin chen grub. In this commentary we find subdivisions and detailed descriptions of the Twenty *Saṃgha*s substantiated with citations of Indian *śāstras*. This style of commenting on the Twenty *Saṃgha*s expanded exponentially with the work of Nya dbon kun dga' dpal and many of his Sa skya pa contemporaries such as Bla ma dam pa bsod nams rgyal mtshan (1312–1375). The expanded AA exegesis of fourteenth-century Tibetan commentators provided detailed examinations of particular topics in the AA. The expansion of investigating AA topics resulted in the topic of the Twenty *Saṃgha*s being investigated independently of the AA. The earliest known evidence of this genre of literature is the *Dge 'dun nyi shu'i mtshan nyid 'phreng ba* by Nu mgo rgyal ba rin chen (1328–1386), an extraordinary scholar from Mi-nyag rab-sgang who is usually identified as a Sa skya pa.[14] However, this work is not available and the other earliest independent treatise on the Twenty *Saṃgha*s is the *Stairway Taken by Those of Lucid Intelligence* (*blo gsal bgrod pa'i them skad*) of Tsong kha pa.

The documentation of these Indian and Tibetan commentators has provided us with the scholastic purview that Tsong kha pa inherited. We have documented both the Indian and Tibetan commentators that were most influential in Tsong kha pa's life, noting the fourteenth-century trend of expanding upon the assimilation of Indian AA commentaries that resulted in progressively encyclopedic Tibetan commentaries. The diagram on page 37 (figure 2.1) charts the lineage of these Indian and Tibetan commentators up until the time of Tsong kha pa. The scholastic atmosphere in Tibet at this time was ready for new developments in AA exegesis as revealed in the early life of Tsong kha pa and his work on the Twenty *Saṃgha*s that we will now document.

THE *ABHISAMAYĀLAṂKĀRA* AND TWENTY *SAṂGHAS* IN TSONG KHA PA'S LIFE AND WORKS

We have traced the lineage of the Indian and Tibetan commentators that preceded Tsong kha pa, documenting the trans-Himalayan tradition that he inherited. In this section we will discuss Tsong kha pa's life in relation to this inherited AA lineage and the circumstances that led to his writing on the Twenty *Saṃgha*s. We will show that Tsong kha's work on the Twenty *Saṃgha*s, through his *Stairway* (*Blo gsal bgrod pa'i them skad*) and *Abbreviated Bestowel* (*Dge 'dun nyi shu rje snang*), most likely represents his first major writings. We will also show how his writing on the Twenty *Saṃgha*s contributed to and formed part of his first major volume, the *Golden Garland* (*Legs bshad gser phreng*).

Much has been written and several books have documented the great philosophical works that Tsong kha pa contributed to Buddhist thought in Tibet. Tsong kha pa blo bzang grag pa (1357–1419) was one of the most profoundly influential and innovative minds in the history

Figure 2.1 Tsong kha pa's Lineage of AA Teachings

Indian	Tibetan
Maitreya	Rngog lo (tsā ba blo ldan shes rab)
Asaṅga	'Bre (shes rab 'bar)
Vasubandhu	Ar (byang chub ye shes)
Ārya Vimuktisena	('Dul 'dzin dkarm mo) gzhon nu tshul khrims
Bhadanta Vimuktisena	(Dkar chung ring mo) shes rab 'bum
Paramasena	(Zhang g.ye pa) byang chub 'bum
Viniyatasena	Gnyal zhig 'jam rdor ('jam pa 'i rdo rje)
Vairocanabhadra	Gzang ring dar tshul
Haribhadra	Brtson 'grus rdo rje
Buddhaśrījñānapāda	Bo dong rin chen
Guṇamitra	Brtson 'grus seng ge
Ratnabhadra	Tsad ma 'i skyes bu (bsod nams mgon)
Candrabhadra	Bu ston thams cad mkhyen
Dhīrava	Mkhas pa nya dpon
Sthirapāla	Rje btsun red mda 'ba
[up to top right]	Tsong kha pa blo bzang grags pa

Note: As recorded in Se ra rje btsun's *Klu dbang gi rol mtsho*: 1b–2b. See also Samten (1997: 837–38).

of Tibetan Buddhism. Born as the fourth child to an ordinary nomadic family, Tsong kha pa would go on to become a prominent figure in Tibetan Buddhist scholarship referred to in the later tradition as "the Second Buddha" (*sang rgyas gnyis pa*). Tsong kha pa, an erudite and thoroughly trained scholar, was also an accomplished practitioner who blended together theory and practice, utilizing both an emphasis on monastic discipline and the techniques of Tantric transformational technology. He is most widely known as the founder of the Dga'-ldan pa school, which later evolved into the present day Dge-lugs pa school. He is recognized for his innovative establishment of a definitive understanding of *Prāsaṅgika Madhyamaka* within Tibet that utilized an integration of Pramāṇa traditions with the *Madhyamaka*. Tsong kha pa wrote over two hundred works in eighteen volumes but his definitive interpretation of *Madhyamaka* philosophy was presented within four major treatises: the *Lam rim chen mo*, "Great Stages on the Path to Enlightenment"; the *Dgongs pa rab gsal*, "Illumination of the Thought"; the *Rigs pa'i rgya mtsho*, "Ocean of Reasoning"; and the *Legs bshad snying po*, "Essence of True Eloquence." His scholastic genius that articulated subtle distinctions of *Prāsaṅgika Madhyamaka* was only superseded by his acknowledgment as an embodiment of the Buddha of Wisdom himself, Mañjuśrī. As van der Kuijp (1983: 45) notes, Tsong kha pa's great contribution to Tibetan Buddhist thought was his reevaluation of Indian Buddhist *sūtra*s and *śāstra*s that not only substantiated his views in regard to *Madhyamaka* philosophy but also elaborated a new hermeneutical system of differentiating definitive and interpretable meaning found in scripture. Besides his innovative contributions to Tibetan scholarship, Tsong kha pa also performed "four great deeds" that shaped Tibetan Buddhist culture: the refurbishing of the Maitreya image at 'Dzing ji (1395), the teaching of the *Vinaya* at Gnam-rtse-ldeng (1400), establishing the Great Prayer Festival in Lhasa (1409), and the founding of Dga'-ldan monastery (1410). The great scholastic and cultural activity that occurred after Tsong kha pa had passed the age of forty is attributed to a transformative enlightenment experience he is said to have had in 1398. As van der Kuijp mentions (1985: 47), this year of 1398 "separates the old from the new Tsong-kha-pa. His enormous literary output from that time up to his demise in 1419 . . . set into motion a series of momentous controversies among his contemporaries and immediate successors. These contributed greatly to the further fragmentation of the Sa-skya-pa school and ultimately resulted in the establishment of the more or less autonomous Dga'-ldan-pa doctrinal entity."

Before this great transformation occurred in Tsong kha pa's life, in which he had a vision of Mañjuśrī and began to construct his special understanding of *Madhyamaka* philosophy, Tsong kha pa went through a period of training and study in which he studied under many teachers and developed his hermeneutical skills. This time of formative training in Tsong kha pa's life is considered to be the first period of his intellectual development and is referred to as the "*Prajñāpāramitā* study period," which culminates with his writing of the *Golden Garland* in May or June of 1389. It is this early period of Tsong kha pa's life in which he composed works on the Twenty *Saṃghas* that we wish to document here.

The Early Years of the Life of Tsong kha pa

Blo bzang grags pa (1357–1419)[15] was born in the northeastern area of Tibet known as A-mdo, in the province of Tsong-kha, "the land of onions," and hence his better known title of Tsong kha pa, "the man from onion valley."[16] Tsong kha pa was born the fourth of six sons amid many alleged wondrous signs and miraculous events. He received *upāsaka* vows as an infant from the Karmapa bla ma Rol pa'i rdo rje and was given his first name of Kun dga' snying po. At the young age of two, Tsong kha pa was entrusted to a Ka-dam-pa monk who would be his first teacher and abbot, Chos rje don grub rin chen, also a native of A-mdo who stayed at Bde-ba-can near Snye-thang. Tsong kha pa received several tantric consecrations of *Hevajra*, *Vajrapāṇi*, and *Cakrasaṃvara*, and received the tantric name Don yod rdo rje. At the age of six, he took the novice (*śrāmaṇera*) commitments under Don grub rin chen and Gzhon nu byang chub. At this time, he was given the name that he is also commonly known under, Blo bzang grags pa'i dpal.

With the intention to give this bright young student the proper education, Don grub rin chen, his teacher, encouraged Tsong kha pa to travel to central Tibet. At the age of fifteen, Tsong kha pa was ready to leave for the study centers of Dbus and Gtsang. Don grub rin chen gave Tsong kha pa some final instructions on the principal course of study, instructions that Obermiller (1934: 323) refers to as a *versus memorialis* and which is found in all the Tibetan biographies. The statement emphasizes the importance of the five texts of Maitreya (*byams chos sde snga*) and most likely reflects the educational sentiments of Don grub rin chen that influenced Tsong kha pa before he even left for central Tibet. The first stanza of what Don grub rin chen is purported to have advised Tsong kha pa is important for our purpose here: "First study with zeal the *Abhisamayālaṃkāra*, which is like an ornament of the three, the Great (*Śatasāhasrikā*), Middle (*Pañcaviṃśatisāhasrikā*), and Abridged (*Aṣṭasāhasrikā*) great Mother (*Prajñāpāramitā sūtras*)."[17]

This injunction to study first the AA, and consequently the AA's special topic of the Twenty *Saṃghas*, is one of the contributing factors explaining why the first works Tsong kha pa composed were on the Twenty *Saṃghas*.

Arriving in central Tibet, Tsong kha pa traveled to 'Bri-khung and underwent the ritual for generating the *Mahāyāna* altruistic thought for highest Enlightenment (*bodhicittotpāda*). He likewise heard from the master Sbyan ngas rin po che chos kyi rgyal po various Tantric teachings, such as the *Vajramālā*, Five Sections on *Mahāmudrā*, and Six Yogas of Nāropa. Then Tsong kha pa studied the healing arts and the eight subjects of medicine under a medical scholar from the district of Tshal called Dpon dkon mchogs skyabs. However, this period of medical study did not last long and Tsong kha pa went on to the monastic college of Bde-ba-can.

At Bde-ba-can, Tsong kha pa would take to heart the advice of his teacher and put his efforts into mastering the AA and its commentaries. He studied AA commentaries under Bkra shis Seng ge, a native of Snye-thang, the reading master Yon tan rgya mtsho, and U rgyan pa. It is said that by the age of seventeen Tsong kha pa had mastered the words of the AA commentarial cycle and by relying on the Sa skya pa commentary of 'Jam skya Nam mkha dPal, a teacher of Bu ston, he understood the essential meaning of the AA. He would also study the rest of the five books of Maitreya, particularly the *Mahāyānasūtrālaṃkāra* under a lama of Bde-ba-can named 'Jam Rin pa. Tsong kha pa completed the initial course of *Prajñāpāramitā* studies within two years. It is at this time that Tsong kha pa is said to have mastered the introductory "coursework" associated with the AA: the cycle of teachings concerned with the levels of concentration in the form and formless realms (*bsam gzugs*), and more importantly, the cycle of teachings concerning the Twenty *Saṃghas* (*dge 'dun nyi shu*) (Kaschewsky, 1971: III, 6r.5–6). At the age of eighteen, he took part in philosophical debate and examinations on the *Prajñāpāramitā* at the great monastic colleges of Gsang-phu and Bde-ba-can.

Tsong kha pa then completed travels in the areas of Gtsang: Snar-thang, Sa-skya, Stod-byang, Jo-mo-nang, Bo-dong, Mar-res-spyi-po-lhas, and Nyang-stod. At many of these places he received teachings or participated in debates concerning difficult matters of doctrine, particularly on the *Prajñāpāramitā*. At Sa-skya and Nyang-stod, Tsong kha pa participated in debates focusing on the subject matter of the *Prajñāpāramitā*. He studied under Chos rje phyogs las rnam rgyal at Jo-mo-nang and received the Bka' gdams pa precepts concerning the gradual stages to Enlightenment at Mar-res-spyi-po-lhas. Tsong kha pa also took part in debate activities at Er and went on to Snar-thang.

Up until this time, Tsong kha pa had focused his studies exclusively on the *Prajñāpāramitā*. However, the AA commentary of 'Jam skya Nam mkha dPal of Sa-skya that Tsong kha pa had studied earlier contained numerous citations of the *Abhidharmakośa*. Wishing to learn the details of the *Abhidharma*, Tsong kha pa requested and received *Abhidharma* teachings from a master at Snar-thang, the teacher-translator Don bzang pa. While at Snar-thang, Tsong kha pa saw the AA commentary of Nya dbon kun dga' dpal (1285–1379; van der Kuijp, 1985: 52) being carried in the arm of one of the *Kalyāṇamitras*. This commentary gave a clearer articulation of the subject matter than that of 'Jam skya Nam mkha dPal and also contained many passages from the *Abhidharmakośa*. Tsong kha pa generated a strong yearning to study the *Prajñāpāramitā* and *Abhidharma* with Nya dbon and set out to study with him. Tsong kha pa was welcomed in Nya-stod (Rnam rgyal, 1967: 121; mKhas grub, 1966: 23) and completed a debate cycle of the *Prajñāpāramitā* in Gnas-rnying. In his nineteenth year, during the summer of the Fire-Dragon year (1376), Tsong kha pa went to Rtse-chen and met with the great master Nya dbon, receiving a new explanation of the AA from the old master. However, with respect to the study of the *Abhidharmakośa*, Nya dbon indicated that his health was not that good and that Tsong kha pa should go and study under one of Nya dbon's brightest students, Red mda' ba gzhon nu blo gros (1349–1412). Tsong kha pa met Red mda' ba at Rtse chen and at that time began with him a systematic study of the *Abhidharmakośa* and its *Bhāṣya*.

Besides Don grub rin chen, Red mda' pa would prove to be a great influence on Tsong kha pa and the two became great colleagues, traveling together for many years. After a summer at Rtse-chen, the student and teacher went to Nyan-stod-bsam-gling where Tsong kha pa would study the *Madhyamakāvatāra*, which was being taught by Red mda' pa. Tsong kha pa traveled on to Dbus, where he studied the *Abhidharmasamuccaya* with the translator Byang chub rtse mo at Po-ta-la. He would go on to Bde-ba-can and then to Skyor-mo-lung. At Skyor-mo-lung, Tsong kha pa met and studied the *Vinaya* and *Abhidharma* under the famous master Bka' bzhi blo gsal. This teacher was a great disciple of a Dge bshes Thag ma. Tsong kha pa was able to gain a complete understanding of the *Vinaya* and its root commentaries. At this time, Tsong kha pa had an extraordinary religious experience concerning the meaning of the *Prajñāpāramitā* while participating in a ritual recitation of the *Heart Sūtra* at the Skyor-mo-lung monastery. He allegedly had a profound realization on the nature of emptiness (*śūnyatā*), the lack of inherent nature in the appearances of all things, and was absorbed in meditative concentration throughout the nine levels of *dhyāna*.[18] This experience relates the intensity of Tsong kha pa's study in the PP at this stage in his life. It shows, at least for his biographers, that his efforts utilized both theory and practice.

Tsong kha pa would study intensely fourteen volumes of related *Vinaya* and *Sūtra* commentaries. At this time, Tsong kha pa also traveled in Gtsang and spent time in Gnas-rnying. In Gnas-rnying it is said that he gave his first teachings on the *Abhidharmasamuccaya*.

In his twenty-first year, the Earth-Male-Horse year (1378), Tsong kha pa met again with Red mda'pa at Sa-skya (Rnam rgyal, 1967: 132). They stayed there for eleven months, during the course of which Tsong kha pa, besides hearing the path and its fruit teachings (*lam 'bras*), studied the *Abhidharmasamuccaya, Pramāṇavārttika*, and *Madhyamakāvatāra*, and received several Tantric teachings as well. From Sa-skya, the student and teacher went through Stod and Byang and stayed in Ngam-ring during the spring and summer. At this time Red mda' pa wrote his commentary to the *Abhidharmasamuccaya*.

After traveling to Dbus, Tsong kha pa planned a trip back to his homeland in Mdo-smad, based on a request from his ailing mother. He went to Mal-gro-lha-lung. However, Tsong kha pa changed his mind; he decided not to go back to his home and reaffirmed a dedication to his studies. As for his mother, it is said that he sent a painted image of himself which spoke to her when she received it, giving her immeasurable joy and happiness (Rnam rgyal, 1967: 133–34).

While staying at Mal-gro-lha-lung, Tsong kha pa began an intensive study of Dharmakīrti's *Pramāṇavārttika* under the Sa skya pa scholar Bson nams grags pa. Tsong kha pa had a profoundly moving spiritual experience while following the *Pramāṇavārttika* commentary of 'U yug pa Rigs pa'i seng ge (ca. 1190–after 1267: van der Kuijp, 1999: 650), specifically in regard to the *Pramāṇasiddhi* chapter. mKhas grub (1966: 36–37) gives a description of this experience:

> On account of his study and insight into [Rigs pa'i seng ge's] *Rigs mdzod* articulation of the *Pramāṇavārttika* and clearly perceiving the section on the second chapter which demonstrates the arrangement of the path, he was overcome with an insuppressible intense force of immeasurable faith in the doctrinal system and reasoning method of Dharmakīrti. During his stay [at Mal gro lha lung] that autumn, merely seeing the *Pramāṇavārttika* text would generate faith such that the hairs on the back of his neck would stand up and he could not hold back his tears.

As we will show, this religious awe for the *Pramāṇavārttika* serves as factor for the circumstantial evidence of when Tsong kha pa composed the *Stairway Taken by Those of Lucid Intelligence*, his foundational work on the Twenty *Saṃghas*.

Writing of the *Stairway Taken by Those of Lucid Intelligence*

After his stay at Mal gro lha lung, Tsong kha pa went back to Bde-ba-can and stayed there for the winter. It was at this time that he composed *Stairway Taken by Those of Lucid Intelligence* (*Blo gsal bgrod pa'i them skas*). Of all Tibetan biographies, only Blo bzang tshul khrims cha har dge bshes (Kaschewsky [1971: III,16v–III,17r]) states this time of composition:

> That winter he stayed in Bde-ba-can having gained insight into many texts. On account of being requested by many seekers, he composed a *śāstra* called *Blo gsal bgrod pa'i them skas* being a presentation of [the types of Noble Beings such as] the Stream-enterer, Once-returner, and so forth.

Working from the colophon of the *Stairway*, Blo bzang tshul khrims quotes a stanza that Tsong kha pa wrote with regard to the importance of study and casting away desire for fame and profit (*Stairway* 1977: 354). Can we adhere to Blo bzang tshul khrims claims that Tsong kha pa composed texts related to the Twenty *Saṃgha*s at Bde-ba-can monastery when he was twenty-one years old? I believe the internal literary evidence gives enough circumstantial evidence to substantiate this claim.

First, the colophon of the *Stairway* (1977: 355) itself mentions that it was composed at Bde-ba-can. Tsong kha pa states, "[This text] was written at the great college Bde-ba-can in the face of being urged on by some possessing clear mindedness searching for meaning."

The place being established, there are several factors that make it most likely that he composed this text after coming to Bde-ba-can from Mal-gro-lha-lung. First, Tsong kha makes exclusive praise to Red mda' pa, unlike the *Golden Garland* where he praises both Red mda' pa and Don grub rin chen. This exclusive praise is significant in that it relates the importance of Red mda' to the subject matter presented in the *Stairway*. The majority of the material in the *Stairway* although correlated to the special topic of the Twenty *Saṃgha*s, is based on research from the *Abhidharmakośa* and *Abhidharmasamuccaya* and their respective subcommentaries. As we have shown above, Red mda' pa was Tsong kha pa's main teacher of *Abhidharma* and was writing and teaching on the *Abhidharmasamuccaya* in the period of time right before coming back to Bde-ba-can. Tsong kha pa purportedly even taught this text before coming back to Sa-skya to study with Red mda' pa. Another important piece of internal evidence is that in the middle of the *Stairway*, Tsong kha pa displays a youthful enthusiasm and knowledge of the *Pramāṇavārttika*'s second chapter. He quotes two sets of stanzas from the *Pramāṇasiddhi* chapter to demonstrate that a Noble trainee (*ārya śaikṣa*: as opposed to an *Arhat*) has the possibility to backslide from his abandonment (*Stairway* 1977: 331–32). In one of the citations Tsong kha pa combines stanzas in a unique manner that demonstrates that he had acquired a firm knowledge of the *Pramāṇasiddhi* chapter through intensive study.[19] As we have mentioned above, his intensive study of the *Pramāṇavārttika* occurred at Mal-gro-lha-lung right before he came back to Bde-ba-can. Finally, the last paragraph of the *Stairway*'s colophon provides almost an autobiographical summation of the years from meeting Red mda' pa, to studying the *Vinaya* at Skyor-mo-lung, up to his study of *Pramāṇa* at Mal-gro-lha-lung. Praising Red mda' pa, Tsong kha pa states:

> [I] obtained illumination of [my] mind in regard to the meaning of all the upper and lower texts of the *Abhidharma* and was able to examine what is correct and incorrect with special confidence in the methods of logical reasoning (*pramāṇa*), and in the *piṭaka*s of *Sūtra* and *Vinaya*. (*Stairway* 1977: 355)

From the above circumstantial and internal literary evidence I propose that Tsong kha pa did indeed write the *Stairway* at Bde-ba-can monastery when he was twenty-one years old.

After his winter stay at Bde-ba-can monastery, Tsong kha pa would spend the next eleven years traveling to various monasteries in central Tibet, taking part in doctrinal debates and study concerning the topics of *Prajñāpāramitā*, *Pramāṇa*, and *Madhyamaka*. It is recorded that he began his main volume on the *Prajñāpāramitā*, the *Golden Garland* (*Legs bshad gser phreng*), during this period when he traveled to Tshal (mKhas grub, 1966: 43). At the age of thirty-one in 1389, Tsong kha pa finished the *Golden Garland* at Tshal and marking the end of his *Prajñāpāramitā* study period. According to a contemporary Dge-lugs-pa oral tradition, at a later time, Tsong kha became dissatisfied with his presentation in the *Golden Garland* and requested his disciple Rgyal tshab dar ma rin chen (1364–1432) to write a study of the *Prajñāpāramitā* from his newly found perspective. One should see van der Kuijp (1985: 52–54) for a discussion of the problems with this oral tradition.

Tsong kha pa most likely utilized his research on the Twenty *Saṃgha*s in the *Stairway* to assist in his compilation of the *Golden Garland*. This is because the first chapter of the *Golden Garland* contains over one hundred pages on the Twenty *Saṃghas*. However, a close look at the material on the Twenty *Saṃgha*s from the *Stairway* and *Golden Garland* reveals that the two texts are complementary. In other words, the subject matter on the Twenty *Saṃgha*s that was not included in the *Stairway* is given in the *Golden Garland* such that the *Golden Garland* completes the topic of the Twenty *Saṃghas*. For example, the *Stairway* gives a presentation solely on the allegorical (*tshon byed dpe)* or *śrāvaka saṃgha*. The presentation found in the *Golden Garland* offers complementary material on the *śrāvaka saṃgha*, but then it also gives a complete presentation of the actual (*tshon bya don*) or *bodhisattva saṃgha* not found at all in the *Stairway*. In fact, with regard to the *śrāvaka saṃgha* described in the *Golden Garland*, Tsong kha pa advises that one should look in the *Stairway* for detail on this type of *saṃgha*. In the *Golden Garland* (1970: 244) regarding his presentation of the *śrāvaka saṃgha*, Tsong kha pa states: "These *Saṃgha*s have been merely roughly described and since I have specifically composed an extensive essay on this topic, one should look there." Therefore, a complementary relationship exists between the *Stairway* and *Golden Garland* with regard to the topic of the Twenty *Saṃgha*s.

I have identified the location where Tsong kha pa wrote the *Stairway* and given my hypothesis as to the time of its composition. The next major question is why did Tsong kha pa focus on the topic of the Twenty *Saṃgha*s and write the *Stairway*? I have already noted that Tsong kha pa states in the colophon that he was "urged on by others" to address this topic. Tsong kha pa also states at the beginning of the *Stairway* (1977: 267–68), aside from the necessary soteriological importance of understanding the essential nature of the *saṃgha*, that

> [I] have applied myself only to the presentation of the great individuals who enter and abide [in the four fruitions] because those who claim to be greatly learned in the teachings from the *Abhidharma* scriptures on the many divisions within these [great individuals] are seen to be mistaken.

I can only conjecture about the actual scholars Tsong kha pa is referring to: he may be making reference to Nu mgo rgyal ba rin chen or another Sa skya pa scholar. Nevertheless, from this statement we can infer that Tsong kha pa is indirectly stating, not only the lack of knowledge among fellow students in his PP debating cycles (*phar phyin gyi grwa skor*), but also and more importantly, the lack of understanding about the teachings of *Abhidharma* among previous Tibetan AA scholars.

As I noted in the previous section on Tsong kha pa's Tibetan scholastic predecessors, beginning with Gnyal zhig 'jam pa'i rdo rje, we see a trend toward the expansion of AA commentary supplemented with an articulation of doctrine based on Indian *śāstra* citation in regard to the topic of the Twenty *Saṃgha*s. I also noted that in the commentaries of Bu ston and Nya dbon the citation and correlation of *Abhidharma* texts is used to define the distinguishing characteristics of the individuals within the Twenty *Saṃgha*s. In the commentaries of Tsong kha pa's predecessors we see a progression of development in which each successive generation cites a wider range of available

Abhidharma texts. For instance, in his section on the Twenty *Saṃgha*s Bu ston utilizes citations from the *Abhidharmakośa* and *Abhidharmakośabhāṣya* and Nya dbon utilizes, in addition, citations from the *Abhidharmasamuccaya* and its *Bhāṣya*. Tsong kha pa's work on the Twenty *Saṃgha*s is more developed than these predecessors from a textual standpoint in his use of the *Abhidharmakośavyākhyā*. We will see that Tsong kha pa clarifies doctrinal problems that he sees in previous scholarship on the Twenty *Saṃgha*s, such as concerning the *Arhat*, utilizing this commentary. Along these lines, we can postulate that Tsong kha pa, having been exposed to the commentaries and subcommentaries of the *Abhidharmakośa* and *Abhidharmasamuccaya* by Red mda' pa, noticed detailed descriptions of the individuals within the Twenty *Saṃgha*s that he had not seen in other AA commentaries he had previously studied. Also, because the AA is traditionally the first textbook studied in the monastic curriculum, the study and debate of controversial points concerning the Twenty *Saṃgha*s may have been a topic of discussion in his early PP debating rounds. Another possible scenario is that along with the AA being the first textbook studied in the monastery, the topic of the Twenty *Saṃgha*s may have been a specialized class within the first year of coursework. Tsong kha pa may have been reacting to monastic textbooks that he studied that were devoted to the Twenty *Saṃgha*s composed by various Sa skya pa scholars that are no longer extant.

SUMMARY

In this chapter I have documented the scholastic purview that Tsong kha pa inherited from his predecessors and the historical circumstances that were influential in his writing about the Twenty *Saṃgha*s. I have demonstrated that Tsong kha pa matured as a scholar at a pivotal point in the Indo-Tibetan history of AA commentarial transmission, a period of time in which the evolution of scholastic commentary had progressed to allow for the possibility of the Twenty *Saṃgha*s being addressed as an independent topic of composition. Within these circumstances, Tsong kha pa's *Stairway* is the earliest extant independent text that we have concerning the Twenty *Saṃgha*s. Along with the *Stairway*, Tsong kha pa addressed the topic of the Twenty *Saṃgha*s in his own AA commentary, the *Golden Garland*. These two texts will be the source material I will employ in the chapter 4 and chapter 5 discussion of the Tibetan Buddhist understanding of the Twenty *Saṃgha*s. Before we actually discuss the Twenty *Saṃgha*s, it is necessary to present the background material needed to understand the overall context in which the AA presents the Twenty *Saṃgha*s and the presumptions of Buddhist doctrine in regard to the path.

3

CONTEXTUAL AND DOCTRINAL PRESUMPTIONS

The Twenty *Saṃghas* is a topic that has been extracted from two verses of the *Abhisamayālaṃkāra*'s first chapter and developed by Tibetan scholars into an encyclopedia of ideal figures. Yet at the same time, the Twenty *Saṃghas* is a subject that is understood through its embedded context within the *Mahāyāna* Buddhist soteriology presented in the AA. An exegesis of the Twenty *Saṃghas* by an Indian or Tibetan author presumes that the reader has background knowledge of *Abhidharma* path structures, categories of mental defilements, meditational attainments, analytical procedures, and cosmology, among other factors. This chapter will present the background material that is needed to properly understand the overall context in which the *Abhisamayālaṃkāra* presents the Twenty *Saṃghas* and the soteriological and cosmological doctrines that Tibetan authors presuppose in studying the topic.

Most of this material can be drawn from the *Abhisamayālaṃkāra* itself following the interpretation given by the Indian commentaries of Vimuktisena and Haribhadra, supplementing these with remarks from Tsong kha pa in his *Golden Garland*. The remarks from these commentaries present a general outline of the material that conforms to the expectations of most Indian and Tibetan commentators. Locating the Twenty *Saṃghas* within the overall schema of the *Abhisamayālaṃkāra*, specifications regarding the *Abhisamayālaṃkāra*'s path and yoga systems, and a brief overview of Indo-Tibetan Buddhist cosmological factors are discussed in this chapter.

LOCATING THE TWENTY *SAṂGHAS* IN THE *ABHISAMAYĀLAṂKĀRA*

The *Abhisamayālaṃkāra* is a *Mahāyāna* Buddhist work that presents the path (*mārga*) to complete unsurpassable awakening (*anuttarasaṃyaksaṃbodhi*) based on the *Prajñāpāramitā Sūtras*. Its full title in Sanskrit is

Abhisamayālaṃkāranāmaprajñāpāramitopadeśaśāstra. The *Abhisamayālaṃkāra* is regarded as an *upadeśaśāstra* ("instructional treatise") because it is viewed as bringing out the hidden or concealed meaning (*sbas don, garbhyārtha*)[1] of the *Prajñāpāramitā Sūtras. Śāstra* here means that which protects (*trāṇa)* the mental continuum of the trainee (*śaikṣa*) and also causes the trainee who has generated the three trainings of morality, concentration, and wisdom to turn away from unsuitable accumulations of body, speech, and mind and engage in that which is suitable for them.[2] *Upadeśa,* translated in Tibetan as *man ngag,* means "specific instruction, teaching, or essential skill-in-means."[3] This rendering implies that the *Abhisamayālaṃkāra* provides the essential advice to easily understand the meaning of the *Prajñāpāramitā Sūtras.* "*Prajñāpāramitā*" refers to, among its many different meanings, three senses of the term. In its (1) direct or primary (*mukhya*) sense, PP refers to the *Buddha Bhagavat* as represented in his *dharmakāya* aspect, the highest nondual wisdom that is like an illusion. In its indirect or metaphorical (*gauṇa*) sense, PP means (2) the path leading to this highest wisdom, and (3) the texts containing the teaching on attaining this path and that nondual wisdom (*advayajñāna*).[4] A fourth meaning is added to this list of three, as the nature (*svabhāva, rang bzhin*) of *Prajñāpāramitā*.[5] In this case, the "essential" *Prajñāpāramitā* is emptiness, the essence, or final nature of all phenomena. The main subject matter of the *Abhisamayālaṃkāra* then is "the path that leads to the attainment of the Perfect Wisdom of a Buddha."

The main title of the text is *Abhisamayālaṃkāra, Ornament for Clear Realization.* In using the word *ornament,* Tsong kha pa utilizes a metaphor from the *Mahāyānasūtrālaṃkāra* in his explanation from the *Golden Garland*:

> The connection with ornament is an illustrative name, for example: just as the lovely body of a natural ornament, adorned with beautifying ornaments like bracelets and so forth, when appearing in a luminous mirror generates happiness for people, likewise, here, when the lovely body of the Mother (PP *sūtras*), the natural ornament, appears [in the sphere of] this *śāstra* that clarifies vividly with the beautifying ornament, the seventy topics [of the AA], wise people generate happiness.[6]

"Ornament" therefore signifies that this instructional treatise adorns the root texts of the PP *sūtras* like jewelry adorns the natural beauty of a woman. Specifically, it is the seventy topics (*don bdun cu*) presented in the *Abhisamayālaṃkāra* that reflect like a mirror the soteriological hidden meaning contained within the natural beauty of the expansive PP *sūtras*.

The term at the beginning of the title, *abhisamaya*, is the most fundamental to the text and is found throughout the *Abhisamayālaṃkāra* and its commentaries with a variety of specific usages. Etymologically *abhisamaya* is comprised of the prefix *abhi* "toward, facing," the prefix *sam* "together" + the verbal root *i* "to go or to understand." The indeclinable prefix *abhi,* drawn from *abhitas* "on all sides" and combined with the indeclinable prefix *sam* "completeness,"[7] implies "comprehensiveness."[8] In combination with the verbal root *i* "to go," which in this case means "to understand," the term *abhisamaya* may be taken to mean "comprehensive understanding" or "clear realization." This is the meaning implied in the sixth chapter of the *Abhidharmakośa.*[9] Therefore, the full title may be translated as *An Instructional Treastise on* Prajñāpāramitā *Called "Ornament for Clear Realization."*

As a technical treastise, the *Abhisamayālaṃkāra* consists of an encyclopedic table of contents, communicating in an abridged form the subject matter of the entire Large *Prajñāpāramitā Sūtra* corpus.[10] It presents a condensed summary of all the instructions, practices, paths, and stages of realization to Buddhahood that are implicitly found in the PP *sūtras*. Each portion of the PP *sūtra*s was interpreted as a specific teaching in regard to the stages on the path to enlightenment. The *Abhisamayālaṃkāra* presents that interpretation on each specific section of the PP *sūtra* in a verse, following the order and succession of topics as they are presented in the *sūtra*. This pattern is designed to allow for an easier understanding of the vast amount of material that is demonstrated in the PP *sūtras*.[11] By providing an easier understanding of the PP *sūtras*, it is thought that all adherents can apply the practices and progress easily toward the goal of Buddhahood. The first two verses of the AA after the homage state this very purpose:

> May the wise behold that path to Total Omniscience, shown by the Teacher here, unperceived by others. And having placed in memory the aim of the *[Prajñāpāramitā] Sūtra,* may they easily progress in the tenfold practice of the Dharma! This is the purpose of my undertaking.[12]
>
> *sarvākārajñātā mārgaḥ śāsinā yo 'tra deśitaḥ /*
> *dhīmanto vīkṣiṣīraṃs tam anālīḍhaṃ parair iti //* (AA 1.1)
>
> *smṛtau cādhāya sūtrārthaṃ dharmacaryāṃ daśātmikāṃ /*
> *sukhena pratipatsīrann ity ārambhaprayojanam //* (AA 1.2)

This versified presentation of the topics based on the PP *sūtras* explains what at first seems to be the strange order of the AA. This text does not give a sequential presentation of the path and its stages occurring in a linear fashion from beginning to end. Rather, the path and its stages are presented with a deliberate degree of repetition. The *Abhisamayālaṃkāra* lays out the same subject matter numerous times, yet with each repetition of the presentation, the subject matter is covered in successively greater detail. The main subject matter of the text is presented five separate times. The (1) homage encapsulates the main principles that flow throughout the whole text. The homage is followed by a reinstatement of these main principles in (2) a condensed presentation (AA I.3–4). These main principles or topics are then slightly expanded and contained in (3) an elucidation of the "body of the text" (AA I.5–17, *śarīra vyavasthānam*, AAV (Pensa, 1967: 14; Pk 5185 fols. 9.2.2–9.4.3); AASPh [Amano, 2000: 8.3]). The fourth repetition is the most expansive and consists of (4) a detailed articulation (AA, I.18-penultimate) of the paths and stages. Finally, (5) summation verses (AA IX.1–2) are given that condense the subject matter of the text into three categories.

The first repetition of the material occurs in the homage, which embodies in a condensed manner the main doctrines that are found in the AA. It is the source by which the presentation is inspired and contains the overall principles that underline the whole *upadeśa śāstra*:

> Homage to the Mother of the Buddha together with *śrāvaka*s and *bodhisattva*s: she who, in the guise of All-knowledge, leads *śrāvaka*s who seek peace to pacification; she who, in the guise of Knowledge of the Paths, causes those who benefit the world to accomplish the welfare of people; [and] possessed of which, Sages teach this all-pervading [dharma] in every aspect.[13]

yā sarvajñatayā nayaty upaśamaṃ śāntaiṣiṇaḥ śrāvakān yā mārgajñatayā jagaddhitakṛtāṃ lokārthasampādikā /

sarvākāram idaṃ vadanti munayo viśvaṃ yayā saṃgatās tasyai śrāvakabodhisattvagaṇino buddhasya mātre namaḥ //

In this homage, *Prajñāpāramitā* manifests herself in three forms of omniscience: All-knowledge (*sarvajñatā, thams cad shes pa nyid*, or *vastujñāna, gzhi shes*), Knowledge of the Paths (*mārgajñatā; lam shes*), and Total Omniscience (*sarvākārajñatā; rnam pa thams cad mkhyen pa nyid*). She is glorified as the "Mother" (*mātṛ; yum*) of the *śrāvaka*s (which implicitly include *pratyekabuddha*s), *bodhisattva*s, and *buddha*s). The name "Mother" (*mātṛ*) may imply a relationship to *mātṛkā*s, early *Abhidharma* terminological lists that clarified the distinguishing points of the Buddha's doctrine that should be known (*jñeya*) or correctly analyzed. Such lists were comprised of topics like the four applications of mindfulness, the four right efforts, the seven limbs of enlightenment, and so forth. This term *mātṛkā,* a secondary formation derived from the ordinary word for "mother" (*mātṛ*), *mātṛkā* (cognate with English "matrix"), is also used figuratively to mean "source" or "origin." The *Abhisamayālaṃkāra* itself may be an early *mātṛkā* of the *Prajñāpāramitā,* serving as a source for the various lists describing paths and stages to full enlightenment.[14]

Traditionally, the name of "Mother" is given to the three kinds of knowledge because each manifestation of knowledge is like a mother who aids her child (the *śrāvaka, bodhisattva,* etc.) in the realization of the desired aim and a mother who fosters the virtuous elements in the spiritual streams of the practitioners.[15] *Prajñāpāramitā* is also considered the mother of the different spiritual types because she is their cause. Just as the mother is one of the two principal causes of a child, so too is wisdom (*prajñā*) one of the two chief causes of enlightenment. The other, of course, is skillful means (*upāya*). Just as a mother must bear the child in her womb for ten (lunar) months, the traditional gestation period, so too does wisdom nurture the adept along the way through the ten *bhūmi*s, the stages of the *bodhisattva* path. Here, in this case, it is the gestation in the mother wisdom's womb that brings about the birth of enlightened beings (Cabezon, 1992: 185). Therefore, whether viewed as a scripture, the spiritual state of mind, the goal of enlightenment, or emptiness, *Prajñāpāramitā* in this Indo-Tibetan tradition is identified as both a feminine force and a maternal one. Manifest in relation to the needs of the aspirant, she incorporates all facets of the path and is synonymous with Total Omniscience.

Because of her relation with the three individuals, this maternal force is explained as *Bhagavatī.* She is one who causes the completion of the desired qualities "leading to peace" and so forth, the final aim for each individual path. The homage illustrates that within the manifestation of the three types of omniscience, she is the Mother of four types of Noble Beings (*ārya*): the Buddha, along with the assemblies of *śrāvaka*s, *pratyekabuddha*s, and *bodhisattva*s.

What are these three manifestations? All-knowledge (*sarvajñatā*) is the Mother of *śrāvaka*s and *pratyekabuddhas,* as *śrāvaka*s and *pratyekabuddha*s are exemplified by the words "*śrāvaka*s, those seeking the peace of *nirvāṇa,* she who is able to lead through pacification of defilement and suffering through the guise of All-knowledge." Knowledge of the Paths (*mārgajñatā*) is the Mother of the *bodhisattva*s and *buddha*s, those who cause benefit to beings, she who causes to achieve the aims of those to be trained in the world. Total Omniscience (*sarvākārajñatā*) is the Mother of the Buddhas, by being well affiliated with knowledge in all its aspects, which understands exactly the manner of reality (*ji lta ba bzhin yod pa, yathāvadbhāvika*) to its fullest possible extent (*ji snyed yod pa, yāvadbhāvikatā*).[16]

The Mother, as *Prajñāpāramitā*, manifests in accord with the disciple's degree of understanding into these three knowledges. However, her nature is not classified into three different natures. She is a mother of the three sons in terms of the disciple's level of training (*gdul bya'i bsam pa'i dbang gyi sras gsum gyi yum yin*), her final nature being only the Mother of Omniscient Buddhahood (PSPh 16a.8–16b.1). The level of training that is engaged in by *śrāvaka*s and *pratyekabuddha*s is the mere realization of selflessness and that engaged in by the *buddha*s and *bodhisattva*s is the realization of the essencelessness of the person (*pudgalanairātmya*) and the essencelessness of things (*dharmanairātmya*).

The AA contains eight chapters of subject matter with a summary of them as the ninth chapter. The three knowledges themselves comprise the subject matter of the first three chapters of the AA and encompass the remaining five realizations (*abhisamaya*) that constitute the text. In this way the praise exalts the Mother, the means of achieving the uncommon goals of *śrāvakas*, *pratyekabuddhas*, *bodhisattvas*, and *buddhas*, along with the subject matter of the *Śāstra*. These eight subjects are illustrated in the third verse of the AA as follows:

> The perfection of wisdom is proclaimed through eight subjects: total omniscience, knowledge of the paths, all-knowledge, the full realization of all aspects, the [realization] that has attained the summit, the progressive [realization], the instantaneous realization, and the *Dharmakāya;* these are the eightfold [perfection of wisdom].
>
> *prajñāpāramitāṣṭābhiḥ padārthaiḥ samudīritā /*
> *sarvākārajñatā mārgajñatā sarvajñatā tataḥ //* (AA 1.3)
>
> *sarvākārābhisambodho mūrdhaprāpto 'nupūrvikaḥ /*
> *ekakṣaṇābhisaṃbodho dharmakāyaś ca te'ṣṭadhā //* (AA 1.4)

The eight subjects (*padārtha*) that comprise the eight chapters (*adhikāra*) of the AA correspond to eight clear realizations (*abhisamaya*) that represent the three meanings of *Prajñāpāramitā* (see Figure 3.1). Each subject is explained by reference to a number of topics (*artha; don*) articulated through the verses of each chapter. The first chapter comprises ten topics within seventy-three verses that mention the necessary practices that lead to the special omniscience of the Buddha, that is, Total Omniscience or the wisdom of all aspects (*sarvākārajñatā; rnam pa thams cad mkhyen pa nyid*). These practices should be performed in order to completely cognize all knowable objects in existence. Total Omniscience is regarded as the fundamental wisdom and the central concept of the *Prajñāpāramitā Sūtras*. This knowledge is attained only by fully enlightened Buddhas. The second chapter of the AA discusses eleven topics in thirty-one verses on the knowledges of all paths (*mārgajñatā; lam shes nyid*), which consists of coming to understand the paths of *śrāvakas*, *pratyekabuddhas*, and *bodhisattvas*, the *bodhisattvas* realizing the knowledge of all the paths. The third chapter makes reference to nine topics through sixteen stanzas that teach the omniscience of objects or knowledge of all things (*sarvajñatā; thams cad shes pa nyid*). This *abhisamaya* is comprehended by *śrāvakas* and *pratyekabuddhas*. Practicing these nine topics leads *śrāvakas* and *pratyekabuddhas* to comprehend the entirety of dharma in which the five aggregates (*skandha*), the twelve sense spheres (*āyatana*), and the eighteen sense objects (*dhātu*) are included. These first three *abhisamayas*, better known as the three kinds of omniscience (*mkhyen gsum*), are the method that one applies to the path.

The path to Buddhahood itself and the detailed means of its application are covered by *abhisamayas* four through seven. The fourth chapter of the AA, the realization of wisdom of all aspects (*sarvākārābhisaṃbodha; rnam rdzogs sbyor ba*), elucidates eleven topics in sixty-three stanzas. This begins the discussion of the one hundred seventy-three aspects of the three forms of omniscience that correspond with the Path of Accumulation (*saṃbhāramārga*). The AA's chapter 5 details in forty-two verses the eight topics pertaining to the summit of full understanding (*mūrdhābhisamaya; rtse sbyor*), or "culminating insight." This *abhisamaya* concurs with the Path of Training (*prayogamārga; sbyor lam*) and the Path of Cultivation (*bhāvanāmārga, sgom lam*) and extends until the instant before the attainment of Buddhahood. The sixth chapter defines, by reference to thirteen topics in one verse, the gradual, full understanding (*anupūrvābhisamaya; mthar gyis sbyor ba*). This *abhisamaya* of "gradual insight" is present, beginning in the path of accumulation, and slowly increases until the final moment before Buddhahood. The seventh *abhisamaya* clarifies the "instantaneous realization" (*ekakṣaṇābhisamaya; skad cig gcig pa'i mngon par rdzogs par byang chub pa*) through five stanzas that discuss four topics. "Instantaneous realization" occurs at the final moment right before Buddhahood. *Abhisamayas* four through seven are known as "the four methods of realization" of the three types of knowledge. The last subject, the fruit of the Path, is the realization of the Dharma-body (*dharmakāyābhisamaya; chos sku mngon rtogs pa*) in its four aspects. This idea is presented in forty verses that make reference to four topics. The realization of the *Dharmakāya* is brought about as a natural cause of the preceding practices. In this way, the eight subjects of the AA are articulated in two hundred and seventy-one verses comprising seventy topics (*don bdun*

Figure 3.1 Relationship of the Eight Subjects (*padārtha*) of the AA

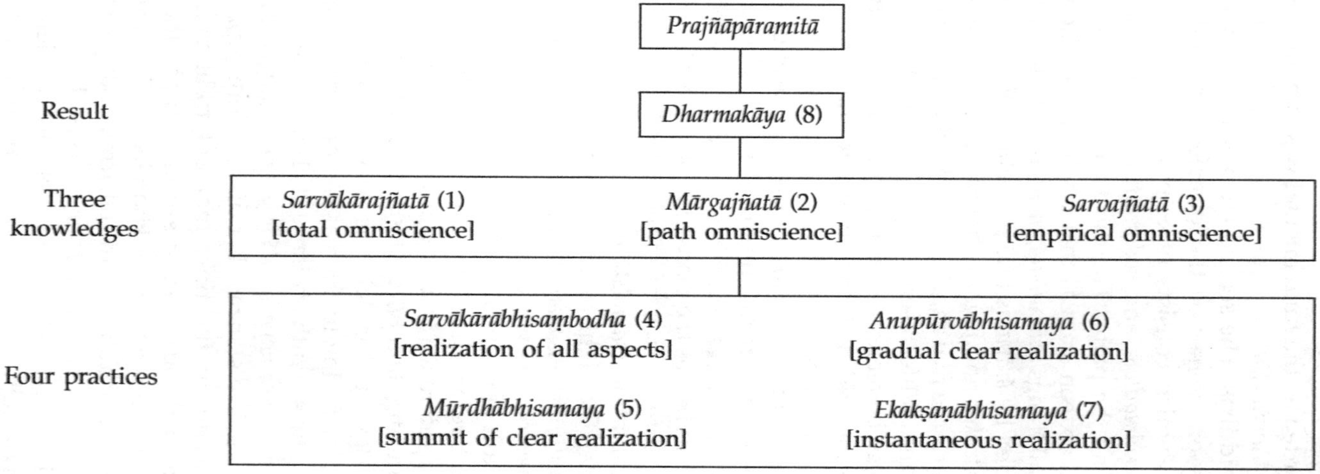

cu). The summation of these subjects occurs at the very end of the *śāstra*, forming a ninth chapter, which has two verses. The AA then contains two hundred and seventy-three stanzas that present the hidden meaning of the *Prajñāpāramitā Sūtras*.

For our purposes here, the contextualization of the Twenty *Saṃghas* within the AA, we need only present a schematic introduction to the material that is discussed in the first chapter.[17]

> Mind generation, special instructions, the four-fold limbs of insight, basis of attaining whose nature is of the *Dharmadhātu*, supports, purpose, the activity of putting on armor and setting out, equipment, along with emergence [comprise] the Total Omniscience of the Sage.
>
> *cittotpādo'vavādaś ca nirvedhāṅgaṃ caturvidhaṃ /*
> *ādhāraḥ pratipatteś ca dharmadhātusvabhāvakaḥ //* (AA 1.5)
>
> *ālambanaṃ samuddeśaḥ saṃnāhaprasthitikriye /*
> *sambhārāś ca saniryāṇāḥ sarvākārajñatā muneḥ //* (AA 1.6)

These verses present a list of the subject matter contained within the first chapter on Total Omniscience (*sarvākārajñatā*). The verses outline a table of contents that includes ten main topics or factors that a *bodhisattva* applies to the path in order to attain the state of total omniscience equal to Buddhahood.

The first factor[18] is (1) the production of the thought for enlightenment (*bodhicittotpāda; byang chub tu sems bskyed*). The *bodhisattva* produces the altruistic mind set on achieving perfect awakening (*saṃyaksaṃbodhi*), a mind having for its essence (*garbha*) emptiness (*śūnyatā*) and compassion (*karuṇā*) and consisting in the twofold stage of resolution (*praṇidhi*) and engagement (*prasthāna*). One who desires to sustain the qualities that are produced from this mind generation must hear and place firmly into his mind (2) special instructions (*avavāda*), such as the practices and applications (*pratipatti*) that develop his advancement in the *Mahāyāna* path. Then, having received the special instructions, a *bodhisattva* cultivates the roots of virtue (*kuśalamūla*), which are characterized by the qualities of faith (*śraddhā*), and so on, conducive to emancipation (*mokṣabhāgīya*) and are obtained by excellence in learning (*śruta*). The *bodhisattva* will then establish (3) the fourfold factors conducive to insight (*nirvedhabhāgīya*).[19] These *nirvedhabhāgīya*, which we shall refer to as "preparatory analytical factors," comprise the path of preparation (*prayogamārga*) and constitute a mundane meditative realization (*laukikabhāvanāmaya*). In addition, they are conducive to a penetrative understanding of the four truths for Noble Beings (*caturāryasatya*). When the mundane factors of penetration, along with the path of seeing (*darśanamārga*) and the path of cultivation (*bhāvanāmārga*) are possessed, a *bodhisattva* becomes a special (4) basis of activity (*pratipattyādhāra*). With advancement into the Noble Path proper, the *bodhisattva* actualizes the *dharmadhātu* nature such that s/he becomes endowed with all (5) previous acquired virtuous qualities as support (*sarvadharmālambanapūrvakaṃ*). This facilitates the development of the *bodhisattva* to have greatness in relation to his/her superior thought for all sentient beings (*sarvasattvāgratācittamahattva*), greatness in the elimination of obstacles (*prahāṇamahattva*), and greatness in comprehension (*adhigamamahattva*). Then, the (6) final purpose (*samuddeśa*) of *Mahāyāna* practices, which is threefold in regard to its goal, is activity based on virtuous dharmas in general, in terms of the three omnisciences (*sarvākārajñatā*, *mārgajñatā*, and *sarvajñatā*). In the terms of the four clear realizations (*sarvākārābhisambodha*, *mūrdhābhisamaya*, *anupūrvābhisamaya*, and *ekakṣaṇābhisaṃbodha*), activity based on the six perfections is applied to each of the four realizations separately.

These four forms of activity correspond to four paths: the activity of putting on the (7) armor (*saṃnāhapratipatti*), which is comprised of vigor (*vīrya*) and is congruent with the path of preparation (*prayogamārga*). The (8) activity of setting out (*prasthānapratipatti*) fulfills all qualities of the *Mahāyāna* (*samastamahāyānadharmābhirohaṇa*) and begins with the path of seeing (*darśanamārga*). The activity that procures the (9) equipment (*saṃbhārapratipatti*) accumulates the necessary spiritual provisions and corresponds to the path of cultivation (*bhāvanāmārga*). Finally, the activity of (10) emergence (*niryāṇapratipatti*) is consistent with the distinctive path (*viśeṣamārga*). These ten topics comprise the gradual comprehensions in the factors necessary to obtain the state of Buddhahood (*buddhatvāvāhakadharmādhigamānukrama*) (see table 3.1).

As we have seen, a *bodhisattva* desires to become a Buddha for the sake of all beings, and generates an altruistic mind to accomplish that desire. In order to sustain and enhance this altruistic mind generation, a *bodhisattva* requests and listens to special instructions (*avavāda*). In general, special instructions are teachings that council meditative equipoise to beings who lack meditative stability and teach liberation to those whose minds have reached meditative equipoise.[20] The AA presents distinctive *Mahāyāna* special instructions that accumulate merit, expand calm abiding (*śamatha*) and special insight (*vipaśyanā*), and help protect all *bodhisattva* qualities that have been obtained so far. A *bodhisattva* will travel to many world realms by means of meditative stabilization, supernormal powers, or attainments for the purpose of serving and hearing doctrinal teachings from innumerable Buddhas.[21] Then having obtained these special instructions

Table 3.1 Ten Factors That Constitute Total Omniscience

Factor	Quality	Purpose
1. Altruistic mind for awakening	Sincere resolution set on achieving full Buddhahood for the sake of all beings	Cultivate the altruistic resolution to achieve Buddhahood
2. Special instructions	Practices and applications that develop the *Mahāyāna* path	Sustain and increase the altruistic mind for awakening
3. Four limbs of insight	Mundane cognitive insight	Gain clear realization of the Nobles' Four Truths
4. Basis of activity	Noble path attainment and supermundane cognitive insight	Actualize *dharmadhātu* Nature
5. Support	Endowed with previous acquired virtuous qualities	Develop greatness in altruism, in elimination of obstacles, and in comprehension
6. Purpose	Active practices and cultivations	Fulfill virtuous qualities in relation to the triple omniscience; achieve four realizations through the six perfections
7. Putting on armor	Vigor	Gain energy through the path of preparation
8. Setting out	The development of all qualities of the *Mahāyāna*	Achieve the *Mahāyāna* path of seeing
9. Accumulating equipment	Procure the spiritual provisions for path of cultivation	Achieve *Mahāyāna* path of cultivation
10. Emergence	Qualities consistent with the distinctive path before attaining Buddhahood	Finalize the realizations and practices to actualize the state of Buddahood

from Buddhas by means of a meditative stabilization called "stream of doctrine," a *bodhisattva* will obtain extensive qualities of quiescence and wisdom.[22] This "stream of doctrine" method of special instruction is reported to be the very manner in which Asaṅga heard the AA from Maitreyanātha. The AA presents ten varieties of special instructions in the first chapter:

> The tenfold special instructions should be known as: practice, truths, the three jewels beginning with the Buddha, non-attachment, indefatigability, fully incorporating [the path], qualities of the five eyes and six supernatural knowledges, the path of seeing, and the path of cultivation.
>
> *pratipattau ca satyeṣu buddharatnādiṣu triṣu /*
> *asaktāv apariśrāntau pratipatsamparigrahe //* (AA 1.21)
>
> *cakṣuḥṣu pañcasu jñeyaḥ ṣaṭsv abhijñāguṇeṣu ca /*
> *dṛṅmārge bhāvanākhye cety avavādo daśātmakaḥ //* (AA 1.22)

These ten subtopics are designed to instruct *bodhisattvas* about the final nature of *Mahāyāna* practices and enhance the altruistic mind generation. Among these ten types, special instructions about (1) practice (*pratipatti; sgrub pa*) are the preceptual advice that progress in the altruistic mind, set on highest enlightenment, progresses through a yoga of nonobservation that is not common to *śrāvakas* (etc.).[23] Next are the special instructions regarding the four (2) truths (*satya; bden pa*). In regard to the truth of suffering, the Buddha advises that the resultant emptiness of form, and so forth, and *Prajñāpāramitā* are one and the same in the nature of suchness, the reality of things. The truth of the origin of suffering gives this advice: Because emptiness and forms (etc.), which are its cause, are not different, forms (etc.) are not subject to origination and cessation, defilement and purity. Emptiness is free of production, cessation, purity, degeneration, and increase. The truth of the cessation of suffering is the special instruction that in emptiness there is no form, up to and including, no arising of ignorance and no cessation of ignorance, no Buddha and no enlightenment. In regard to the truth of the path, there is the special instruction that emptiness of the inner (etc.) is the activity of practice. This emptiness is neither joined with nor not joined with perfect generosity, (etc.), with emptiness of the outer (etc.), or with the earlier or later limits, and vice versa.[24]

Special instruction regarding the (3) three jewels (*triratna; dkon mchog gsum*) involves advice about the nature of the Buddha, Dharma, and *Saṃgha*. It is from this set of instructions that the special topic of the *Saṃgha* is derived. In particular, this instruction enumerates the twenty varieties of the *Saṃgha* Jewel. As for the special instruction concerning the Buddha Jewel, there is a knowledge of the observed and observer being the same thing. This is because the Buddha and the experience of enlightenment are the same. Therefore, one cannot find the knowledge of all aspects, the defining property of the Buddha, as anything separate. The special instruction for the Dharma Jewel is that there is a lack of intrinsic being of all the included dharmas, which are subsumed under the totality of entities, antidotes, and aspects included within the three omniscient knowledges. In general, instructions regarding the *Saṃgha* Jewel concern the community of irreversible Noble *Bodhisattva*s (*āryāvaivartikabodhisattva*). We will discuss the special instruction in regard to the *Saṃgha* Jewel in the next section.

With progress in the previously mentioned aims and initial enthusiasm, the practitioner may be longing for such things as physical ease, causing the *bodhisattva* to become complacent in his or her development. Therefore, there is special instruction in (4) nonattachment (*asakta; ma zhen*) relating that the body (etc.) lacks an intrinsic nature (*svabhāva*).

When the desired aim is not forthcoming, even after trying for a long time, weariness may arise and a sense of defeatism may set in. In this case, the AA offers a special instruction for (5) indefatigability (*apariśrānti; yongs su ngal ba med pa*), which demonstrates that there is no intrinsic knowledge from form (etc.) up to perfect complete enlightenment.

The mind may be susceptible to anguish when one is receiving instruction on each separate aspect of the path taught by all the various Buddhas. For this there is special instruction about (6) fully embracing the *Mahāyāna* path (*pratipatsaṃparigraha; lam yongs su bzungs ba*). This contains the advice that all dharmas are naturally unproduced.

Next there are special instructions regarding the (7) five eyes (*pañcacakṣu; spyan lnga*). This is instruction that progress is in terms of oneness, from the point of view of the truly real, of the fleshly matured (*māṃsavaipākika*), divine (*divya*), wisdom (*prajñā*), dharma, and Buddha eyes, which focus, respectively, on (i) specific entities (*pratiniyata vastu*), (ii) the demise and rebirth of all beings (*sarvasattvacyutyupapatti*), (iii) on nonimagination of any dharma (*sarvadharmāvikalpana*), (iv) on the realization of every Noble Being (*sarvāryapudgalādhigama*), and (v) on the awakened comprehension to all dharmas in every aspect (*sarvākārasarvadharmābhisambodha*).

In the special instructions concerning (8) the six supernatural knowledges (*ṣaḍabhijñā; mngon shes drug*) is the guidance that magical apparition, divine ear, reading others' minds, recollection of previous lives, the composite divine eye, and realization of the extinction of contamination that performs functions like shaking the earth (etc.), hearing faint and nonfaint sounds existing in all world spheres, knowing the minds of others in their state of longing (etc.), recollecting one's and other's many earlier lives, seeing all forms, and bringing about the removal of the defilements and obscurations to knowledge are understood to actually be in a state of primordial calmness.

The ninth special instruction is given to the practitioner who cultivates the path of seeing (*darśanamārga; mthong lam*) through realizing that all dharmas lack intrinsic nature (9). This path consists of sixteen thought-moments construed in agreement with the four noble truths. It is comprised of eight moments of "intellectual receptivity" (*kṣānti*) and eight moments of knowledge (*jñāna*) associated with comprehension (*jñāna*) and subsequent comprehension (*anvayajñāna*) of the doctrine in accordance with each truth of suffering, arising, path, and cessation. This path is cultivated as an antidote to intellectually acquired defilements.

The tenth instruction involves the path of cultivation (*bhāvanāmārga, sgom lam*). The supposition of a real difference between composite and noncomposite phenomena is not possible since the ultimate nature of one is the ultimate nature of the other. Likewise seeing and cultivation are not separate because the above-mentioned path of seeing's support is an entity made manifest that does not differ from the path of seeing. Therefore, there is no establishment of (10) the path of cultivation through a distinctive mark. Nevertheless, the path of cultivation is practiced as an antidote to entities that have the nature of dependent origination, which this path is to remove.

In this way, there are ten topics mentioned as special instructions to Total Omniscience in regard to *Prajñāpāramitā*. These ten special instructions concern the attributes implied by the generation of an altruistic mind set on enlightenment and the qualities that should be incorporated to enhance and protect that mind generation. In relation to this mind, these ten are (1) practices that have an unperceived aspect (*anupalambhākāra*); (2) its support (*ālambana*), the four truths [for] Noble Beings (*catvāry āryasatyāni*); (3) the foundation (*āśraya*), the three refuges; (4) the cause of special advancement (*viśeṣagamanahetu*), nonattachment; (5) the cause of nonretreating advance (*avyāvṛttigamanahetu*), indefatigability; (6) the cause of not advancing in other [lesser] vehicles (*ananyayānagamanahetu*), fully embracing the path; (7) the five eyes, which are the cause of advance independent of reliance on others (*aparapratyayāgāmanahetu*); (8) the six supernatural knowledges, which are the cause of bringing Total Omniscience to full completion (*sarvākārajñatāparipūrihetu*); (9–10) and the [*Mahāyāna*] paths of seeing and cultivation, which are the causes of advancement to the final stage (*pratipattiniṣṭhāhetu*).[25]

The special instructions of the Buddha's Jewel (etc.), which are regarded to be the "support of the *Mahāyāna* practices," are the third

Table 3.2 Ten Special Instructions for *Bodhisattvas*

Instruction	Object	Advice	Purpose
1. Practice	Altruistic bodhimind development	Rare aspiration not common to other vehicles	Nonconceptualized practices
2. Truths	Suffering Arising Cessation Path	Forms are suchness Emptiness is free of production, etc. All things, even Buddahood, are empty Practices lack intrinsic existence	Support
3. Three Jewels	Buddha Dharma Saṃgha	Buddhahood and Bodhi are the same All things lack intrinsic existence Twenty varieties of the *saṃgha*	Foundation
4. Nonattachment	Complacency	Things such as the body lack intrinsic existence	Cause of special advance
5. Indefatigeability	Weariness	All knowledge up to Awakening lack intrinsic existence	Cause of nonretreating advance
6. Full incorporation	Anguish	All things are naturally unproduced	Cause of not advancing in other vehicles
7. Five eyes	Eyes of flesh, divine, wisdom, dharma, and Buddha	All forms of vision are undifferentiated	Nonreliance on others
8. Six supernatural knowledges	Magical apparition, divine ear, reading others' minds, previous life recollection, extinction of contamination	All supernatural knowledges are in a state of primordial calmness	Bring total omniscience to completion
9. Path of seeing	Antidote to acquired defilements	All dharmas lack intrinsic nature	Cause advancement to Buddhahood
10. Path of cultivation	Antidote to conceptualizing entities	Path of cultivation does not have a distinctive mark	Cause advancement to Buddahood

subtopic. These practices enable the student to fulfill the accomplishment of the motivating thought of the first topic, the goal of perfect complete enlightenment for all other living beings. The support (*āśraya*) is made up of the Three Jewels (*triratna*) that consist of the Buddha, Dharma, and *Saṃgha*. What concerns us here are the instructions on the support of the *Saṃgha* Jewel, from which the special topic of the twenty varieties of the *Saṃgha* Jewel arises (see table 3.2).

Saṃgha in Early Buddhism and in the *Abhisamayālaṃkāra*

The term *saṃgha*[26] literally refers to an assembly, crowd, group, or community. The term was used in pre-Buddhist India to refer to a merchants' or artisan's guild, the ruling council of a royal family, or to a religious community. *Saṃgha* also referred to a group of seekers who gathered around a master in order to attain, with his help, spiritual knowledge and realization of the highest truth. Śākyamuni Buddha was sometimes described as the leader and teacher of a body of monks and his "*saṃgha*" consisted of at first monks (*bhikṣu*), novices (*śrāmaṇera*), lay followers (*upāsaka*), and later on nuns (*bhikṣuṇī*). Since the way of life of Śākyamuni's *saṃgha* was determined by rules established in the *Vinaya* code, the term *Saṃgha* in this context meant a religious body adhering to particular views and rules of discipline (*diṭṭhisīlasāmaññasaṃghātabhāvena saṅgho*).[27]

Śākyamuni Buddha's *saṃgha*, or community of followers, took part in certain disciplines that set them apart, including keeping certain precepts, living the homeless life, and the begging of food. Early on at some point in the course of Buddhism's development, the community became known as "worthy of worship, worthy of offerings, etc." and the term *saṃgha* came to refer to an object of veneration and a "place of refuge." The *saṃgha* evolved into one of the three essential components, along with Buddha and Dharma, of Śākyamuni's doctrine, and together these were known as the "three jewels" (*triratna; ratnatraya*). An early standard definition of the *saṃgha* as one of the three jewels, according to the *Nikāya* tradition, was as follows:

> Well-directed is the Saṅgha of the Lord's disciples, of upright conduct, on the right path, on the perfect path; that is to say the four pairs of persons, the eight kinds of individuals. The Saṅgha of the Lord's disciples is worthy of offerings, worthy of hospitality, worthy of gifts, worthy of veneration, an unsurpassed field of merit in the world. (MN 7.7 *Vatthūpama Sutta*)

The *saṃgha*, often called the "congregation," is compared to the nurses or medical assistants of the Buddha.[28] They are meant to have successfully taken in the Buddha's teaching and to be faithfully administering it to other beings. Tibetan scholars classify the *saṃgha* into two general categories: the conventional *saṃgha* (Tib. *kun rdzob pa'i dge'dun*) and the *saṃgha* in the highest sense (Tib. *don dam pa'i dge'dun*). The conventional *saṃgha* usually signifies a group or five or more monks (Skt. *bhikṣu*; Tib. *dge long*) who perform rituals and recite the *Pratimokṣa* vows together. The *saṃgha* in the highest sense signifies individuals who have achieved the Path of Seeing (*darśanamārga*) and are actualizing the Truth of Cessation (*nirodhasatya*) and the Truth of the Path (Skt. *mārga*; Tib. *lam*).[29]

Tsong kha pa in his AA commentary, the *Golden Garland* (220.12), examines the *saṃgha* from a Tibetan perspective in which various Indian Buddhist sources are compiled together to form a unified exposition. He divides the definition of the *Saṃgha* Jewel into two parts, the system according to the *śrāvaka* vehicle and that according to the *Mahāyāna*. First, for the *śrāvaka* vehicle method, Tsong kha pa draws from the *Abhidharmakośa* (AK iv.32), "One who takes the triple refuge takes refuge in the dharmas of the *Aśaikṣa* which produce the Buddha, in the dharmas of both types which produce the *saṃgha*, and in *nirvāṇa*."

In regard to taking the *saṃgha* as a refuge, the *saṃgha* is composed of the qualities of those who are training on the path (*śaikṣa*) and those who are no longer training (*aśaikṣa*), not including the Buddha. This refers to the qualities that are acquired by the eight Noble individuals (*aṣṭāryapudgala*) who, by being unbreakable from the path, are called "*saṃgha*."[30] One takes refuge in the uncontaminated continuity of the eight holy individual's five aggregates, but any remnant left over from that is not a refuge since it is not the *saṃgha*.

In defining the *Mahāyāna Saṃgha* Jewel, Tsong kha pa incorporates the tradition of Maitreyanātha's *Ratnagotravibhāga Mahāyānottaratantraśāstra* into his catholic exegesis. The *Mahāyāna Saṃgha* Jewel consists of irreversible (*avaivartika*) *bodhisattvas* who possess four unsurpassable qualities: (1) seeing reality just as it is (*yathāvat*), and (2) to its utmost extent (*yāvat*), visions which consist of (3) pure introspective pristine cognitions (*adhyātmajñāna*), and (4) the qualities that arise from these visions. For Tsong kha pa, seeing reality "just as it is" means to have a strong cognition into the suchness of entities, that is, the essencelessness of the person (*pudgalanairātmya*) and things (*dharmanairātmya*). To perceive this suchness itself as pervading all sentient beings is to see reality to its utmost extent. In this way, the first vision cognizes the true nature of reality (*dharmatā*) and the latter cognizes where it is established. These two visions are perceived in an introspective manner (*rang rig pa'i tshul*) and are purifying to defilement obscurations like attachment and obscurations to knowledge. The *Uttaratantra* states: "Because of its pure vision [consisting of] pristine cognitions which are introspective, [that sees] reality just as it is and [reality] to its extent, the assembly of irreversible sages [is endowed] with unsurpassable qualities."[31]

The *Mahāyāna saṃgha* consists of irreversible sages, those *bodhisattvas* who perceive *bodhi* with wisdom and sentient beings with compassion and who are much more spiritually evolved than ordinary people (*pṛthagjana; so so skye bu*). These *bodhisattvas* enter into and practice whatever is beneficial to achieving the path, while cognizing that these activities are from the very beginning unproduced (*anutpattika*). As we will see in chapter 5, the enumeration of this *Mahāyāna saṃgha* depends upon imputing the names or designations of the *śrāvaka saṃgha* on to *bodhisattvas*. These *bodhisattvas* are merely nominally designated (*tsam po pa'i ming gis btags nas*) and exist with this designation through possessing the name only (*ming can*). There are three who nominally abide in the result of Stream-enterer, Once-returner, and Non-returner and four who nominally are enterers to the results of Stream-enterer, Once-returner, Non-returner, and *arhat* making seven great individuals. These seven great individuals together with the *pratyekabuddha* make eight. Here it is necessary to count the nominal abider in the result of *arhat*, one who is beyond *Mahāyāna* training (*mahāyānāśaikṣa*), as being part of the Buddha Jewel. This is because *arhat* in this context of the *Prajñāpāramitā Sūtras* and *Abhisamayālaṃkāra* means "fully enlightened Buddha."[32]

The *Mahāyāna arhat* therefore is not to be counted among the *saṃgha* of trainees (*śaikṣasaṃgha*). The *saṃgha* of noble irreversible *bodhisattva* trainees (*āryāvaivartika-bodhisattvaśaikṣa saṃgha*) at its base is counted as these eight individuals. When divided according to weak or sharp faculties and so forth, it includes twenty individuals. Haribhadra summarizes these factors while commenting on the jewel of the *saṃgha* in his *Abhisamayālaṃkāravṛtti Sphuṭārthā*:

> As regards the jewel of the *saṃgha*, with the exception of the [*Mahāyāna*] *arhat* who is to be regarded as the jewel of the Buddha, there are seven great individuals among the divisions of enters [to the first three results] and abiders [in all four results], to which an eighth, viz. the *pratyekabuddha*, is included. In classifying through the division of weak faculties and so forth there are altogether twenty varieties. These Noble irreversible trainee *bodhisattvas* occur as [ultimately] unproduced.[33]

Haribhadra emphasizes here that going for refuge in the *saṃgha* necessitates "entering into the unproduced essence" of the *saṃgha*, that is, the *saṃgha's* emptiness of existing as an absolutely or truly existing phenomena.

This "going forth by way of the unproduced" (*anutpādatayā pravṛttiḥ*) relates to the tenets of the *Prajñāpāramitā* and *Madhyamaka* systems. All phenomena are presented in the PP as ultimately being unoriginated, unproduced, unarisen, and so on; yet, from the conventional side, phenomena have some sort of merely designated existence where we can posit something in dependence upon a name. This conventional existence of designations comprises the "implicit" aspect of the PP, the main topic of the AA, which presents stages, aspects, and systems of the path. These principles are also applied to the twenty varieties of the *Saṃgha* Jewel. Not only do these irreversible trainee *bodhisattvas* go forth by way of the unproduced, they are constituted by the unconditioned (*asaṃskṛtaprabhāvita*).

Noble Beings are distinguished by cognitive knowledge of the unconditioned. Ārya Vimuktisena (AAV 77), Haribhadra (AAĀ 78), as well as Tsong kha pa (Hopkins, 1980: 181) will interpret this to mean that Noble Beings are constituted by direct, noncontaminated, and nonconceptual knowledge, a gnoseological constitution (Ruegg, 1989: 37). For such thinkers, whether Buddhas are present or not, the ultimate mode of reality is unproduced, nonceasing, nonstatic, and unconditioned like space. *Mahāyāna* philosophers consider the cognition of the unconditioned to be a direct nonconceptual cognition of the suchness (*tathatā*) of things. This type of knowledge occurs in relation to a nonimplicative negation of the erroneous conceptual construction that arises from contaminated cognition of objects. This type of knowledge constitutes irreversible trainee *bodhisattvas*.

AVAIVARTIKA-SAṂGHA AS REFUGE IN THE *ABHISAMAYĀLAṂKĀRA*

The members of the *Saṃgha* Jewel that are understood to be the most definitive object of veneration in the AA system are the "irreversible community" (*avaivartika saṃgha*). This type of *saṃgha* is mentioned in both the commentaries of Ārya Vimuktisena and Haribhadra before articulating the characteristic of the *Saṃgha* Jewel in general and enumerating the divisions within the *Saṃgha* Jewel in particular (AAV 39. AAĀ 32. 28. AASph [Amano 2000: 13]). Later in the AA, Haribhadra (AAĀ 665.5–8.) distinguishes three types of irreversible *bodhisattvas*: (1) those who abide on the path of preparation [while cultivating] the preparatory analytical factors (*nirvedhabhāgīyaprayogamārgastha*); (2) those who abide on the path of seeing, consisting of [eight moments of] receptivity and [eight moments of] knowledge (*kṣāntijñānasaṃgṛhītadarśanamārgastha*); and (3) those who abide on the path of cultivation which follows (*prābandhikabhāvanāmārgastha*). These divisions are likewise characterized in the AA itself:

> Here, that assembly of those who are irreversible is those Bodhisattvas who have acquired the limbs of penetration, who abide in paths of vision and familiarization.
>
> *nirvedhāṅgāny upādāya darśanābhyāsamārgayoḥ /*
> *ye bodhisattvā vartante so'trāvaivartiko gaṇaḥ //* (AA 4.38)

The term *irreversible, avaivartika* in Sanskrit, is an epithet most often applied to the *bodhisattva* who dwells in the eighth *bhūmi,* the *Acalā,* of the ten stages entailed in reaching supreme and complete Buddhahood. An *avaivartika bodhisattva* possesses the irreversible certainty (*avaivartikadharmakṣāntilabdha*) to attaining highest enlightenment. This epithet can also be applied to the *bodhisattvas* in his entry on to the *bhūmis* or again at the preparatory stage. The concept of the irreversible *bodhisattva* is mentioned in many *Mahāyāna sūtras* such as the *Saddharmapuṇḍarīka, Śūraṃgamasamādhi, Vimalakīrti,* and others, and is considered to be one of the most problematic subjects in *Mahāyāna* Buddhism.[34] In the context of the AA and its related commentaries, all the *bodhisattvas* who are training in the path of *prajñāpāramitā* are considered to be irreversible. This theory assumes many overlapping aspects of *Mahāyāna* soteriology such as the ideas of *ekayāna, gotra, tathāgatagarbha,* and so forth, that are perhaps too complex for our purposes here.[35]

In summary, the Twenty *Saṃghas* is a topic that occurs within the context of the first chapter of the AA and corresponds with special topics that *bodhisattvas* need to learn in order to acquire Total Omniscience. From the soteriological standpoint of the AA, these Twenty *Saṃghas* are irreversible *bodhisattvas.*

PATH AND YOGIC SYSTEMS OF THE *ABHISAMAYĀLAṂKĀRA*

We have so far given a contextual schema of the location and role that the special topic of the Twenty *Saṃghas* has in the AA. This special topic presumes many factors of Buddhist doctrine, particularly in regard to the path. In this section we will discuss these presumptions.

The AA itself documents a highly complex schema of "classical *Mahāyāna* path systems" that assumes an understanding of Buddhist soteriological doctrine along with a knowledge of the *Prajñāpāramitā Sūtra*'s contents. Edward Conze (1957: 21–36) provides a summary of how the path unfolds in the AA with its relationship to the *Prajñāpāramitā Sūtras,*

> The AA treats the contents of the PP as statements of spiritual experiences . . . the spiritual world is an essentially hierarchical structure, and

> the Absolute must appear different on different levels of attainment. Buddhist tradition had, by 350 AD, evolved a clear and detailed picture of the Path which a Buddhist Saint has to traverse through countless aeons, and to each meditation it finds in the PP, the AA assigns its appropriate place on the path. The reader of the AA must constantly bear in mind the position from which events are observed. What at first sight seems to be a dry and scholastic treatise does then become a fascinating contribution to transcendental psychology.

The AA has an intimate relationship with these *sūtra*s and standing on its own appears to be no more than lists of topics summarized from them. However, beginning with Ārya Vimuktisena and particularly Haribhadra's commentaries, we begin to see a trend in giving detailed definitions while commenting on particular subjects found in the AA. These are supported by the testament of doctrinal digests, such as the *Abhidharmakośa* and *Pramāṇavārttika*, and through expanded discourses on doctrinal points that may or may not be directly related to the AA or the PP *sūtras*. By the time the AA commentarial tradition had reached its apex in mid-fifteenth-century Tibet, this all-inclusive methodology allowed for Tibetan AA commentaries to evolve into a tour de force of encyclopedic Buddhist doctrinal knowledge where even minor topics became expanded essays of catholic exegesis.

Our discussion of AA path system, however, will be brief and not comprehensive, and we will comment on the various presuppositions of the path that are implicit within the topic of the twenty divisions of the *Saṃgha* Jewel.

The Variegated System of the "Path" in the AA

The Buddhist tradition in almost every aspect revolves around the concept of the "path" and the processes, stages, and doctrines of training it entails. Just as a route that leads to a certain place or enables one to search out a place is called in conventional usage a "path" (*mārga*), so too, that which leads to the city of Nirvāṇa or enables one to search out (*mṛg*) *nirvāṇa* is referred to as the "path."[36]

The "path" therefore has a goal-directed nature that leads to and produces higher states of being. Incorporating the secondary (*gauṇī*) characteristics of *Prajñāpāramitā* into its interpretation, the Tibetan Buddhist tradition provides a general definition of the "path":

> The clear realization of the manner of things which is conducive to the attainment of enlightenment, *nirvāṇa,* and the liberation from the fetters of existence. Its synonyms are "the way to final deliverance," "path of liberation," pristine cognition, clear realization, Mother, and vehicle."[37]

Tsong kha pa himself (*Golden Garland* 1970: 5) has stated in his collected works that "the sole path which is taken by all Victors is [the one found in] the precious *Prajñāpāramitā Sūtras.*" Tsong kha pa also attributes the special instructions of the AA with providing the fundamental basis for his composition of his *Great Stages of the Path* (*lam rim chen mo*).[38]

Now, what exactly is this "sole path taken by all Buddhas"? This is the subject expressed in the *Prajñāpāramitā Sūtras*. Explicitly, the subject matter of the PP is *śūnyatā* (emptiness) and is expounded upon in the "Six Collections of Reasoning" (*rigs tshogs drug*).[39] Implicitly, the subject matter of the PP is the path and is explained in the verses of the AA. The path structure of the PP assimilates a variety of *Abhidharma* categories: numerous meditative states, cosmic realms, or cognitive stages; varieties of individuals associated with each state, realm, or stage; specific techniques of spiritual practice, and the powers and attainments that occur with these practices. With this assimilation, the path structure that is represented in the PP by the AA becomes exceedingly complicated and elaborate, with numerous divisions and subdivisions. Nevertheless, the path system of the AA and its commentaries incorporates a generally accepted *Mahāyāna* soteriological system of five paths:[40]

1. the path of acquiring the provisions (*sambhāramārga*)
2. the path of preparation (*prayogamārga*)
3. the path of seeing (*darśanamārga*)
4. the path of cultivation (*bhāvanāmārga*)
5. and the path of no more training (*aśaikṣamārga*)

The first two are mundane paths (*laukika*) and the latter three are considered to be supramundane (*lokottara*), as they generate the attainments of Noble Beings (*ārya*). The paths of preparation, seeing, and cultivation will be the main concern for our purposes here, as they represent the preparation phase for abandoning afflictions and the actual paths where afflictions are abandoned (*prahāṇamārga*).

In the system of the AA there is also a threefold division of individuals who progress on the fivefold division of the path: that of *śrāvakas*, *pratyekabuddhas*, and *bodhisattvas*. This division of individuals into three provisional lineages (*gotra*)[41] accords with a categorization of the type of faculties, realizations, manner of abandonments, and goals individuals have when they engage in the path of the PP. This distinction is also made from the transformations of the Mother *Prajñāpāramitā* into three types of omniscience (i.e., *sarvākārajñatā*, *mārgajñatā*, *sarvajñatā*) that manifest due to the force of the thoughts of trainees to be trained. As it says in the *Pañcaviṃśatiprajñāpāramitā*: "The *śrāvaka* vehicle, *pratyekabuddha* vehicle, and the vehicle of perfectly complete Buddhahood are extensively taught from this *Prajñāpāramitā*."[42]

The AA does discuss these three vehicles but only in relation to the training of the *bodhisattva*. The AA's main purport and path structure is for the training of *bodhisattvas* to attain unsurpassable complete awakening (*bla na med pa'i yang dag par rdzogs pa'i sangs rgyas*) through cognizing Total Omniscience (*sarvākārajñatā*). In order for *bodhisattvas* to accomplish this goal, they must train in acquiring an understanding of all paths, both *Hīnayāna* and *Mahāyāna*.[43] This understanding of all paths is called "path omniscience" (*mārgajñatā*) and is acquired when the *bodhisattva* reaches the *Mahāyāna* path of seeing (*theg chen mthong lam*). Therefore, the presentation of the paths within the AA is from the viewpoint of what the *bodhisattva* needs to discern from all paths in order to generate, know, and complete the paths of various trainees.

Along with the AA's discussion of the paths, most commentators fill in details or expect readers to understand path-system specifications that were already established in the Indian and Tibetan Buddhist scholastic environment. These details of the path are usually supplied with quotations or inferences drawn from such texts as the *Abhidharmakośa*, *Abhidharmasamuccaya*, *Mahāyānasūtrālaṃkāra*, and so on.

The reader will need to keep in mind as we present the path systems of the AA that we have to unpack these paths in two layers: The first layer is the details of each path as they are presented in the AA and its commentaries, the second layer being the presumed understood factors that may or may not be expressed in the commentaries. Our presentation here for the most part will cover the basic fivefold path structure as it pertains to *śrāvakas*. All three vehicles have the same path structure but differ in terms of meditative objects, goals, faculties, and so forth (see Table 3.6). After presenting the *śrāvakas* path structure, we will then offer some brief comments about the distinctive features of the *pratyekabuddha* and *bodhisattva* vehicles and their paths as it is understood in the context of the AA.

Śrāvaka*'s Path System*

Śrāvakas, translated as "Auditors," "Disciples," or "Hearers," are those who strive for the realization of Omniscience (*sarvajñatā*).[44] They are individuals who seek peace (*śāntaiṣiṇaḥ*) from the suffering of conditioned existence and have the aim to achieve *nirvāṇa* merely in the sense of emancipation from this suffering. A brief definition of this vehicle is given in the *Abhidharmasamuccaya*:

> Who is an individual that belongs to the *śrāvaka* vehicle? This is a person who, whether having attainments or not, dwells in the doctrine of the *śrāvaka*s, having by nature weak faculties, is fixed upon his own liberation through the means of cultivating detachment, depending on the canon of the *śrāvaka*s, practices the minor and major virtues through energetic cultivation, [and then] obtains the end of suffering.[45]

In regard to seeking their own liberation, the *śrāvaka* is viewed as having a selfish aim, but nevertheless a spiritual one.

The sixteen aspects of the Nobles' Four Truths. In the system of the AA, being situated in the doctrine of the *śrāvaka*s means that the course of this individual's path is to be totally fixated upon the Nobles' Four Truths (*catvāri āryasatyāni*) with particular emphasis on their sixteen aspects.[46] These sixteen are divided by way of four aspects for each Truth and are thoroughly summarized by Haribhadra in his *Ālokā*:

> Here, through the qualities of production and disintegration there is (1) impermanence (*anitya*). Because contaminated entities are unpleasant there is (2) misery (*duḥkha*). . . . Because of the emptiness of self and other there is (3) selflessness (*anātma*). Since there is not a self which is independent there is (4) emptiness (*śūnyatā*). [These are] the aspects of the truth of suffering. Through fundamental (5) causes (*hetu*) which are like the seed of a fruit there is disease. Through the (6) driving force (*samudaya*) of suffering there is excrescence. Through the (7) condition (*pratyaya*) of suffering there is irritation. There is misfortune because of extensive destruction through the successive (8) process (*prabhava*) of suffering. There is an other through the occurrence of hostile forces. Because there is a destructive quality with the hostile entity, there are destructive objects. Thus these two are an aspect of aversion for each one of the truths of suffering and origin. Through the unsteadiness in its own nature there is agitation. Through disintegrating by nature without relying on a cause there is decay. These two are an aspect which is free from attachment for each one [of these truths]. Through the occurrence of a place of pain in this world and others there is dread. Through the occasion of torment by obnoxious demons there is disease. Through the occurrence of a place becoming disturbed through the turbulence and jolt of the great elements there is calamity. The aspects of cessation have each one of these. In this way, *śrāvaka*s will enter [the path] because of aversion, detachment, and cessation. This is the meaning of the scripture that has been discussed. Through being separated from afflictions there is (9) selflessness. Through the pacification of suffering there is (10) pacification. Through the entities of happiness and purity there is (11) isolation. If by the entities of permanence and benefit there is (12) emptiness, signlessness, wishlessness, and lack of accomplishment. Thus are the aspects of the truth of cessation. Through causing to obtain the

city of Nirvāṇa there is a (13) path (*mārga*). Through being a collection of antidotes to all afflictions there is a (14) method. Through the purpose of unmistakable achievement of the mind there is (15) achievement (*pratipatti*). Through going to a permanent place which lacks imaginative constructions there is (16) deliverance (*nairyāṇika*). [These are] the aspects of the truth of the path.[47]

A *bodhisattva* will cognize the Nobles' Four Truths without perceptually grasping on to their aspects. This is because even though a *bodhisattva* recognizes the aspects of disease, calamity, and so forth, he/she does not become attached to these aspects for the purpose of escaping *saṃsāra* as does a *śrāvaka*.

If a *śrāvaka* understands these sixteen aspects of the Truths, this leads to aversion and detachment to *saṃsāra*. These qualities are dominant throughout most of this lineage's fivefold path system. With these aspects of the Truths as meditational objects, the *śrāvaka*s spiritual career abandons emotional afflictions (*kleśāvaraṇaprahāṇa; nyon mongs spangs bya*) and realizes the selflessness of the person (*pudgalanairātymādhigamana; gang zag gi bdag med rtogs pa*).

Śrāvaka *path of acquiring the provisions*. The path of acquiring provisions (*sambhāramārga*) is the first of the paths and it is that which accumulates the provisions necessary to achieve the awakening of one's vehicle.[48] It mainly consists of various practices that are considered to be the necessary preliminaries to the cultivation of the path proper, the noble path (*āryamārga*). For *śrāvaka*s this involves the acquisition of "noble attitudes" (*āryavaṃśa*), such as contentment, and the full development of an ordinary individual's (*pṛthagjana*) moral character. This is characterized by the control of the sense faculties, moderation of food and sleep, and the beginning meditative development of quiescence (*śamatha*) and special insight (*vipaśyanā*). The *śrāvaka* also begins to develop the wisdoms (*prajñā*) of study (*śrutimayī*), reflection (*cintāmayī*), and cultivation (*bhāvanāmayī*), which gives rise to the full cognition of the "Word of the Doctrine" (*dharmābhisamaya; chos mngon rtogs*) in its twelve limbs (*dvādaśāṅga*).[49] This accumulation phase of the path culminates in the practice of the cultivation of the loathsome (*aśubhābhāvanā*) and mindfulness of breathing (*ānāpānasmṛti*).[50] The practices of what is loathsome (*aśubhā*) and mindfulness of breathing (*ānāpānasmṛti*) result in quiescence (*śamatha*) or concentration (*samādhi*), and it is at this point that a *śrāvaka* begins to develop the four stations of mindfulness (*smṛtyupasthāna*).[51] With the beginning development of these accumulations characterized by the said practices, a *śrāvaka* enters the path of preparation (*prayogamārga*).

Śrāvaka *path of preparation.* The path of preparation, also called the path of training, is that which literally "links" or "joins" (*prayoga*) the practitioner to the process of directly perceiving the Nobles' Truths. Yet because it still precedes the actual cognition of the Truths, it is a mundane path (*laukikamārga*) and is characterized as "the cognition of the meaning of the Doctrine" (*don mngon rtogs*). At this point one gathers a rough connotation of selflessness through the experience of meditating upon the Doctrine.[52] In the *Abhidharmakośa*, the path of preparation arises from the practice of the fourth station of mindfulness, which gives rise to the four roots of virtue (*kuśalamūla*) called "preparatory analytical factors" (*nirvedhabhāgīya*). As Haribhadra in his *Sphuṭārthā* mentions, for *śrāvakas*, these four roots of virtue allow for a rough perception of Nobles' Four Truths. They are involved with aspects of impermanence and so forth that cure the view of a self, are for the sake of realizing their own vehicle, lack assistance, and arise without the four types of concepts.[53] The "preparatory analytical factors" (*nirvedhabhāgīya*) constitute the path of preparation proper and have four divisions: heat (*uṣmagata*), summit (*mūrdhagata*), forbearance (*kṣānti*), and the stage that constitutes the peak of the mundane path, the highest worldly dharma (*laukikāgradharma*). Each of these has three degrees: weak, medium, and strong. Heat is called as such because it is similar to heat being the first indication of the Noble Path, a fire that burns the fuel of the defilements.[54] As Obermiller states (1932: 20), heat (*uṣmagata*)

> represents a state of complete mental quiescence, connected with transcendental analysis (*vipaśyanā*), during which the light of knowledge revealing for the first time the essential nature of the four Truths of the Saint and their sixteen aspects is obtained.

Summit (*mūrdhan*), or also "head," is known as such because it is the most elevated of the unstable roots of virtue. It is a higher achievement than basic virtues and from these one can ascend to higher states.[55] These first two preparatory analytical factors are weak because, being unstable, one can degenerate from them.[56] Certainty (*kṣānti*)[57] denotes perseverance in regard to perceiving the Nobles' Four Truths and is considered to be the moderate level of the *nirvedhabhāgīyas*. Highest worldly dharma is understood to be the supreme of mundane achievements and the strongest of the preparatory analytical factors; yet, it is still considered worldly (*laukika*) and impure (*sāsrava*). These preparatory analytical factors are developed only in the preliminary threshold to full concentration (*dhyāna*), the *anāgamya*, ("not-incapable"; compare to Pāli, *upacāra*) or in the concentrations themselves [i.e., *dhyānāntara*], but they are not developed in the four formless attainments.[58] At this point one sees the suffering of existence and has reached a level of disgust such that one is fully prepared to enter into the path of seeing (*darśanamārga*) and cognize the Nobles' Four Truths in their entirety.

Śrāvaka *path of seeing*. As soon as one reaches the *śrāvaka* path of seeing (*darśanamārga*), one begins the supermundane path (*lokottaramārga*) and the beginning of the Noble Path (*āryamārga*) proper, the path that abandons the defilements (*prahāṇamārga*).[59] In the *Abhidharmakośa*, the path of seeing is characterized by a direct knowledge of seeing something that has not been seen before.[60] The Tibetan tradition regards the knowledge gained on the *śrāvaka's* path of seeing as the fact that the person lacks a permanent, unique, independent self (*gang zag rtag rang dbang can gyi bdag gis stong pa*).[61] The knowledge gained on the path of seeing causes the removal of defilements that are to be abandoned by direct seeing (*darśanaprahātavya; mthong spang bya ba*) of the selflessness of the person. These are learned defilements (*nyon sgrib kun brtags*)[62] that are acquired by incorrect philosophical views and intellectual predispositions formed primarily by the study of non-Buddhist tenet systems. In this way, the path of seeing is an especially Buddhist path and is exclusively supermundane. It is a path that consists of sixteen thought-moments (*ṣoḍaśa kṣaṇāḥ*) of clear realization applied to the Nobles' Four Truths (*satyābhisamaya*). These sixteen moments of consciousness are made up of a series of alternating moments of intellectual receptivity (*kṣānti*), or acquiescences, and knowledges (*jñāna*). This series is also divided into uninterrupted paths (*ānantaryamārga*) and paths of liberation (*vimuktimārga*) (see Table 3.3).

The uninterrupted path is the path by which obstacles are abandoned[63] and is characterized as "the clear realization of the truth for a *śrāvaka* which acts as a direct antidote to imputed afflictional obstacles."[64] The uninterrupted path consists of eight moments of consciousness in which one gains an intellectual receptivity (*kṣānti*) toward understanding the Nobles' Four Truths. These eight moments of intellectual receptivity are divided into four moments of receptivity to the doctrine (*dharmajñānakṣānti; chos bzod*) of the Four Truths in the realm of desire, and then a continuance of this receptivity in understanding (*anvayajñānakṣānti; rjes bzod*) of the Four Truths carried on into the form and formless realms. In these moments of consciousness, the Four Truths serve as cognitive objects to implement a direct realization of the selflessness of the person. The moments of intellectual receptivity represent the subject, the consciousness in which there is an intellectual cognition of the selflessness.[65]

The path of liberation is the first path that arises after an obstacle is abandoned by means of the uninterrupted path.[66] It is characterized

Table 3.3 Path of Seeing's (*darśanamārga*) Moments of Consciousness [*read from bottom to top*]

Nobles' Four Truths	Moment of consciousness	Realm affected
IV. Regarding the Path [*Mārge*]	16. subsequent knowledge (*anvayajñāna*)	Form and Formless
	15. subsequent intellectual receptivity (*anvayajñānakṣānti*)	
	14. knowledge of the doctrine (*dharmajñāna*)	Desire
	13. intellectual receptivity to the doctrine (*dharmajñānakṣānti*)	
III. Regarding Cessation [*Nirodhe*]	12. subsequent knowledge (*anvayajñāna*)	Form and Formless
	11. subseqent intellectual receptivity (*anvayajñānakṣānti*)	
	10. knowledge of the doctrine (*dharmajñāna*)	Desire
	9. intellectual receptivity to the doctrine (*dharmajñānakṣānti*)	
II. Regarding Origin [*Samudaye*]	8. subsequent knowledge (*anvayajñāna*)	Form and Formless
	7. subseqent intellectual receptivity (*anvayajñānakṣānti*)	
	6. knowledge of the doctrine (*dharmajñāna*)	Desire
	5. intellectual receptivity to the doctrine (*dharmajñānakṣānti*)	
I. Regarding Suffering [*Duḥkhe*]	4. subsequent knowledge (*anvayajñāna*)	Form and Formless
	3. subseqent intellectual receptivity (*anvayajñānakṣānti*)	
	2. knowledge of the doctrine (*dharmajñāna*)	Desire
	1. intellectual receptivity to the doctrine (*dharmajñānakṣānti*)	

as "the clear realization of the truth for a *śrāvaka* who is liberated, having abandoned the learned afflictional obstacles."[67] A moment of consciousness that consists of a path of liberation follows immediately after a moment of an uninterrupted path. This amounts to a series of moments that alternate from an uninterrupted path to a path of liberation. Therefore, the path of liberation, like the uninterrupted path, consists of eight knowledges (*jñāna*). These are divided into four kinds of knowledge of the doctrine (*dharmajñāna*), corresponding to each of the four truths as applied in the desire realm. Then, after each one of the four knowledges is applied in the desire realm, there occurs a continuance of knowledge (*anvayajñāna*) that is sustained into the form and formless realms.

With this structure of the eight knowledges and eight moments of intellectual receptivity in mind, we can see how it is applied through a specific examination of these moments as applied to the first Nobles' Truth on the path of seeing. After the highest worldly dharma that is the last of the four phases of the path of preparation, during meditative equipoise, a period of acquiescence arises in which one develops an intellectual receptivity to the knowledge of the truth of the doctrine as it pertains to suffering (*duḥkhe dharmajñānakṣānti*).[68] This is a pure moment, the first of the eight periods of intellectual receptivity on the uninterrupted path. This moment of intellectual receptivity is likened to a battle in which one must withstand learned afflictions (*nyon sgrib kun brtags*) that act as forces against realizing the object of personal selflessness as it pertains to the truth of suffering in the desire realm. Because the period of intellectual receptivity cannot be hindered in its elimination of these afflictional forces, it is therefore called an "uninterrupted path" (*ānantaryamārga*). Then after the moment of intellectual receptivity comes the knowledge or certitude relating to the truth of suffering in the desire realm (*duḥkhe dharmajñāna*), all doubt having disappeared. In this moment, one takes hold of the cutting off or destruction of these afflictional forces and therefore is liberated from them; thus this second moment is a path of liberation (*vimuktimārga*). The relationship between the moments of intellectual receptivity, consisting of uninterrupted paths, and the knowledges, consisting of paths of liberation, is described by the image of expelling a thief and then closing the door. Through cutting off the possession of the afflictional obstacles, there is expulsion of the thief by the uninterrupted path; then, through this disconnection there is the closing of the door by the path of liberation.[69] In the third and fourth moments, one subsequently sees the Nobles' Truth of Suffering as it relates to the suffering of the form and formless realm. In the third moment there is an intellectual receptivity that is a continuance of knowledge (*anvayajñānakṣānti*), and in the fourth moment there is a continuance of knowledge (*anvayajñāna*). These moments maintain the same alternation between a moment consisting of an uninterrupted path followed by a moment consisting of a path of liberation. This same type of four moments applies to each of the Four Truths adding up to sixteen moments.

The path of seeing is therefore a succession of moments of consciousness in which one gathers a complete comprehension of the fundamental truths of Buddhist doctrine. It is through this comprehension that non-Buddhist intellectual predispositions are eliminated and artificial afflictional obstacles concerning wrong view are removed. These obstacles will be discussed in the next chapter. Here we should note that even though there are sixteen moments of intellectual receptivity and knowledge, according to the system of *Abhidharmakośa*, the first fifteen moments of comprehension (*abhisamaya*) make up the path of seeing and the sixteenth moment is considered to be the first moment of the path of cultivation.[70]

According to Tsong kha pa, however, the path of seeing as defined in this system of the *Abhisamayālaṃkāra* and the *Abhidharmasamuccaya* consists of sixteen moments.[71] It is generally understood that the system of the *Abhidharmasamuccaya* is used to explain the *Mahāyāna* path of seeing (which will be mentioned below). However, Tsong kha pa indicates in his *Stairway* and *Golden Garland* that the moments that demarcate the boundaries of the path of seeing as understood from the *Abhidharmasamuccaya* should be used in order to facilitate "the method which generates in the mental continuum a clear realization for the individuals of all three vehicles."[72] This implies that in the system of the AA, sixteen moments of the path of seeing apply to *śrāvaka*s and *pratyekabuddha*s. This is in fact explicitly stated in the *Abhisamayālaṃkāra* within the chapter of empirical Omniscience (*sarvajñatādhikāra*)[73] and implicitly understood from remarks made by Haribhadra at the beginning of his brief outline of the Twenty *Saṃgha*s in his *Ālokā*.[74]

The *śrāvaka* arrives at a clear intellectual comprehension of the Nobles' Four Truths through sixteen moments of consciousness and removes only the artificial defilements in the path of seeing. This path of seeing is pure (*anāsrava*) and supermundane (*lokottara*) and can only be traversed by the Buddhist yogi.

Śrāvaka *path of cultivation.* The next category of the path, the path of cultivation (*bhāvanāmārga*), is by nature "repeated practice" (*abhyāsa*) or "repeated confrontation" (*punaḥ punar āmukhīkaraṇa*).[75] It is at this point in the path that one cultivates and refines through absorption what has been previously understood in an intellectual manner. The path of cultivation has many divisions and subdivisions, which makes it almost too complicated to summarize briefly. A fundamental division of the path of cultivation is that between the mundane (*laukika*) and the supermundane (*lokottara*).[76]

Mundane path of cultivation. The mundane path of cultivation (*laukikabhāvanāmārga*) may be briefly said to include those meditative practices, Buddhist or non-Buddhist, which are not related to cultivating a repeated analysis of the sixteen aspects of the Nobles' Four Truths.[77] The discussion of the path of cultivation, whether mundane or supermundane, centers around the ancient Indian cosmological division of the spheres that constitute cyclic existence (*saṃsāra*) into the three worlds (*triloka*) or three realms (*traidhātuka*): the desire realm (*kāmadhātu*), the four stages of the realm of form (*rūpadhātu*), and the four levels of the formless realm (*ārūpyadhātu*). These nine realms are also considered to be states of meditative consciousness as well as cosmological realms. We will investigate this cosmology briefly below. Here, the mundane path of cultivation is seen as a progression through these cosmological stages and corresponding states of consciousness by means of meditative absorption (*dhyānas*). This is achieved by a cultivation of developing distaste and detachment for one's current state of existence in comparison with the apparent peacefulness of the upper realms. The Tibetan tradition refers to this practice as the cultivation bearing on the aspects of calmness and coarseness (*śāntaudārika; zhi rags*).[78] In this mundane cultivation, the paths of deliverance enable the yogi to experience the higher spheres of meditative absorption as calm, excellent, and liberating. Through the uninterrupted paths, or paths of abandoning, the yogi experiences the lower spheres as coarse, bad, and as like a barrier.[79] This method of meditation allows for the yogi to detach himself from the first eight of the nine levels of meditative absorption because there is no higher stage to which the ninth can be compared.[80] Through this successive process of detachment from the various realms, the yogi acquires separation from the defilements that belong to each realm. However, this separation, since it is by means of a mundane path, is itself only mundane and therefore is only a temporary removal of the defilements. On the other hand, the experience of removing defilements by the mundane path of cultivation before engaging in the path of seeing may enable a yogi to advance more rapidly toward *nirvāṇa*. We will identify and discuss these individuals in the next chapter.

Supermundane path of cultivation. The supermundane path of cultivation (*lokottara bhāvanāmārga*) is uncontaminated (*anāsrava*) and can only be entered by the individual who has already advanced through the path of seeing. In the AA, the supermundane path of cultivation is described as "repeatedly considering, assessing, and contemplating [that which is beheld] within the preparatory analytical factors, the path of vision, and the path of cultivation."[81] In the case of the *śrāvaka*, this is familiarization (*abhyāsa*) and concentrated awareness (*samāhita-jñāna*) of the realization of personal selflessness through the meditative objects of the Nobles' Four Truths (*satyabhāvanā*).

Like the path of seeing, the supermundane path of cultivation is divided into the uninterrupted path and path of liberation. These corresponding divisions differ in respect to the defilements to be abandoned. The supermundane path of cultivation removes those defilements to be abandoned by cultivation (*bhāvanāprahātavya; sgom spang bya ba*), the innate afflictional obscurations (*sahajakleśāvaraṇa; nyon sgrib lhan skyes*).

These innate defilements are categorized in sequence with the fundamental division of existence into the realm of desire (*kāmadhātu*), the first, second, third, and fourth absorptions (*dhyāna*) of the form realms (*rūpadhātu*), and the realms of infinite space (*ākāśānantyāyatana*), infinite consciousness (*vijñānānantyāyatana*), nothingness (*ākiṃcanyā-yatana*), and peak of existence (*bhavāgra*) of the formless realms (*ārūpyadhātu*). In each of these nine realms there are three fundamental categories of the defilements, subtle (*mṛdu*), medium (*madhya*), and coarse (*adhimātra*). Each one of these fundamental categories is in turn subdivided into subtle, medium, and coarse, yielding a paradigm of nine categories: subtle-subtle, subtle-medium, subtle-coarse, medium-subtle, medium-medium, medium-coarse, coarse-subtle, coarse-medium, coarse-coarse. Therefore, with nine categories of defilements in each of the nine realms of existence there is a total of eighty-one defilements to be removed by the supermundane path of cultivation.[82]

Each of these eighty-one defilements is abandoned by a corresponding number of uninterrupted paths and paths of liberation. These varieties of the defilements are removed in reverse order: a weak-weak path of cultivation has the power to act as the antidote to the coarse-coarse defilement, and so on, up to a strong-strong path having the power to act as the antidote to the subtle-subtle defilement. This is because it is not possible to begin the path with a strong-strong path and it is not possible to have a coarse-coarse defilement when there is a strong-strong path. Vasubandhu employs two heuristic analogies to describe this procedure. First, he compares the process of removing these defilements in this way to the process of washing a piece of cloth. The coarse or greater stains on the cloth, the defilements, are the easier to remove and, thus, are washed out first. The more subtle stains on the cloth require a stronger cleansing agent. Hence, the subtle defilements are removed by strong paths. The other analogy is that a great amount of darkness can be dispelled by a small amount of light; whereas a great amount of light is required to dispel a small amount of darkness.[83]

These defilements to be removed by the supermundane path of cultivation may be removed in one of two ways: gradually or simultaneously. The gradual method involves the abandonment of first, the nine categories of defilement specific to the desire realm, then, of the nine categories specific to the first level of the form realm, and so on sequentially through the remaining realms of the *triloka*. The simultaneous method of abandonment involves the instantaneous removal of defilements in relation to their density. That is to say, all the coarse defilements with regard to the desire, form, and formless realms are removed first. Then all the intermediate defilements related to the three realms are removed. Finally, all the subtle defilements of the desire, form, and formless realms are removed. With this latter method, all the defilements to be removed by cultivation can be accomplished in nine steps. We will investigate the types of individuals who abandon defilements gradually or simultaneously in the next chapter. The final removal of the last category of the defilements to be abandoned by the supermundane path of cultivation is achieved by the "diamond-like concentration" (*vajropamasamādhi*). This occurs at the fourth and last sphere of the formless realm, called "peak of existence."[84] This final abandonment is immediately followed by the path of no more training (*aśaikṣamārga*).

Śrāvakas *path of no more training*. Once the final abandonment of the last category of the defilements is accomplished by the *vajropamasamādhi*, there arises a path of deliverance in which one possesses the knowledge that all defilements have been destroyed (*kṣayajñāna*)[85] and the knowledge that such defilements will not originate once again in the future (*anutpādajñāna*).[86] These two knowledges are considered to be the final enlightenment of the *śrāvaka*.[87] This phase of the path is described as the end of the course of training, the final knowledge in which there is no longer any training, and is synonymous with the achievement of the state of an *Arhat*. However, in the *ekayāna* system propagated by AA commentators such as Haribhadra and Tsong kha pa, the *śrāvaka* has merely attained the termination of his own vehicle and will necessarily proceed into the *Mahāyāna* vehicle for the sake of obtaining full unlocated *nirvāṇa*.[88]

Summary of the Śrāvaka *Path in the* Abhisamayālaṃkāra. The above outline of the fivefold path system of the *śrāvaka* forms the underlying path system that is presumed in Indian and Tibetan scholasticism (see table 3.4). In the context of underlying path systems, Tsong kha pa draws attention to how the *śrāvaka* path is represented in the AA. He does this by rearranging certain points of the text to show that the AA

Table 3.4 Path Structure Overview [*read from bottom to top*]

Individual	Path Type	Path	Path Practices	Cognition	Result
Noble Being (*ārya*)	Supramundane (*lokottara*)	Path of no more training		All defilements have been destroyed and will not arise again	*Aśaikṣa arhat*
		Path of cultivation	Repeated uncontaminated awareness on Nobles' Four Truths	Selflessness	*Arhat*-enterer Non-returner Non-returner enterer Once-returner Once-returner enterer Stream-enterer
		Path of seeing	Sixteen Moments on the Nobles' Four Truths	Selflessness	Stream-enterer enterer
Ordinary individual (*pṛthagjana*)	Mundane (*laukika*)	Path of preparation	Highest worldly dharma Certainty Summit Heat	Preparatory analytical factors Meaning of the doctrine	Four roots of virtue
		Path of acquiring provisions	Four stations of mindfulness Mindfulness of breathing Cultivation of the loathsome Noble attitudes: contentment, moderation	Word of the doctrine	Wisdoms of study, reflection, cultivation

is as soteriological relevant for *śrāvakas* as it is for *bodhisattvas*. This discussion encompasses knowledge of the *śrāvakas* goal of basic empirical Omniscience (*vastujñāna*) that, in the context of the AA, a *bodhisattva* will also gain.

Tsong kha provides in his *Golden Garland* a summary of the types of *śrāvaka* knowledge that a *bodhisattva* gains. First, the foundation of the *śrāvaka*'s path knowledge is indicated in the AA by thirty-seven auxiliaries of enlightenment. These occur in the discussion of one hundred ten aspects related to Total Omniscience presented in the fourth chapter of the AA. Next, sixteen of those aspects indicate the *śrāvaka*'s path of seeing. Twenty characteristics occur in AA's chapter 4 that describe basic empirical Omniscience. The *śrāvaka*'s path of preparation is indicated in chapter 2 of the AA. The *śrāvaka*'s path of seeing, which arises from the path of preparation is indicated in chapters 2 and 3. Finally, even though the results of the *śrāvaka*'s path are not directly indicated in the AA, it is suitable to demonstrate them through the section that discusses the Twenty *Saṃghas*.[89] The *bodhisattva*'s knowledge of the *śrāvaka*'s path in the AA, in brief, is elucidated in this manner. Tsong kha pa provides this account to demonstrate the coherence of the AA in being soteriologically efficacious for all three vehicles. The last emphasis placed upon the results of the *śrāvaka*'s path is of interest to us here and will be related in the next chapter.

The Path of the Pratyekabuddha

The next type of vehicle mentioned in the AA is that of the *pratyekabuddha*. A *pratyekabuddha* in this system is similar to the *śrāvaka* in that he/she seeks peace and achieves empirical Omniscience (*vastujñāna, sarvajñatā*). The basic structure of the *pratyekabuddha*'s path system for the most part also mirrors that of the *śrāvakas*, having five divisions beginning with the path of accumulation and so forth and achieving the abandonment of defilements through the paths of seeing and cultivation.[90] However, several characteristics of lineage, objects of meditative cultivation, and meditative realizations distinguish the *pratyekabuddha*'s vehicle from other vehicles (see table 3.5).

The *pratyekabuddha* possesses three main characteristics that differentiate it from other vehicles. First, the *pratyekabuddha* by nature has fewer afflictions and therefore with that type of mind does not enjoy society but enjoys a solitary existence. Second, a *pratyekabuddha* does not have much compassion and therefore does not teach the mind of compassion nor seek the welfare of sentient beings. Third, the *pratyekabuddha* has moderate faculties along with an arrogant behavior pattern, which therefore leads a *pratyekabuddha* to desire to be awakened through his or her own efforts and without the aid of a teacher.[91] In its solitary existence, a *pratyekabuddha* does not wish to hear anything, views verbalization as a distraction, and will communicate if necessary in a nonverbal manner.[92] A *pratyekabuddha*'s meditative knowledge is self-arisen due to self-realization and therefore does not depend on the verbal instruction from Buddhas as does *śrāvakas*.[93]

A *pratyekabuddha* with these character traits will focus on six types of objects to be mastered while training in his spiritual career. *Pratyekabuddhas* thoroughly learn the subjects of the aggregates (*skandha*), sensory spheres (*āyatana*), elements (*dhātu*), dependent coarising (*pratītyasamutpāda*), that which is appropriate and inappropriate (*gnas dang gnas ma yin pa*), and the Nobles' Four Truths.[94]

Through its mastery of these six objects to be learned, the most distinguishing feature of a *pratyekabuddha* is his or her abandonment of the conceptualization of these objects to be apprehended (*grāhyārtha*), yet at the same time he fails to abandon the conceptualization of that which apprehends (*grāhaka*).[95] In other words, by realizing that external objects of knowledge lack inherent existence, a *pratyekabuddha* abandons the conceptualization that grasps at external or sensory objects as being real. Likewise, by failing to realize that the experience of cognition also lacks inherent existence, a *pratyekabuddha* does not abandon the conceptualization which grasps at experience in the subjective domain as being real.[96] For example, although a magical creation or illusion does not actually exist as a real object, there is a mental cognition of its appearance. Accordingly, although *pratyekabuddhas* realize that the sensory phenomena of this illusion do not have a nature, they do not realize that the cognition itself does not truly exist.[97]

With these distinctions in realization, a *pratyekabuddha* is understood to be superior to a *śrāvaka* and inferior to a *bodhisattva*. A *pratyekabuddha* is superior to a *śrāvaka* in that, not only does he realize the selflessness of the person (*gang zag gi bdag med*), but through his abandonment of the conceptualization of objects, a part of the obstacles to knowledge is removed (*jñeyāvaraṇaikadeśagrāhyavikalpaprahāṇād*), albeit a very rough aspect of the knowledge obstacles (*shes sgrib rags pa*). Because of the inefficient removal of knowledge obstacles, a *pratyekabuddha* is considered to be inferior to the *bodhisattva*, who totally removes knowledge obstacles through his realization of both the selflessness of the person and the essencelessness of things (*dharmanairātmya*).

At the time when the eighty-one defilements to be removed by the path of cultivation are abandoned, the *pratyekabuddha*'s spiritual pursuit culminates in the path of no more training (*aśaikṣamārga*), where the goal of *pratyekabuddha arhat*ship is achieved.

Mahāyāna *soteriological theory and the one ultimate vehicle.* In the *Mahāyāna* tradition that is followed by AA commentators such as Haribhadra and Tsong kha pa, the conclusion of the *śrāvaka*'s and *pratyekabuddha*'s path in their goals of *arhat*ship does not represent the final termination of their respective vehicles.[98] The *śrāvaka arhat*'s and *pratyekabuddha arhat*'s achievement of *nirvāṇa,* with or without remnant (*sopadhiśeṣani-rupadhiśeṣanirvāṇa*), is said to be only a state of peaceful trance in which the *arhat* is engaged for a countless period of time. This apparent *nirvāṇa* is called "*nirvāṇa* resembling an extinguished light" (*pradī-panirvāṇaprakhyanirvāṇa*). In this instance, although their karmic propensities to take rebirth in the three spheres of existence (*traidhātuka*) have ceased, these *arhat*s take rebirth by means of uncontaminated karma (*zag med kyi las*) in Buddha-fields of utmost purity that resemble the petals of lotus flowers. They abide in this uncontaminated realm (*anāsravadhātu*) with mental bodies (*yid kyi lus*), engaged in meditative absorption, until they are roused from their *samādhi* by Buddhas, and urged on to enter into the *Mahāyāna* path.[99] On this point, both Haribhadra and Tsong kha pa describe the situation of the *śrāvaka* and *pratyekabuddha arhats,* based on Candrakīrti's *Triśaraṇasaptati*:

> Having attained two aspects of enlightenment, those [*hīnayāna arhat*s] whose minds are frightened by existence, rejoice in the expiration of life thinking they have attained *nirvāṇa.* [But] they do not [actually] possess *nirvāṇa.* Although rebirth in the three spheres does not exist for them they nevertheless abide in the uncontaminated realm. Later, they are urged on by the buddhas for the purpose of abandoning unafflicted ignorance. Accumulating the provisions of enlightenment, they will become leaders of the world.[100]

In this way, it is understood in this *Mahāyāna* system that those who have taken up the paths of the lower vehicles and achieved the consummation of those paths are urged out of their apparent catalepsy and into the single ultimate vehicle of the *bodhisattvas.*

Mahāyāna *Path of the* Bodhisattva *in the* Abhisamayālaṃkāra

Innumerable *Mahāyāna sūtra*s and *śāstra*s discuss the attributes of the *bodhisattva,* the spiritual aspirant of the *Mahāyāna* path who is said to achieve the "inconceivable liberation." By the complex and abstract account of the *bodhisattva*'s spiritual career given in the AA, one could also characterize the *bodhisattva* as traveling the "inconceivable path." In any case, we shall give here a brief account of the *bodhisattva*'s path structure because a detailed presentation of the *bodhisattva*'s path will not be necessary in our discussion of the Twenty *Saṃghas*.

The basic structure of the *Mahāyāna* path as discussed in the AA is the same fivefold division that was mentioned earlier in regard to the *śrāvaka* vehicle. The fundamental difference from the other vehicles is that the *Mahāyāna* is considered to be superior in its aspiration, abandonment, and realization (see table 3.5). *Bodhisattvas* are superior in that they aspire to unsurpassable complete awakening (*anuttarasaṃyaksaṃbodhi*), not only for themselves but also for the sake of all other beings. With emphasis on the altruistic intention of others' purpose, one primary distinction over other vehicles is that *bodhisattvas* have great compassion (*mahākaruṇa*). They abandon not only the afflictional obscurations (*kleśāvaraṇa*) but also the obstacles that impede complete knowledge (*jñeyāvaraṇa*). The understanding that actuates their abandonment, is not only cognizing the essencelessness of the person (*pudgalanairātyma*), but also realizing the essencelessness of things (*dharmanairātmya*) through the apprehension of emptiness (*śūnyatā*). In the course of cognizing the two types of essencelessness and abandoning the two types of obscurations, a *bodhisattva* will travel through ten levels or stages (*daśabhūmi*). Through the *bodhisattva's* abandonment of the knowledge obstacles they achieve Total Omniscience (*sarvākārajñatā*), enabling them to help all beings through their achievement of Buddhahood.

The individual who travels the *Mahāyāna* path may be of two types: the *bodhisattva* who from the very beginning is firm in the *Mahāyāna* lineage (*rigs nges*), and the *hīnayāna arhat*, either *śrāvaka* or *pratyekabuddha,* who is not firm in the lineage (*rigs ma nges pa*) and subsequently enters into the *Mahāyāna* path. The foundation of the *Mahāyāna* path is the seed potential for enlightenment, the *tathāgatagarbha,* which is considered to be latent in all sentient beings. This seed potential that naturally exists in all living beings must be activated by means of special reflection concerning the nature of *saṃsāra* such that this potential becomes engaged in the process of spiritual development.[101]

The special reflection that takes place is the aspiration to achieve full awakening for one's own benefit and for the sake of other beings. This is known as the generation of the thought for enlightenment (*bodhicittotpāda; byang chub tu sems bskyed*).[102] A *bodhisattva* produces an altruistic mind set on achieving perfect awakening (*saṃyaksaṃbodhi*), consisting in the twofold stage of resolution (*praṇidhi*) and engagement (*prasthāna*), for the sake of all beings. Production of this altruistic mind marks the beginning of the *Mahāyāna* path and the phase of the path called the "path of accumulation." In the AA, this phase is referred to as "factors conducive to liberation" (*mokṣabhāgīya*) and it is in this stage of the path that a *bodhisattva* begins to collect the provisions necessary to make the aim of that altruistic intention possible. Here one develops faith, enthusiastic perseverance in giving, mindfulness, stabilization, and wisdom.[103] A *bodhisattva* will acquire a whole series of provisions, or equipment, throughout his career in order to attain highest enlightenment and the AA enumerates seventeen types of provisions.[104] Also in this phase of the path, a *bodhisattva* who wishes to sustain and expand the qualities that are produced from altruistic mind generation must hear, through dependence on meditative absorption of the stream of the doctrine (*srotānugatasamādhi*), special instructions (*avavāda*) such as the ten topics beginning with application (*pratipatti*) and so forth. Having received special instruction and developed the roots of virtue (*kuśalamūla*), which are characterized by the qualities of faith (*śraddhā*) (etc.), one becomes possessed of the factors that constitute emancipation (*mokṣabhāgīya*). At this point, one has gathered a rough understanding of the essencelessness of things and begun the unified path of calm abiding and special insight (*śamathavipaśyanāyuganaddha*). The *bodhisattva* is ready to enter into the *Mahāyāna* path of preparation.

The next phase of the path begins when the *bodhisattva*, who is still an ordinary individual (*pṛthagjana*), obtains for the first time a forceful experience of special insight directed at the emptiness of all things (Obermiller, 1932: 34). As with the paths of the *śrāvaka* and *pratyekabuddha*, this stage of developing insight on the path of preparation consists of the fourfold preparatory analytical factors (*nirvedhabhāgīya*).

These four factors of the *nirvedhabhāgīya* are heat (*uṣmagata*), peak (*mūrdhagata*), forbearance (*kṣānti*), and highest mundane dharma (*laukikāgradharma*), and they constitute a mundane meditative realization (*laukikabhāvanāmaya*), even though they focus on realizing truths for Noble Beings (*caturāryasatya*). Each of these four preparatory analytical factors has a subdivision into soft, medium, and great. They are considered to be superior to the *hīnayāna nirvedhabhāgīya*'s because of five factors: (1) distinctive in terms of objective support, (2) in terms of mode of cultivation, (3) of causing realization of all three paths, (4) in terms of having a spiritual friend characterized by skill-in-means, and (5) having divisions correlated with the stages of dissolving the bifurcation of conceptualized subject and object.[105]

Haribhadra provides the following description of these four preparatory analytical factors and the meditative stabilizations associated with each factor. When the mind is in meditative equipoise discerning things and there is a cultivation of the essencelessness of all things, through a slight illumination of wisdom (*jñānāloka*) on account of the lack of imaginative entanglement in various external objects, one sees merely the mind and at this time one is absorbed in the stage of heat (*uṣmagata*). This meditative stabilization is called "attaining illumination" (*ālokalabdha*). One has begun to develop the fire of nonconceptual wisdom that will penetrate the truths. When that very illumination for dharma expands through extensive effort in cultivating the meditative object of essencelessness, there is some clarity and a moderate illumination of wisdom is cultivated, and at this time one is absorbed in the stage of peak (*mūrdhagata*). The peak or end of the roots of virtue (*kuśalamūla*) become stabilized. This state is a meditative stabilization that is called "expanded illumination" (*vṛddhāloka*). Then, through absorption, the mental continuum generates a particularly clear illumination of knowledge where there is no imaginative entanglement at all, and at this time one becomes absorbed in the stage of forbearance (*kṣānti*). A more pronounced serviceability in regard to emptiness (*śūnyatā*) is developed at this point, as one no longer has fear of this concept. At this point one develops the meditative stabilization that understands suchness one-sidedly. One attains for the first time cognition of the emptiness of objects, but one has not yet perceived the emptiness of subjects. The stabilization is one-sided with respect to emptiness. After this stage, when one gathers a complete illumination of wisdom in which there is no appearance at all that grasps at objects, then one is absorbed in the stage known as the highest of mundane dharmas (*laukikāgradharma*). One now cultivates the uninterrupted meditative stabilization. This is so called because in the same session of meditative equipoise, the *bodhisattva* will proceed without interruption to the path of liberation on the *Mahāyāna* path of seeing.[106]

During the *Mahāyāna* path of preparation, the experience of the preparatory analytical factors begins to dissolve the bifurcation of conceptualized subjects and objects. The conceptualization of objects (*grāhya*) and the conceptualization of subjects (*grāhaka*) are each divided into two to make four kinds of concepts. The two kinds of objects concern entities (*vastu*) and their antidotes (*pratipakṣa*). This involves the conception that things that are pursued truly exist (*pravṛttipakṣādhiṣṭhānagrāhyavikalpa; 'jug gzung rtog*) and that things that should be turned away from truly exist (*nivṛttipakṣādhiṣṭhānagrāhyavikalpa; ldog gzung rtog*). The two kinds of subjects concern substantially existing persons (*pudgaladravya*) and nominally existing beings (*prajñaptipuruṣa*). This takes in the conception of true existence for the mind, which conceives of the person to be substantially existent (*rdzas'dzin rtog*), and the conception of true existence for the mind, which conceives the person to imputedly exist (*btags 'dzin rtog*). Comprehensions connected with these four types of concepts, formative in the path of preparation, become the dominant focal point on the *Mahāyāna* paths of seeing and cultivation.

Haribhadra and Tsong kha pa present the *Mahāyāna* path of seeing in the AA according to the system of the *Abhidharmasamuccaya*. It is similar to the paths of seeing in the lower vehicles in that there are sixteen moments of consciousness directed at the Nobles' Four Truths. However, the elements of existence within the context of these Truths are directly cognized as not being merely selfless, and not merely unreal as external objects, but as being dependently co-arisen and having no essence of their own. This cognition occurs as a meditative stabilization and comprehension consisting in the nonperception of the bifurcation of that which is apprehended and that which apprehends. This comprehension understands what is apprehended and what apprehends as being completely the same, or nondifferentiated. In this instance, "nonperception" means the cessation of ordinary dualistic appearances and the manifestation of ultimate reality (*dharmadhātu*). Relating to the sixteen moments, the moments of *intellectual receptivity in regard to knowledge of the doctrine* (*dharmajñānakṣānti*) and *knowledge of the doctrine* (*dharmajñāna*) comprehend what is apprehended, while the *subsequent moment of intellectual receptivity* (*anvayajñānakṣānti*) and *subsequent knowledge* (*anvayajñāna*) comprehend that which apprehends. As Vimuktisena notes in his AAV (1967: 45), intellectual receptivity in regard to knowledge of the doctrine (*dharmajñānakṣānti*) for a *bodhisattva* is receptivity toward understanding that dharmas are unproduced (*anutpattidharmakṣānti*). The *bodhisattva*'s vision (*darśana*) and knowledge (*jñāna*) perceives and passes through (*avekṣyātikrāmati*) all *śrāvaka* and *pratyekabuddha* stages. Likewise, all *śrāvaka* and *pratyekabuddha* realizations are fulfilled in the *bodhisattva*'s path of seeing.

Through this manner of comprehension, a *bodhisattva* will abandon artificial defilements and imputed knowledge obstacles on the path of seeing. In regard to artificial defilements to be abandoned by the path of seeing, there are ten afflictions for each of the Nobles' Truths in the desire realm. There are six fundamental afflictions consisting of desire, anger, pride, ignorance, doubt, and wrong view. Wrong view is in turn divided into five types: [false] view of the perishable aggregates (*satkāyadṛṣṭi*), extreme view (*antagrāhadṛṣṭi*), false view (*mithyādṛṣṭi*), holding a [wrong] view as supreme (*dṛṣṭiparāmarśa*), and holding [wrong] ethics and rituals as supreme (*śīlavrataparāmarśa*). These ten afflictions separately occur with respect to each of the four truths such that within the desire realm there are forty artificial defilements. With the exception of anger (*pratigha*), which does not arise in the form or formless realms, the remaining afflictions likewise occur for each of the four truths in the two upper realms, allowing for seventy-two artificial defilements. The forty artificial defilements of the desire realm and the seventy-two of the form and formless realm make for one hundred and twelve artificial defilements to be removed by the *Mahāyāna* path of seeing. Along with these artificial defilements, there are one hundred and eight imputed knowledge obstacles that are removed by the *Mahāyāna* path of seeing. This number of imputed knowledge obstacles is calculated by multiplying the four types of conceptions times nine varieties that occur within each type of conception from among the divisions of desire, form, and formless realms. The removal of these imputed obstacles to knowledge correlates with the first *bodhisattva* ground known as "joyous" (*pramuditā*).

The *Mahāyāna* path of cultivation is a continuation of the comprehensions that were beheld during the preparatory analytical factors of the path of preparation and the sixteen moments of the path of seeing.[107] This path of cultivation repeatedly considers, assesses, and contemplates the four types of concepts that proliferate subject/object dichotomization throughout the serviceable levels of meditative stabilization. Similar to the *hīnayāna* paths of cultivation, the most weak of the weak paths are antidotes to most of the coarse defilements, and the most strong of the strong paths are antidotes to the most subtle of the subtle defilements.[108] By means of this repeated practice or familiarization, the path of cultivation abandons the instinctual or innate afflictional obscurations and innate knowledge obstacles. There are sixteen innate defilements to be removed by the path of cultivation. Six fundamental afflictions are associated with the desire realm: desire, anger, pride, ignorance, (false) view of the perishable aggregates, and extreme view. Then, with the lack of anger in the upper realms, there are five each in the form and formless realm, resulting in sixteen. There are one hundred and eight innate knowledge obstacles in correlation with the concepts of subjects and objects, by divisions of the desire, form, and formless realms, each with nine aspects for each of the four concepts.[109]

These sixteen innate afflictional obscurations and one hundred and eight innate obstructions to omniscience are gradually abandoned by the path of cultivation in nine stages, consonant with the *bodhisattva* stages two through ten. When the *bodhisattva*, abiding on the tenth stage, attains the last of the uninterrupted paths, the innate afflictional obscurations and innate obstructions to omniscience are simultaneously abandoned. This is known as the simultaneous illumination (*ekakṣaṇābhisaṃbodha*) and the culmination of the *bodhisattva*'s development. The *bodhisattva* at this time reaches the *Mahāyāna* path of no more training. In this moment, the differentiation into subject and object ceases, the latent subtle seeds of ignorance are totally removed, and the state of highest enlightenment is attained (*anuttarasamyaksaṃbodhi*).

COSMOLOGICAL FACTORS

Besides the presuppositions of the path system we have reviewed above, the special topic of the Twenty *Saṃgha*s necessarily involves knowledge of traditional Buddhist cosmology, particularly the classes

Table 3.5 Vehicles (*yāna*) in the *Abhisamayālaṃkāra*

Vehicle	Faculty	Goal	Object of Cultivation	Abandonment	Realization	Knowledge	Result
Bodhisattva	Sharp	Buddhahood for the sake of all beings	Dissolution of subject/object dichotomization along with concepts and imprints via the *Mahāyāna* paths of seeing and cultivation within Nobles' Four Truths	Obscurations to knowledge and afflictional obscurations	Lack of essence in things and persons	Total omniscience Path omniscience	Buddhahood *Mahāyāna arhat*
Pratyekabuddha	Moderate	Solitary Peaceful *Nirvāṇa*	Aggregates, sense spheres, elements, dependent co-arising, appropriate/inappropriate Nobles' Four Truths	Concepts of apprehended objects	One part of obstacles to knowledge Selflessness of person	Empirical omniscience	*Pratyekabuddha arhat* [provisional]
Śrāvaka	Weak	Peaceful *Nirvāṇa*	Nobles' Four Truths in sixteen aspects	Afflictional obscurations	Selflessness of person	Empirical omniscience	*Śrāvaka arhat* [provisional]

of heavenly realms. An understanding of this cosmology is relevant because the path of cultivation (*bhāvanāmārga*), in which the abandonment of instinctual defilements takes place, occurs in various levels of concentration (*dhyāna*) that are also considered to be cosmological realms. The Buddhist spiritual aspirant, whether a *śrāvaka* or *bodhisattva*, is believed to journey throughout the realms of ancient Indian cosmology to reach *nirvāṇa*. We shall give below a brief outline of this cosmology only for the sake of future reference, and one may find details of this cosmology in other works.[110]

As we have mentioned above, the basic cosmological arrangement that constitutes cyclic existence (*saṃsāra*), or the universe as a whole, is divided into the three worlds (*triloka/tridhātu*): the desire realm (*kāmadhātu*); the realm of form (*rūpadhātu*), consisting of four stages; and the formless realm (*ārūpyadhātu*), which also has four stages. Buddhism accepts that there are five types of living beings who live within these worlds: gods (*deva*), human beings (*manuṣya*), animals (*tiryañc*), hungry ghosts (*preta*), and hell denizens (*nāraka*). Sometimes a sixth type is added to this list as *asuras*. We are concerned with only the worlds in which Noble Beings (*ārya*) travel and they transmigrate only through human and god realms.

Within the desire realm, humans are subdivided among the four continents and eight subcontinents. The four continents are set around the *axis mundi*, or central mountain, Mount Meru. To the east is the continent *Videha*; to the west is *Godānīya*; to the south is our own continent called *Jambudvīpa*; and to the north is the continent *Kuru*. The gods of the desire realm live among six different abodes. These are the heavens of the Four Great Kings (*caturmahārājakāyika*), of the Thirty-three gods (*trāyatriṃśa*), the land without combat (*yāma*), the Joyous (*tuṣita*), Enjoying Emanation (*nirmāṇarati*), and Controlling Others' Emanations (*paranirmitavaśavartin*). The five objects of sensory desire heavily influence beings in these abodes: form (*rūpa*), sound (*śabda*), smell (*gandha*), taste (*rasa*), and touch (*spraṣṭavya*).

The form realm has seventeen divisions that are classified into four main areas correlated in ascending order with the levels of concentration (*dhyāna*). The first concentration marks the beginning of the form realm and is composed of three abodes. The first is the *Brahmakāyika*; the second, *Brahmapurohita*; and the third, *Mahābrahma*. The second concentration has three abodes. They are, in ascending order, called *Parīttābhā*, *Apramāṇābhā*, and *Ābhāsvara*. The third concentration also has three abodes, which are, in ascending order, *Parīttaśubha*, *Apramāṇaśubha*, and *Śubhakṛtsna*. These first three realms of concentration are similar in that the mental quality of delight remains within them. They are therefore

Table 3.6 Realms Traveled by Noble Beings on the Path

World (*dhātu*)	Realm		Consciousness Level
Formless world (*ārūpyadhātu*)	*Naivasaṃjñānāsaṃjñānāyatana*		Formless sphere mind
	Akiṃcanyāyatana		
	Vijñānānantyāyatana		
	Ākāśānantyāyatana		
Form worlds (*rūpadhātu*)	*Akaniṣṭha*	Five pure heavens	Fourth *dhyāna*
	Sudarśana		
	Sudṛśa		
	Atapa		
	Abṛha		
	Bṛhatphala		
	Puṇyaprasava		
	Anabhraka		
	Śubhakṛtsna		Third *dhyāna*
	Apramāṇaśubha		
	Parīttaśubha		
	Ābhāsvara		Second *dhyāna*
	Apramāṇaśubha		
	(no *Āryas* born in first *dhyāna*)		First *dhyāna*
World of five senses (*kāmadhātu*)	*Paranirmitavaśavartin*	Six heavens of desire realm	Sense sphere mind (*kāmāvacara*)
	Nirmāṇarati		
	Tuṣita		
	Yama		
	Cāturmahārājakāyika		
	Trāyatriṃśa		
	Uttarakuru	Human realm	
	Aparagodānīya		
	Pūrvavideha		
	Jambudvīpa		

called *sukhopapatti*, "realms generating delight." The last main area of the form realm is the domain of the fourth concentration. It consists of eight abodes with the first three being called, in ascending order, *Anabhraka*, *Puṇyaprasava*, and *Bṛhatphala*. The remaining five abodes of the fourth concentration are known as the *Śuddhāvāsakāyika* ("the pure places"). This is because only Noble Beings (*ārya*) can be reborn in these areas. Noble Beings are born in these five pure places through cultivating a form of meditation in which one alternates between moments of uncontaminated (*anāsrava*) and contaminated (*sāsrava*) concentrations. Through varying moments of these contaminated and uncontaminated concentrations, a Noble Being will take rebirth in the abodes of either *Abṛha*, *Atapas*, *Sudṛśa*, *Sudarśana*, or *Akaniṣṭha*.

Above the form realm is the formless realm (*ārūpyadhātu*). This realm has four levels that correspond to four kinds of meditative absorption. The first is called *Ākāśānantya* ("limitless space"); the second is called *Vijñānānantya* ("limitless consciousness"); the third is called *Akiṃcanya* ("nothingness"); and the fourth is called *Naivasaṃjñānā-saṃjñāyatana* ("neither perception nor nonperception"). This fourth level is also known as *Bhavāgra* ("peak of existence"). These divisions within the desire, form, and formless realms constitute the areas where Noble Beings are reborn due to the forces of their previous actions (karma) and meditative ability. Table 3.6 is provided for reference.

SUMMARY

In this chapter we have given an account of the tacit assumptions and soteriological presuppositions that are necessary in approaching the special topic of the Twenty *Saṃgha*s. The first part of the chapter highlighted the basic structure and contents of the AA. We identified the position the topic of the Twenty *Saṃgha*s has in relationship to the AA's structure and content so as to show how the topic of the Twenty *Saṃgha*s fits into the overall soteriological schema that the AA presents. The second half of the chapter explained the complex schema of path and yogic presuppositions. This *Mahāyāna* path schema was presented for the purpose of understanding the theoretical mechanisms through which soteriological results can take place. With an understanding of these assumptions of structure and soteriology, we are now ready to proceed to an articulation and examination of our main topic, the Twenty *Saṃgha*s.

4
Analysis of the Twenty *Saṃghas*

We are now ready to thoroughly examine the Twenty *Saṃghas*, having surveyed the contextual and doctrinal presumptions surrounding this topic in the AA. Our analysis and exegesis consists of three main parts: an introduction to the topic from the foundational text of the AA and the PP *sūtras*; a detailed discussion and exposition of the *Allegorical Saṃghas*, Tsong kha pa's exegesis of ideal figures in mainstream Buddhism; and finally in chapter 5, an articulation of the *Mahāyāna* community of Noble Irreversible *bodhisattvas* and the conclusions to our study.

An Introduction to the Topic from the Root Texts

In this section we introduce the topic of the Twenty *Saṃghas* from the foundational text of the AA and its appearance in the *Pañcaviṃśati*. We provide a preliminary translation of the AA verses along with charts comparing the denaturalized terminology of the AA with other relevant Indian Buddhist texts. As we have seen, this special topic is an instruction (Skt. *avavāda;* Tib. *gdams ngag*), and within the context of the *saṃgha* jewel, it is the instruction giving a detailed articulation of twenty types of Noble Individuals (*āryapudgala*).

The topic of the Twenty *Saṃghas* is mentioned in the twenty-third and twenty-fourth verse of the AA's first chapter:

> 23a–b. *mṛdutīkṣṇendriyau śraddhādṛṣṭiprāptau kulaṃkulau* /
> c–d. *ekavīcyantarotpadya kārākārākaniṣṭhagāḥ* //
>
> 24a–b. *plutās trayo bhavasyāgraparamo rūparāgahā* /
> c–d. *dṛṣṭadharmaśramaḥ kāyasākṣī khaḍgaś ca viṃśatiḥ*[1] //

If we were to give a literal translation outside the contextual understanding of our Indo-Tibetan commentarial tradition, these stanzas might be translated as follows:[2]

> There are Twenty [categories]: those with dull and sharp faculties, those who have attained faith and vision, those who are born from family to family, those born with one interval, those who are born in the intermediate state, those who are born, with effort and effortlessly, those who go to Akaniṣñha, three who leap, those who go to the upper limit of the world, those who destroy attachment to the form [realm], those who pacify visual phenomena, the bodily witness, and the rhinoceros.

Conze (1957: 31) mentions that leading experts on the Sanskrit language note that, from a grammatical point of view, these cryptic verses do not give sufficient hints to allow us to sort out the twenty types of Noble Beings. The difficulty lies in the fact that these twenty types are really a subdivision of the eight *āryapudgala*s, which are not explicitly mentioned in the verses. Within the text of the *Pañcaviṃśati* (Dutt, 1934: 60–71; Conze, 1975a: 66–73) there are twenty-four topic headings, most likely inserted into the *sūtra* by Haribhadra, of which four do not represent any of the Twenty *Saṃgha*s mentioned in the AA. These four are (in Conze's listing): A. *bodhisattvāṣṭamakaḥ* (= i. Candidate to the First Fruit); B. *sakṛdāgāmī* (= iv.); C. *anāgāmī* (vi); and D. *arhattvapratipannaka* (= vii). Likewise the fifth variety of the Non-returner, the *ūrdhvaṃsrotas*, is not mentioned in either the *Pañcaviṃśatisāhasrikā* or the *Abhisamayālaṃkāra*.

The *Pañcaviṃśati* (60; Conze, 1975a: 66) lists the various types of *bodhisattva*s, from which the AA derives the Twenty *Saṃgha*s, according to the circumstances of their rebirth, beginning with the section that states: "The *bodhisattva*, the great being who dwells through dwelling in perfect wisdom, having left from which state, is he reborn here, or deceased here, where will he be reborn?"

We will see how the various Indian and Tibetan commentators deal with the discrepancies between the AA and *Pañcaviṃśati* later in this chapter. Having briefly introduced the topic from the foundational texts, we wish to chart a comparison of the denaturalized terminology found in the AA with other Indian Buddhist texts.

The paradigm of soteriological typologies listed in AA i.23–24 that represent the Twenty *Saṃgha*s most likely embodies a category of *Abhidharmic* scholasticism carried into the PP literature. With this hypothesis in mind, we will chart a comparison of the denaturalized terminology found in the AA with other Indian Buddhist sources to demonstrate that, at least from a terminological standpoint, the Twenty

Saṃghas represents a classification of Noble Beings fairly well established by the sixth century in India.

Table 4.1 on pages 96 and 97 demonstrates the comparison of nomenclature used by various Indian Buddhist texts. The numbers occurring within each column represent the order of the terminology as it occurs in each text. The first page of table 4.1, beginning from the left column, lists the nomenclature of the Twenty *Saṃghas* as it is found from a literal reading of the AA verses. Then the terminology as is found in the topic headings of the revised *Pañcaviṃśati* is listed as representative of the terminology used in the PP *sūtras*. The third column represents terminology from the *Nikāya/Āgama* traditions. The *Nikāya* tradition knows of eight Noble Beings (*aṣṭāryapudgala*) grouped into four pairs (AN II: 56; IV: 373): the candidates for and those who abide in the four main results. In particular, the *Aṅguttaranikāya* (1: 220–21) enumerates nine different classes of Noble Beings according to their removal of fetters (*saṃyojana*). Another *sutta* of the *Aṅguttara* (4: 379) enumerates nine individuals (*puggala*) worthy of worship (*dakkhiṇeya*). The individuals who are worthy of worship represent the Community of disciples (*śrāvakasaṃgha*), which is similar to an aspect of the Twenty *Saṃghas* we will present later in this chapter. This Community can be divided into two classes: those still in training (*śaikṣa*) and those who have no more to train in (*aśaikṣa*). The terminology we list here is from the *Madhyamāgama* (T 26, ch. 40, 616a) which distinguishes eighteen kinds of *śaikṣas*. The fourth column lists the nomenclature used by the *Puggalapaññatti*, a Pāli *Abhidhamma* work that comprises the fourth work of the *Abhidhamma Piṭaka*.

The second page of table 4.1 gives the nomenclature as listed from the verses of the *Abhidharmakośa* and sections of the *Abhidharmasamuccaya*. Tsong kha pa relies predominately on these two texts to define the distinguishing characteristics of the Twenty *Saṃghas*. Finally, the last column represents the listing of terminology for the stages of *śrāvaka* individuals (*śrāvakapudgalakramāḥ*; *nyan thos kyi gang zag gyi rim pa'i ming la*) found in the *Mahāvyutpatti*, a lexicon of Sanskrit and Tibetan formulated during the reign of Khri gtsug lde bstan ral pa chan (reign 815–839).

A brief comparison of the nomenclature from table 4.1 reveals that the system of terminology employed by the AA is related to the *Sarvāstivādin-Vaibhāṣika* school, as the terms are most similar to the list from the *Abhidharmakośa*. However, the Tibetan tradition classifies the interpretation of the AA verses on the Twenty *Saṃghas* into two separate systems: Ārya Vimuktisena and Haribhadra. Ārya Vimuktisena is understood to follow his interpretation of the AA verses in correlation with the *Abhidharmakośa*, and Haribhadra is understood to construe these

Table 4.1 Terminology Comparison of Indian Buddhist Texts

AA	*Pañca*	*Madhyamāgama-Śaikṣas*	*Puggala*
mṛdu-indriya	*bodhisattvāṣṭamaka* *śraddhānusārin*	1. *śraddhānusārin*	10. *gotrabhū* 36. *saddhānusārin*
tīkṣṇa-indriya	*dharmānusārin*	2. *dharmānusārin*	35. *dhammānusārin*
śraddhāprāpta	*śraddhādhimukta*	3. *śraddhādhimukta*	No term
dṛṣṭiprāpta	*dṛṣṭiprāpta sakṛdāgāmin* *anāgāmin*	4. *dṛṣṭiprāpta* 11. *sakadāgāmin* 13. *anāgāmin*	33. *diṭṭipatto* 48. *sakadāgāmin* 49. *anāgāmin*
manuṣyakulaṃkula	*manuṣyakulaṃkula*	6. *kulaṃkula*	38. *kolaṅkolo*
devatākulaṃkula	*devatākulaṃkula*	No terms	No terms
ekavīcya	*ekavīcika*	7. *ekavīcika*	39. *ekabījin*
antara	*antarāparinirvāyin*	14. *antarāparinirvāyin*	42. *antarāparinibbāyin*
utpadya	*upapadyaparinirvāyin*	15 *upapadyaparinirvāyin*	43. *upahacca-parinibbāyin*
kāra	*abhisaṃskāraparinirvāyin*	16. *sābhisaṃskāraparinirvāyin*	45. *sasaṅkhāra-parinibbāyin*
ākara	*anabhisaṃskāra*	17. *anabhisaṃskāraparinirvāyin*	44. *asaṅkhāra-parinibbāyin*
akaniṣṭha	*akaniṣṭhaparama*	18. *ūrdhvaṃsrotas-rūpopaga*	46. *uddhaṃsota akaniṭṭhaga*
plutas-traya #1	*pluta*	No terms	No terms
#2 (implied)	*ardhapluta*		
#3 (implied)	*sarvasthānacyuta*		
bhavasyāgraparama	*bhavāgraparama*		
rūparāgahā	*rūpavītarāga*		
dṛṣṭadharmaśrama	*dṛṣṭadharmaparinirvāyin*		
kāyāsākṣin	*kāyasākṣin*	5. *kāyasākṣin*	32. *kāyasakkin*
khaḍga	*arhattvapratipannaka* *pratyekabuddha*	No terms	29. *paccekasambuddho*

Table 4.1 *(Continued)*

AA	*Abhidharmakośa*	*Abhidharmasamuccaya*	*Mahāvyutpatti*
mṛdu-indriya	(*mṛdu-indriya*) *śraddhānusārin*	*śraddhānusārin*	1021. *śraddhānusārin*
tīkṣṇa-indriya	(*tīkṣṇa-indriya*) *dharmānusārin*	*dharmānusārin*	1022. *dharmānusārin*
śraddhāprāpta	*śraddhādhimukta*	*śraddhādhimukta*	1023. *śraddhādhimukta*
dṛṣṭiprāpta	*dṛṣṭiprāpta* *saptakṛtvaparama*	*dṛṣṭiprāpta sakṛdāgāmin*	1024. *dṛṣṭiprāpta* 1012. *sakṛdāgāmin*
manuṣyakulaṃkula	*kulaṃkula sakṛdāgāmin*	*kulaṃkula*	1011. *kulaṃkula*
devatakulaṃkula	No terms	No terms	No terms
ekavīcya	*ekavīcikaḥ anāgāmin*	*sakṛdāgāmin ekavīcika*	1012. *sakṛdāgāmin* 1013. *ekavīcika*
antara	*antarāparinirvāyin*	*anāgāmin* *antarāparinirvāyin*	1014. *anāgāmin* 1015. *antarāparinirvāyin*
utpadya	*upapadyaparinirvāyin*	*upapadyaparinirvāyin*	1016. *upapadyaparinirvāyin*
kāra	*sābhisaṃskāraparinirvāyin*	*abhisaṃskāraparinirvāyin*	1017. *abhisaṃskāraparinirvāyin*
ākara	*anabhisaṃskāraparinirvāyin*	*anabhisaṃskāra*	1018. *anabhisaṃskāra*
akaniṣṭha	*akaniṣṭhaga*	*ūrdhvaṃśrotas*	1019. *ūrdhvaśrotas*
plutas-traya #1	*pluta*	No terms	No terms
#2 (implied)	*ardhapluta*		
#3 (implied)	*sarvacyuta*		
bhavasyāgraparama	*bhavāgraga*		
rūparāgahā	No terms		
dṛṣṭadharmaśrama			
kāyāsākṣin	*kāyasākṣin*	*kāyasākṣin*	1020. *kāyasākṣin*
khaḍga	Verse vi.24 *khaḍga*	*pratyekajnina*	1006. *pratyekabuddha*

Note: AA = *Abhisamayālaṃkāra*; *Pañca* = the topic headings of *Pañcaviṃśatisāhasrikā*; *Madhyamāgama-Śaikṣa* = *śaikṣa* listed from the *Madhyamāgama*; *Puggala* = the number heading in the first listing of *puggalas* in *Puggalapaññatti*.

categories in correlation with the *Abhidharmasamuccaya*. We will investigate the doctrinal foundations of the Twenty *Saṃghas* in the next section to demonstrate how these various interpretations are possible.

THE ALLEGORICAL *SAṂGHA* OF *ŚRĀVAKAS*

Tsong kha pa begins his presentation of the Twenty *Saṃghas* in his *Golden Garland* (1970: 224), based on a distinction between the *saṃgha* that serves as an example (*mtshon par byed pa'i dpe'i dge 'dun*), or *allegorical saṃgha,* and the *actual saṃgha* to be indicated (*mtshon par bya ba'i don gyi dge 'dun*). This distinction represents a standardized hermeneutical device used by the Tibetan tradition that can only be traced back textually to Bu ston rin po che's *Lung gyi nye ma* (1978: 349). This heuristic distinction allows the Tibetan tradition to articulate the types of Noble Beings in all three vehicles—that is, *śrāvakas*, *pratyekabuddhas*, and *bodhisattvas*. It is also a skillful exegetical technique that provides the background material necessary to understand the commentaries on the Twenty *Saṃghas* by Ārya Vimuktisena and Haribhadra, and ultimately to understand the meaning of the Twenty *Saṃghas* in the *Abhisamayālaṃkāra* itself.

The *saṃgha* that serves as an example (*mtshon par byed pa'i dpe'i dge 'dun*) represents an articulation of the Twenty *Saṃghas* by means of the classic *Abhidharma* categories of the *śrāvaka saṃgha* as enumerated in the sixth chapter of the *Abhidharmakośa* and the first part of the *prāptiviniścaya* section (*pudgalavyavasthāna*) of the *Abhidharmasamuccaya*. The enumeration of this type of *saṃgha* serves as a model to illustrate the *actual saṃgha* of *bodhisattvas* mentioned in the AA.

The *actual saṃgha* indicated (*mtshon bya don gyi*) represents the "real" *saṃgha* that is presented in the AA—the *Mahāyāna* spiritual community in its definitive sense. This *actual saṃgha* is the *Mahāyāna* community of Noble Irreversible *bodhisattvas* (*avaivartika; phyir mi ldog pa*) who are destined for the state of Buddhahood through attaining *anuttarasaṃyak-saṃbodhi*. They are the *actual saṃgha* mentioned in the *Pañcaviṃśatiprajñāpāramitāsūtra*. Tsong kha pa, along with the Indian commentators Ārya Vimuktisena and Haribhadra, correlates the relationship between these two distinctions of *saṃgha* with the analogies given in the *Avaivartikadharmacakrasūtra* (AAV 46; AAĀ 36).

In this section we will present Tsong kha pa's articulation of the *allegorical saṃgha*. Tsong kha pa examines the *allegorical saṃgha* primarily in his *Stairway* and has complementary remarks regarding this *saṃgha* in his *Golden Garland*. The *allegorical saṃgha* serves as an analogical template for the *actual saṃgha* of *bodhisattvas*. Chapter 5 will articulate the *actual saṃgha* of *bodhisattvas* and its semiotic relationship with the *allegorical saṃgha*.

The Allegorical Saṃgha (mtshon par byed pa'i dpe'i dge 'dun)

The *allegorical saṃgha* is an illustration of the *saṃgha* that is composed of individuals from within the *śrāvakayāna*. Before we discuss the details and specifics of this type of *saṃgha*, I would like to give a brief sketch of the general doctrinal principles and soteriological structures in which the matrix of the *śrāvaka saṃgha* takes place.

In the previous chapter, we discussed how *śrāvaka*s become averse to the sufferings of conditioned existence and wish to escape *saṃsāra*, the endless cycle of rebirth that beings go through. The goal for *śrāvakas* is to obtain *nirvāṇa*, spiritual emancipation that is the cessation of suffering and rebirth. *Nirvāṇa* for *śrāvaka*s is understood in terms of extinguishing the causes for rebirth and suffering. The causes that generate karma and contribute to the continuation of rebirth are defilements (*kleśa*). Therefore, the most important factor and organizing principle in the construction of the *śrāvaka* path is the abandoning of defilements.

In the systemized *Abhidharma* tradition that Tsong kha pa follows, based on the *Sarvāstivāda-Vaibhāṣika* school, defilements are referred to generically as: fetters (*saṃyojana*), bonds (*bandhana*), latent defilements (*anuśaya*), and afflictions (*kleśa*). In general ten basic defilements are to be abandoned: belief in the perishable aggregates (*satkāyadṛṣṭi*), doubt (*vicikitsā*), the belief that ethics and rituals are supreme (*śīlavrataparāmarśa*), sensual pleasure (*kāmarāga*), hostility (*vyāpāda*), desire for existence in the form realm (*rūparāga*), desire for existence in the formless realm (*ārūpyarāga*), pride (*māna*), delusion (*moha*), and excitability (*auddhatya*). These defilements are divided into different enumerations depending on how they are removed. Tsong kha pa follows the enumeration that is calculated in relation to how the defilements are removed by the path of seeing (*darśanamārga*) and the path of cultivation (*bhāvanāmārga*).

A *śrāvaka* progresses to the goal of *nirvāṇa* through successively abandoning defilements that are associated with an established sequence of cosmic realms and meditative stages. A result of practice is a stage on the way to *nirvāṇa* that is defined in accordance with the abandonment of specific defilements associated with specific realms. For example, in order to become a Once-returner one must abandon the sixth path of cultivation defilement of the desire realm. The variety of defilements are correlated with three cosmic realms—the realm of desire, the realm of form, and the formless realm. Each defilement in each realm is specified according to whether it is to be abandoned by the path of seeing (*darśanamārga*) or the path of cultivation (*bhāvanāmārga*). Abandonment occurs by progressing through successive stages of seeing the Nobles' Four Truths in the path of seeing and then repeated practice in the path of cultivation of what was seen in the path of seeing. Therefore, comprehensive realization (*abhisamaya*) of the Nobles' Four Truths characterizes both the path of seeing and the path of cultivation.

The path of seeing involves sixteen thought-moments (*cittakṣaṇa*) in which sixteen aspects of the Nobles' Four Truths are cognized. The path of cultivation involves a removal of defilements through a repeated familiarization with the Nobles' Four Truths. The defilements of the path of cultivation are calculated as eighty-one: Each of the nine stages of the cosmic realm—the realm of desire, four concentration levels of the realm of form, and four spheres in the form realm, possesses nine varieties of defilements (coarse-coarse, coarse-moderate, coarse-subtle, etc.). The first nine path-of-cultivation defilements are important to note because they exist in the desire realm and mark the boundary to progressing into the form and formless realms. The paths of seeing and cultivation are demarcated by the character of the defilements to be abandoned, the frequency of practice each path requires, and the type of individual engaged in the path.

In general, there are two types of individuals: ordinary people (*pṛthagjana*) and Noble Beings (*ārya*). These two types of individuals are differentiated in relation to the sixteen moments of the path of seeing. Generally, at the beginning of the first sixteen moments of the path of seeing, one becomes a Noble Being (*ārya*) and various results of spiritual praxis can be attained, depending on the categories of defilements that have been, or still need to be, abandoned through practicing the path of cultivation. One has to pass through the moments of the path of seeing only once, whereas one must pass through the stages of the path of cultivation repeatedly. Ordinary individuals (*pṛthagjana*) practice only the mundane path of cultivation, while Noble Beings (*ārya*) may practice both the path of seeing and the supermundane path of cultivation. When ordinary persons abandon certain defilements by practicing the path of cultivation, it is referred to as a mundane path (*laukikamārga*). Abandoning defilements as an ordinary person on the mundane path obviates the need to abandon them once again as a Noble Being (*ārya*) on the path of seeing. Defilements removed by a Noble Being after completing the path of seeing occur in the supermundane path of cultivation (*lokottarabhāvanāmārga*).

At the sixteenth moment of the path of seeing, a Noble Being achieves the result known as Stream-enterer; one will never be reborn again as a hell-being, hungry ghost, or animal. While making effort to abandon the first six of the nine desire realm defilements, one is a candidate for the result of Once-returner. At this point a practitioner is approaching or entering into the next result. We will apply the term *enterer* to those individuals who are approaching or entering into a given result. When the sixth desire realm defilement is removed, an individual obtains or abides in the result of Once-returner. We will apply the term *abider* to an individual who is "staying in a certain status" (*phalastha*), that is, residing or abiding (*viharati*) in a given result on the way to *nirvāṇa*. A Once-returner will return to the desire realm by the force of unabandoned defilements one more time, will then strive to abandon the three remaining defilements of the desire realm, and will become an enterer to the result of Non-returner. At the time when an individual has removed the ninth defilement of the desire realm, he is known as an abider in the result of Non-returner. A Non-returner will never take rebirth in the desire realm again and has removed all the path of cultivation defilements associated with the desire realm. However, a Non-returner may take birth in various form or formless realm heavens, depending on defilements that need to be abandoned. At this point one takes rebirth in the form and formless realms to remove the remaining seventy-two defilements of the path of cultivation. When an individual makes effort to abandon the remaining seventy-two defilements of the form and formless realms, he becomes an enterer to the result of *Arhat*. One becomes an abider in the result of *Arhat* with the removal of all eighty-one defilements of the path of cultivation, and this result is synonymous with the *śrāvaka* goal of *nirvāṇa*—that is, emancipation from the suffering of *saṃsāra*.

Tsong kha pa mentions both in the *Stairway* (268) and *Golden Garland* (224) that these four principal results of Stream-enterer, Once-returner, Non-returner, and *Arhat* compose the *allegorical saṃgha*. These four results are also known as the four pairs of persons (*skyes bu zung bzhi*). When enumerating the *allegorical saṃgha* according to entering into and abiding in the four principal results, the *saṃgha* is referred to as the eight great individuals (*mahāṣṭapudgala; gang zag chen ya brgyad*):[3] the enterers to (*pratipannakāḥ; zhugs pa rnams*) and abiders in (*phalasthā; gnas pa rnams*) the results of the Stream-enterer (*srota-āpanna; rgyun du zhugs pa*), the Once-returner (*sakṛdāgāmin; lan cig phyir 'ong*), the Non-returner (*anāgāmin; phyir mi 'ong*), and the *Arhat* (*dgra bcom pa*). Tsong kha pa also includes the *Pratyekabuddha* (*rang sangs rgyas*) in this *saṃgha*.

Tsong kha pa provides a detailed examination of this type of *saṃgha* through his investigation of *Abhidharma* digests that were available to him. Tsong kha pa's interpretation is primarily based on the *Abhidharmakośabhāṣya* and *Vyākhyā* and the *Abhidharmasamuccaya* and its *Bhāṣya*. Tsong kha pa's system of this aspect of the Twenty *Saṃgha*s represents a synthesis of the doctrinal points from texts correlated to the system of the AA. In utilizing the methodology of presenting an *allegorical saṃgha* as the basis of the *actual saṃgha*, Tsong kha pa will be able to demonstrate an understanding of the *saṃgha* from the viewpoint of all three vehicles. More importantly, Tsong kha pa will be able to demonstrate how the principles and terminology utilized for the community of *Mahāyāna bodhisattvas*, as found in the presentation of the *actual saṃgha*, are principles extended from basic *Abhidharma* categories found in the definition of the *śrāvaka saṃgha*. This approach to defining the *Saṃgha* Jewel reveals a systematic coherence between scholastic categories of the *śrāvakayāna* and the *bodhisattvayāna*. It illustrates that the *Mahāyāna Saṃgha* Jewel reappropriates the defining elements of the *śrāvaka saṃgha* and extends those elements to the more demanding and strenuous *bodhisattva* path to full Buddhahood.

Having given a brief outline of the general principles of the *śrāvaka saṃgha*, and before we proceed with the details of Tsong kha pa's articulation of these *saṃgha*s, we must briefly present several specific doctrinal presumptions that Tsong kha pa assumes of the reader that provide the soteriological structure of how fruition within the *śrāvaka* vehicle functions.

Fruition within the Śrāvaka *Vehicle: The Results of* Śrāmaṇya

The four general results of the religious life within the *śrāvaka* vehicle are based on what is known as *śrāmaṇya* (*dge sbyong gi tshul*), rendered in Tibetan as literally the "method of training [in] virtue." *Śrāmaṇya* is the stainless (*amala*) and uncontaminated, uninterrupted path (*anāsravānantaryamārga*).[4] A traditional etymology (*nirukti*) relates *śrāmaṇya* to one who pacifies (*śamayati*) the afflictions.[5] The AKBh states that *śrāmaṇya* is understood as such because "one who thoroughly pacifies all the various pollutions and unvirtuous qualities [that extend] from rebirth up to old age and death is known as a *śrāmaṇya*."[6] Yaśomitra comments that *śrāmaṇya* is a purifying activity like the cleaning of a cloth and he also defines the term *śrāmaṇya* from "pacifying" (*śamayati*) the afflictions (*kleśa*).[7]

Śrāmaṇya is understood to be equal to the "uncontaminated uninterrupted path," and it causes the Noble Being (*ārya*) who abides on an uncontaminated path to be a "true *śramaṇa*" (*paramārthaśramaṇa*), one who pacifies the defilements in an absolute sense. When a fruition from *śrāmaṇya* is attained, the uninterrupted path (*ānantaryamārga*), there is a result of *śrāmaṇya* (*śrāmaṇaphala*) that is both conditioned (*saṃskṛta*) and unconditioned (*asaṃskṛta*). The conditioned result is the path of liberation (*vimuktimārga*) and the unconditioned result is a true cessation (*nirodhasatya*). The path of liberation is the result of a homogeneous cause (*sabhāgahetu*), and it consists of outflowing results (*niṣyandaphala*) and results through effort (*puruṣakāraphala*). True cessation as result of *śrāmaṇya* is the disconnection (*visaṃyoga*) of that path and the abandonment of afflictions at the corresponding level. In other words, true cessations result in the mental continuum becoming bereft of afflictions.

The conditioned paths of liberation (*saṃskṛtavimuktimārga*) are eighty-nine in number. There are eight paths of liberation which abandon the eight afflictions (*kleśa*) to be removed by the path of seeing (*darśanaheyaprahāṇa*). The eight afflictions removed by the path of seeing comprise the defilements removed within the desire realm and upper realms of the form and formless heavens. These are abandoned by seeing the truths of suffering (*duḥkha*), arising (*samudāya*), cessation (*nirodha*), and the path (*mārga*). Therefore there are eight paths of liberation correlated to the path of seeing.

There are eighty-one paths of liberation that remove the eighty-one afflictions abandoned by the path of cultivation (*bhāvanāheyaprahāṇa*). These comprise the nine—three coarse, three medium, and three subtle—afflictions abandoned by the path of cultivation (*bhāvanāheyakleśa*) within the realm of desire. Likewise there are nine—three coarse, three medium, and three subtle—afflictions abandoned by the path of cultivation in each of the first, second, third, and fourth concentrations of the form realm, the realms of infinite space, infinite consciousness, nothingness, and peak of existence of the formless realms. Therefore, there are eighty-one paths of liberation that abandon these eighty-one afflictions (*kleśa*). There are also eighty-nine unconditioned true cessations (*asaṃskṛtanirodhasatya*), according to a similar method of counting. In this way the *Abhidharmakośa* states: "*Śrāmaṇya* is the stainless path, the result is conditioned and unconditioned, there are eighty-nine, the path of liberation along with the cessations."[8]

Even though there are eighty-nine twofold results of *śrāmaṇya*, it is not contradictory to classify them into four results such as the Stream-enterer, Once-returner, Non-returner, and *Arhat*. Classifying the results of *śrāmaṇya* into four results involves numbering the results according to the principle proclivities to be abandoned in order to achieve emancipation. These are the three fetters (*saṃyojanas*) abandoned by the path of seeing (*mthong spang kun sbyor gsum*), the five "inferior" fetters (*avarabhāgīya*), and the five "superior" fetters (*ūrdhvabhāgīya*). The three fetters abandoned by the path of seeing are the view of the perishable aggregates (*satkāyadṛṣṭi; 'jig tshogs la lta ba*), holding the belief that ethics and conduct are supreme (*śīlavrataparāmarśa; tshul khrims dang brtul zhug mchog 'dzin*), and doubt (*vicikitsā; the tshom nyon mongs can*). Abandoning these fetters leads to the result of Stream-enterer. The five inferior fetters include the three of the first set, along with sensual desire (*kāmacchanda*) and hatred (*vyāpāda*). Through abandoning most of the *avarabhāgīya*, the result of Once-returner is attained and through abandoning all of the *avarabhāgīyasaṃyojana* the result of Non-returner is attained. The five superior fetters (*gong ma'i cha dang mthun lnga*) are the two, craving of the form and formless realms, conceit (*māna*), excitability (*auddhatya*), and delusion (*moha*).[9] The result of *śrāmaṇya* based on abandoning all the fetters is the stage of *Arhat*.

Another manner of establishing four results is based on the enumeration of five reasons. This is the method that Tsong kha pa uses in both the *Stairway* (352) and *Golden Garland* (1970: 244). Tsong kha pa bases the five reasons for four results entirely according to the *Abhidharmakośa*:

> In the explanation of the four results five causes exist: letting go of the previous path of result, obtaining another path, a collected cessation, obtaining the eight knowledges, and realizing the sixteen aspects [of the four noble truths].[10]

As Tsong kha pa comments in the *Stairway* (352):

> One posits four results as follows: (1) there is the release from a *previous path of result*; (2) obtaining the *path of another result*; and (3) a *collected cessation*, or collected abandonment, as in acquiring a single attainment which consists of all the abandonments to be abandoned by the path of seeing at the time of the sixteenth moment; (4) *eight knowledges* to be obtained are the four dharma knowledges [on the truths of suffering, origination, cessation, path] and the four subsequent knowledges; (5) one also obtains the *sixteen* uncontaminated *aspects*, impermanence and so forth [of the Nobles' Four Truths]. Attainment of these five distinct states is posited in the four results.

Tsong kha pa therefore reasons that the results of *śrāmaṇya* are arranged into four results of the Stream-enterer (etc.), because it is set forth accordingly by these five causes: (1) That each of the four fruits has its own previous path of entrance; (2) that one attains the realization of abiding on a result other than entrance into those paths; (3) that there is an acquisition of an abandonment, which is like a single attainment that allows one to be free of all objects to be abandoned by the path of seeing; (4) that there is an acquisition of the set of eight knowledges—that is, the eight paths of liberation; and finally, (5) that there is the acquisition of the knowledge that realizes the sixteen aspects of the Nobles' Four Truths, impermanence, and so on.

Basic enumeration of the allegorical Saṃgha. As we have mentioned, the *allegorical saṃgha*, which is demonstrated as a model of the *actual saṃgha* of the AA, is comprised of four pairs of individuals that are eight persons: the enterer to and abider in the result of Stream-enterer, the Once-returner enterer and abider, the Non-returner enterer and abider, and the *Arhat* enterer and abider.

Tsong kha pa notes (*Stairway* 268; *Golden Garland* 224) that, according to the *Abhidharmakośa*, these eight persons are Noble Beings (*āryas*). This is because even the lowest cognitive threshold for entering to the result of Stream-enterer is explained as abiding on no later than the "persevering receptivity to the doctrine in regards to the truth of suffering" (*duḥkhe dharmakṣānti*) on the path of seeing, that is, the first moment of the path of seeing. Tsong kha pa also states that the two enterers who skip fruitions have attained the path of seeing; the three later enterers to the results of Once-returner, Non-returner, and *Arhat* who progress gradually attain the path of cultivation. This is because the abiders in the first three results have attained the path of cultivation and because at the sixteenth moment, the subsequent knowledge with regard to the truth of the path (*mārge anvayajñāna*) is considered in the *Abhidharmakośa* system to be the path of cultivation (*bhāvanāmārga*).

According to the *Abhidharmasamuccaya*, the enterer of the Stream-enterer and the two enterers of the skipper fruition are on the path of preparation (*prayogamārga*). The Stream-enterer and the abider who skips results, those two are on the path of seeing because the sixteenth moment in the system of the *Abhidharmasamuccaya* is considered to be the path of seeing. Tsong kha pa notes these two different points of reference because it has consequences for how the results of Stream-enterer and those who skip fruitions (*thod rgal*) are defined.[11]

General classifications of individuals within the results of śrāmaṇya. Tsong kha pa utilizes certain classifications throughout both the *Stairway* and *Golden Garland* as a method of categorizing the divisions within the results of *śrāmaṇya*. I would like to provide basic descriptions of these terms here as a reference point to the specific descriptions in later sections. Tsong kha pa employs five different types of terminology to categorize the results of *śrāmaṇya*: (1) Those who skip fruitions (*thod rgal pa*); (2) those who have previously separated from attachment (*chags 'bral sngon song ba*); (3) those who attain results gradually (*'bras bu rim gyis pa*); (4) those who gradually abandon defilements (*spang bya rim gyis pa*); and (5) those who abandon defilements instantaneously (*spang bya cig car ba*).

(1) Those who skip fruitions (*thod rgal pa*) are individuals who remove defilements to be abandoned by the path of cultivation by a mundane path before reaching the path of seeing. At the moment of reaching the sixteenth moment of the path of seeing, they "skip over" lower results based on the number of defilements removed previously

by a mundane path of cultivation (*laukikabhāvanā mārga*). Tsong kha pa (*Golden Garland* 225) mentions that the term *thod rgal* (*skipper*) is applied to the terms *One who is separated from attachment for the most part* (*bhūyovītarāga; phal cher chags dang bral ba*) and *One who is separated from attachment in the desire [realm]* (*kāmavītarāga; 'dod chags dang bral ba*). These terms are from the *Abhidharmakośabhāṣya* and Tsong kha pa employs the designation *skipper* (*thod rgal ba*), although the actual term *skipper* in the *Abhidharmakośa* is in the context of a name of a meditative attainment (*vyutkrāntakasamāpatti; thod rgal gyi snyoms par 'jug pa*).[12]

(2) Those who have previously separated from attachment (*chags 'bral sngon song ba*) are those who, in the period previous to the path of seeing, separate from attachment to the desire realm *kleśas*.

(3) Those who gradually attain results (*'bras bu rim gyis pa*) are those individuals who gradually achieve the four fruitions in a progressive and sequential manner. (4) Those who gradually abandon defilements (*spang bya rim gyis pa*) are those individuals who abandon gradually the nine most subtle of the subtle obstacles within the desire, form, and formless realms to be removed by the path of cultivation. (5) Those who abandon defilements instantaneously (*spang bya cig car ba*) are individuals who abandon instantaneously the nine most subtle of the subtle afflictions of the desire, form, and formless realms to be removed by the path of cultivation.

Tsong kha pa utilizes these general classifications in his analysis of the *Saṃgha* Illustration comprised of the *śrāvakasaṃgha*. The specific types of individuals that are placed within these general classification will be discussed below.

The path parameters of śrāmaṇya. Along with the assumptions related to the topic of *śrāmaṇya* that we have discussed so far, Tsong kha pa also provides a brief discussion in the *Golden Garland* (1970: 227) concerning parameters of the path in which the results of *śrāmaṇya* are attained. These parameters are mentioned from four points of view: (1) The acquisition of results having relied on a certain meditative state; (2) the path from which the acquisition of results takes place; (3) the realms in which the attainment of *śrāmaṇya* take place; and (4) the time of attainment. These topics are briefly mentioned in the *Golden Garland* as a point of reference. Each of these topics could be expanded to the encyclopedic proportions that are characteristic of Tibetan scholasticism, but this is not necessary in our articulation of the Twenty *Saṃghas*.

(1) As regards the acquisition of results by having relied on a certain meditative state: Most of the results are obtained by having relied on the "not-incapable" preparation (*anāgamyasāmantaka*) of the first concentration or the fourth concentration itself. Tibetan traditions

refer to the *anāgamya* as "that which is not-incapable" based on the *Sgra sbyor bam po gnyis pa*. According to this lexical text, it is called "'not-incapable,' since it is without the inability to abandon all the afflictions of the three realms through the mind of meditative absorption on the first concentration."[13] This interpretive gloss may be related to the *Abhidharmakośa*'s statement that "One becomes detached from all spheres by means of pure *anāgamya*."[14] Briefly, the not-incapable (*anāgamya*; *mi lcogs pa med pa*) preparation is the first preparatory concentration. The fundamental (*maula*) concentrations of the four *dhyānas* and the four *ārūpyas* each have a preliminary threshold called *sāmantaka* (*nyes bsdogs*), the one before the first concentration being known specifically as *anāgamya*. The theory of *anāgamya* and its use in detachment (*vairāgya*) is based on the principle that a meditator cannot enter concentration without being free from the defilement of a lower sphere, and that one cannot, while in the same lower sphere, become free from the said lower sphere defilements. Therefore it is necessary to have a threshold that is preliminary to concentration. In other words, a meditator cannot be free of desire realm defilements if his mental awareness is stuck in the desire realm by being attached to various sensual pleasures. At the same time, if a meditator's mental awareness is at the level of the first concentration, the meditator experiences the joy and bliss that comes with the first attainment of that concentration and will therefore not be able to abandon defilements. The *anāgamya* then is a threshold between desire realm mental awareness and first concentration mental awareness in which the conditions are possible for the removal of defilements. The *anāgamya* is considered to be deficient in *śamatha*, or quiescence, while the *ārūpya* concentrations lack the quality of *vipaśyanā* (AKBh vi.66b).

(2) The second parameter mentioned by Tsong kha pa concerns the path in which results take place. The three results of Stream-enterer, Once-returner who skips fruitions, and the Non-returner who skips fruitions, attain a result from merely relying on the path of seeing, because they attain the result having relied on just the subsequent persevering receptivity (*anvayajñānakṣānti*) in regard to the truth of the path; that is, the fifteenth moment on the *śrāvaka* path of seeing. The Once-returner who progresses gradually and the Non-returner who progresses gradually attain results relying on the path of cultivation (*bhāvanāmārga*). That is because the Once-returner who progresses gradually practices to a great extent special insight (*vipaśyanā*) and attains the actual antidote of the sixth affliction of the desire realm, having relied on an uninterrupted path. The Non-returner who progresses gradually attains the actual antidote of the ninth affliction of the desire realm having relied on an uninterrupted path. These two results can also be attained by relying on a mundane path (*laukikabhāvanāmārga*) because an

individual who is empowered to a great extent by the practice of quiescence (*śamatha)* relies on a meditative cultivation that alternates between grossness and peacefulness (*zhi rags*) and can remove either the sixth or ninth affliction previous to the path of seeing. The result of *śrāvaka arhat* is attained by relying only on the supermundane path of cultivation (*lokottarabhāvanāmārga*). This is because the essential antidote of the ninth affliction of the peak existence (*bhavāgra*) can only be attained by having relied on the uninterrupted path that corresponds with the peak of existence.

(3) The third parameter concerns the realms in which the attainment of *śrāmaṇya* takes place. It is clear that the result of Stream-enterer and Once-returner are achieved in states of existence within the desire realm. These two results are not born in the upper realm states of existence, the form and formless realms, since it is not possible for them to become detached from the attachment of the desire realm (*kāmadhātu*). However, it is important to keep in mind that these results can be attained within the heavens of the classes of gods within the desire realm. Also, the path of seeing is absent above the desire realm because it is not possible to carry out analysis in the form and formless realm (see AK, chapter 6); perhaps the mental continuum in the upper realms are too "spaced out" to perform reasoning. Nevertheless, as a result of the lack of a path of seeing in upper states of existence, a person detached from the desire realm and reborn in a higher abode cannot attain the state of Non-returner. The result of Non-returner therefore is attained in a desire realm state of existence because one cannot achieve the causes for state of Non-returner in the upper realms. The result of the *śrāvaka arhat* can be attained in a state of existence within the desire realm. This is because it is possible to manifest this result in a desire realm state of existence by the Stream-enterer who simultaneously abandons obstacles. The *śrāvaka arhat* can also be manifest in the abode of the form realm because the Non-returner who transmigrates to the form realm passes beyond the fifth affliction and by having undertaken this in the realm of desire one is caused to make achievement in the realm of form. The *śrāvaka arhat* can also be manifest in formless realm states of existence because there are Non-returners who transmigrate in the formless realms. Although Tsong kha pa does not mention his source, the above statements concerning how results are attained within each sphere are derived from the *Abhidharmakośa*: "Three are obtained in the desire realm, the last in the three [realms], in the upper [realms] there is not a path of seeing, there is not disgust because from the *sūtra*: 'here [one] sets out, there one achieves.' "[15]

(4) The fourth and final parameter concerns the time of attainment. The Stream-enterer and the Once-returner and Non-returner

who skip fruitions attain a result at the time of obtaining the sixteenth moment of the path of seeing. The Once-returner and Non-returner who skip fruitions obtain the result at the sixteenth moment of the path of seeing by having previously abandoned the sixth or ninth desire realm defilement to be abandoned by the mundane path of cultivation. If the sixth defilement to be removed by the path of cultivation is not abandoned and one abandons up to the first five defilements, one obtains only the result of Stream-enterer at the sixteenth moment. Therefore, the Once-returner or Non-returner who skip fruitions can be counted as a first result, since they do not previously release from, or proceed onward from, either the result of Stream-enterer or Once-returner. The two middle fruitions who gradually progress—that is, Once-returner and Non-returner—manifest the result after obtaining the sixteenth moment of the path of seeing and obtain the result when abandoning either the sixth or ninth desire realm defilement to be abandoned by the path of cultivation. In this way, with regard to the gradual progressor, although it is possible to abandon previous to the path of seeing one to five defilements, the sixth and ninth defilements can only be abandoned after the sixteenth moment of the path of seeing. Those who skip fruitions abandon either six or nine defilements previous to the path of seeing.

These parameters mentioned above serve as reference points for when and where various results can be attained. We have incorporated these path parameters into tables on the following pages to facilitate a graphical reference of the divisions of the four results that comprise the Twenty *Saṃgha*s. There are four basic tables, one for each of the four results of Stream-enterer (table 4.2); Once-returner (table 4.3); Non-returner (table 4.4); and *Arhat* (table 4.5). Each table has a number of columns, reading from left to right, that indicate the result, the process of either entering to or abiding in a result, the realm where the results are achieved, the path that engenders a process or achieves a result, the specific type of Noble Being in a given process or result, and the number of path-of cultivation-defilements removed. The dark sections indicate areas of exclusion that are not applicable to a given process or result. Non-dark sections are the parameters applicable for a given process or result. We will need to keep these parameters in mind for the next section in which the characteristics of each of the categories of Noble Beings are described.

Descriptions of Each Type of Noble Being

We will now present descriptions of the distinguishing characteristics of each type of Noble Being (*ārya*) within the *allegorical saṃgha* of *śrāvaka*s. Tsong kha pa bases his detailed examination of this type

Table 4.2 Stream-enterers

Result	Process	Realm	Path	Type	Defilements Removed
srotā-apanna (Stream-enterer)	*pratipannaka* (enterer)	*kāma* (desire)	*darśana* (seeing)	*mṛdu indriya śraddhānusārin* or *dharmānusārin tīkṣṇa indriya*	
			bhāvanā (cultivation)		1 to 5
		rūpa (form)	*darśana*		
			bhāvanā		
		ārūpya (formless)	*darśana*		
			bhāvanā		
	phalastha (abider)	*kāma* (desire)	*darśana*	*saptakṛtvaparama*	0
			bhāvanā	*kulaṃkula*	3 or 4
		rūpa (form)	*darśana*		
			bhāvanā		
		ārūpya (formless)	*darśana*		
			bhāvanā		

Table 4.3 Once-returners

Result	Process	Realm	Path	Type	Defilements Removed
sakṛdāgāmin	*pratipannaka*	*kāma*	*darśana*		
			bhāvanā	*sakṛdāgāmin pratipannaka*	1 to 5
		rūpa	*darśana*		
			bhāvanā		
		ārūpya	*darśana*		
			bhāvanā		
	phalastha	*kāma*	*darśana*		
			bhāvanā	*sakṛdāgāmin phalastha*	6
		rūpa	*darśana*		
			bhāvanā		
		ārūpya	*darśana*		
			bhāvanā		

Table 4.4 Non-returners

Result	Process	Realm of attainment	Path	Type		Realm of *nirvāṇa*	Mode of progress	Defilements removed
anāgāmin	*pratipannaka*	*kāma*	*darśana*					
			bhāvanā	*ekavīcika*		desire realm deities	gradual	7 or 8
		rūpa	*darśana*					
			bhāvanā					
		ārūpya	*darśana*					
			bhāvanā					
	phalastha	*kāma*	*darśana*					
			bhāvanā	*anāgāmin phalastha*				9
		rūpa	*darśana*					
			bhāvanā	*antarāparinirvāyin*		form realm intermediate state	by means of intermediate state	
				upapadyaparinirvāyin		form realm	by rebirth	
				abhisaṃskāraparinirvāyin		form realm	with effort	
				anabhisaṃskāraparinirvāyin		form realm	without effort	
				ūrdhvaṃsr-otas	*akaniṣthaga* 1. *pluta* 2. *ardhapluga* 3. *sarvacyuta*	*Akaniṣṭha* heaven	alternating concentration	
					bhavāgra-paramaga	Peak of Existence		
		ārūpya	*darśana*					
			bhāvanā	*ārūpyaga*	*upadadya-parinirvayin*	formless realm	form realm detachment	9+
					abhisaṃskāra-parinirvāyin			
					anabhisaṃskāra-parinirvāyin			

Table 4.5 *Arhat*s

Result	Process	Realm	Path	Type	Defilements Removed
arhat	*pratipannaka*	*kāma*	*darśana*	*arhat* enterer	73–80
			bhāvanā		
		rūpa	*darśana*		
			bhāvanā		
		ārūpya	*darśana*		
			bhāvanā		
	phalastha	*kāma*	*darśana*	*arhat*	81
			bhāvanā		
		rūpa	*darśana*		
			bhāvanā		
		ārūpya	*darśana*		
			bhāvanā		

of *saṃgha* through his investigation of *Abhidharma* digests that were available to him: the *Abhidharmakośabhāṣya* and *Vyākhyā* and the *Abhidharmasamuccaya* and its *Bhāṣya*. Tsong kha pa's system of articulation represents a synthesis of these texts and consists of complex descriptive analysis and interpretation. In addition to noting textual parallels, we will also note comparisons of terminological definitions with the *Mahāvyutpatti* and *Puggalapaññati*. These two texts represent definitions of Noble individuals from an eighth-century Indian/Tibetan collaboration and a comparable *Abhidhamma* text from the Pāli tradition. Tsong kha pa divides his exegesis of the individual descriptions of the *saṃgha* of *śrāvakas* from three standpoints: those who progress gradually in the path (*rim gyis pa*), those who skip over fruitions (*thod rgal ba*), and those who are simultaneous abandoners (*cig car ba*).

Gradual progressors (rim gyis pa). As mentioned above, gradual progressors are those individuals who sequentially and in a progressive manner attain results one by one. Tsong kha pa classifies those who progress gradually into four basic categories: Stream-enterers, Once-returners, Non-returners, and *Arhats*.

Stream-enterers (Rgyun du zhugs pa, Srota-āpanna). For individuals who progress gradually, the first result is the stage of Stream-enterer (*srota-āpanna*). In the *Abhidharma* tradition that Tsong kha pa follows, the contextual etymology (*nirukti*) of *srota-āpanna* (*rgyun du zhugs pa*) refers to "one who has entered (*āpanna; zhugs pa*) into the river or stream (*srotas, rgyun*), the stream of the path leading to *nirvāṇa*."[16] The Stream-enterer is explained from two aspects: the enterer to the result of Stream-enterer and the abider in the result of Stream-enterer. Tsong kha pa begins his description of the enterer to the result of Stream-enterer (*rgyun zhugs zhugs pa*) in the *Stairway* with an analysis of the characterization of the path of seeing (*darśanamārga*) from among two textual systems available to him. These two textual systems are the *Vaibhāṣika*, based on the *Abhidharmakośa*, and the system of the Ārya Asaṅga, from the *Abhidharmasamuccaya*. The system of the *Abhidharmakośa* (vi.29–30) considers the path of seeing to consist of fifteen moments. Therefore the parameter in this system of the enterer to the result of Stream-enterer is considered to be up to the intellectual receptivity on the truth of the path (*mārge anvayajñānakṣānti*)—that is, fifteenth moment of the path of seeing. The threshold point of the first enterer in the system of the *Abhidharmasamuccaya* (AS 88) is considered to be located in the path of preparation (*prayogamārga*) from among the preparatory analytical factors (*nirvedhabhāgīya*). Tsong kha pa characterizes this boundary based on the *Abhidharmasamuccayabhāṣya*, which states that "holding from a single session meditative equipoise of the 'preparatory analytical factors' up to the first result there is no attainment."[17]

Tsong kha pa notes in the *Stairway* (269) that the single session of meditative equipoise (*sbyor lam stan gcig*) is not exactly defined other than that an enterer must have continual effort and activity that puts forth effort for the purpose of abandoning defilements. The *Stairway* (269) also states that it is not evident from the source texts which of the four preparatory analytical factors generates the single session of meditative equipoise. However, the *Golden Garland* (1970: 231) states, without a textual reference, that it is generated from the first preparatory analytical factor of heat (*uṣmagata*). Tsong kha pa concludes from his comparison of these two textual systems in the *Stairway* (270) that

> Accordingly, on account of proposing two discordant [systems] in terms of a single basis of analysis, the enterer to the result of Stream-enterer, it is not reasonable for both systems to be correct. If both [systems] are incorrect what is the definite meaning to be accepted? Because it will be damaging to the explanation, the first opinion is not to be admitted. Accordingly it is just that system of the *Abhidharmasamuccaya* that is not flawed.

He bases this statement on the premise that one should explain the method of entrance into the first result that generates in the mental continuum a realization that is consonant for the individuals of the three vehicles: *śrāvakas*, *pratyekabuddhas*, and *bodhisattvas*. In other words, it is important for Tsong kha pa to establish a *Mahāyāna* understanding of the first enterer based on the *Abhidharmasamuccaya* (AS). As we will see later in this chapter, Tsong kha wishes to demonstrate how the AA interpretation of the Twenty *Saṃghas* is consonant with the *Abhidharmasamuccaya,* both of which are considered to be *Mahāyāna* texts. The AA and AS encompass doctrines pertaining to the three vehicles, while the *Abhidharmakośa* accounts for only the *śrāvaka* vehicle—that is, *śrāvakas* and *pratyekabuddhas*. This distinction will allow Tsong kha pa to demonstrate the difference of interpretation between Ārya Vimuktisena and Haribhadra in the section concerning the *actual saṃgha* of *bodhisattvas*. Tsong kha pa therefore defines the parameter of the enterer to the result of Stream-enterer from the heat of the path of preparation up to the subsequent intellectual receptivity on the truth of the path. After comparing these two textual systems, Tsong kha pa defines the enterer to the result of Stream-enterer in the *Stairway* (271):

> Thus, a person of the inferior vehicle who makes effort for the sake of obtaining the result of Stream-enterer either does not abandon the series

> of obstacles to be removed by the path of cultivation in the desire realm or abandons the first up to the fifth but does not [abandon] the sixth [defilement]; as previously explained, an enterer to the result of Stream-enterer is one who abides from the path of preparation of one meditative session up until the time of abiding in the subsequent intellectual receptivity of the path.

In these moments of the path of seeing that lead up to attaining the result of Stream-enterer, there are two types of enterers that are characterized by their strength of faculties (*indriya*). Tsong kha pa correlates the division of enterers found at the beginning of AA i.23 *mṛdutīkṣṇendriyau* ("those with dull and sharp faculties") with that found in the *Abhidharmakośa* (iv.30cd): "the ascetics of weak and sharp faculties (*mṛdutīkṣṇendriyau*) are the ones who follow by faith (*śraddhānusārin*) and the ones who follow by doctrine (*dharmānusārin*) (*mṛdutīkṣṇendriyau teṣu śraddhādharmānusāriṇau*)." Tsong kha pa therefore classifies these enterers to the first result by means of faculty: the weak faculty enterer of Stream-enterer is a follower through faith (*śraddhānusārin*); the one that has sharp faculties is a follower through dharma (*dharmānusārin*).

The *Abhidharmakośa* provides a contextual etymology of the *śraddhānusārin* as *śraddhayā anusāraḥ* = *śraddhānusāraḥ*, "pursuit by reason of faith." One is known as such because while in the state of being an ordinary individual (*pṛthagjana*), a person pursues the Truths under the impulse of another, through having confidence in another.[18] Tsong kha pa states basically the same definition but relies upon the *Abhidharmasamuccaya:* "Who is the follower of faith? One who, having acquired the provisions, having weak faculties, practices for the sake of clearly realizing the truth, having recollected the teaching [given] by others."[19]

Likewise, the *dharmānusāraḥ* is explained in a similar manner from the *Abhidharmakośa*: *dharmair anusāraḥ* = *dharmānusāraḥ*, "pursuit by means of dharma." This is one who pursues the Truths by himself, without relying on another, by means of the twelvefold scriptures, *sūtras*, and so forth.[20] Tsong kha pa accepts the definition from the *Abhidharmasamuccaya*: "Who is the follower of the doctrine? One who, having acquired the provisions, having sharp faculties, practices the clear realization of the truth, having recollected the doctrine dominated by the truth by himself."[21]

The *Stairway*, in addition to these definitions, notes from the *Abhidharmakośabhāṣya* that if these followers of faith and doctrine have not previously abandoned the defilements to be abandoned through the mundane path of cultivation (*laukikabhāvanāmārga*), they are known as one who is "bound by all the bonds" (*sakalabandhana*). If it is the case that these two types of followers have previously abandoned the obstacles to be removed by the mundane path of cultivation, up to the fifth category of desire realm defilements, they are still the same as enterers to the first result.[22] Tsong kha pa concludes his discussion of the enterer to the result of Stream-enterer in the *Stairway* with the following descriptive stanza: "Not having abandoned six obstacles of the desire realm, from the meditative period of the path of preparation up to the subsequent patience of the path, that abider, is an enterer [to the result] of Stream-enterer."[23]

After describing the enterer to the result of Stream-enterer, Tsong kha pa examines those who abide in the result of Stream-enterer (*rgyun zhugs gnas pa, srota-āpannaphalasthā*). The *Stairway* provides a general definition for the abider in the result of Stream-enterer as "one of an inferior vehicle who abides on the realization of the sixteenth [moment] and does not abandon the sixth obstacle to be removed by the path of cultivation in the desire realm."[24]

The *Stairway* (269) notes that the sixteenth moment on the path of seeing abandons all the obstacles to be removed by the path of seeing and that one attains the result of Stream-enterer by merely that moment. The result of Stream-enterer may also be divided into two categories by means of abandoning defilements: one who abandons obstacles in the path of cultivation gradually (*spang bya rim gyis pa*) or simultaneously (*spang bya cig car pa*). The one who abandons simultaneously is considered to be more prominent in realization. We will discuss this type of Stream-enterer in the section on the simultaneous abandoners.

Tsong kha pa categorizes an abider in the result of Stream-enterer who abandons defilements gradually into two types: the mere abider in the result (*'bras bu tsam la gnas pa*) and the abider in the result who has superior distinction (*khyad par can*). The mere abider in the result refers to the Stream-enterer who takes, at most, seven rebirths (*saptakṛtvaparama*), and the abider with distinction refers to the Stream-enterer who goes from family to family (*kulaṃkula*). The difference between these two, the mere abider and superior abider, is based on the continual effort to further abandon defilements. Tsong kha pa, citing the AKBh and AKV,[25] states that an abider in the result of Stream-enterer who does not forcefully abandon the obstacles to be removed by the path of cultivation in the desire realm and likewise does not achieve in the abandoning of the first five defilements, or who does not put forth effort in further abandonment, is merely an abider in the result of Stream-enterer. As the *Stairway* (273) states: "It is indicated that the abider in the result of Stream-enterer, if not making effort in the application of abandonment, does not enter to the upper fruitions and does abide in the [superior] distinction of the [Stream-enterer] result."

Mere abider in stream-entry: Saptakṛtvaparama. A mere abider in the result of Stream-enterer does not abandon any of the obstacles to be removed by the path of cultivation and accumulates the karma of definitely experiencing seven existences at the time of each rebirth. This individual is called "one who takes existence seven times." One does not achieve realization in an eighth existence in the desire realm because by the seventh existence the mental continuum is considered to be fully matured. The path is exhausted by seven desire realm existences similar to the way a certain snake is called "the seven-footed serpent" or similar to how the sickness called "four-day fever" lasts four days. According to the AKV a seven-footed serpent is a snake whose bite kills a person after he has taken seven steps; likewise one is called a seven-timer by being reborn up to a possibility of seven times. If all rebirths are taken, the classification utilized is *seven times at the most* (*saptakṛtvaparama*) and the abider in the result is considered to be the *lowest of all* Noble Beings. An individual who takes seven times by not exhausting the obstacles to be removed by the path of cultivation, and by taking seven times, is said to be the lowest of the seven-timers. In this way, the *Stairway* explains this mere abider in the result of Stream-enterer as one who

> being an abider in the result [of Stream-enterer] explained previously, [does] not abandon firmly the defilements to be abandoned by the path of cultivation, and accumulates the karma which definitely experiences seven rebirths in the desire realm at the time of each rebirth is an abider in the result of *Saptakṛtvaparama* (Stream-enterer which takes up to seven times).[26]

Tsong kha pa cites the AKBh and the AKV to demonstrate that the *Saptakṛtvaparama* does not necessarily take rebirth seven times. Just as the *Ūrdhvaṃsrotas* (a type of Non-returner that will be discussed below) does not necessarily transmigrate up to the *Akaniṣṭha* heaven or the Peak of Existence, likewise the *Saptakṛtvaparama* does not necessarily take up to seven existences.[27] The term *saptakṛtvaparama* does not exclusively refer to Noble Beings (*ārya*), as there are others who may have their mind-stream ripened before achieving an eighth desire realm existence. As Tsong kha pa states:

> The ordinary individual seven-times-at-the-most and the Ārya Stream-enterer seven-times-at-the-most are the two [types]. The first [type] in that life's path of preparation or on a childish [path] definitely manifests *nirvāṇa* while not achieving an eighth existence and the second [type], as stated above, is of two [divisions] definitely or not definitely [taking seven rebirths].[28]

What is a seven-times existence? Tsong kha pa goes to great lengths (*Stairway* 277–81) to demonstrate that a seven-times existence refers to taking up to twenty-eight existences: seven existences among humans, seven intermediate state existences, seven existences among gods, and then seven intermediate state existences. One reborn up to "seven times" therefore refers to the series or cycles of seven existences as like a monk who is "wise in seven objects" (*saptasthānakuśala*) or like a tree called "seven petaled" (*saptaparṇa*). A "seven-petaled" tree does not have just seven leaves. Rather, it is called such since it grows leaves that have seven petals. Likewise, the *Saptakṛtvaparama* Stream-enterer takes up to seven rebirths in cycles of seven existences. The series of seven rebirths that this type of Stream-enterer takes is only counted for the desire realm. If this Stream-enterer goes on to take an eighth existence in the form or formless realm, Tsong kha pa (*Stairway* 280) maintains that there is no problem because the cycle of seven rebirths is only counted for rebirths among gods and humans of the desire realm. What is the manner in which this type of Stream-enterer takes rebirth? Tsong kha pa (*Golden Garland* 233) posits, based on the *Abhidharmakośabhāṣya,* his own theory of the manner in which the *Saptakṛtvaparama* takes rebirth. In this instance, a *Saptakṛtvaparama* Stream-enterer achieves emancipation in the same type of life support in which the individual first achieved the result of Stream-enterer. In this regard the *Golden Garland* (233) states:

> As to the manner of taking rebirth, when obtaining [the result of] Stream-enterer in the embodiment of a human, taking six times as a human, seven times as a god, finally having been born as a human, one is emancipated. When obtaining [the result] in the embodiment of a god, taking six times as a god, having been reborn seven times as a human, finally one is emancipated in the embodiment of god. Likewise, fourteen existent rebirths among gods and humans plus fourteen intermediate existences equals taking twenty-eight and, because it is similar to the series seven, one is called a "seven-timer."

Tsong kha pa sums up the *Saptakṛtvaparama* by stating that the gradualist Stream-enterer who does not abandon even a single defilement to be abandoned by the path of cultivation takes at least two rebirths in the desire realm, that in general the cycle of rebirths is seven times at the most, and that the certainty of taking seven times is mentioned as a distinction. These characteristics are applied at the beginning of the mere Stream-enterer's career because by abandoning a single affliction and taking a single rebirth, the characteristics of this type of Stream-enterer are left behind.

Distinctive abider in stream-entry: Kulaṃkula. An abider with distinction refers to the Stream-enterer who goes from family to family (*kulaṃkula*). The *Stairway* (283) considers that the abider in the distinctive result of Stream-enterer makes the effort to abandon the first to the sixth desire realm obstacles to be removed by the path of cultivation. Tsong kha pa notes that the embodiments of the abider in the result of Stream-enterer, when passing away and manifesting as a Once-returner or Non-returner, takes rebirth in either the form or formless realm. The implication from this is that one who goes from family to family, a *Kulaṃkula,* cannot be reborn in either the results of Once-returner or Non-returner and does not transmigrate in the upper form and formless realms. He states that one born from family to family needs to have three distinctive qualities: the distinction related to abandoning afflictions, the distinction in the manner of taking birth, and the distinction of obtaining a relative. These qualities are from the *Abhidharmakośa* which states: "Delivered from three or four categories, destined for two or three rebirths, is one who goes from family to family (*Kulaṃkula*)."[29]

In relation to the distinction of abandoning afflictions, a *Kulaṃkula* needs to definitely abandon the third defilement to be removed by the path of cultivation, and although it may abandon the fourth defilement, the *Kulaṃkula* definitely does not abandon the fifth defilement. The fourth defilement is an option because the *Kulaṃkula,* who is more than a mere Stream-enterer, does not aspire to remove just the first and second defilements. However, if it were the case that the fifth defilement was abandoned, one would definitely abandon the sixth defilement and become a Once-returner. The idea here is that when the fifth category of defilement is abandoned, since it is not necessary to pass over or leave from the desire realm to abandon the next category of defilement, the sixth category also becomes abandoned. If one were to abandon the sixth defilement, one would then be a Once-returner and not take two rebirths as a single desire realm transmigrator. Therefore, Tsong kha pa reasons that to abandon the fifth category of the path of cultivation defilements is not suitable for one who goes from family to family.

The *Stairway* (285) notes for the distinctive manner of taking birth that it is necessary to take two rebirths in a single transmigration sequence within the desire realm because that is the conventional or expressed meaning of one who is born from family to family (*Kulaṃkula*). Tsong kha pa states that a *Kulaṃkula* may or may not take three rebirths but that one definitely does not take four rebirths because the *Abhidharmakośabhāṣya* says a *Kulaṃkula* has "two or three lives remaining."[30]

With regard to the distinction of antidote, the *Kulaṃkula* obtains the uncontaminated path antidotes that abandon the above-mentioned obstacles. According to Tsong kha pa, the aforementioned quote from the *Abhidharmakośa*, "delivered from three or four categories," explicitly demonstrates two qualities—the quality of abandoning afflictions and the quality of taking rebirth—while the quality of obtaining the antidote to the afflictions is implicitly understood. Tsong kha pa reasons that after the Stream-enterer abandons one category of the defilements, the antidote of those defilements, which consists in the attaining of the uncontaminated path, although not mentioned in the text, will be realized because an individual does not abandon afflictions without an antidote and also because an individual attains an uncontaminated path as a Noble Being (*ārya*). This is based on the *Abhidharmakośabhāṣya*, which states that "within the verse only two [qualities] are mentioned, for when abandoning the afflictions after [attaining the result of] Stream-enterer, one obtains the antidote of that [result], the faculty of the uncontaminated, although not spoken, is achieved."[31]

After clarifying the above distinctions, the *Stairway* (285–86) provides a general definition of the *Kulaṃkula*:

> Accordingly, if not abandoning the sixth obstacle of the desire realm to be removed by the path of cultivation, possessing the application of abandoning afflictions, abiding on the subsequent knowledge on the truth of the path, liberated having definitely taken two births in a single transmigration of the desire realm, that one is a family-to-family Stream-enterer (*kulaṃkula srota-āpanna*).

Following the *Abhidharmakośabhāṣya*, Tsong kha pa accepts that there are two types of *Kulaṃkula*: one that is born family to family among gods (*devakulaṃkula*) and one that is born family to family among humans (*manuṣyakulaṃkula*). A *Devakulaṃkula* is a one who, having obtained the status of Stream-enterer in a suitable embodiment from among the six types of desire realm gods, having been born two times among a lineage of the first class of gods or whatever suitable other five classes of desire realm gods, then achieves emancipation. A *Manuṣyakulaṃkula* is one who, having obtained the status of a Stream-enterer in an embodiment within *Jambudvīpa*, having been born two times as a human, born in the *Jambudvīpa* continent itself or a suitable eastern or northern continent, then achieves *parinirvāṇa*.

The *Stairway* sums up in a stanza the definition of a *Kulaṃkula*:

> Definitely abandoning three afflictions and definitely taking two rebirths gradually, the fourth abandonment and the third rebirth may or may

> not be abandoned or taken. Four rebirths and five abandonments are definitely not taken nor abandoned. This particularity of the *Kulaṃkula* should be realized by the wise in the doctrine.[32]

Once-returners (Sakṛdāgāmin). The second result of those who progress gradually is the state of Once-returner (*Sakṛdāgāmin*). A Once-returner is classified into an enterer and an abider. Tsong kha pa states in the *Stairway* (292) that one who, having obtained the sixteenth moment and not abandoning the sixth desire realm affliction, makes effort at abandoning the first through the sixth desire realm afflictions is called "an enterer to the result of Once-returner." This is synonymous with possessing a distinction in abiding in the result of Stream-enterer.

Tsong kha pa remarks also that in a similar fashion, according to the *Abhidharmakośabhāṣya*, the remaining enterers are differentiated from the three abiders in a result. Thus, not counting the first enterer to the result of Stream-enterer, the three later enterers, gradually, are spoken of as possessing distinction in abiding in the results of Stream-enterer, Once-returner, and Non-returner.

Tsong kha pa compares the definitions between the *Abhidharmakośa*[33] and the *Abhidharmasamuccaya*[34] for this enterer and determines that they are congruent. Like the definition above, the *Golden Garland* (234) defines an enterer to the result of Once-returner as an abider in the result of Stream-enterer, who, when making effort for the sake of obtaining the result of Once-returner, does not abandon whichever defilement up to the fifth to be removed by the path of cultivation nor makes effort to abandon the sixth defilement. Tsong kha pa provides a summary of this type of enterer in the *Stairway* (293): "Making effort to abandon up to the sixth [aspect], and making effort to abandon the sixth definitely, [one] is called a Once-returner enterer, as explained in the system of the two, upper and lower, *Abhidharma*s."

The abider in the result of Once-returner is that enterer who abandons the sixth desire realm affliction. The *Stairway* defines the Once-returner as "the lesser vehicle [person] who does not abandon the ninth [affliction] and who abandons the sixth desire realm affliction on obtaining the sixteenth moment."[35]

The Once-returner abider has two aspects: the abider in the mere result (*'bras bu tsam la gnas pa*) and the abider in the distinctive result (*'bras bu khyad par can la gnas pa*). Tsong kha pa considers that the one who merely abides in the Once-returner result does not abandon other than the sixth desire realm affliction and does not try to abandon the upper realm afflictions. The *Golden Garland* (234) notes that when abiding on the path of liberation (*vimuktimārga*) that abandons the sixth defilement, one is a mere abider in the result and when making effort in abandonment up to the ninth defilement, one possesses distinction (*viśeṣa; khyad par can*).

Distinctive Once-returner: Ekavīcika. The Once-returner who has distinction is called an *Ekavīcika.* This one makes effort to abandon from the seventh up to the ninth defilements to be abandoned by the path of cultivation and is synonymous with the Non-returner enterer. Tsong kha pa defines the *Ekavīcika* in the *Stairway* (293):

> One who has distinction as an abider in the result of Once-returner obtains the result of Non-returner by abandoning the seventh and eighth desire realm afflictions and is obstructed by a single affliction and obstructed by a single life for obtaining emancipation.[36]

Here it is noted that in exhausting the seventh affliction there is a single interval and that an interval is the principle hindrance to the result of Non-returner because an interval is itself also the ninth defilement. The *Golden Garland* (235) explains that the *Abhidharmasamuccayabhāṣya* relates that the meaning of one interval (*eka vīci*) is an interruption between one rebirth. The ASBh states:

> The *Ekavīcika* Once-returner is only an enterer to the result of Non-returner who, having transmigrated a single existence among the gods, is emancipated. For one who has "one interval" means the intermediate state, the intermediate time between birth (*janmāvakāśaḥ*), that is the *Ekavīcika.*"[37]

With one interval to go, the *Ekavīcika* at the time of already abandoning the seventh and eighth affliction will not become a Non-returner from abandoning the ninth affliction. However, abandoning the ninth affliction at the time of death manifests the result of Non-returner and by manifesting *nirvāṇa* in that very embodiment itself, one is obstructed by a single affliction for the result of Non-returner and is obstructed by one life for *nirvāṇa.* The Non-returner is unable to be obstructed for attainment in that life by the ninth affliction. Why is the situation of the *Ekavīcika* not similar to that of the *Kulaṃkula* mentioned earlier who, if abandoning the fifth affliction, would undoubtedly also abandon the sixth affliction? Tsong kha pa reasons that an *Ekavīcika* is unable to pass over the desire realm, which is necessary to abandon afflictions that allow acquisition of a passage to the form realm and the state of Non-returner. However, the category of defilements to be abandoned by a *Kulaṃkula* to reach the state of Once-returner are within the desire realm. According to the texts available to Tsong kha pa, an *Ekavīcika* does not appear to be born in the upper transmigrations of the form and formless realms. Tsong kha pa cites the *Abhidharmasamuccaya*: "Who is the *Ekavīcika*? A Once-returner who, just among the gods, obtains the end of suffering."[38]

The *Ekavīcika* therefore obtains emancipation in the embodiment of a desire realm deity. The *Stairway* (295) states, however, that the distinction of rebirth does not apply for the mere abider in the result of Once-returner, for a mere Once-returner is reborn as a human and will return back one time because of not coming back more than a single time in a single transmigration. The general characteristic of the Once-returner is that he/she comes back one time to the desire realm. In the *Stairway*, Tsong kha pa gives (295) the following condensed verse to provide a summary of the distinctive Once-returner: "That *Ekavīcika* Once-returner, abandoning the seventh and eighth affliction, is shown to make manifest *nirvāṇa* in the embodiments of desire realm gods when dying."

We have so far discussed the first two results of *śrāvaka*s who progress gradually in the results of *śrāmaṇya*.

Non-returners (Anāgāmin). The third result of *śrāmaṇya* is the state of Non-returner. A Non-returner may also be initially divided into an enterer and an abider. As Tsong kha pa states in the *Stairway* (296): "Who is the enterer to the result of Non-returner? That same abider in the result of Once-returner formerly explained who makes application of abandoning from the seventh to ninth [afflictions]."

Therefore, an enterer to the result of Non-returner is essentially an *Ekavīcika*. If that enterer abandons the ninth defilement to be abandoned on the path of cultivation, he is then a Non-returner. The *Stairway* explains the abider in the state of Non-returner: "The lesser vehicle trainee who, obtaining realization of the sixteenth [moment] abandons the ninth [affliction] to be abandoned by the path of cultivation in the desire realm."[39]

In regard to the state of Non-returner, Tsong kha pa emphasizes that if one does not apply oneself to abandoning the afflictions of the upper realm, one is a mere abider in the Non-returner result. To engage in the application of abandoning the afflictions contained within the first concentration up to the ninth affliction of the peak of existence, one is then considered an abider in the distinctive Non-returner result and possesses the foundation for entering into the state of *Arhat*. Once again, in Tsong kha pa's system, it is necessary to constantly apply effort in abandoning defilements in order to progressively advance to the upper stages of the path. Tsong kha pa divides the distinctive Non-returner into four principle divisions: a Non-returner who transmigrates in the form realm (*rūpopaga*), one who transmigrates in the formless realm (*arūpyopaga*), one who achieves emancipation in the present life (*dṛṣṭadharmaśramaḥ*), and a bodily witness (*kāyasākṣī*). Tsong kha pa (*Stairway* 296) explains that although it is acceptable to classify these Non-returners as distinctive abiders in the result, they are not to be understood as definitely abandoning the remaining afflictions to be abandoned by the path of cultivation. As we will see, the examination of distinctive Non-returners who progress gradually involves a system of categorizing that differentiates them in regard to the levels of the form or formless realm they transmigrate through and differentiates them in correlation with the different levels of meditative concentration they have mastered. Table 4.6 (p. 126) presents the four general divisions in which Tsong kha pa divides the distinctive Non-returners of the *saṃgha illustration* or *allegorical saṃgha*. We note here that these divisions are applied to the Non-returners of the *saṃgha illustration* because these categories are not divided the same way in the AA system of the *actual saṃgha* of *bodhisattvas*. Table 4.6 also illustrates the various subdivisions found within each of the four general categories of Non-returners classified by Tsong kha pa and serves as a reference for the Non-returners presented in this section.

Rūpopaga: *Non-returners in the form realm.* The first division of distinctive Non-returners consists of those that transmigrate in the form realm (*rūpopaga*). The *Stairway* (297) provides a general definition of such Non-returners: "The Non-returner who possesses a desire realm embodiment that obtains *nirvāṇa* having definitely taken rebirth in the form realm."

This implies that one who progresses gradually reaches toward the state of Non-returner in the desire realm and takes rebirth in the form realm to achieve emancipation. Tsong kha pa notes that a karmic connection (*mtshoms sbyor*) that establishes a rebirth existence itself in the form realm is not necessary because of the absence of such a connection for the Non-returner (i.e., *Antarāparinirvayin*) who achieves emancipation in the intermediate state between death in the desire realm and rebirth in the form realm.

Tsong kha pa also explains that it is not necessary to achieve *nirvāṇa* in a form realm embodiment because of the emancipation process of the Non-returner who may go to the Peak of Existence (*Bhavāgraparama*).

Tsong kha pa classifies three types of transmigrators in the form realm: the *Antarāparinirvāyin* (Non-returner who achieves emancipation in the intermediate state), *Upapadyaparinirvāyin* (Non-returner who achieves emancipation through birth), and the *Ūrdhvaṃsrotas* (Non-returner who achieves emancipation through going higher). These three

Table 4.6 Tsong kha pa's Division of Distinctive Non-returners (*Anāgāmin*) in the *Śrāvaka Saṃgha* Illustration

<table>
<tr><td rowspan="10">(1) Rūpopaga
(transmigrator in the form realm)</td><td rowspan="3">Antarāparinirvāyin
(one who achieves nirvāṇa in the intermediate state)</td><td colspan="2">Āśuparinirvāyin
(immediately in the intermediate state)</td></tr>
<tr><td colspan="2">Anāśuparinirvāyin
(not immediately in the intermediate state)</td></tr>
<tr><td colspan="2">Ciraparinirvāyin
(after a long time)</td></tr>
<tr><td rowspan="3">Upapadyaparinirvāyin
(one who achieves nirvāṇa through birth)</td><td colspan="2">Abhisaṃskāraparinirvāyin
(one who achieves through effort)</td></tr>
<tr><td colspan="2">Anabhisaṃskāraparinirvāyin
(one who achieves without effort)</td></tr>
<tr><td colspan="2">Upapadyaparinirvāyin</td></tr>
<tr><td rowspan="4">Ūrdhvaṃsrotas
(one who goes higher)</td><td rowspan="3">Akaniṣṭhaga
(Non-returner who goes up to Akaniṣṭha)</td><td>Pluta (Jumper)</td></tr>
<tr><td>Ardhapluta
(half-jumper)</td></tr>
<tr><td>Sarvasthānacyuta
(one who dies in all abodes)</td></tr>
<tr><td colspan="2">Bhavāgraparamaga
(one who may go up Peak of Existence)</td></tr>
<tr><td rowspan="2">(2) Arūpyopaga
(transmigrator in the formless realm)</td><td>Ūrdhvaṃsrotas</td><td colspan="2"></td></tr>
<tr><td>Upapadyaparinirvāyin
(3 types)</td><td colspan="2"></td></tr>
<tr><td>(3) Dṛṣṭadharmaśrama
(one who is emancipated in the present life)</td><td></td><td colspan="2"></td></tr>
<tr><td>(4) Kāyasākṣin
(bodily witness)</td><td></td><td colspan="2"></td></tr>
</table>

are essentially differentiated based on the karmic bonds that propel them into various form realms. The *Antarāparinirvāyins* possess the karma of coming into being (*abhinirvṛttikarma*), while the *Upapadyaparinirvāyins* have karma that will necessitate the experience of rebirth (*upapadyavedanīyakarma*), and the *Ūrdhvaṃsrotas* possess karma that will be experienced at another time (*aparaparyāyavedanīyakarma*). Tsong kha pa defines an *Antarāparinirvayin* as follows:

> This is one who goes in the form realm obtaining *nirvāṇa* in that embodiment itself which is connected to whatever suitable of the sixteen intermediate states, not counting the intermediate state of the *Mahābrahma* heaven of the form realm.[40]

Based on the AKBh, Tsong kha pa explains that there are three aspects to the *Antarāparinirvayin*: those who obtain *nirvāṇa* quickly in the intermediate state (*Āśuparinirvāyin*), not quickly (*Anāśuparinirvāyin*), and after a long time in the intermediate state (*Ciraparinirvāyin*). These three are thought to either obtain *nirvāṇa* immediately upon taking rebirth in the intermediate state, in the middle time of the intermediate state, or at the end period of the intermediate state. Tsong kha pa bases his interpretation of these three types of *Antarāparinirvayin* through the examples given in the *Sūtra Showing the Seven Transmigrations of Holy Individuals* (*Saptasatpuruṣagatī*) found in Yaśomitra's AKV.[41] As Tsong kha pa explains in the *Stairway* (298):

> What are these three illustrations? In the manner of three stages: like a spark of hay that is immediately extinguished, like a spark of iron struck by the hammer of an iron smith that ascends up towards the sky and is extinguished, and like a flaming iron spark, having turned up towards the sky, is extinguished before hitting the ground.

These three examples also occur in the *Aṅguttaranikāya* (AN iv.70) and *Śrāvakabhūmi* (ŚBh). La Vallèe Poussin (1906: 446) has made a comparison between the AKV and the AN. Wayman (1974) has translated the Sanskrit from the *Śrāvakabhūmi*, which Masefield (1986: 110ff) has compared with the AN. The AN, AKV, and ŚBh present similes that are very much alike, although the Sanskrit and Pāli traditions widely differ in interpreting them (see Masefied, 1986). Nevertheless, Tsong kha pa interprets the three aspects of the *Antarāparinirvāyin* from the explanation of Asaṅga found in the *Abhidharmasamuccaya*.[42] Tsong kha pa explains:

> [F]irst, manifesting the path at the same time of achieving the intermediate state, one abandons the remaining abandonments and obtains *nirvāṇa;* or one achieves an intermediate existence and the desire of transmigrating into a rebirth merely does not occur, one manifests the path and achieves *nirvāṇa;* or having achieved an intermediate state existence, one manifests the path when there is desire to pass through an abode of rebirth, then obtains *nirvāṇa;* these [*Antarāparinirvāyins*], although abandoning the afflictions of actual birth in the god abodes of the form realm, since they do not abandon the afflictions of achieving the intermediate state existence, take rebirth in the intermediate state. (*Stairway* 208)

That Non-returner *Antarāparinirvāyin* who possess a desire realm embodiment refers to the four *Antarāparinirvāyin* of the first concentration. There are sixteen in the intermediate state of *Brahmakāyika* heaven and so forth. The states of Stream-enterer and Once-returner are without an *Antarāparinirvāyin*. According to Tsong kha pa, this is because of not being accustomed for very long on the path and not having few afflictions. The *Stairway* (313) quotes the *Vaibhāṣikas* as stating that the Stream-enterer and Once-returner have nonvirtuous afflictions of the desire realm and many form and formless realm afflictions not explicitly demonstrated in the scripture to abandon in order to attain other results of the path. It is necessary for the Stream-enterer to obtain three results and the Once-returner to obtain two results. Since both have many realms to pass over, these realms are unable to be made by them, because they abide in the intermediate state for a short time.

The next type of *śrāvaka* Non-returner who transmigrates in the form realm is the *Upapadyaparinirvāyin*. This is a Non-returner who obtains *nirvāṇa* through birth in the form realm. The *Stairway* states: "A transmigrator in the form realm who, in that very first embodiment itself in whatever suitable sixteen abodes of form realm gods, obtains *nirvāṇa*."[43]

Tsong kha pa classifies these into three: those who obtain *parinirvāṇa* having been liberated from mere birth, without effort and with effort. These distinctions are also explained (*Stairway*, 300) based on the *Sūtra Showing the Seven Transmigrations of Holy Individuals*. According to this *sūtra*, there are three *Antarāparinirvāyins*, three *Upapadyaparinirvāyins*, and the *Ūrdhvaṃsrotas*. Tsong kha pa follows the system of that *sūtra* in positing a succession of three *Upapadyaparinirvāyins*: those that arise first in liberation by the manifesting *nirvāṇa* without effort (*Anabhisaṃskāraparinirvāyin*),[44] and the distinction just the opposite from that, one who achieves through effort (*Abhisaṃskāraparinirvāyin*).[45] The third type has the distinction of being liberated through mere birth and without accomplishment, the *Upapadyaparinirvāyin*. These arise by a more spontaneous path and their abandonments are weaker than those without accomplishment. Tsong kha pa considers that the succession and the distinction of these three *Upapadyaparinirvāyins* is again based on the *Sūtra Showing the Seven Transmigrations of Holy Individuals.* Establishing this *sūtra* as the source for the Non-returners who transmigrate in the form realm is important for Tsong kha pa so that he can demonstrate that Vasubandhu and Asaṅga have a unified understanding of these types of Non-returners based on the same *sūtra*. Tsong kha pa accepts only the following sequence for these types of Non-returners: one without accomplishment and then one with accomplishment. He considers that these individuals generate in their mental continuum a path that does not rely on great accomplishment for the purpose of quickly achieving *nirvāṇa* (*Stairway* 302).

In regard to the *Upapadyaparinirvāyins* and *Antarāparinirvāyins,* Tsong kha pa examines whether they achieve *nirvāṇa* with remnant (*sopadhiśeṣa*) or *nirvāṇa* without remnant (*nirupadhiśeṣa*), based on the discussion in the AKBh and AKV.[46] The *Stairway* (302) reasons that the *Upapadyaparinirvāyin* does not have the ability to obtain *nirvāṇa* without achieving the end of life because it is necessary to have the power for abandoning life by means of the concentration known as *prāntakoṭicaturthadhyāna*. The *Upapadyaparinirvāyin* does not have the power to abandon life through the force of *prāntakoṭicaturthadhyāna* because, according to the AKBh (Pradhan, 420), only the embodiment of an individual of the three continents (*dvīpa*) or a woman has that power. Based on this, Tsong kha pa states that the *Upapadyaparinirvāyin* has a *nirvāṇa* with remnant (*sopadhiśeṣa*) and the *Antarāparinirvāyin* has a *nirvāṇa* without remnant (*nirupadhiśeṣa*). As regards the *Antarāparinirvāyin,* the *Stairway* (303) explains that it does not matter whether an *Antarāparinirvāyin* has the power to abandon life or not. Tsong kha pa considers death in the intermediate state to not really be a death, but rather an uncompleted lifetime, because the intermediate state is cast by a single karma that puts forth an intermediate state existence and two rebirth existences. Therefore, the *Antarāparinirvāyin* has connections in that very abiding rebirth for *nirvāṇa* without remnant, since releasing the conditionings of the previous life immediately abandons all the afflictions. Otherwise, the *Antarāparinirvāyin* previously obtains a *nirvāṇa* with remnant that abandons all afflictions and at that time of death has a *nirvāṇa* without remnant.

The third type of Non-returner that Tsong kha pa classifies as achieving *nirvāṇa* in the form realm is the *Ūrdhvaṃsrotas*. The *Stairway* (303) provides a general definition: "Who is the *Ūrdhvaṃsrotas*? One who goes in the form realm, not obtaining *nirvāṇa* in the embodiment of first birth in the form realm but going higher to upper [realms] obtains *nirvāṇa*."[47]

Tsong kha pa notes in the *Golden Garland* (236) that an *Ūrdhvaṃsrotas* is a Non-returner who is emancipated in the form realm, having passed through at least two rebirths of existence within the form realm. Tsong kha pa (*Stairway* 304) divides the *Ūrdhvaṃsrotas* into two primary categories: the transmigrator up to the limit of *Akaniṣṭha* heaven and the transmigrator up to the limit of the Peak of Existence, *Bhavāgra*. If it is an *Ūrdhvaṃsrotas* who has the possibility of transmigrating to the limit of the realm of form, then that Non-returner is called an *Akaniṣṭhaga*. If the Non-returner has the potential to travel up to the edge of the formless realm, then it is a *Bhavāgraparamaga*. The *Golden Garland* (236) also classifies an *Ūrdhvaṃsrotas* by means of cause, alternating or not alternating concentrations and an *Ūrdhvaṃsrotas* by means of result, transmigrating up to *Akaniṣṭha* heaven or to *Bhavāgra*. I will explain the process of "alternating concentrations" below. I note that each general type of *Ūrdhvaṃsrotas* has the "potential" to transmigrate up to its respective realms, similar to the situation of the *Saptakṛtvaparama* not taking seven rebirths, since they do not necessarily go up to those realms to achieve emancipation.

Since these Non-returners progress through the form realm, we should quickly review Buddhist form realm (*rūpadhātu*) cosmology. The form realm has seventeen divisions that are divided into four main areas, correlated in ascending order with the levels of concentration (*dhyāna*). The first concentration marks the beginning of the form realm and is composed of three abodes. The first is the *Brahmakāyika*; the second, *Brahmapurohita*; and the third, *Mahābrahma*. The second concentration has three abodes. They are, in ascending order, called *Parīttābhā*, *Apramāṇābhā*, and *Ābhāsvara*. The third concentration also has three abodes, which are, in ascending order, *Parīttaśubha*, *Apramāṇaśubha*, and *Śubhakṛtsna*. The last main area of the form realm is equal to the fourth concentration and consists of eight heavens with the first three called, in ascending order, *Anabhraka*, *Puṇyaprasava*, and *Bṛhatphala*. The remaining five abodes of the fourth concentration are collectively known as *Śuddhāvāsakāyika*. It consists of the heavens *Abṛha*, *Atapas*, *Sudṛśa*, *Sudarśana*, and finally *Akaniṣṭha* (see the chart in chapter 3, table3.6). With these form levels in mind, we can now see how Tsong kha pa defines the various divisions of the *Ūrdhvaṃsrotas* called *Akaniṣṭhaga*.

The *Stairway* (304) follows the AKBh in defining the transmigrator up to the limit of *Akaniṣṭha* heaven: "That is the *Ūrdhvaṃsrotas* who possesses the lineage of obtaining *nirvāṇa* in an embodiment of *Akaniṣṭha* heaven. For that there are three types: the jumper (*pluta*), half-jumper (*ardhapluta*), and the jumper who dies in all places (*sarvasthānacyuta*)."[48]

Tsong kha pa explains in the *Stairway* that a jumper (*pluta*) is a transmigrator to the limit of *Akaniṣṭha* heaven who, having been born in *Brahmakāyika* heaven, has the characteristic of shifting to a embodiment of *Akaniṣṭha* heaven by jumping over all other form realm heavens in between the first heaven of *Brahmakāyika* and the last form realm heaven of *Akaniṣṭha*. The half-jumper (*ardhapluta*) is a transmigrator up to the limit of *Akaniṣṭha* heaven who has the characteristic of obtaining *nirvāṇa* in *Akaniṣṭha* heaven through jumping over rebirth in the *Brahmakāyika* heaven up to the interval for rebirth in the first three *Śuddhāvāsa* realms. The jumper who dies in all abodes (*sarvasthānacyuta*) is a transmigrator to the limit of *Akaniṣṭha* heaven who transmigrates through all abodes in the form realm, not counting *Mahābrahma* heaven, in order to obtain *nirvāṇa* in an embodiment of *Akaniṣṭha* heaven (*Stairway* 304). Tsong kha pa (*Golden Garland* 236) cites the AKBh as to why Noble Beings (*ārya)* are not born in *Mahābrahma* heaven: "A [*śrāvaka*] *ārya* is not reborn among the *Mahābrahma*s because this heaven is a place of [wrong] view: [one considers *Mahābrahma* as the creator there]; and because only one leader can be found there: an *ārya* would be superior to *Mahābrahma* there."[49]

In both the *Stairway* (305) and *Golden Garland* (236), Tsong kha pa notes that these three jumpers first have had a desire realm embodiment that generates the cause of rebirth in the *Śuddhāvāsa* heavens, the cultivation that alternates the fourth level of concentration. Through falling from the three later concentrations, one experiences the first concentration and as a result takes rebirth in *Brahmakāyika*. At this point, through the force of previous familiarization with alternation of the fourth concentration, one passes over either, all, some, or none of the heavenly realms in between, takes rebirth in *Akaniṣṭha* heaven, and achieves emancipation. Practicing the alternating cultivations of the fourth concentration is a cause to be reborn in the *Śuddhāvāsa* heavens. With regard to the latter two jumpers, Tsong kha pa states that one takes rebirth in the upper levels from *Brahmakāyika* heaven up to the *Bṛhatphala* heaven in an upper realm embodiment, having generated the higher absorption, and then, having generated the alternation of cultivation in a *Bṛhatphala* heaven embodiment, one is reborn successively in the *Śuddhāvāsa* heavens.

The discussion of these types of Non-returners begs the question, What is alternating cultivations (*spel ma bsgom pa, vyavakīrṇabhāvanā*)? Alternating cultivations is a meditative technique that consists of mixing contaminated and uncontaminated moments of concentration that causes rebirth in the *Śuddhāvāsa* heavens. In both the *Stairway* (306–10) and *Golden Garland* (236–39), Tsong kha pa utilizes the discussion from the AKBh (on vi.42a–43b) to explain this meditative technique. We will give a brief summary of alternating cultivations based on Tsong kha pa's exegesis.

This meditative technique of mixing contaminated and uncontaminated moments of concentration is only cultivated by the Non-returner and liberated in two ways (*Ubhayatogbhāgavimutka*) *Arhat*. The reason is that since it is necessary to alternate with uncontaminated concentration, the cultivation that is necessary for the Noble Being (*ārya*) is unable to be cultivated by the Stream-enterer and Once-returner because they do not obtain an actual concentration. Non-returners with sharp faculties cultivate the technique of alternating concentrations for the sake of birth in the *Śuddhāvāsakāyika* heavens and for the sake of abiding in bliss for this life. Alternating concentrations is necessary for the Non-returners with weak faculties so that they may not backslide from a result, generate more afflictions, or take rebirth in the formless realms. *Arhat*s with sharp and weak faculties cultivate for the sake of abiding in bliss for this life and for the sake of abandoning degeneration through fear of the afflictions. Tsong kha pa considers the *Vaibhāṣika*s to accept the degeneration of the *Arhat*'s immovable liberation. However, Tsong kha pa does not accept this type of *Arhat* degeneration and the cultivations are not necessary for the *Arhat* for this reason. We will discuss specifics regarding the *Arhat* in the next section.

One first cultivates this technique in a desire realm embodiment and then later cultivates it in a form realm embodiment. The first period of alternation is only in the fourth concentration since there is an equilibrium of calming and special insight, making this level the most suitable from among all meditative stabilizations. Later on one can make alternation with other levels of concentration.

Tsong kha pa states that the grounds for achievement in this meditative technique are based on the moments in which one mixes or alternates the contaminated and uncontaminated moments. This is based on the *Abhidharmakośa*, which states: "Achievement is by a combination in moments."[50] Tsong kha pa also defines the achievement of alternation from the *Abhidharmakośabhāṣya*: "With the exception of a Buddha, it is impossible to alternate [thoughts] in a single moment, because of that, [alternation of concentrations] is achieved by means of entering, for as long as one wants into three continuous [concentrations]."[51]

In this manner, first having alternated the fourth concentration, one also alternates other concentrations. The actual alternation is the result, the cause of birth in the five *Śuddhāvāsa* heavens, which has five alternating cultivations—that is, from alternating three thoughts up to alternating fifteen thoughts. What is the manner of these alternations? First one alternates three weak thoughts. After that, one alternates six medium thoughts, alternates nine strong, alternates twelve stronger, and then fifteen strongest. Tsong kha pa follows Yaśomitra in the manner of how alternated moments are mixed. For instance, to say that one alternates six thoughts, one enumerates as follows: one counts the three moments as uncontaminated, contaminated, and uncontaminated, and again three moments as uncontaminated, contaminated, and uncontaminated. This manner of counting applies to nine, twelve, and fifteen moments also.

In regard to this alternation, the cause of rebirth in the *Śuddhāvāsa*s is contaminated thought, since uncontaminated thought cuts off existence. The *Golden Garland* (239) notes that the contaminated aspect of the alternating concentration is the mundane cultivation that focuses on comparing the peacefulness and grossness between the upper and lower realms. This contaminated aspect is a pure mundane virtue. It is a path of liberation from the lower realms because a contaminated fundamental threshold is contradictory as being a path of abandonment. Any Non-returner who takes rebirth within the *Śuddhāvāsa* heavens must practice the technique of alternating cultivations to be born there.

Along with the transmigrator up to the limit of *Akaniṣṭha* heaven, the other category of the *Ūrdhvaṃsrotas* is the transmigrator up to the limit of the *Bhavāgra*, the *Bhavāgraparamaga*. The *Stairway* (310) defines this Non-returner:

> An *Ūrdhvaṃsrotas* who, from *Brahmakāyika* heaven, not counting *Mahābrahma* heaven, is connected in all [heavens] up to the *Bṛhatphala* heaven, from that, having gone gradually in the four formless [realms], possesses the lineage of obtaining *nirvāṇa* in an embodiment of the Peak of Existence (*Bhavāgra*).

The *Golden Garland* (239) states that one who transmigrates to *Bhavāgra*, although not definitely transmigrating up to *Bhavāgra*, is necessarily thought to be emancipated in a formless realm embodiment. Tsong kha pa considers that the *Bhavāgraga*, although not counted as one of the nine Non-returner transmigrators who achieve emancipation in the form realm, is actually a transmigrator in the form realm. He states that the meaning is not that the *Bhavāgraga* achieves emancipation in a form realm embodiment, but that it was caused to be born there on account of desire.

Tsong kha pa notes that the above presentation of the first two Jumpers (i.e., *Pluta* and *Ardhapluta*), along with the *Bhavāgraparamaga* and *Akaniṣṭhaga* derived from the third Jumper, is difficult to determine. This is because there are not any *sūtra*s that support the defining characteristics of these individuals. Tsong kha pa casts the blame on the *Vaibhāṣika*s for not stating the *sūtra*s that support the *Abhidharma* interpretation. However, he notes (*Stairway* 312) that in the *Abhisamayālaṃkāra*, the source *sūtra*s are also not taught. Nevertheless, Tsong kha pa bases his articulation of the Non-returners who transmigrate in the form realm on the *Saptasatpuruṣagatīsūtra,* from which the *Vaibhāṣika*s enumerate a single *Ūrdhvaṃsrotas* and from which Asaṅga, as a follower of that *sūtra,* arranges the Jumpers and *Ūrdhvaṃsrotas.* Tsong kha pa therefore sees a coherent arrangement of these Non-returners, based on the *Abhidharmakośa* and the *Abhidharmasamuccaya,* although neither one of these *śāstra*s gives scriptural reference for the subdivisions they provide.

At the end of the discussion of form realm Non-returners, Tsong kha pa addresses how many types of Non-returners are possible. He does this through the example of counting the number of possible *Antarāparinirvāyin*s and then applying it to other form realm Non-returners. Tsong kha pa's calculation is as follows. The *Antarāparinirvāyin* can pass through any of the sixteen intermediate states of the form realm and can be divided by means of lineage (*gotra*),[52] separation from attachment (*vairāgya*), and faculty (*indriya*). The lineage consist of six different types, consonant with that of the six different *Arhat*s (discussed below): these are, the lineages of the *Parihāṇadharman, Cetanādharman, Anurakṣaṇadharman, Sthitākampya, Prativedhanādharman,* and an *Akopyadharman.* Each of the six lineages, the *Antarāparinirvāyin* of the first concentration, from the one bound by all bonds in not abandoning the nine obstacles to be removed by the paths of cultivation of the first concentration up to the one abandoning the eight abandonments to be removed by the path of cultivation, has nine aspects. In similar fashion, for the three later concentrations there are nine and nine times six groups making fifty-four. These fifty-four times the number of form realm heavens (sixteen) will make eight hundred sixty-four. Then, by dividing the *Antarāparinirvāyin* into three kinds of faculty—dull (*mṛdu*), moderate (*madhya*), and sharp (*adhimātra*): three times eight hundred sixty-four makes two thousand five hundred and ninety-two *Antarāparinirvāyin* Non-returners. This manner of calculation also applies to the three types of *Upapadyaparinirvāyin*s and the *Ūrdhvaṃsrotas.* Therefore, five types of Non-returners each have the possibility of two thousand five hundred and ninety-two to make twelve thousand nine hundred sixty types of Non-returners who transmigrate in the form realm.[53] Tsong kha pa gives the following verse as a summary of the Non-returners in the form realm (see Figure 4.1): "The transmigrator in the realm of form has ten aspects, divisions in the desire realm embodiment and the five alternating cultivations causing rebirth in the *Śuddhāvāsa*s, explained to the intention of the masters [Asaṅga and Vasubandhu]."

Other types of Non-returners. Along with the Non-returners who transmigrate in the form realm, Tsong kha pa enumerates other types of

Figure 4.1 Ten Aspects of the Form Realm Transmigrator

Antāraparinirvāyin (One achieves *nirvāṇa* in the intermediate state)
(1) *Āśuparinirvāyin* (Immediately in the intermediate state)
(2) *Anāśuparinirvāyin* (Not immediately in the intermediate state)
(3) *Ciraparinirvāyin* (After a long time)
Upapadyaparinirvāyin (One who achieves *nirvāṇa* through birth)
(4) *Abhisaṃskāraparinirvāyin* (One who achieves through effort)
(5) *Anabhisaṃskāraparinirvāyin* (One who achieves without effort)
(6) *Upapadyaparinirvāyin* (One who achieves through rebirth)
Ūrdhvaṃsrotas (One who goes higher)
Akaniṣṭhaga ([Non-returner] who goes up to *Akaniṣṭha*)
(7) *Pluta* (Jumper)
(8) *Ardhapluta* (Half-jumper)
(9) *Sarvasthānacyuta* (One who dies in all abodes)
(10) *Bhavāgraparamaga* (One who may go up Peak of Existence)

Non-returners that either progress in the formless realm (*ārūpyadhātu*) or in the desire realm (*kāmadhātu*). Tsong kha pa explains in the *Golden Garland* (224) the *śrāvaka* who transmigrates in the formless realm: "[A Non-returner in the formless realm,] having the force of exhausting the fetter of the form realm, does not transmigrate in the form realm, and takes rebirth in the formless realm."

Tsong kha pa notes that since a rebirth in the formless realm lacks an intermediate state, there are only four types of these Non-returners: One who is emancipated from mere rebirth *(Upapadyaparinirvāyin)*, one who is emancipated with effort (*Abhisaṃskāraparinirvāyin*), one emancipated without effort (*Anabhisaṃskāraparinirvāyin*), and the one who goes higher (*Ūrdhvaṃsrotas*). Tsong kha pa states that the definitions of these Non-returners resemble the corresponding definitions given for transmigrators in the form realm, except that these Non-returners progress through the four levels of the formless realm. However, Tsong kha pa (*Stairway* 317) notes that some scholars believe that one should not count the *Ūrdhvaṃsrotas* and the three jumpers among the formless realm Non-returners. This is because there are no scriptural citations for supporting these types of formless realm Non-returners and their meaning cannot be determined through reasoning because there is not a formless realm heaven in which to count the half-jumper.

Tsong kha pa enumerates Non-returners that progress in the desire realm according to the third category he gives for Non-returners as those that obtain peace in this very existence (*Dṛṣṭadharmaparinirvāyin*) and as well as the fourth category of the one who witnesses with the body (*Kāyasākṣin*) (see table 4.6). The *Golden Garland* (235) explains that one who achieves nirvāṇa in the desire embodiment itself (*'dod pa'i rten de nyid la 'da' ba*) is, in general, a Non-returner who obtains peace in this very existence (*Dṛṣṭadharmaparinirvāyin*) and a *Kāyasākṣin* is one who has not degenerated from the attainment of cessation (*nirodhasamāpatti*) with the body.

A *Dṛṣṭadharmaparinirvāyin* is characterized as actualizing *nirvāṇa* at the time of attaining the path of seeing (*mthong lam*). A *Dṛṣṭadharmaparinirvāyin* is a type of Non-returner that obtains *nirvāṇa* in the very embodiment in which one obtained the Non-returner state. The *Golden Garland* (242) mentions that this Non-returner does not take rebirth in the upper realms and also does not take rebirth in the desire realm. In the brief discussion of this type of Non-returner, Tsong kha pa (*Stairway* 317) mentions that the *Dṛṣṭadharmaparinirvāyin* attains the state of *Arhat* in an embodiment that first has already obtained the result of Stream-enterer or Once-returner.

Tsong kha pa classifies a Non-returner who obtains cessation into three types: one who during this life does not fall from the attainment of cessation, one who having fallen away from the attainment of cessation is reborn in the form realm and attains *nirvāṇa* there, and one who, having been reborn in the form realm, generates the attainment of cessation, and then having died, passes to the Peak of Existence (*Bhavāgra*). The first is the bodily witness who pacifies in the present life (*mthong chos zhi'i lus mngon byed*). The second is a Non-returner who has restored their attainment after backsliding while abiding in a desire realm embodiment and becomes a transmigrator to the form realm (*gzugs su nyer 'gro, rupagaḥ*) but is not a bodily witness. The third type is a Non-returner who, having generated the attainment of cessation in the embodiment that is reborn in the form realm, at that time, having died, actualizes *nirvāṇa* in the formless realm and is thought of as being a bodily witness (*Kāyasākṣin*).

Tsong kha pa also defines the Non-returner who witnesses with the body (*Kāyasākṣin*) directly from the *Abhidharmasamuccaya*: "Who is the bodily witness? One in the course of training who concentrates on the eight liberations."[54]

Tsong kha pa therefore accepts the definition of a bodily witness as the Non-returner who is able to enter into absorption of the eight liberations.[55] In the discussion on the *bodhisattva saṃgha*, the *Golden Garland* (1970: 260) describes the *śrāvaka kāyasākṣī*:

> When the [Noble Being] emerges from the absorption of cessation, from the moment when thinking, "This cessation is calm like *nirvāṇa*," a calmness of the afflicted body which has consciousness is obtained that was never previously acquired. In this way one directly witnesses by the body [the calmness of extinction].[56]

Tsong kha pa considers the *Kāyasākṣī* to be unsuitable as a Non-returner who has terminated rebirth in the desire realm (*parivṛttajanmā anāgāmin*). This is because for the one who has terminated rebirth in the desire realm, transmigration in the upper realms does not exist. Tsong kha pa bases this assertion on statements from the *Abhidharma-kośabhāṣya* and *Abhidharmakośa* that a Noble Being (*ārya*) who terminates rebirth (*parivṛttajanma*) in the desire realm does not transmigrate to another realm. A Noble Being who terminates other rebirths in the desire realm does not transmigrate to another realm because in that birth itself, having obtained the result of Non-returner, one achieves *parinirvāṇa*.[57] Tsong kha pa defines the Non-returner who terminates rebirth in the desire realm based on the *Abhidharmakośabhāṣyavyākhyā*: "A Non-returner who terminates rebirth is one that in the first birth, having obtained the result of Stream-enterer or the result of Once-returner, in the second birth becomes a Non-returner."[58]

Therefore, for Tsong kha pa, a *Dṛṣṭadharmaparinirvāyin* may also be classified as a Non-returner who terminates rebirth based on whether or not they have previously achieved the state of Stream-enterer or Once-returner.

Arhats. The fourth division of those who progress gradually in the results of *śrāmaṇya* is the state of *Arhat*. It is important to keep in mind that the *Arhat*s discussed here belong to the *śrāvaka* vehicle and are primarily seeking emancipation from suffering through realizing the sixteen aspects of the Nobles' Four Truths.

In the *Stairway* (321), the *Arhat* enterer is considered to be synonymous with the distinctive Non-returner abider whom we have just discussed in the previous section. The *Golden Garland* (242) states that an *Arhat* enterer is "an abider in the result of Non-returner who makes effort to abandon the first defilement to be abandoned by the path of cultivation of the form realm up to making effort to abandon the ninth defilement of the peak of existence." Tsong kha pa follows the *Abhidharmasamuccaya* in defining the abider in the result of *Arhat*: "The lesser vehicle person who abandons all nine afflictions of the Peak of Existence."[59]

Tsong kha pa divides *Arhat*s by means of several different classifications. *Arhat*s classified according to how they abandon defilements are two: the *Prajñāvimukta* and the *Ubhayatobhāgavimukta*. *Arhat*s classified according to whether they fall or do not fall away from abiding in the bliss of concentration are six:[60] *Parihāṇadharman* (one who can fall away), *Cetanādharman* (one who can put an end to his worldly existence), *Anurakṣaṇadharman* (one who can protect himself), *Sthitākampya* (one who firmly holds his ground and is unshakable), *Prativedhanādharman* (one who can penetrate at will), and an

Akopyadharman (one who is immovable). When classified by means of faculty, there are two types of *Arhat*s: an *Arhat* who is liberated dependent upon particular occasions (*samayavimukta*) and an *Arhat* who is liberated regardless of occasion (*asamayavimukta*).

Regarding these classifications, Tsong kha pa considers that *Arhat*s who are not able to enter the meditative absorption on the eight liberations are called *Prajñāvimukta*[61] (liberated by wisdom), because they do not abandon obscurations through entering absorption but are liberated from obscurational afflictions by the wisdom that cognizes selflessness. Those able to enter the meditative absorption on the eight liberations are *Ubhayatobhāgavimukta*,[62] because they are liberated from both the obscuration of entering absorption and the obscurations of the afflictions (*Stairway* 321).

Tsong kha pa states that of the classification consisting of six divisions, the first five *Arhat*s are without distinction and have dull faculties. The characteristics of these *Arhat*s are to be divided by whether or not they degenerate from abiding in bliss of body and mind in this life by the meditative stabilization of mundane concentration. Tsong kha pa explains each of these first five *Arhat*s by means of their name. So, a dull faculty *Arhat* that is a *Parihāṇadharman* (one who can fall away), when differentiated by gratification of the senses, definitely degenerates from concentration or does not fall away if not gratified through the senses. The *Cetanādharman* is one who can put an end to his existence; if not putting an end to the mental continuum by oneself, the *Arhat* degenerates and if putting an end to the mental continuum by oneself, the *Arhat* does not continuously degenerate. Likewise, an *Anurakṣaṇadharman* is one who can protect himself; if protecting the mind from sensual gratification, the *Arhat* does not degenerate, and if not increasingly protecting the mind, the *Arhat* degenerates. These *Arhats*, successively from the *Parihāṇadharman* up to the *Prativedhanādharman*, may change from dull to sharp faculties. In this case, Tsong kha pa states that whether or not one protects from sensual gratification, there is an *Arhat* for whom it is not possible to degenerate and not change from dull to sharp faculties, the *Akopyadharman*. Tsong kha pa cites the *Abhidharmasamuccaya*: "Who is the *Akopyadharman*? This is one who has by nature sharp faculties, distracted or not, reflective or not, does not possess the fortune of falling from abiding in bliss for the present life."[63]

Thus, Tsong kha pa classifies these six types of *Arhat*s based on whether they have sharp or dull faculties. Tsong kha pa states that the *Parihāṇadharman* and so forth can be located in the realm of desire. The *Sthitākampya* and the *Akopyadharman* can be located in the form and formless realms because these realms are without degeneration, volitional thought, and the ability to change faculties.

According to Tsong kha pa, the *Vaibhāṣika*s assert the first five *Arhat*s to exist as Stream-enterers when degenerating from the state of *Arhat*. The *Sautrāntika*s, on the other hand, assert that it is not possible to degenerate from the state of *Arhat* and that the *Arhat* degenerates from merely abiding in bliss for the present life.

Tsong kha pa has an extended discussion in the *Stairway* (326–35) in which he demonstrates the arguments and scriptural citations that the *Vaibhāṣika*s utilize to prove that one may degenerate from the state of *Arhat*. The *Vaibhāṣika*s assert that each one of these six *Arhat*s are distinguished from each other according to whether their faculties, lineage, or practice degenerates. The distinction of faculty is that the first five go previously aspiring by faith and have dull faculties and the sixth obtains by seeing and has sharp faculties. The distinction of lineage is based on the individual who abides in the lineage from the beginning or the individual who although not in a lineage from the beginning changes lineages later. The first kind is the sharp faculty *Akopyadharman* and the second kind is for the later five lineages.

Tsong kha pa also states that the *Vaibhāṣika* position is that one cannot degenerate from a first result, one obtained either by gradual progress (i.e., a Stream-enterer) or one obtained by skipping fruitions (i.e., the results of Once-returner or Non-returner), although one may fall away from the result of *Arhat*. This is because the abandonment of the first three fruitions is made firm by both a mundane and supermundane path. In regard to the gradual progressor, the *Vaibhāṣika* holds that they will degenerate from the result of *Arhat* and turn into a Non-returner by producing in the continuum the upper realm afflictions. The *Arhat* will turn into a Once-returner by producing the upper seven desire realm afflictions, and will turn into a Stream-enterer by producing the lower six desire realm afflictions. However, *Vaibhāṣika*s posit that it is not possible to degenerate from the result of Stream-enterer or either of the skipper results. The abandonments of the Stream-enterer are irreversible since the obstacles to be abandoned by the path of seeing, the root of the false view of the imaginary self (*ātmadarśana*), is removed by a Noble Being because of directly perceiving the selflessness of the imaginary self and therefore does not produce the afflictions from the view of the self. On the other hand, the basis of the obstacles to be removed by the path of cultivation, desire and anger, may reoccur. Tsong kha pa (*Stairway* 329-31) shows that the *Vaibhāṣika*s rely on four scriptural sources to assert the possibility of degenerating from the state of *Arhat*. These are found in the AKBh and the AKV. The first has to do with five conditions that may hinder an *Arhat*. The second concerns the *Arhat* being interrupted by fame and fortune. The third scriptural source is the *Aṅgārakarṣūpama Sūtra* (= SN i.120) in which the Venerable Gautika (Godhika) kills himself. The fourth concerns the eight powers of the monk who is an *Arhat*. Through quoting their interpretation of the principles given in these *sūtras*, Tsong kha pa demonstrates that the *Vaibhāṣikas* propose there to be a possibility of degenerating from the state of *Arhat*.

Tsong kha pa counters each of the arguments and meticulously examines the scriptural citations quoted by the *Vaibhāṣikas* to demonstrate that it is not possible to degenerate from the state of *Arhat*. Tsong kha pa asserts that if an *Arhat* does degenerate, it is merely degenerating from abiding in bliss for the present life. Tsong kha pa follows the statements in the *Abhidharmakośabhāṣyavyākhyā*:

> Not only is there no degeneration by abandoning that to be abandoned by the path of seeing, but there is also no degeneration from [the result of] *Arhat* itself. Not from the first [result], but there is falling from the result of Once-returner and Non-returner because those attainments can occur by a mundane path. That is the intended meaning.[64]

Tsong kha pa explains (*Stairway* 331) that for Vasubandhu both the first and last result do not degenerate because they are obtained only from a supermundane path. However, it is possible to fall away from the two middle fruitions since the Noble Being may obtain them by a mundane path, and the abandonment by a mundane path is reversible. Tsong kha pa (*Stairway* 332) also demonstrates, through quoting the *Pramāṇavārttika* of Dharmakīrti, that since the abandonment of the Buddha is irreversible and complete, a Buddha is superior to outsiders (*bāhya*), Buddhist trainees (*śaikṣa*), and those Buddhists beyond training (*aśaikṣa*). Tsong kha pa understands this to implicitly show that the defilements abandoned by a Noble trainee (*āryaśaikṣa*) may reoccur but not the defilements abandoned by an *Arhat*.

Tsong kha pa cites this scriptural statement for the nondegeneration from the state of *Arhat*: "In this way Monks, abandonment is abandonment through *āryan* wisdom."[65]

Tsong kha pa considers the abandonment mentioned in this *sūtra* to be definite abandonment since *ārya* wisdom does not allow for the possibility of afflictions regenerating. Tsong kha pa also states that it is taught that "a *śaikṣa* should cultivate vigilance"[66] but that the Buddha did not state that the *Arhat* should cultivate vigilance. In other words, a *śaikṣa* must still observe training but an *Arhat* no longer needs to train in abandoning defilements. Tsong kha pa holds that the *Abhidharma* teaches the collection of three causes and conditions that generate the latent defilements of the desire realm: the latent defilement (*anuśaya*) of sensual desire that has not been completely known and has not been abandoned, the qualities that appear favorable to the increase of sensual desire, and erroneous judgment.[67] Since an *Arhat* abandons all latent defilements, it cannot fulfill the three causes of generating these defilements. Tsong kha pa argues that since an *Arhat* produces meditative antidotes that do not generate the seed of afflictions, how can it degenerate? If an *Arhat* does not eradicate the seed of afflictions, how can an *Arhat* be called a *"kṣīṇāsrava,"* one who exhausts (*kṣīṇa*) the vices (*āsrava*). Therefore, Tsong kha pa surmises that there is no degenerating from the state of *Arhat*.[68]

What about the intention of those *sūtra*s cited by the *Vaibhāṣika*s? For Tsong kha pa, these *sūtra*s refer to occasional degeneration, and the meaning of the *sūtra*s in this instance is to degenerate from the meditative stabilization of the fourth concentration. Tsong kha pa notes that one *sūtra* (see *Stairway* 329.4) states that "a degeneration from the four concentrations that arise from superior intellect" may occur. In regard to the third *sūtra*, the *Aṅgārakarṣūpamasūtra*, Tsong kha pa states that Gautika kills himself, having repeatedly degenerated from meditative stabilization; he does not kill himself having repeatedly degenerated from the state of *Arhat*. Gautika, although having experienced concentration at the time of training, because of weak faculties, has repeatedly degenerated from concentration and from disgust stabs himself with a dagger. At the moment of death, he attains the state of *Arhat* and achieves *nirvāṇa*. Finally, Tsong kha pa demonstrates that the meaning of the fourth *sūtra* applies to the qualities of Noble trainees (*śaikṣa*) not *Arhat*s. The quality of the *Arhat* has the distinction of having qualities that are preeminent (Skt. *prakarṣa*).[69] At the conclusion of these arguments in the *Stairway* (334), Tsong kha pa states:

> The Second Buddha [*Vasubandhu*] extensively explained the refutations eloquently with reasoning and scripture of the bad ideas of the *Vaibhāṣika*s who say, "the *Arhat* reverses abandonment." Fearing it would be too prolific, I have not extensively presented the proofs of the refutations. Have no doubt though, for I have properly explained the intentions of the *Abhidharmakośabhāṣya* and *Bhāṣyavyākhyā*.

Tsong kha pa finally discusses the *Arhat* from the point of view of whether it is occasionally delivered (*samayavimukta*)[70] and not-occasionally delivered (*asamayavimukta*).[71] The first five lineages of *Arhat*s are considered to have the possibility of degenerating from meditative concentration because it is possible to fall away at a certain occasion that abandons liberation. The sixth lineage of *Arhat* is not possible to fall away because there is not an occasion for which it will degenerate. Tsong kha pa follows the *Abhidharmakośabhāṣya*[72] in interpreting the statement "the *Arhat* who is liberated occasionally" to refer to one who, because of weak faculties, will be directly facing meditative stabilization with respect to time. The opposite is called liberation that is not connected with time.

Tsong kha pa concludes this section on *Arhat*s by stating that these *Arhat*s that have been explained above are also classified as the "nine *aśaikṣas*," the nine Noble Beings who are no longer subject to training on the *śrāvaka* path. Tsong kha pa cites a *sūtra* from the AKV: "Who are the nine *aśaikṣas*? The *Parihāṇadharman, Aparihāṇadharman, Cetanādharman,* up to the *Akopyadharman, Prajñāvimukta,* and *Ubhayatobhāgavimukta,* these are called the nine *aśaikṣas*.[73]

Those who skip fruitions. Besides those Noble Beings who actualize through progressive fruition and abandon defilements by progressive abandonment—that is, gradual progressors (*ānupūrvaka*), Tsong kha pa also classifies Noble Beings (*ārya*) of the *saṃgha illustration* into those who skip fruitions (*thod rgal, vyutkrāntika*) and those who simultaneously abandon defilements (*cig car pa, sakṛnnairyāṇika*). In regard to this classification, as we mentioned earlier in the chapter, there are two that either gradually obtain or skip over in obtaining fruitions and two that, either gradually or simultaneously, abandon defilements. Tsong kha pa states in the *Stairway* (338) that one who skips fruitions is not in contradiction to those who gradually abandon defilements, but those who gradually progress in fruition are definitely contradictory to be simultaneous abandoners.

As we mentioned earlier, those who skip fruitions (*thod rgal pa*) are individuals who remove defilements to be abandoned by the path of cultivation by a mundane path before reaching the path of seeing. At the moment of reaching the sixteenth moment of the path of seeing, they "skip over" lower results based on the number of defilements removed previously by a mundane path of cultivation (*laukikabhāvanāmārga*). The classification of fruition skipper applies only for the four enterers and abiders of the two middle fruitions. A fruition skipper is characterized as skipping over former results at the time of first obtaining the sixteenth moment, and there is not a former result for the result of Stream-enterer to skip over. Also, the result of *Arhat* is unable to be obtained at the time of the sixteenth moment of the path of seeing because one cannot abandon the path-of-cultivation abandonments of the Peak of Existence previous to the path of seeing and because one on the path of seeing is unable to abandon those path-of-cultivation defilements. Tsong kha pa mentions in the *Golden Garland* (225) that the term *skipper* (*thod rgal*) is construed to be consonant with the terms *Bhūyovītarāga* and *Kāmavītarāga* found in the AKBh. These fruition skippers, although skipping over results, are regarded as gradual progressors in the fruit. Tsong kha pa notes that the AKBh in stating that even though there are from a nominal standpoint eight Noble Beings (four enterers and four abiders), essentially there are only five. The *Abhidharmakośabhāṣya* states: "In actuality there are five aspects, the first enterer and four abiders in the result because the remaining enterers are not differentiated from the three abiders in the result. It is explained thus because of obtaining by gradual progression."[74]

In this manner of counting, the enterers to the three later results—Once-returner, Non-returner, and *Arhat*—are not regarded as categorically different from the first three abiders in the results of Stream-enterer, Once-returner, and Non-returner and are in substance set forth as five construed through the domain of gradual progression. These five are the Stream-enterer enterer and the four abiders in the result. Tsong kha pa (*Stairway* 340) states that although this method of counting is in agreement with the system of gradual progression, if a Noble Being is a fruition skipper, an enterer to a later result is not certain to be an abider in a former result. For example, the results of the fruition skipper Once-returner enterer and Non-returner enterer are not definitely considered to be Stream-enterers or Once-returners. The AKBh states in this regard: "The *Bhūyovītarāga*s and *Kāmavītarāga*s are, in the path of seeing, enterers to the fruit of Once-returner and Non-returner but also are not [necessarily] Stream-enterers or Once-returners."[75]

Tsong kha pa construes a classification scheme based on this statement along with implicitly reading into the following statement of Yaśomitra in the *Abhidharmakośabhāṣyavyākhyā*:

> That being the case, in actuality there are seven: the three enterers to the results of Stream-enterer, Once-returner, and Non-returner and the four abiders in the result. However, one should realize that one [of the eight,] the enterer to the result of *Arhat*, is not different from the result of Non-returner.[76]

Tsong kha pa notes here that the gradual progressor (*ānupūrvaka*) in substance is five, but along with that we have two fruition skipper enterers—that is, enterers to the results of Once-returner (*Bhūyovītarāga)* and Non-returner (*Kāmavītarāga)*—who are different from the abiders in the result and, if including these, there will be essentially seven Noble individuals who enter and abide in the results of *śrāmaṇya*. This list of seven is enumerated by counting a single enterer to the first result in the period of the gradual progressor along with the two skipper fruition enterers to make three individuals who enter into the first three fruitions and then adding the four abiders in a result. Tsong kha pa states that the enterer to the result of *Arhat* is only a gradual progressor and that undifferentiated from the Non-returner means the state that is let go of before attaining *Arhat*ship. The following list depicts how Tsong kha pa enumerates essentially seven Noble Beings.

TSONG KHA PA'S ENUMERATION OF ESSENTIALLY SEVEN NOBLE BEINGS

1. Stream-enterer enterer (*srota-āpanna pratipannaka*) [*ānupūrvaka*]
2. Once-returner enterer [skipper] (*bhūyovītarāga*)
3. Non-returner enterer [skipper] (*kāmavītarāga*)
4. Stream-enterer abider (*srota-āpannaphalasthā*) [*ānupūrvaka*]
5. Once-returner abider (*sakṛdāgāminphalasthā*) [*ānupūrvaka*]
6. Non-returner abider (*anāgāminphalasthā*) [*ānupūrvaka*]
7. *Arhat*

The *Stairway* (340) states that all sections of the *Abhidharma* concerning the fruition skipper mention only two: those separated from attachment to a great extent (*bhūyovītarāga; phal cher las 'dod chags dang bral pa*), consonant with the Once-returner, and those who have previously separated from desire-realm attachment (*kāmavītarāga; 'dod pa las 'dod chags dang bral pa*), consonant with the Non-returner. For these two types of fruitions, Tsong kha pa posits both an enterer and abider.

The *Golden Garland* (1970: 229) defines the enterer to the state of Once-returner who skips fruitions:

> [One] who abandons the six defilements of the desire realm to be abandoned by the mundane path of cultivation previous of the path of seeing, although the seventh or eighth defilement may or may not be abandoned, that one does not abandon the ninth [defilement] and abides in whatever suitable [level] from the doctrinal forbearance on suffering up the subsequent forbearance on the [truth of the] path possessing both the quality of realization and the realization of abandonment.

Tsong kha pa notes (*Stairway* 341) that when entering a result, in addition to the abandoning of the path of seeing abandonments, one engages in the abandonment of the path of cultivation abandonments and enters the three later fruitions. If abandoning a single abandonment of the path of seeing, one enters only the result of Stream-enterer. Here, when one abandons six (but does not abandon nine) of the path-of-cultivation abandonments of the desire realm by a mundane path previous to the path of seeing and abides in the first fifteen moments of the path-of-seeing, one is considered an enterer to the Once-returner result. When that individual obtains the sixteenth moment of the path of seeing, having abandoned all path-of-seeing defilements and discards the path of cultivation's sixth abandonment, then that individual first obtains a result and is considered a fruition skipper

Once-returner. The individual skips over the result of Stream-enterer because of obtaining the result of Once-returner.

The *Golden Garland* (229) defines the enterer to the Non-returner fruition skipper as:

> [One] who abandons the ninth defilement of the desire realm to be abandoned by the path of cultivation previous of the path of seeing and [who] possesses, as like the former [enterer], the quality of realization and abandonment from the first concentration, being separated or not separated from attachment, [up] to the realms lower than Nothingness.

The *Stairway* (342) adds that one definitely abandons the nine afflictions of the desire realm by a mundane path previous to the path of seeing and is separated from attachment from the first concentration up to the realm of nothingness. Tsong kha pa states that if abiding on the first fifteen moments of the path of seeing, one is an enterer to the result of Non-returner. Likewise, if abandoning nine defilements by a mundane path of cultivation and then obtaining the sixteenth moment of the path of seeing, one is a Non-returner.

Concerning these skippers, the *Golden Garland* (230) explains that after those abandonments of each one of these enterers who skip fruitions is obtained, at the time of reaching the sixteenth moment, one will be abiding in the result of Once-returner or Non-returner; the previous enterers, dull faculty followers of faith and sharp faculty followers of doctrine, after obtaining the result, will respectively have the conventional name of "One who aspires by faith (*śrāddhādhimukta*)" and "One who obtains by seeing (*dṛṣṭiprāpta*)." Tsong kha pa follows the *Abhidharmakośa*, which states: "In the sixteenth [moment], [whichever enterer becomes] an abider, at that time, those of dull and sharp faculties become respectively 'One who aspirers by faith' and 'One obtains by seeing.' "[77]

When one is called "Once-returner" through skipping fruitions and abandons the sixth defilement on the sixteenth moment of the path of seeing, one is not yet considered an enterer to the result of Non-returner. Tsong kha pa states that if at the sixteenth moment, one abides in a mere result but does not enter to a path that causes a higher result, one is not called "an enterer to later fruitions." This also applies to the case of the Non-returner result. The *Abhidharmakośa* remarks in this regard: "At the moment of obtaining a result, a path of a higher result is not obtained, therefore, the abider in a result does not make effort for and is not an enterer to a superior result."[78]

The category of the fruition skippers is important because it allows for the inclusion of non-Buddhist meditative practices by crediting mundane meditative stabilization with some soteriological value.

However, a fruition skipper still must pass through the sixteen moments of the Buddhist path of seeing and the previously established mundane meditative experience; whether propeling one to the result of Once-returner or Non-returner, these attainments are subject to degeneration. This category is also important in that the system of skipping fruitions is established only in the *Abhidharmakośa* and its commentaries. In the section on the *actual bodhisattva saṃgha,* we will see how this system from the *Abhidharmakośa* affects the interpretation of the *Abhisamayālaṃkāra* verses, as opposed to an interpretation based strictly on the *Abhidharmasamuccaya.*

The simultaneous abandoner. The final classification of the *saṃgha illustration* that Tsong kha pa employs is the distinction of simultaneous abandoner (*sakṛtprahāṇaka; spang bya cig car ba*). This class of Noble Beings is found only in the exegesis of the *saṃgha illustration* and is completely based on a statement from the *Abhidharmasamuccaya.* In regard to the simultaneous abandoner, the *Stairway* (338) states:

> The simultaneous abandoner is established as two: the first and last fruitions; [they are so defined] because [1] the Once-returner is without abandoning the afflictions of the upper realms and because [2], if not abandoning the ninth [affliction] of the desire realm, [one] will not be a Non-returner and if abandoning the ninth, [one] abandons all nine of the three realms and then becomes an *Arhat.*

Tsong kha pa's articulation of the simultaneous abandoner in both the *Stairway* (346) and *Golden Garland* (243) relies on a citation from the *Abhidharmasamuccaya*:

> One who is liberated simultaneously, is a person who, having made the comprehension of the truth, having relied on [the liminal absorption of] that which is not-unable, by the supermundane path, abandons simultaneously the afflictions which are committed in the three realms. Here are distinguished two [results], the result of the Stream-enterer and the result of *Arhat.* Ordinarily, in the present life or at the time of death, one obtains perfect knowledge itself. If it is the case that one does not do so, one possesses the power of resolution. By the power of resolution, [one] takes birth just in the desire realm. If a Buddha does not appear, one will be a *pratyekajina.*[79]

Tsong kha pa analyzes this citation and the simultaneous abandoner from five points of view: (1) from the time or circumstance; (2) by the level of path; (3) the method for simultaneous abandonment;

(4) the type of individuals who achieve simultaneous abandonment; and (5) the method that generates this type of abandonment.

(1) A Simultaneous abandoner practices from the time of the sixteenth moment of the path of seeing that completes the realization of the four noble truths. This is because it is not possible to abandon simultaneously the defilements in the mundane path of cultivation previous to the path of seeing and because, during the path of seeing, the defilements removed by the path of cultivation are not abandoned. (2) Simultaneous abandonment by the supermundane path of cultivation (*lokottarabhāvanāmārga*) relies on only the "not-incapable" (*anāgamya*) preparation of the first concentration from among the nine levels of the three realm's existence. For Tsong kha pa, those who do not rely on this level of the path are not capable of achieving simultaneous abandonment. The supermundane path is necessary because the mundane path of cultivation is unable to abandon defilements simultaneously. (3) In general there are two types of defilements to be abandoned: the defilements to be abandoned by the path of seeing and the defilements to be abandoned by the path of cultivation. The *Stairway* (349) states that the defilements to be abandoned by seeing the Nobles' Four Truths are not simultaneously abandoned. For Tsong kha pa, only the defilements to be abandoned by the path of cultivation have the possibility of either being abandoned simultaneously or gradually. The path-of-cultivation defilements of the three realms can therefore be abandoned simultaneously. (4) Both the text of the AS and ASBh mention that only the result of Stream-enterer and *Arhat* have the possibility of simultaneous abandonment. This excludes the enterers of those two results. (5) When one has abandoned all afflictions, in the present life, at the time of circumstance previous to death, or at the time of death, the state of *Arhat* is obtained. If it is the case that one is not able to abandon all afflictions, when one dies and takes rebirth in the desire realm through the force of resolution, one may obtain *Arhat*ship in a situation where there are no Buddhas nor teachings of the *śrāvaka*s at the time of the last *saṃsāric* existence. In this situation, one will be a *pratyekajina* because it is a characteristic of this lesser vehicle person to manifest enlightenment in the desire realm while not relying on others. Tsong kha pa states that at the time of abandoning simultaneously, one is not a *pratyekajina*, although after such abandonment, one may become a *pratyekajina*.

The Pratyekabuddha. We have seen above how simultaneous abandonment may provide the germinative cause for the possibility of a *pratyekabuddha* to occur. Tsong kha pa emphasizes that the *pratyekabuddha* is not a simultaneous abandoner and that this has been a point of confusion for previous Tibetan scholars. The *Golden Garland* does not address the definition of the *pratyekabuddha* in the section concerning the *saṃgha illustration*. Yet in the *Stairway* (350), Tsong kha pa asks whether it is suitable to count a *pratyekajina* among the eight enterers and abiders. He points out that earlier Tibetan scholars claimed that the *pratyekajina* is not placed in the two middle results and that they asserted the *pratyekajina* result's paths of liberation as definitely being seventeen—that is, above a Non-returner abider. Tsong kha pa provides a description of the *pratyekajina* from the *Abhidharmasamuccaya*:

> Whether not generating or generating the preparatory analytical factors, whether obtaining a result previously or not, where a Buddha has not arisen, when manifesting the path by one's self one will be like [the horn of a] rhinoceros abiding solitarily, or one will be as a *pratyekajina* obtaining the end of suffering when practicing in a group.[80]

Tsong kha pa sees the *pratyekajina*[81] therefore as having two aspects based on whether or not one previously releases from the *śrāvaka* path. The first aspect is a *pratyekabuddha* who does not generate the preparatory analytical factors in a former time period and is solitary like the horn of a rhinoceros (*khaḍgaviṣāṇakalpaḥ*).[82] The second aspect of a *pratyekabuddha* has two divisions. One may either previously attain the path of preparation and not obtain a result then become a *pratyekabuddha*, or having obtained only the result of Stream-enterer one becomes a *pratyekajina*. Tsong kha pa states that the Noble Being who lives in solitude and abides like the horn of a rhinoceros is not tormented with fierce effort and thus has previously developed only the path of the ordinary individual (*pṛthagjana*). The latter two divisions of the *pratyekajina* are known as "abiding within a group (*vargacāri*)."[83] Tsong kha states that in Tibet they are also called "the greater and smaller practicing within a group (*tshogs che chung*)." These later two types of *pratyekajina* are either a Once-returner or Non-returner because, having obtained merely the result of Stream-enterer, one becomes a *pratyekajina*, and then, having abandoned the sixth desire realm affliction, one becomes a Once-returner or, if abandoning the ninth desire realm affliction, one becomes a Non-returner.

5

An Assembly of Irreversible *Bodhisattvas*

The Actual *Saṃgha* of *Bodhisattvas*

The *saṃghas* we have discussed in chapter 4 consist of the *saṃgha illustration* or *allegorical saṃgha* (*mtshon byed dpe'i dge 'dun*) of *śrāvakas*, those individuals seeking emancipation from *saṃsāra* through realizing the sixteen aspects of the Nobles' Four Truths. The path of Noble Beings within the *allegorical saṃgha* culminates in the result of *śrāvaka arhat*. However, as mentioned above, the goal of this type of *arhat*ship is not final according to the *Mahāyāna* theory of *ekayāna*. The *allegorical saṃgha* serves as an analogical template that exemplifies the *actual* (*don gyi*) *saṃgha*. The *actual saṃgha* is composed of irreversible (*avaivarttika*) *bodhisattvas*, those Noble Beings who are striving to be completely awakened into unsurpassable full enlightenment (*anuttarāṃ samyaksaṃbodhim abhisaṃbudhyante*) and to achieve the state of *Mahāyāna arhat*—that is, Buddhahood.[1] These *bodhisattvas* have generated the altruistic mind (*bodhicitta*) to achieve full enlightenment for the sake of all beings (AA i.18) and thereby strive to cultivate great compassion (*mahākaruṇā*), to practice the six perfections (*ṣaṭpāramitā*), and to master various meditative concentrations and absorptions. *Bodhisattvas* implement skill-in-means (*upāyakauśalya*), or tactical dexterity, in not actualizing the results of their meditative mastery and eventually gain the skill to travel from Buddha-field to Buddha-field through voluntary rebirth in the long, arduous path to attaining full Buddhahood.

The *actual saṃgha* of irreversible *bodhisattvas* is mentioned in the *Prajñāpāramitā sūtra* after the section concerning methods of training and special instructions (*avavāda*) concerning the precious jewel of the Dharma. As mentioned earlier, our commentators presuppose that when *bodhisattvas* practice in accord with previous special instructions of the PP *sūtras*, then the Buddha teaches the characteristics of these *saṃghas* in response to Śāriputra's questions, "When deceased, is a *bodhisattva* reborn here? Where will a *bodhisattva* be reborn?" The dialogue in the PP *sūtra* concerns the circumstance of rebirth for a *bodhisattva*, who takes rebirth to a great extent through skillful means in order to practice the perfections and help beings. This notion of "rebirth as skillful means" will be important to keep in mind for understanding the relationship between the *allegorical* and *actual saṃghas*. Tsong kha pa (1970: 244) considers that the *saṃghas* taught in the PP *sūtras* are condensed into two verses of the *Abhisamayālaṃkāra* for the sake of easily understanding and remembering the many different types of *bodhisattvas* in the *Mahāyāna saṃgha*.

Tsong kha pa (1970: 245) states that many Indian AA scholars, such as Ārya Vimuktisena, Ācārya Haribhadra, Kulandatta, Prajñākaramati, Buddhaśrījñāna, and Abhayākaragupta, assert that the foundation for the irreversible *bodhisattvas* divisions is derived from the community of Noble Beings (*āryasaṃgha*). This implies that the community of *bodhisattvas* to be counted among the Twenty *Saṃghas* includes those Noble *Mahāyāna* Beings who have reached the path of seeing. However, Tsong kha pa notes that other Indian scholars such as Śāntipa explain these divisions as beginning from the preparatory analytical factors (*nirvedhabhāgīya*). The *Golden Garland* (245) notes that Śāntipa considers "the first two [individuals] are on the path of preparation, four [individuals] are on the path of seeing, and then fourteen [individuals] are on the path of cultivation." Along these lines, Tsong kha pa notes that Ratnākaraśānti, when commenting on the meaning of the PP *sūtra* line, "The *bodhisattva*, the great being, who dwells in this abode of perfect wisdom, deceased in this world . . . he is reborn here," states in the *Śuddhamatī* that "abiding in the perfection of wisdom" is consonant with the preparatory analytical factors (*nirvedhabhāgīyas*). According to Tsong kha pa, the identification of whether *bodhisattvas* of the *actual saṃgha* first dwell in the paths of preparation, seeing, or cultivation, does not appear in any other text but the *Śuddhamatī*. Tsong kha pa accepts the boundary from the path of preparation as stated by Ratnākaraśānti, but adds that Haribhadra explains these *saṃghas* as only Noble Beings (*ārya*; *'phags pa*). According to Tsong kha pa, Asaṅga explains that the *saṃgha*, as one of the three jewels of refuge, consists of those who have entered to a spiritual level (*bhūmi*; *sa*). The *Golden Garland* (246) therefore concludes that only the "preparatory analytical factors" (*nirvedhabhāgīyas*) are suitable as a path boundary for the irreversible *saṃgha* (*avaivartikasaṃgha*), although it is not suitable for the precious jewel of the *saṃgha* (*ratnasaṃgha*) in general.

ENUMERATING *BODHISATTVAS* IN THE *PRAJÑĀPĀRAMITĀ*

The Twenty *Saṃghas*, in terms of the *actual saṃgha* of *bodhisattvas*, represents an enumeration of irreversible *Mahāyāna* Noble Beings drawn from the *Prajñāpāramitā sūtras*. According to the PP manuscripts that Tsong kha pa had in front of him, there are three principal PP *sūtras* that enumerate lists of *bodhisattvas*—the *Śatasāhasrikā* (100,000 verse), *Pañcaviṃśatisāhasrikā* (25,000), and *Aṣṭādaśasāhasrikā* (18,000). The lists of *bodhisattvas* occur in each one of these *sūtras* where the section states: "Having deceased in other Buddha-fields, among deities of *Tuṣita* heaven, or among humans, one should know [the *bodhisattva*] to be reborn here."[2]

For commentators like Tsong kha pa, the enumeration of *bodhisattvas* may or may not correlate to the *Abhisamayālaṃkāra*'s presentation of the Twenty *Saṃghas* based on these statements from the PP *sūtra*.

The System That Does Not Correlate to the Abhisamayālaṃkāra

The system of enumerating *bodhisattvas* without any correlation between the PP *sūtra* and the *Abhisamayālaṃkāra* occurs mainly in the *Śatasāhasrikā* and an Indian commentary associated with it. Tsong kha pa notes that there are forty-eight *bodhisattvas* mentioned in the *Śatasāhasrikā* (266–81). In regard to this enumeration, Tsong kha pa bases his interpretation on a commentary called *Conquering Harm to the Three Mothers*.[3] This commentary states that the first three *bodhisattvas* that occur in the PP *sūtras* are explained as supreme, moderate, or deficient by means of either sharp, middling, or dull faculties. According to Tsong kha pa the first three *bodhisattvas* are briefly explained and the remaining forty-five are demonstrated in detail. The *Golden Garland* quotes from the *Conquering Harm to the Three Mothers*:

> Having grouped together [*bodhisattvas*] into two: those with skill-in-means and those who do not have skill-in-means, those [*bodhisattvas*] who do not have skill-in-means take rebirth among the long-lived deities and in the desire realm, the remaining forty-three are said to have skill-in-means. In this way, having construed [the *bodhisattva*] who does not have skill-in-means as two, only this factor is harmonious or non-harmonious to both in counting forty-five. Accordingly, in whichever of the three *sūtras*, the *bodhisattva* on the side of the forty-three [with skill-in-means] generates the first [altruistic] thought [for enlightenment], engages in the perfections, and does not let go of the path of ten virtues until obtaining the stage of being irreversible (*avinirvartanīyabhūmi*).[4]

In this way, with three *bodhisattvas* listed at first and then forty-five spoken later, according to the above method, a total of forty-eight *bodhisattvas* are demonstrated. These *bodhisattvas* are classified according to whether they have skill-in-means or not and whether they take rebirth among long-lived deities. Although the *Conquering Harm to the Three Mothers* and Tsong kha pa appear to accept this enumeration to be applied to the three aforementioned PP *sūtras*, this enumeration appears to be only consonant with the *Śatasāhasrikā Prajñāpāramitā*.

The System in Correlation with the Abhisamayālaṃkāra

The other system of enumerating *bodhisattvas* related to the *Prajñāpāramitā* pertains directly to the Twenty *Saṃghas* mentioned in the *Abhisamayālaṃkāra*. The enumeration of the Twenty *Saṃghas* occurs within the context of correlating the sections of the PP *sūtra*, primarily the *Pañcaviṃśatiprajñāpāramitāsūtra*, to the AA through either a literal or nonliteral interpretation. The translation that was given at the beginning of chapter 4 accords with a literal interpretation of the Twenty *Saṃghas* given in the AA. Conze is not the only scholar to read the verses on the Twenty *Saṃghas* in this manner, as the *Golden Garland* (247) states that Buddhaśrījñāna and Śāntipa also draw out Twenty *Saṃghas* literally from the *Abhisamayālaṃkāra*. Tsong kha pa does not comment on this method of exegesis, and we can assume that he does not see this method as a feasible interpretation of the Twenty *Saṃghas*. This is most likely because a literal interpretation of the AA verses does not allow for the correspondences required by the *allegorical saṃgha* model. A literal reading of the AA verses concerning the Twenty *Saṃghas* is also not consonant with the readings from the corresponding sections of the *Pañcaviṃśatiprajñāpāramitāsūtra*. This will become evident in the next section, where we discuss Ārya Vimuktisena's exegesis of the Twenty *Saṃghas*. Ārya Vimuktisena and Haribhadra are the two main commentators Tsong kha pa describes as providing a nonliteral interpretation of the AA verses on the Twenty *Saṃghas*. Both of these commentators note that *bodhisattvas* come to take on the nomenclature of the various *śrāvakas* in the *allegorical saṃgha* only in a nominal sense, that is, through sharing similar qualities. The subcommentaries that follow Ārya Vimuktisena, Ratnākaraśānti's *Śuddhamatī*, and Abhayākaragupta's *Marmakaumundī* and *Munimatālaṃkāra*, attempt to explain the meaning of these *bodhisattvas* with analogies to fit into the framework of *Mahāyāna* soteriology. We will see these analogies as we examine Ārya Vimuktisena's system of the *actual saṃgha* of *bodhisattvas*.

Ārya Vimuktisena's system. Ārya Vimuktisena's system of articulating the Twenty *Saṃghas* is intimately related to the *Pañcaviṃśatiprajñāpāra-*

mitāsūtra. Ārya Vimuktisena directly correlates sections of the *Pañcaviṃśati* with statements in the *Abhisamayālaṃkāra* while having a methodological approach that reflects the style of delineation of the *śrāvaka saṃgha* given in the *Abhidharmakośa*. Tsong kha pa (1970: 247–60) demonstrates that Ārya Vimuktisena interprets sixteen *saṃghas* to be explicitly stated from the root text of the AA and then fills in four *saṃgha*s that are implicit—that is, not directly stated in the root text. The four implicitly mentioned *saṃgha*s are the eighth (*aṣṭamaka*), Once-returner, Non-returner, and enterer to the state of *Arhat*. Ārya Vimuktisena also posits the foundation of the Twenty *Saṃgha*s as the *irreversible saṃgha* (AAV 39). In order to properly understand Ārya Vimuktisena's system, Tsong kha pa divides his articulation into four divisions of *bodhisattva*s: those who possess the name of the Eighth, those who are separated from attachment previous to the path of seeing (*vītarāgapūrvin*), those who remove defilements to be removed by the path of cultivation serially (*anupūrvin*), and the *Pratyekajina*.

The Eighth Ārya. The Eighth (*aṣṭamaka)* is the first *bodhisattva* that is mentioned in the *Pañcaviṃśati* and is considered by Ārya Vimuktisena to be the basis from which one construes the two, followers through faith (*śraddhānusārin*) and followers through doctrine (*dharmānusārin*). Tsong kha pa notes that the *bodhisattva* follower of the path by faith has dull faculties (*mṛdu indriya*) and abides on the first fifteen thought-moments of the path of seeing. The *Pañcaviṃśati*[5] states:

> The *bodhisattva, mahāsattva* who, deceased among humans, has the destiny to be reborn among them, has dull faculties (*dhanvānīdriyāṇi*); excluding the *bodhisattva, mahāsattva* who is *irreversible*, [this one] does not make effort to quickly practice the yoga of perfect wisdom and even through the doors of *dhāraṇī* or the doors of meditative stabilization (*samādhi*) will not quickly manifest [perfect wisdom].[6]

Ārya Vimuktisena comments here that "directly saying 'irreversible' means that ground is obtained through only the path [followed with] sharp faculties."[7] This means that the irreversible seventh *bodhisattva* ground, the *avivartacaryā bhūmi* among the ten *bodhisattva* stages, is obtained only by one with sharp faculties. A *bodhisattva* with sharp faculties (*tīkṣṇendriya*) is the follower of the path by doctrine, who is also within the fifteen moments of the path of seeing.

> The *bodhisattva, mahāsattva* who, deceased in other Buddha-fields (*buddhakṣetra*) and reborn here, has sharp faculties (*tīkṣṇānīndriyāṇi*) and will quickly achieve this yoga, the present yoga of perfect wisdom. The *bodhisattva, mahāsattva* who, deceased from among the *Tuṣita* heaven

deities and reborn here, will have especially sharp faculties, practices nothing but the perfections, and will directly face [perfect wisdom] with all the doors of *dhāraṇī* and doors of meditative stabilization."[8]

The basis of these two followers of faith and doctrine is regarded in Ārya Vimuktisena's *Abhisamayālaṃkāravṛtti* as being the Eighth. The *Pañcaviṃśati* describes the Eighth: "The *bodhisattva, mahāsattva* who abides in the abode of perfect wisdom, deceased in other Buddha-fields, *Tuṣita* heaven, or in this world, should be understood as being reborn here."[9]

Ārya Vimuktisena connects the Eighth *bodhisattva* together with the first two followers of faith and doctrine. The section of the *Pañcaviṃśati* concerning the two followers is not distinguished from the section on the Eighth and Ārya Vimuktisena therefore construes these two followers as enterers to the result of Stream-enterer. Tsong kha pa posits these followers to abide on the fifteenth moment of the path of seeing, even though Ārya Vimuktisena himself states that they are within the first sixteen thought-moments.[10] This is because Tsong kha pa wishes to correlate the presentation of Ārya Vimuktisena with that of the *Abhidharmakośa* presented in the *allegorical saṃgha*. Why Tsong kha pa posits this correlation will become clearer below. Along these lines of interpreting the followers of faith and doctrine, Ārya Vimuktisena asserts that if the two followers abandon the path of cultivation defilements, from the sixth defilement of the desire realm up to the eighth, previous of the path of seeing, then those two followers are Once-returners. If they may abandon the ninth path of cultivation defilement previous to the path of seeing, then they will be a Non-returner enterer. As Tsong kha pa interprets, at whatever time either of these two obtain the sixteenth thought-moment, at that time those two will abide in either the result of Once-returner or Non-returner. When this occurs, one who previously had dull faculties (*mṛdvindriya*) will become one who aspires by faith (*śraddhādhimukta*) and one who previously had sharp faculties (*tīkṣṇendriya*) will become one who obtains by seeing (*dṛṣṭiprāpta*). However, the two followers in Ārya Vimuktisena's system of interpretation are not considered to be enterers to a result for the first time who progress through serial progression (*ānupūrvika*). Rather, they are considered to be enterers who are separated from attachment previous to the path of seeing (*vītarāga-pūrvin*). The *Abhisamayālaṃkāravṛtti* states: "The enterer to the second and third result is spoken with reference to the one who aspires by faith (*śraddhādhimukta*),"[11] and "The enterer to the second and third result is spoken with reference to the one who obtains by seeing (*dṛṣṭiprāpta*)."[12]

Tsong kha pa (1970: 252) states that although there is one enterer who is separated from attachment previous to the path of seeing, this enterer is symbolically represented by either one who aspires by faith or one who obtains by seeing. The interpretation of these two types is that even though they are two followers who have sharp or dull faculties, the intention is that they are of one lineage, the lineage of those who have faculties. The *Abhisamayālaṃkāravṛtti*, immediately after quoting the *sūtra* on the one who aspires by faith and the one who obtains by seeing, quotes the *sūtra* in regard to the two abiders in the result of Once-returner and Non-returner. It therefore correlates four enterers and abiders in the result who are separated from attachment previous to the path of seeing. Therefore, when AA 23a states "those of sharp and dull faculties" (*mṛdutīkṣṇendriyau*), Tsong kha pa considers Ārya Vimuktisena to demonstrate implicitly the first enterer and explicitly the second and third enterers who are separated from attachment previous to the path of seeing. When AA 23b states "those who aspire by faith and who obtain by seeing" (*śraddhādṛṣṭiprāptau*), Ārya Vimukuktisena demonstrates the two abiders in the result of either Once-returner or Non-returner (see figure 5.1, p. 166).

As Tsong kha pa will show, the enterers for the two middle results, which progress gradually, are illustrated by the distinguished Stream-enterer, the one who goes family to family (*kulaṃkulaḥ*). The distinguished Once-returner is demonstrated by the *Ekavīcika*, and the Non-returners beginning with the *Upapadyaparinirvāyin* Non-returners and so forth are considered to be *Arhat* enterers. Tsong kha pa provides a summary in the *Golden Garland* (253) of the main points of Ārya Vimuktisena's system of interpreting the *actual saṃgha* of *bodhisattvas*:

> When construed in this manner, the first two enterers are counted as one called "the Eighth," the two dull and sharp faculty enterers who are separated from attachment previous [to the path of seeing] are counted as two; and having counted the two abiders in the result of that [fruition] as two, subtracting the *Akaniṣṭhagaḥ* since it is the basis for the division of the three Jumpers, the other [*Saṃghas*] are to be counted literally [according to the text].

Tsong kha pa explains that these *saṃgha*s are explained based on the *Abhidharma* and are taught using similar terminology because they have similar qualities. The first part of the AA verse (23ab *mṛdutīkṣṇendriyau śraddhādṛṣṭiprāptau*) is explained by Ārya Vimuktisena based on the *Abhidharmakośa*.[13] Ārya Vimuktisena next counts three enterers, classifying them according to how many defilements have been removed previous to the path of seeing, and then in a similar manner, counts two abiders in the result of either Once-returner or Non-returner. Therefore, according to Tsong kha pa's reading, in Ārya Vimuktisena's system those who are separated from attachment previous to the path of seeing are presented in a similar manner to those who skip fruitions in the *allegorical saṃgha*. Next, we will describe those types of *bodhisattvas* who are separated from attachment previous to the path of seeing.

Vītarāgapūrvin: *Those previously separated from attachment*. Those *bodhisattvas* who are separated from attachment previous to the path of seeing (*vītarāgapūrvin*) have a fundamental classification of being either an enterer or an abider. An enterer separated from attachment previous to the path of seeing consists of two subdivisions. First, there is a dull faculty one who shares a similar lineage with the aspirer by faith (*śraddhādhimukta*), entering into either the state of Once-returner or Non-returner. The second subdivision consists of the sharp faculty one who shares a similar lineage with one who obtains by seeing (*dṛṣṭiprāpta*), entering into either the state of Once-returner or Non-returner. In regard to the first subdivision the *Pañcaviṃśati* states:

> There are *bodhisattvas*, *mahāsattvas*, who are not skilled-in-means (*anupāyakauśalya*), although they achieve the four concentrations (*dhyāna*), engage in the perfections, and in obtaining concentration, take rebirth among long-lived deities or among humans; they will delight the [Buddha] *Bhagavāns*. They will be with dull faculties and will not have sharp faculties.[14]

The *Pañcaviṃśati* describes the second subdivision, the sharp faculty one who possesses the same lineage of one who obtains by seeing, as an enterer to either the result of Once-returner or Non-returner as:

> There are *bodhisattvas*, those who have skill-in-means (*upāyakauśalya*), who enter into the concentrations and formless attainments, engage in the thirty-seven limbs of enlightenment, they are not reborn by the force of concentrations and so forth but through skill-in-means, they are reborn where they can please the Buddha *Bhagavāns* and nourish them. Since they are not separated from the yoga of perfect wisdom, they will become completely fully awakened in unsurpassable complete enlightenment in this very *Bhadrakalpa*.[15]

In this section of the *sūtra* one can plausibly count four enterers, but as Tsong kha pa reasons, by means of classifying via faculties, there are only two that can be counted because this section of the *sūtra* makes a distinction into only dull or sharp faculties. The distinction between having dull or sharp faculties is also correlated to whether *bodhisattvas* have skill-in-means or not. *Bodhisattvas* that have skill-in-means gain the ability to control their mode of rebirth and not actualize the results of meditative concentration. The second division of those who are separated from attachment previous to the path of seeing (*vītarāgapūrvin*)] consists of abiders. This type of abider also has two subdivisions. The first subdivision mentioned by Tsong kha pa (1970: 254) is the *bodhisattva* among the two who either aspires by faith or who obtains by seeing and who abides in the result of Once-returner that is separated from attachment previous to the path of seeing. The *Pañcaviṃśati* describes this *bodhisattva*:

> There are *bodhisattvas*, *mahāsattvas* who are obstructed by one life (*ekajātipratibaddha)*, course in perfect wisdom, and with skill-in-means, engage in the four concentrations, the four immeasurables (*catvāryapramāṇāṇi*), four formless attainments (*ārūpyasamāpatti)*, thirty-seven limbs of enlightenment, the three doors of liberation and not influenced by the force of these, having directly perceived the *Buddha Bhagavāns*, please them, practicing the celibate holy life under them, take rebirth again for a kalpa among the gods of *Tuṣita* heaven, where they abide until the end of their lifespan. Then, with non-defective faculties, mindful and conscientious, in front of and surrounded by hundreds of thousands of *niyutas* of *koṭis* of gods, take rebirth here and are fully awakened in various Buddha-fields.[16]

The *Golden Garland* (255) states that this type of *bodhisattva* comes back one time to this world, and then achieves enlightenment in another world.[17] The second subdivision is the *bodhisattva* among the two who either aspires by faith or who obtains by seeing, and who abides in the result of Non-returner that is separated from attachment previous to the path of seeing. The *Pañcaviṃśati* states:

> The *bodhisattvas, mahāsattvas*, who obtain the six supernatural knowledges (*abhijña)*, and who are not reborn in the desire realm, form realm, or formless realm, but they pass on from Buddha-field to Buddha-field, honoring, respecting, revering, and worshiping the *Tathāgata*, *Arhat*, are fully enlightened *Buddhas*.[18]

This type of *bodhisattva* does not return to this world and achieves enlightenment by being reborn in the upper heavens of the form and formless realm.

Ānupūrvika: *Those who progress gradually*. Ārya Vimuktisena counts those who remove defilements to be removed by the path of cultivation serially (*anupūrvin*) into three divisions: the members of the *bodhisattva saṃghas* who possess the name of Stream-enterer, Once-returner, and Non-returner.

Bodhisattva *stream-enterers*. The abider in the result of Stream-enterer is described in the *Abhisamayālaṃkāravṛtti*: "That one who is spoken of by saying, 'Stream-enterer' should be understood in the two aspects of those who go from family to family (*kulaṃkula*)."[19] The two aspects of the *bodhisattva* Stream-enterer according to Ārya Vimuktisena are the *bodhisattva* who is born family to family (*kulaṃkula*) among humans and the *bodhisattva* who is born family to family among gods. In regard to the *bodhisattva* who is born family to family among humans, abider in the result of Stream-enterer, the *Pañcaviṃśati* states:

> There are *bodhisattvas*, *mahāsattvas* who, having generated the four concentrations, the four immeasurables, and the four formless attainments, and with skill-in-means, having turned away from [the beneficial results of the] concentrations, meditative stabilizations, and attainments, take rebirth in the desire realm and for the sake of maturing beings are reborn, as like within a great *Śāla*, in families of householders, Brahmins, and royalty.[20]

As for the *bodhisattva* who is born family to family among gods:

> There are *bodhisattvas*, *mahāsattvas* who, having entered into the four concentrations, the four immeasurables, and the four formless attainments, by the power of skill-in-means are not reborn under the force of concentrations, meditative stabilizations, and attainments, who take rebirth among the gods from the abode of the Four Great Kings (*Cāturmahārājakāyika*) to the abode of Controlling Others Emanations (*Paranirmitavaśavartin*) and please [the *Tathāgatas*].[21]

Bodhisattvas who go from family to family therefore take rebirth in wealthy households among humans or in the upper five heavens of the desire realm among celestial families. Tsong kha pa explains in the *Golden Garland* (255) that the *Śatasāhasrikāvivaraṇa* classifies the *Bodhisattva* who is born family to family among gods into two types or categories: those born among desire realm deities and those born among form realm deities. *Bodhisattvas* work for others and please the Buddhas but are differentiated according to defilements removed. These two types of *bodhisattvas* that go family to family abandon the third and fourth affliction of the desire realm, obtain the antidote of those afflictions, the uncontaminated faculty, and are distinctive since two or three rebirths remain. The *Abhisamayālaṃkāravṛtti* mentions the one who goes family to family as more distinctive than a mere Stream-enterer because of having these three qualities.[22]

Bodhisattva *Once-returners*. The second division of *bodhisattvas* who progress gradually is the Once-returner. Ārya Vimuktisena enumerates this one as the *Ekavīcikaḥ*: "That one who is spoken of by saying 'Once-returner' is itself an *Ekavīcikaḥ*."[23] The *Pañcaviṃśati* gives the following description of the *bodhisattva* who is an *Ekavīcika*:

> There are *bodhisattvas*, *mahāsattvas* who obtain the four concentrations up to the eighteen special qualities of a Buddha, they course in compliance with them. They also obtain the Nobles' Four Truths and yet they do not penetrate them. *Śāriputra*, these *bodhisattvas*, *mahāsattvas* should be understood to be obstructed by one life (*ekajātipratibaddhā*).[24]

This *bodhisattva* abandons the seventh or eighth affliction, obtains the antidote of that, the uncontaminated faculty, and has distinction with one extra rebirth remaining. The *Abhisamayālaṃkāravṛtti* mentions the *Ekavīcika* as more distinctive than a mere Once-returner because of having these three qualities.[25] The *Golden Garland* (256) explains the meaning of *Ekavīcika* from the *Abhidharmasamuccayabhāṣya*[26] as denoting an interval (*vīci*) between achieving *nirvāṇa* by one (*eka*) rebirth. This meaning is similar to the one mentioned in the *allegorical saṃgha* and is consonant with this *sūtra* in that the *Ekavīcika bodhisattva* has one interval for full enlightenment. Tsong kha pa states that even though Abhayākaragupta explains this *bodhisattva* to be on the seventh or eighth ground, it is evident that this *bodhisattva* would be on the tenth ground if relying on the *sūtra,* because it explains the *bodhisattva* as one who is obstructed by one rebirth (*ekajātipratibaddha*). Tsong kha pa also notes that the intention from the *sūtra* saying "obtaining the four concentrations up to the eighteen special qualities" is that the *Ekavīcika* has the distinction in the lineage or ability to obtain these qualities.

Bodhisattva *Non-returners.* The third and final division of *bodhisattvas* who progress serially in Ārya Vimuktisena's system is the Non-returner. The Non-returner is described as: "That one who is spoken of by saying, 'the Non-returner who abandons nine afflictions,' should be understood in five aspects."[27] The Non-returner here is initially enumerated in five principal aspects: *Antarāparinirvāyin*, *Upapadyaparinirvāyin*, *Abhisaṃskāraparinirvāyin*, *Anabhisaṃskāraparinirvāyin*, and *Ūrdhvaṃsrotas*. This is in agreement with the general enumeration given in the *Abhidharmakośa*.[28] Tsong kha pa, based on these principal divisions, classifies the *bodhisattva* Non-returner in Ārya Vimuktisena's system into eight subdivisions.

The first subdivision consists of the *bodhisattva* Non-returner who attains full enlightenment in the intermediate state (*antarāparinirvāyin*). The *Pañcaviṃśati* states:

> There are *bodhisattvas*, *mahāsattvas* who, from the generation of the first thought of enlightenment obtain the concentrations, the immeasurables, the formless attainments, the thirty-seven limbs of awakening, the [ten] powers [of a *Tathāgata*], fearlessness, the analytical knowledges, and the eighteen special qualities [of a Buddha]. With skill-in-means, they take rebirth among *Brahmakāyika* gods up to the gods of *Akaniṣṭha* heaven. Having become fully enlightened there, they work for the sake of beings.[29]

Tsong kha pa (*Golden Garland*, 256) explains this *bodhisattva* through the analogy that it becomes fully enlightened instantly in whichever suitable form realm abode, the intermediate of the three realms. The form realm is considered here to be the intermediate of the three realms—that is, desire, form, and formless realms—analogous to the intermediate state between death and future birth.

The second division of Non-returners accords with the *bodhisattva* Non-returner who attains full enlightenment as soon as they are reborn (*upapadyaparinirvāyin*).

> There are *bodhisattvas*, *mahāsattvas* who, by that very generation of the first thought of enlightenment become awakened into full enlightenment and turn the wheel of Dharma, and having performed the purpose of countless immeasurable beings, achieve full *nirvāṇa* in the sphere of *nirvāṇa* which leaves no aggregates behind. These [*bodhisattva*'s] sacred Dharma remains for an aeon or more after they have achieved *nirvāṇa*.[30]

Tsong kha pa explains, based on the *Śuddhamatī*, that this *bodhisattva* generates the first thought of enlightenment, then comes down from *Akaniṣṭha* heaven into *Tuṣita* heaven and thereafter descends into the human realm, renounces the homelife, and then sits cross-legged beneath the Bodhi tree. Tsong kha pa gives the analogy that since this *bodhisattva* immediately gives birth to the mind of enlightenment and then achieves *nirvāṇa*, or full enlightenment, with remnant (*sopadhiśeṣa nirvāṇa*), the *bodhisattva* is therefore called "one who achieves *nirvāṇa* by birth."

The third division of the *bodhisattva* Non-returner is one who achieves full enlightenment with great effort. The *Pañcaviṃśati* describes this Non-returner:

> There are *bodhisattvas*, *mahāsattvas*, who, practicing the six perfections, pass on from world system to world system and there fully establish beings into enlightenment. These *bodhisattvas* always make effort for the sake of sentient beings and never speak purposeless words. Always making effort for the sake of beings, they travel from Buddha-field to Buddha-field.[31]

Tsong kha pa states that the analogy here is that since this *bodhisattva* puts forth great effort for the sake of sentient beings, he or she is called "one who achieves *nirvāṇa* with great effort." Tsong kha pa's AA teacher, Nya dbon kun dga' dpal, compares this type of *bodhisattva* Non-returner to tenth-stage *bodhisattvas* such as Avalokiteśvara, Tārā, and Mañjuśrī based on the *Munimatālaṃkāra*.[32] However, as we will see, Tsong kha pa *will not* accept this type of comparative interpretation.

The fourth division of the *bodhisattva* Non-returner is the *bodhisattva* who achieves *nirvāṇa* without effort. The citation from the *sūtra* states: "There are *bodhisattvas, mahāsattvas,* who, by the generation of the first thought of enlightenment itself, completely pass beyond from the faults of a *bodhisattva* and while definitely abiding on the irreversible stage, achieve all the qualities of a Buddha."[33] Following the *Munimatālaṃkāra* and the *Śuddhamatī,* Tsong kha pa explains that this *bodhisattva* has the distinction of lineage because of becoming enlightened quickly, with a great roar[34] and with little activity. On account of these qualities, the *bodhisattva* is called "one who achieves *nirvāṇa* without effort." Indian scholars like Dharmamitra (ca. ninth century) and Tibetan scholars such as Rong ston shes bya kun rig (1367–1449) will compare this type of *bodhisattva* Non-returner to the *bhikṣu* who became the Buddha Akṣobhya and the Brahmin rgya mtsho'i rdul.[35]

Tsong kha pa explains that in the *Abhisamayālaṃkāravṛtti* and the *Munimatālaṃkāra* both the *bodhisattva* Non-returner who achieves *nirvāṇa* by being born (*upapadyaparinirvāyin*) and the *bodhisattva* who achieves *nirvāṇa* with effort (*sābhisaṃskāraparinirvāyin*) enter into the path with great exertion and the *bodhisattva* who achieves *nirvāṇa* without effort (*anabhisaṃskāraparinirvāyin*) enters the path without exertion.[36]

The fifth division of the *bodhisattva* Non-returner in the system of Ārya Vimuktisena is the *Ūrdhvaṃsrotas* who has two subdivisions:[37] a *bodhisattva* who goes up to *Akaniṣṭha* heaven (*akaniṣṭhaparama*) and the *bodhisattva* who goes up to the Peak of Existence (*bhavāgraparama*). Ārya Vimuktisena explains the first division, the *Akaniṣṭhagaḥ*: "This one is an *Ūrdhvaṃsrotas* who transmigrates to the end of *Akaniṣṭha* heaven having three aspects."[38]

Ārya Vimuktisena takes the *Akaniṣṭhagaḥ* as the base for three Jumpers. The *sūtra* states:

> There are *bodhisattvas, mahāsattvas* who, practicing the six perfections, have become Universal Monarchs (*cakravartin*). Having taken the perfection of giving for their guide, they provide all beings with everything that brings happiness, like "food for those desiring food" up until having established beings in the path of the ten virtuous actions. Having taken rebirth from among the gods of *Brahmakāyika* heaven up until the gods of *Akaniṣṭha* heaven, they will become enlightened in various Buddha-fields.[39]

The *bodhisattva* Non-returner who transmigrates to *Akaniṣṭha* heaven has three Jumpers: a Jumper, Half-jumper, and Jumper who dies everywhere. Tsong kha pa does not give the details from the *Abhisamayālaṃkāravṛtti* regarding these three divisions, most likely because they are similar to those in the *allegorical saṃgha,* and Ārya Vimuktisena's system *is not* the commentator who Tsong kha pa adheres to. Tsong kha pa, therefore, merely cites the corresponding *Pañcaviṃśati* sections in explaining these three Jumpers.

Ārya Vimuktisena explains the *bodhisattva* Jumper as one who, having degenerated from the first three concentrations, achieves the first concentration and takes rebirth in *Brahmakāyika* heaven. Then through the force of previous familiarization, the Jumper alternates with the fourth concentration, and as a consequence when he dies, takes rebirth as a deva in *Akaniṣṭha* heaven. This *bodhisattva* is called a "Jumper" because of jumping all of the intermediate heavens between *Brahmakāyika* and *Akaniṣṭha.*[40] The *sūtra* states:

> There are *bodhisattvas, mahāsattvas* who, accomplished in the four concentrations, when degenerating from the concentrations become accomplished in the first concentration and [as a consequence] take rebirth among the gods of *Brahmakāyika* heaven. Then these [*bodhisattvas*], having achieved the concentrations again from rebirth in *Akaniṣṭha* heaven, will become fully awakened into unsurpassable complete enlightenment in various Buddha-fields.[41]

The *bodhisattva* Half-jumper, having passed away in *Brahmakāyika* heaven, takes birth in the *Śuddhāvāsa* heavens, and having jumped over one heaven in between, enterers into *Akaniṣṭha* heaven.[42] The *sūtra* describes this Half-jumper:

> There are *bodhisattvas, mahāsattvas* who, deceased from the world of *Brahma,* take rebirth among the gods of *Śuddhāvāsakāyika* heavens. Having jumped over one or two abodes of *Śuddhāvāsakāyika,* taking rebirth in *Akaniṣṭha* heaven they will become fully awakened into unsurpassable complete enlightenment in various Buddha-fields.[43]

The *bodhisattva* Jumper Who Dies Everywhere is one who, having traversed through all other abodes of the form realm, enters into *Akaniṣṭha* heaven and then achieves enlightenment.[44] The Jumper Who Dies Everywhere is described in the *sūtra*:

> There are *bodhisattvas, mahāsattvas* who, having emanated their own body like the spiritual body of a *Tathāgata,* purified the abode of *Tuṣita* heaven, take rebirth among the gods of *Brahmakāyika* heaven up to the gods of

> *Akaniṣṭha* heaven, and with skill-in-means teach the Dharma to hell-realm beings, and teach the Dharma in the animal realm and in the world of *Yama*.[45]

The second division of the *Ūrdhvaṃsrotas* in the system of Ārya Vimuktisena is the *bodhisattva* who transmigrates to the Peak of Existence. This is a *bodhisattva* Non-returner who is distinguished by entering into all the heavens and engaging in absorption, but does not enter into the *Śuddhāvāsas* heavens, gradually enters into the formless realms, and having gone to the Peak of Existence, achieves enlightenment in various Buddha-fields.[46] The *sūtra* states here:

> There are *bodhisattvas, mahāsattvas* who, in consequence of having accomplished the concentrations and formless realm attainments, take rebirth among the gods of *Brahmakāyika* heaven up to rebirth among the gods of *Śubhakṛtsna* and then take rebirth in the realm of limitless space (*Ākāśānantyāyatana*) up to the Peak of Existence (*Bhavāgra*).[47]

Tsong kha pa explains that since the *sūtra* states "*Śubhakṛtsna*," and the *Abhisamayālaṃkāravṛtti* comments that "In not entering only the *Śuddhāvāsa* heaven having taken rebirth in all other abodes, gradually produces the formless realm [attainments],"[48] that therefore this *bodhisattva* transmigrates up to the *Bṛhatphala* heaven. It is crucial to note here that in dividing these *bodhisattvas* in the above manner, Ārya Vimuktisena treats AA 23d–24ab *akaniṣṭhagāḥ / plutās trayo bhavasyāgraparamo* / as five subdivisions counted under the *Ūrdhvaṃsrotas*. These *bodhisattvas* therefore comprise only one count among the Twenty *Saṃghas* in the system of Ārya Vimuktisena (see Figure 5.1, p. 166).

The sixth division of *bodhisattva* Non-returners is the *bodhisattva* who destroys the attachment to form, transmigrator to the formless realms. The *sūtra* describes this *bodhisattva*: "There are *bodhisattvas, mahāsattvas* who, obtaining the concentrations and formless realm attainments, take rebirth in the realm of limitless space up to the Peak of Existence and then will be reborn in various Buddha-fields."[49]

Tsong kha pa does not discuss this *bodhisattva* other than following Ārya Vimuktisena's statements that this Non-returner, having deceased in this realm, does not go to the form realm but takes rebirth in the formless realm.[50]

The seventh division concerns the *bodhisattva* who is pacified in this present life and achieves *nirvāṇa* (*dṛṣṭadharmaparinirvāyī*).[51] Ārya Vimuktisena does not explain this *bodhisattva* other than the description provided by the *sūtra*:

> There are *bodhisattvas, mahāsattvas* who, at the time of practicing the six perfections, their bodies ornamented with the thirty-two marks of a

> Great Individual, come to possess unsurpassably complete pure faculties and will never take rebirth in fallen states of bad transmigrations and do not praise themselves nor deprecate others. These *bodhisattvas*, by being endowed with completely pure faculties, will become pleasing and dear to many individuals. Whatever beings see these *bodhisattvas*, *mahāsattvas*, they, through extreme happiness in mind, gradually attain full *nirvāṇa* through the three vehicles.[52]

Tsong kha pa explains that in the *allegorical saṃgha*, the *hīnayāna śrāvaka* who pacifies in the present life achieves *nirvāṇa* in the embodiment that first obtains the Noble path (*ārya mārga*). However, based on the statement from the *sūtra*, the implication is that the *bodhisattva* who pacifies in the present life, causes whoever sees him/her to achieve *nirvāṇa*. Therefore, according to Tsong kha pa, this *bodhisattva* directly pacifies others in the present existence. The *Golden Garland* (259) notes that Abhayākāragupta provides another interpretation in the *Munimatālaṃkāra*: "Because the continuity of giving, morality, and so forth is not cut off in all lives, [one] is completely enlightened in the present life."

The eighth and final division of *bodhisattva* Non-returners is the *bodhisattva* who is a Bodily Witness (*kāyasākṣī*). The *sūtra* explains this *bodhisattva*:

> There are *bodhisattvas*, *mahāsattvas* who, practicing perfect wisdom, obtain the four concentrations, four immeasurables, four formless attainments, and playing with these, enter into the first concentration. Emerging from that concentration, they enter into the absorption of cessation (*nirodhasamāpatti*). Likewise [engaging and emerging] up to the Peak of Existence. *Śāriputra*, in this way, *bodhisattvas*, *mahāsattvas* who possess skill-in-means while practicing perfect wisdom, since they attain and increase again and again these concentrations, immeasurables, meditative stabilizations, and attainments, enter into the attainment which skips over [at will from one abode to the next] and will become enlightened in various Buddha-fields.[53]

Tsong kha pa notes that Ārya Vimuktisena refers to this one as a "bodily witness" since when the *bodhisattva* achieves the attainment of cessation, which has a quality similar to *nirvāṇa* and is without mind, it directly witnesses with the body.[54] Tsong kha pa accepts this explanation to be consonant with that of the *Vaibhāṣikas* and Vasubandhu.[55] The next type of *bodhisattva* mentioned by Ārya Vimuktisena and the *Pañcaviṃśati* is the enterer to the result of *Arhat* (*arhatvaphala-pratipannaka*). However, Tsong kha pa does not discuss in detail this type of *bodhisattva* in the system of Ārya Vimuktisena. As we have briefly mentioned, Tsong kha pa considers the *bodhisattva* Non-returners in this system, beginning with the *Upapadyaparinirvāyin* Non-returner, to be synonymous with the *Arhat* enterer. Ārya Vimuktisena briefly states that a Non-returner who has removed the eighth affliction of the Peak of Existence is considered to be an *Arhat* enterer.[56] This is the same definition that Tsong kha pa accepts when presenting the Twenty *Saṃghas* system of Haribhadra.

Bodhisattva Pratyekabuddha. The fourth and final division in which Tsong kha pa classifies *bodhisattvas* according to the system of Ārya Vimuktisena is the *bodhisattva* who is like the horn of the rhinoceros. The *sūtra* states:

> *Śāriputra,* there are *bodhisattvas, mahāsattvas* who, in Buddha-less world-systems where there are no disciples, will become fully enlightened in the *pratyekabuddha* enlightenment. These [*bodhisattvas*], with skill-in-means, having matured many hundreds of thousands of *niyutas* of *koṭis* of living beings in the three vehicles, will become completely awakened in unsurpassable fully complete enlightenment.[57]

The *pratyekabuddha* has similar characteristics to the *pratyekabuddha* of the *allegorical saṃgha* in that they appear where there are no Buddhas nor *śrāvaka* disciples. Tsong kha pa notes, according to the *Śuddhamatī* and *Munimatālaṃkāra,* that the *pratyekabuddha* has two aspects. The first is much like the *allegorical saṃgha pratyekabuddha,* having the quality of becoming enlightened without listening to teachings from others. The second aspect of the *pratyekabuddha* takes on the appearance of a *pratyekabuddha.* Here we are reminded of the story in the *Śūraṃgamasamādhisūtra* (1998: 214–16) of Mañjuśrī manifesting "the figure (*saṃsthāna*), colors (*varṇa*), and bodily attitudes (*īryāpatha*) of a *pratyekabuddha*" as a form of skillful means to help deliver beings.[58] That *sūtra* (1998: 111) states that a *bodhisattva* "manifests the figure, colors, and bodily attitudes of a *pratyekabuddha,* but without ever straying inwardly from the thought of great compassion (*mahākaruṇācitta*) of the Buddhas."

These aforementioned divisions of the Twenty *Saṃghas* comprise the system of Ārya Vimuktisena. The *Abhisamayālaṃkāravṛtti* quotes twenty-four *saṃghas* from the *sūtra,* condensing them into Twenty *Saṃghas,* sixteen of which are explicitly stated and four of which are implicit. Figure 5.1 (p. 166) depicts Ārya Vimuktisena's system.

Ācārya *Haribhadra's and Tsong kha pa's System.* The second system of the *actual saṃgha* of *bodhisattvas* is that of Haribhadra. This is the system whose intention (*dgongs pa, abhiprāya*) Tsong kha pa accepts in the

Figure 5.1 Twenty *Saṃghas* According to Ārya Vimuktisena

1. *Aṣṭamaka* (*srota-āpannapratipannaka* implicit in AA 23a *mṛdutīkṣṇendriyau*) on path of seeing with dull and sharp faculties (*vītarāgapūrvin*)
2. Once-returner enterer (*sakṛdāgāmi pratipannaka*) and Non-returner enterer (*anāgāmi-pratipannaka*) on path of seeing with dull faculties (23a *mṛdvindriya*) (*vītarāgapūrvin*)
3. Once-returner enterer (*sakṛdāgāmi pratipannaka*) and Non-returner enterer (*anāgāmi-pratipannaka*) on path of seeing with sharp faculties (23a *tīkṣṇendriya*) (*vītarāgapūrvin*)
4. Once-returner abider (*sakṛdāgāmi phalastha*) and Non-returner abider (*anāgāmi-phalastha*) with dull faculties (23ab *śraddhāprāpta*) (*vītarāgapūrvin*)
5. Once-returner abider (*sakṛdāgāmi phalastha*) and Non-returner abider (*anāgāmi-phalastha*) with sharp faculties (23ab *dṛṣṭiprāpta*) (*vītarāgapūrvin*)
6. Stream-enterer abider (*srota-āpanna phalastha*) who goes from family to family among humans (23b *manuṣyakulaṃkula*) (*anupūrvin*)
7. Stream-enterer abider (*srota-āpanna phalastha*) who goes family to family among devas (23b *devakulaṃkula*) (*anupūrvin*)
8. Once-returner enterer (23b implicit *anupūrvin*)
9. *Ekavīcika* Once-returner (23c "*ekavīci*")
10. Non-returner abider (23c implicit *anupūrvin*)
11. *Antarāparinirvāyin* (23c "*antara*")
12. *Upapadyaparinirvāyin* (23c "*utpadya*")
13. *Abhisaṃskāraparinirvāyin* (23d "*kāra*")
14. *Anabhisaṃskāraparinirvāyin* (23d "*akāra*")
15. *Ūrdhvaṃsrotas*
    a. *Akaniṣṭhaga*
    b. *Pluta*
    c. *Ardhapluta*
    d. *Sarvasthānacyuta*
    e. *Bhavāgraparama*

15. *Rūparāgahan*

17. *Dṛṣṭadharmaśama*

18. *Kāyasākṣin*

19. *Arhat* enterer (implicit from AA 23c to 24c)

20. *Pratyekabuddha* (AA 24d)

Golden Garland. Haribhadra's articulation of the Twenty *Saṃghas* is mentioned in his *Abhisamayālaṃkārasphuṭārthāvṛtti* (Amano, 2000: 15) and *Abhisamayālaṃkārālokā* (Wogihara, 1932: 35–36). Unlike Ārya Vimuktisena, neither one of Haribhadra's commentaries are directly related to the *Pañcaviṃśatiprajñāpāramitāsūtra*. The AAĀ is correlated to the *Aṣṭasāhasrikāprajñāpāramitā* while the AASPh, perhaps representing a summary of the AAĀ, comments on the verses of the *Abhisamayālaṃkāra* alone. Both of the commentaries present a brief exegesis of the Twenty *Saṃghas* and as a consequence, Tsong kha pa's presentation of "our own system" (*rang lugs*) is concise as well. While following the commentaries of Haribhadra, Tsong kha pa divides his exegesis of the *actual saṃgha* into five classifications: the Stream-enterer, Once-returner, Non-returner, *Arhat* enterer, and *Pratyekabuddha*. Tsong kha pa mentions each one of these types of *bodhisattvas* as merely "possessing the name" (*ming can*) of "Stream-enterer" and so forth. We will discuss the relationship between the *allegorical saṃgha* and *actual saṃgha* in the next section.

The first of the five divisions of the *actual saṃgha* in Tsong kha pa's system consists of the Stream-enterer, which has three subdivisions: a Stream-enterer enterer, a mere abider in the result of Stream-enterer, and a distinctive abider in the result of Stream-enterer.

First, the *bodhisattva* who has the name of enterer to the result of Stream-enterer (*srota-āpanna pratipannaka*) has a division of two followers: those with dull faculties and those with sharp faculties. These are individuals who strive for the abandonment, realization, and achievement of the status of Stream-enterer. They rely on the first fifteen of the sixteen thought-moments within the path of seeing that are arranged in the second chapter of the AA within the context of path omniscience. Tsong kha pa states that they have two aspects, sharp (*tīkṣṇa*) or dull (*mṛdu*) faculties, from either understanding quickly or understanding after a long time and being previously well trained or not well trained.[59] Second is the *bodhisattva* who possess the name of the mere abider in the result of Stream-enterer (*srota-āpanna phalastha*) and who is characterized according to faculties like the enterers just mentioned. This is an abider on the sixteenth thought-moment of the path of seeing who, according to Tsong kha pa, does not abandon even one single defilement of the desire realm to be abandoned by the path of cultivation.[60] The third classification within the first division is that abider in the result of Stream-enterer who is a distinctive abider in the result, the one who goes from family to family (*kulaṃkula*) either among gods or among men. Tsong kha pa only mentions that this one is labeled according to the root abandonment that is obtained by the path of cultivation, while Haribhadra mentions that a *Kulaṃkula* has abandoned up to the fourth defilement of the path of cultivation.[61]

Altogether Tsong kha pa accepts five types of Stream-enterers: two who enter the first result with dull or sharp faculties, the mere abider in the result, and two who may have distinction in the result.

The second principal division, which consists of the *bodhisattva* who has the name of Once-returner (*sakṛdāgāmī*), has three subdivisions: an enterer, a mere abider in the result, and a distinctive abider in the result. The first subdivision from among the three, an enterer to the result of Once-returner, consists of the aspirer by faith (*śraddhādhimukti*) who has dull faculties and one that obtains by seeing (*dṛṣṭiprāpta*) who has sharp faculties. Either one of these make effort for the sake of obtaining the result of Once-returner, having abandoned the fifth desire realm affliction by the path of cultivation. According to Tsong kha pa, who is following Haribhadra, the two enterers to Once-returner are counted only as one among the divisions of the Twenty *Saṃghas*.[62] The second subdivision consists of a Once-returner who is a mere abider in the result abiding on the path of liberation that abandons the sixth desire realm affliction.[63] The third subdivision is the distinctive abider in the result of Once-returner who is called an *Ekavīcika*. This Once-returner, distinctive because of its abandonment, has one rebirth remaining among the gods.[64]

The third division that Tsong kha pa employs regards the *bodhisattvas* who have the name of Non-returner (*anāgāmī*). Non-returners have two divisions: an enterer and an abider. First, the Non-returner enterer, who may have either sharp or dull faculties, abandons the seventh or eighth desire realm defilement and makes effort for the sake of abandoning the ninth defilement. In a similar manner to the Once-returner enterer, the Non-returner enterer is counted only once among the Twenty *Saṃghas*.[65] The question may arise as to how one can interpret one enterer to the two middle fruitions while having earlier counted separately each one of the sharp and dull faculty enterers to the first result. The *Golden Garland* (268), following the remarks of Byang chub ye shes, states that each one is counted separately when entering the first result because it is definite to have either dull or sharp faculties and that there is no time to change faculties when the path of seeing is generated uninterruptedly. Since faculties can be changed at the time of the path of cultivation, when entering to the result of Once-returner or Non-returner, the faculty is not definite for each one and therefore it is to be counted as only one among the Twenty *Saṃghas*.

The second principal division among the *bodhisattvas* who have the name of Non-returner is the Non-returner abider (*anāgāmiphalastha*). The Non-returner abider is one who abandons the ninth desire realm affliction and consists of five subdivisions.[66] The first of the Non-returner subdivisions is comprised of the Non-returner who achieves *nirvāṇa* in the intermediate state (*antarāparinirvāyin*). This nominal *bodhisattva*, by abandoning the fetter that achieves birth in the form realm but not abandoning the fetter that achieves the intermediate state of whichever suitable form realm, obtains the end of suffering through manifesting the path in an intermediate state.[67] Tsong kha pa notes that this Non-returner, according to the *Prasphuṭapadā*, "will be enlightened having accumulated merit by that very embodiment that has taken rebirth in the world of *Brahma*." Tsong kha pa states that the *Śuddhamatī* interprets the phrase "that very embodiment" to refer to *Akaniṣṭha* heaven and not to the continent of *Jambu*. The second of the Non-returner abiders is the one who achieves *nirvāṇa* by birth (*upapadyaparinirvāyin*). This Non-returner obtains the end of suffering by taking rebirth in the form realm because it does not abandon either the fetter of taking rebirth or the fetter of becoming.[68] Tsong kha pa adds a curious statement, stating that this Non-returner will be enlightened in that life alone, having achieved the last existence after immeasureable lives. The third subdivision of the nominal *bodhisattva* Non-returner abider is the one who achieves *nirvāṇa* with activity (*sābhisaṃskāraparinirvāyin*) and the fourth subdivision is the Non-returner who achieves *nirvāṇa* without activity (*anabhisaṃskāraparinirvāyin*).[69] These two Non-returners achieve *nirvāṇa* either through manifesting the path with diligent effort when taking rebirth in the form realm, or achieve *nirvāṇa* in just the opposite manner of having effort. With the inclusion of these two Non-returners, Tsong kha pa states (*Golden Garland* 269) that there are a total of four *parinirvāyin* Non-returners.[70]

The fifth type of Non-returner consists of the *Ūrdhvaṃsrotas* and has two aspects: the Non-returner who transmigrates up to *Akaniṣṭha* heaven (*akaniṣṭhaparama*) and the Non-returner who may transmigrate up to the Peak of Existence (*bhavāgraparama*).[71] The first aspect, the Non-returner who transmigrates finally to *Akaniṣṭha* heaven, has three subdivisions: A Jumper (*pluta*) to *Akaniṣṭha* who avoids abiding in realms from *Brahmakāyika* to *Akaniṣṭha* heaven, a Half-jumper (*ardhapluta*) who enters to *Akaniṣṭha* skipping over only the abodes from *Brahmakāyika* up to the *Śuddhāvāsakāyika*, and One who dies in All Abodes (*sarvasthānacyuta*) when entering to *Akaniṣṭha*, having continued on in all the abodes of the form realm.[72] Tsong kha pa states that other than the Non-returner who goes higher by transmigrating to the Peak of Existence (*ūrdhvaṃsrotas bhavasyāgraparamagaḥ*) there are only three aspects to the *Ūrdhvaṃsrotas*. The second aspect, the Non-returner who transmigrates to the Peak of Existence is one who is separated from attachment of the form realm and destroys the attachment of form (*bhavāgraparamaś ca rūpavītarāgaḥ*). When this Non-returner is classified, there are two aspects other than the transmigrator to *Akaniṣṭha* heaven, one who obtains *nirvāṇa* in this life seeing the qualities of pacification (*dṛṣṭadharmaśamaḥ*) and one who witnesses with the body the absorption of cessation (*kāyasākṣī*). On this manner of interpreting AA I.24b–c, Tsong kha pa directly quotes Haribhadra in the *Golden Garland* (270) from the *Abhisamayālaṃkārālokā*: "The one who transmigrates to the Peak of Existence is separated from the attachment to forms and is of two aspects: one for whom there is peace in this life and one who witnesses [absorption] with the [physical] body."[73]

Tsong kha pa also notes the method of exegesis of these two in the *Śatasāhasrikā Prajñāpāramitā*. He states that these two, in sequence, abandon the form realm defilements to be abandoned by the path of seeing and the form realm defilements to be abandoned by the path of cultivation in a desire realm embodiment, and then obtain the four formless attainments. When either one dies, they may either pass over the form realm and take rebirth in the formless realm, or, possessing the seven treasures of a *bodhisattva,*[74] not take another body, and become enlightened in one life. The later one, who does not take another body, is explained as the supreme *bodhisattva*.

The fourth principal division among the Twenty *Saṃgha*s construed according to the system of Haribhadra consists of the *arhat* enterer. The *bodhisattva* who has the name of enterer to the result of *arhat* abandons the eighth defilement of the Peak of Existence to be removed by the path of cultivation and makes effort to abandon the ninth defilement.[75]

The fifth and final division among the Twenty *Saṃgha*s concerns the *pratyekabuddha*. When one manifests the path oneself, through focusing on the *śrāvaka* scriptures, and when a Buddha does not occur, one will be as a *pratyekajina*.[76] Tsong kha pa explains that when the text states "will be a *pratyekabuddha*" in the *Abhisamayālaṃkārālokā*, Haribhadra is not referring to a *Mahāyāna arhat*. Rather, if one does interpret this statement as referring to an *arhat*, it is correct to interpret this nominal *bodhisattva* as one who possesses the name of a *śrāvaka arhat* by means of a similar cause. Tsong kha pa concludes his discussion from the *Prasphuṭārthapadā*: "Finally, it is taught in three stages, [one] who makes effort for the sake of oneself, others, and both [self and others]. The *bodhisattva* who [makes effort for both] is taught as supreme."[77]

Therefore, Tsong kha pa follows the principles of categorizing the Twenty *Saṃgha*s through the interpretation given by the *Abhisamayālaṃkārālokā*. In this system, seventeen *saṃgha*s are taught explicitly in the *Abhisamayālaṃkāra* and three *saṃgha*s are taught implicitly. The *Abhisamayālaṃkārālokā* concludes: "The individuals who abide in the first and second results and those who enter to the fourth result, since they are easy to understand, are not [explicitly] explained in the arrangement [of Twenty *Saṃgha*s]." [78]

The system of Twenty *Saṃgha*s that Tsong kha pa concludes from the *Golden Garland* (271) is the definition accepted by contemporary Tibetan scholarship: "There are five Stream-enterers, three Once-returners, ten Non-returners, an enterer to the result of *arhat*, and *pratyekabuddha*, which makes Twenty [*Saṃgha*s]."[79]

As noted above, these Twenty *Saṃgha*s have been explained according to the *Abhisamayālaṃkārālokā*, which Tsong kha pa notes is the same system as that of Dharmakīrtiśrī, a teacher of Atiśa Dipaṃkāraśrījñāna. The *Golden Garland* (271) also notes that Prajñākaramati explains afflictions abandoned by the *bodhisattva ūrdhvaṃsrotas* are abandoned by a mundane path of cultivation. However, Tsong kha pa rejects this interpretation because it is not discussed by either Ārya Vimuktisena or Haribhadra. Based on the above interpretation of Tsong kha pa and Haribhadra, the *Abhisamayālaṃkāra* verses on the Twenty *Saṃgha*s would be translated in the following manner:

> 23a–b. *mṛdutīkṣṇendriyau śraddhādṛṣṭiprāptau kulaṃkulau /*
> c–d. *ekavīcyantarotpadya kārākārākaniṣṭhagāḥ //*
> 24a–b. *plutās trayo bhavasyāgraparamo rūparāgahā /*
> c–d. *dṛṣṭadharmaśramaḥ kāyasākṣī khaḍgaś ca viṃśatiḥ //*

> There are Twenty [categories]: the [(1) Stream-enterer enterer] with dull and [(2) Stream-enterer enterer] with sharp faculties, [(3) the Stream-enterer abider,] the [(6) Once-returner and (9) Non-returner enterer] who have attained faith and vision, [the Stream-enterer abider] born from family to family [(4) among gods and (5) among humans], (7) one born with an interval, [(8) the Once-returner abider,] (10) those who are born in the intermediate state, (11) those who are born, (12) with effort and (13) effortlessly, those who proceed to *Akaniṣṭha*, the (14–16) three who leap, those who go to the upper limit of the world destroying attachment to the form realm being the (17) one who pacifies in the present and the (18) bodily witness, [(19) the *arhat* enterer,] and the (20) one who is like the horn [of a rhinoceros].

Figure 5.2 (p. 172) depicts this system of interpretation.

RELATIONSHIP BETWEEN THE ACTUAL *SAṂGHA* AND THE ALLEGORICAL *SAṂGHA*

We have so far given a detailed description of the *allegorical saṃgha*, comprised of *śrāvaka*s and *pratyekabuddha*s, and the *actual saṃgha*

Figure 5.2 Twenty *Saṃgha*s According to Haribhadra and Tsong kha pa

1. Stream-enterer enterer with dull faculties (23a)
2. Stream-enterer enterer with sharp faculties (23a)
3. Stream-enterer abider (23a implicit)
4. Stream-enterer abider *Kulaṃkula* among humans (23b)
5. Stream-enterer abider *Kulaṃkula* among devas (23b)
6. Once-returner enterer with dull and sharp faculties (23ab)
7. *Ekavīcika* Once-returner (23c)
8. Once-returner abider (23b implicit)
9. Non-returner enterer with dull and sharp faculties (23ab)
10. *Antarāparinirvāyin* (23c)
11. *Upapadyaparinirvāyin* (23c)
12. *Abhisaṃskāraparinirvāyin* (23d)
13. *Anabhisaṃskāraparinirvāyin* (23d)

Following three are *Akaniṣṭhaparama* (23d–24a)

14. *Pluta*
15. *Ardhapluta*
16. *Sarvasthānacyuta*

Following two are *Bhavāgraparama* and *Rūparāgahan* (24ad)

17. *Dṛṣṭadharmaśama*
18. *Kāyasākṣin*
19. *Arhat* enterer (23d–24c implicit)
20. *Pratyekabuddha* (24d)

constituted by *irreversible bodhisattvas*. The relationship between these two types of *saṃgha* is discussed by only the Tibetan tradition since our principal Indian commentators, Ārya Vimuktisena and Haribhadra, present these *saṃgha*s as irreversible (*avaivartika*) *bodhisattvas*. Tsong kha pa therefore examines all the relevant Indian source material before him and combines various strands of *sūtra* and *śāstra* to provide a coherent explanation of how to properly understand the *actual saṃgha* (*mtshon bya don gyi dge 'dun*).

One of the first remarks Tsong kha pa states in regard to the relationship between the *actual saṃgha* and *allegorical saṃgha* relates to the *Abhidharmic* scholasticism that influenced the two major Indian AA commentators, Ārya Vimuktisena and Haribhadra. In relation to Ārya Vimuktisena, Tsong kha pa states:

> The Ārya [Vimuktisena] explains both the [one who] skips [fruitions] and the [one who progresses] gradually. Along with this, there are two who have sharp and dull faculties and two, one who aspires by faith

> and one who obtains by seeing, making four abider and enterers who skip [fruitions] and since the remaining [*saṃghas*] are connected with [those who progress] gradually, these *saṃghas* are explained in harmony with the *Abhidharmakośa*. (*Golden Garland* 260)

As we have seen, in the *allegorical saṃgha* those who skip fruitions are defined from the *Abhidharmakośa*, and Ārya Vimuktisena interprets four of the Twenty *Saṃghas* to be those who are previously separated from attachment (*vītarāgapūrvin*). Tsong kha pa therefore correlates these two ways of enumerating the Twenty *Saṃghas*, one in regard to the *allegorical saṃgha* and the other to the *actual saṃgha*, to be consonant.

Tsong kha pa depicts the relationship between enumerating the *allegorical saṃgha* and the *actual saṃgha* according to Haribhadra in the following manner: "Ācārya [Haribhadra] in his *Abhisamayālaṃkārālokā* explains all the *Saṃghas* similar with [those who progress] gradually and [his] explanation is principally in harmony with the *Abhidharmasamuccaya*" (*Golden Garland* 260).

Tsong kha pa in both his *Stairway* and *Golden Garland* has made an effort to direct his interpretation of the *allegorical saṃgha* and *actual saṃgha* to be in agreement with statements from the *Abhidharmasamuccaya* and Haribhadra. Tsong kha pa wishes to correlate the manner of presentation of this text and author in order to articulate a homogeneous system of interpreting the Twenty *Saṃghas* from both the perspectives of the *allegorical saṃgha* and of the *actual saṃgha*. Along these lines, Tsong kha pa notes that neither of the aforementioned commentarial methods demonstrates a correlation of the simultaneous abandoners in the *allegorical saṃgha* to the *actual saṃgha*.

Tsong kha pa relates that previous commentators have explained that there are three qualities of resemblance between the *actual saṃgha* of irreversible *bodhisattva* and the *allegorical saṃgha* of *śrāvakas:* the qualities of abandonment, realization, and the manner of taking rebirth. Tsong kha pa states that the method of explaining the quality of abandonment between the *actual saṃgha* and *saṃgha illustration* is explained in the two great commentaries of Haribhadra, the *Abhisamayālaṃkārālokā* and *Sphuṭārthā*, the *Durbodhāloka* of Kulandatta, the *Abhisamayālaṃkāravṛttipiṇḍārtha* of Prajñākaramati, the *Munimatālaṃkāra* and *Marmakaumudī* of Abhayākaragupta, and the *Prasphuṭapadā* of Dharmamitra. This quality has been documented above in the presentation of Haribhadra's system.

Tsong kha pa examines other distinctive qualities of the *actual saṃgha* through analyzing the difficult points of the PP *sūtra*, the levels (*bhūmi*) to which the various *actual saṃgha* members are thought to correspond, and the intention that is meant when the characteristics and designations of the *śrāvaka saṃgha* are applied to the *actual saṃgha*. The first point concerns the sections of the PP *sūtra* that are difficult to interpret in relation to *Mahāyāna* doctrine. For instance, *bodhisattva*s are thought to avoid rebirth in the heavens of long-lived deities in order to help beings. Tsong kha pa cites the *Sūtra of Expanded Gnosis (jñānavistarasūtra)* in support of this opinion:

> Monks! Only one who is called "equally abiding in all objects" is a vessel of the *Mahāyāna*. It will also be eloquent to say that "*Nirvāṇa* is the goal of human rebirths since there are not others to be trained when taking rebirth among long-lived gods."[80]

However, there are sections of the PP *sūtra* that mention *bodhisattva*s taking rebirth among the long-lived deities. Tsong kha pa states that rebirth in the heavens of long-lived deities is generally outside the scope of the Noble Being (*ārya*) *bodhisattva* since rebirth there generates improper views and is considered an inopportune rebirth. However, Tsong kha pa states that ordinary individual *bodhisattva*s who are reborn there by the force of wisdom do not generate wrong view. Tsong kha pa quotes from the *Conquering Harm to the Three Mothers* to demonstrate his interpretation:

> Formerly, with no skill-in-means, although making effort in the practice of the concentrations and the practice of the perfections, because [one] does not have skill-in-means, [one] takes rebirth among the long-lived gods and in the interval of a single existence at that time will not be making effort in the perfections, later at the time of rebirth among humans, practicing in the perfections, although making forceful effort of practice, [one] will have dull faculties.[81]

Tsong kha pa therefore explains that it is only in previous lives that one is born among long-lived gods and that later, having taken rebirth among humans and obtaining the Noble Path, one is established as having dull faculties.

Tsong kha pa states that it is also incorrect to assert that the *bodhisattva* Non-returner who is characterized as a transmigrator to the Peak of Existence and destroyer of the attachment to form (*bhavāgraparama* and *rūparāgahan*) takes rebirth in the formless realm. This is based on a citation from the *Ratnaguṇasaṃcayagāthā*: "The good qualities of enlightenment come through practicing the perfections. Therefore one does not take pains for the purpose of birth in the formless realms."[82]

Tsong kha pa notes that this type of *bodhisattva* Non-returner is called a "transmigrator up to the Peak of Existence" because this one is able to obtain the formless realm absorption, the cause of rebirth there, and therefore is referred to as such because of his meditative ability. However, through skill-in-means (*upāyakauśalya*) this type of *bodhisattva* Non-returner does not take rebirth in the formless realm. In relation to this issue, Tsong kha pa cites the *Abhidharmasamuccaya*, which states that a *bodhisattva* "possesses the concentrations which abandon the aspect of the formless realm."[83] In other words, *bodhisattvas* master a meditative attainment but do not actualize the results on account of other being's welfare. The *Abhidharmasamuccayabhāṣya* states: "The *bodhisattva* practices in the desire and form [realms] but does not practice in the formless realm because it is not an abode in which to fully ripen sentient beings. Those attaining the specialty of force are not born there."[84]

The second topic Tsong kha pa addresses relates to the spiritual levels (*bhūmi*) to which the various *actual saṃgha* members are thought to correspond. Tsong kha pa (*Golden Garland* 265) articulates the explanation given by Abhayākaragupta in his *Munimatālaṃkāra*. Abhayākaragupta appears to equate the removal of the path-of-cultivation defilements with the attainment of various *bodhisattva* spiritual levels. In this text, while the two enterers who have either weak or dull faculties abide on the first fifteen thought-moments of the path of seeing, the two who go from family to family (*kulaṃkula*) are located from the second *bhūmi* up to the fifth *bhūmi*. Abhayākaragupta regards the Once-returner enterer to be located on the sixth *bhūmi* while the Once-returner and *Ekavīcika* reside on the seventh *bhūmi*. The Non-returner enterer is positioned on the eighth or ninth *bhūmi* and the Non-returners, from the one who achieves *nirvāṇa* in the intermediate state (*antarāparinirvāyī*) up to the Bodily Witness, are situated on the tenth *bhūmi*. Tsong kha pa comments that the *Marmakaumudī* of Abhayākaragupta places the *Ekavīcika* on either the seventh or eighth *bhūmi* and that the five Non-returners, from the one who achieves *nirvāṇa* in the intermediate state up to the *Ūrdhvaṃsrotas*, abandon the path of cultivation defilements and are *Arhat* enterers. The spiritual level for the *pratyekabuddha* does not occur in either of these two commentaries.

Another commentator that Tsong kha pa examines is Rngog lo tsa ba blo ldan shes rab (1059–1109 CE). Rngog blo ldan shes rab correlates the levels of the *actual saṃgha* members within four different *bhūmis*: *prathamacittotpādika*, *caryāpratipanna*, *avaivartika*, and *ekajātipratibaddha*. This articulation corresponds closely to the oldest systems of articulating *bodhisattva* levels (La Vallèe Poussin, 1910a: 744). Rngog blo ldan shes rab, in articulating the twenty members of the *actual saṃgha*, posits a set of five Stream-enterers who are considered to have generated the first supermundane thought (*prathamacittotpādika*). The two enterers and abiders in the result of Once-returner, along with two Non-returner enterers, comprise four that have entered into the activity (*caryāpratipanna*). There are nine different types of abiders in the result of Non-returner that are considered irreversible (*avaivartika*). According to Tsong kha pa, Rngog blo ldan shes rab asserts the *arhat* enterer to be obstructed by one rebirth (*ekajātipratibaddha*) and the *pratyekabuddha* to be arranged into whichever of these four levels.[85]

Tsong kha pa himself, however, rejects the association of these *saṃgha*s to the stages of spiritual levels (*bhūmi*s). As an example of why this is not feasible, Tsong kha pa cites from the section of the *Pañcaviṃśati sūtra* where the Dharma follower and the *Ekavīcika* are stated to be *bodhisattvas* who are obstructed by one birth (*ekajātipratibaddha*). Other than this example, Tsong kha pa does not go into detail as to why he rejects the *bhūmi*s to be applied to these *saṃgha*s. This will become clearer when we discuss how the characteristics and designations of the *śrāvaka saṃgha* are applied to the *actual saṃgha* of *bodhisattva*s.

The final point Tsong kha pa discusses concerning the *actual saṃgha* relates to how the characteristics and designations of the *śrāvaka saṃgha* are applied to the *actual saṃgha*. Since the members of the *actual saṃgha* are not correlated with the *bhūmi*s, a question arises: Are the *bodhisattva*s that have been explained as Stream-enterers and so forth actual "Stream-enterers" in a literal sense, or are they special designations—that is, denaturalized terminology, used to insinuate something more? Along these lines, Tsong kha pa quotes first the scholar Byang chub Ye shes:

> Just as entering to the path which is the stream of *nirvāṇa* in the time period of the *śrāvaka,* is posited as the characteristic, arranged as a Stream-enterer and so forth, likewise, it is established as a Stream-enterer and so forth for entering to the path which is the stream of *Buddhahood*.[86]

Therefore, Tsong kha pa accepts that just as one uses terms like *Stream-enterer* to indicate those *śrāvaka*s who are progressing toward a *nirvāṇa* that is an emancipation from *saṃsāra*, the terms *Stream-enterer* and so forth can be applied to *bodhisattva* individuals who are progressing toward *anuttarasaṃyaksaṃbodhi*—that is, Buddhahood.

Tsong kha pa states that in the *Prajñāpāramitā sūtra*s, the *bodhisattva* is not demonstrated by scholastic denaturalized terminology such as Stream-enterer, Once-returner, Non-returner, or *pratyekabuddha*. However, Tsong kha pa (*Golden Garland* 265) considers that Maitreyanātha, in commenting on the meaning of the *Prajñāpāramitā sūtra* through the *Abhisamayālaṃkāra,* employs well-known scholastic denaturalized terminology, such as *śraddhānusārīn, dharmānusārīn, ekavīcikaḥ,* and so forth, as a form of skillful means to generate awareness for the *bodhisattva* *saṃgha*. Tsong kha pa explains that since scholastic terminology is well known in the commentarial literature of the *śrāvaka* vehicle to elucidate the *saṃgha*, that Maitreya has also utilized this terminology to illuminate the *saṃgha* of *bodhisattvas*.

In order to clarify the hermeneutics of Maitreyanātha's approach, Tsong kha pa cites and analyzes another *sūtra* that he claims utilizes a similar interpretative technique, the *Avaivartikacakrasūtra*. This *sūtra* is also referred to in the *Abhisamayālaṃkāravṛtti* (AAV 1967: 46) and *Abhisamayālaṃkārālokā* (AAĀ 1932: 36), although it is not discussed at any length in either commentary. The *Avaivartikacakrasūtra*[87] (Pk. 906, Taipei 240) is a *Mahāyāna sūtra* said to have been preached by the Buddha, at Śrāvastī, in the Jeta Grove of Anāthapiṇḍada. The *sūtra* depicts the Buddha teaching the "wheel of the irreversible doctrine" (*avaivartikadharmacakra*) where all beings are destined for Buddhahood. Among the topics in this *sūtra*, the Buddha articulates to Ānanda what is meant when he states *śraddhānusārīn, dharmānusārīn*, and so forth. Tsong kha pa paraphrases a brief passage from the *sūtra* in order to demonstrate this: "[These] nine terms: the two followers [of faith and doctrine], the Eighth, Stream-enterer, Once-returner, Non-returner, *arhat*, *śrāvaka*, and *pratyekabuddha* are employed in [reference to the] *bodhisattva*."[88]

Tsong kha pa explains, however, that the discourse in this *sūtra* is not definitive in meaning and is not to be taken literally. If it was, the *śrāvaka*, *pratyekabuddha*, and *arhat* who are mentioned as *bodhisattvas* may cause one to be confused and combine the individuals of the three vehicles together. Tsong kha pa paraphrases another section of the *sūtra* to demonstrate the intention the Buddha has in utilizing this terminology:

> Monks, as in the example of establishing the perception of water in the waterless *Jetavana* grove, the four results of Stream-enterer and the *pratyekabuddha* and so forth are not identified as these [results], the *bodhisattva*, for the sake of removing identification with these results, is explained as the Eighth, and so forth.[89]

Tsong kha pa notes here that those who are in the lineages of the *śrāvaka* and *pratyekabuddha* vehicles are satisfied by obtaining the results among the four fruitions and the result of self-liberation and do not have the resolution or inspiration to achieve anything more than that. This *sūtra* has the intention to guide beings toward the *Mahāyāna* vehicle, and therefore, as a form of skill-in-means, the Buddha teaches these individuals themselves to be *bodhisattvas*.

Tsong kha pa cites a series of stanzas from the *Avaivartikacakrasūtra* in order to demonstrate the intentional and scriptural basis of the

Buddha's methodology in teaching *bodhisattvas* identified through scholastic terminology. However, each stanza is taken from a separate section of the *sūtra* in which a certain type of individual is discussed by the Buddha to Ānanda. In the *sūtra*, the Buddha gives a whole discourse on a certain type of *bodhisattva* who obtains the name from *śrāvaka* terminology, say for instance *śraddhānusārin*, the "follower by way of faith." After the Buddha gives a discourse as to why a *bodhisattva* takes up the name of whichever *śrāvaka*, he follows the discussion with a series of stanzas that serve as a summary of the topic. Tsong kha pa (*Golden Garland* 266) cites the first summary verse of each type of individual:

> There is no attachment when seeing the Buddha and that causes faith for immeasurable sentient beings; they have no attachment for him. Therefore, the intelligent "follow by faith" (*śraddhānusārin*).[90]
>
> The stream of dharmas are inconceivable, yet one does not pass beyond that stream, that very dharma is subsequently obtained. Therefore, one is called a "Dharma-follower" (*dharmānusārin*).[91]
>
> Well beyond the eight faults, and touching upon the eight liberations, there is no desire for the eight purities. Therefore, one is called "the Eighth" (*aṣṭamaka*).[92]
>
> Definitely proclaiming "a stream for the path," although Buddha's path is unthinkable, whoever abides here, the [Buddha] and those [people] are diligent for the stream (Stream-enterer).[93]
>
> Whoever excellently teaches the many conditions which will achieve enlightenment, saying "these conditions should be known," there is a returner searching for these [conditions] (Once-returner).[94]
>
> Above even the three transmigrations, that one does not return or transmigrate when obtaining the qualities of a Buddha. That one is called a "Non-returner."[95]
>
> Whoever destroys all the afflictions of sentient beings who suffer exceedingly, liberating beings from the afflictions, one who does that is called an "*arhat.*"[96]
>
> Caused to proclaim without difficulty, the unelaborated, pacified, Enlightenment, proclaiming in immeasurable lives, one who does that is called a "*śrāvaka.*"[97]
>
> Ignorance is just like space and all dharmas are without a distinguishing characteristic; when one directly perceives this [that person] is called a "*pratyekabuddha.*"[98]

As one can see, outside the sphere of the *Avaivartikacakrasūtra* itself and the background discussion of each verse, these stanzas are cryptic and terse and do not reveal the complete intention that stands behind them. These stanzas most likely represent word plays on the Sanskrit ideal figure terminology lost in the Tibetan translation. Nevertheless, Tsong kha pa does not wish to give a full discourse on that *sūtra* and its meaning. He merely wishes to show the type of intention that is presented by the *Avaivartikacakrasūtra* through briefly demonstrating how terms such as the *Eighth*, *Stream-enterer*, and so forth, that usually refer to *śrāvaka* Noble Beings, are posited in relation to *bodhisattvas*.

Bodhisattvas take on the name and quality of the various *śrāvaka* Noble Beings through mere nominal designation.[99] The *Prajñāpāramitā* literature repeatedly states that while coursing in the practice of *prajñāpāramitā*—that is, viewing things through cognizing emptiness—*bodhisattvas* see the various stages from Stream-enterer up to Buddhahood as being like an illusion.[100] A *bodhisattva*, if obtaining a result such as Stream-enterer, does not think "I have obtained the result of Stream-enterer."[101] A *bodhisattva* acts and lives in a nondual unity of emptiness and awareness, fused with compassion for all beings. As Subhūti states to Śāriputra near the end of the first chapter of the *Pañcaviṃśati* (1934: 261):

> Honorable Śāriputra, the goal and full realization do exist, but not both [in an everyday and ultimate sense.] Honorable Śāriputra, both the goal and full realization are posited through transactional conventions of the everyday world. The [goals of] Stream-enterer, Once-returner, Non-returner, *arhat*, *pratyekabuddha*, *bodhisattva*, and [even] Buddha are [mere] transactual conventions of the everyday world. In the perspective of the highest meaning, there is neither goal nor realization, no Stream-enterer, no Once-returner, no Non-returner, no *arhat*, no *pratyekabuddha*, no *bodhisattva*, no Buddha.

Therefore, all stages are ultimately seen as like illusions, like a fictitious person. Yet, even though these results are like an illusion, through skill-in-means, a *bodhisattva* assumes the gestures, guises, and appearances of various types of Noble Beings in order to spiritually mature sentient beings. Moreover, *bodhisattvas* master, accomplish, and play with all the meditational attainments and realizations of all the various *śrāvaka* stages in order to mature beings who are training in those types of stages. As Ārya Vimuktisena states, *bodhisattvas* "do not obtain through such paths the results of Stream-enterer and so forth that are attained through a *śrāvaka*'s path or achieve the status of a *pratyekabuddha* through a *pratyekabuddha*'s path. Rather, they help establish beings in the results of Stream-enterer up to the awakening of a *pratyekabuddha*."[102] *Bodhisattvas* cause beings to attain results according to their inclinations and capacities. Likewise, *bodhisattvas* share similar nomenclature with Noble Beings of the *śrāvaka* vehicles for the sake of developing sentient beings' awareness for the *Mahāyāna saṃgha* of irreversible *bodhisattvas* destined for *anuttarasaṃyaksambodhi* (complete Buddhahood).

Therefore, based on the example of the *Avaivartikadharmacakrasūtra*, Tsong kha pa can then correlate the methodology of how these nine individuals from the *sūtra* are established as *bodhisattvas* to the manner in which the Twenty *Saṃghas* in the *Abhisamayālaṃkāra* are also *bodhisattvas*. The *Golden Garland* cites the *Marmakaumudī*, which comments on this methodology: "The similarity of names with *śrāvaka* individuals is for the purpose of gaining conviction in the [*avaivartika bodhisattva*] *saṃgha*."[103]

Tsong kha pa explains that some individuals may think, *The* saṃgha *is only the four pairs of* śrāvaka *individuals* and will not have any resolution for the *saṃgha* of irreversible *bodhisattvas*. Tsong kha pa asserts that Maitreyanātha has employed the denaturalized terminology describing the *śrāvaka* Noble Beings, the four pairs of individuals and so forth, for the sake of reversing the improper understanding that may arise in regard to the *Mahāyāna saṃgha*.

However, even with this articulation of how *bodhisattvas* are presented in relation to the Twenty *Saṃghas*, Tsong kha pa explains that this understanding may hold the possibility of belittling the correct understanding of the *Mahāyāna bodhisattva*. This may occur through the consequence of mixing together the vehicles of *śrāvakayāna*, *pratyekabuddhayāna*, and *bodhisattvayāna* if taking the aforementioned explanations in a literal and strict manner. To demonstrate this, Tsong kha pa quotes from the *Abhidharmasamuccaya*:

> Why will the *bodhisattva*, by entering into immaculate *bodhi*, not become a Stream-enterer? Because entry into the stream is imperfect in regards to the practice [of the path]. Why will [the *bodhisattva*] not become a Once-returner? Because in [attaining the good] thought [the *bodhisattva*] accepts unlimited rebirths. Why will [the *bodhisattva*] not become a Non-returner? Because after abiding in the concentrations, [the *bodhisattva*] takes rebirth in the desire realm.[104]

Therefore, even though a *bodhisattva* may take on the terminology that is representative of the various types of *śrāvakas*, the *bodhisattva* will not carry the strict defining characteristics that may pertain to a particular type of *śrāvaka*.

CONCLUSION

Our task has been to provide an exegetical presentation of the Tibetan interpretation of the Twenty *Saṃgha*s based on the works of Tsong kha pa blo bzang grags pa. The topic of the Twenty *Saṃgha*s is important because it provides the defining characteristics of one of the three essential components—*Buddha*, *Dharma*, and *Saṃgha*—that are accepted as objects of refuge universally among Buddhists. More specifically, the topic of the Twenty *Saṃgha*s incorporates methods of taxonomic organization through which the list of the twenty individuals provides a worldview where soteriological results of the Buddhist path, whether that path be individual liberative in scope or universally liberative in scope, are possible.

I have been guided throughout this study of the Twenty *Saṃgha*s by Tsong kha pa's texts and the Indo-Tibetan literature related to this topic. I have employed an emic approach to the materials in "thinking along" with this tradition of scholarship. I have tried to avoid, in my scholarly approach to the materials, what J. Z. Smith (1982: 43) has referred to as the "ultimate act of imperialism, the removal of all rights to interpretation from the native, and the arrogation of all such rights to" the historian of religion. I am reminded of Lévi-Strauss's remark (1966: 43) regarding a professional biologist who once noted in relation to taxonomic systems of biological classification, "how many errors and misunderstandings . . . could have been avoided, had the older travelers been content to rely on native taxonomies instead of entirely new ones."

The Twenty *Saṃgha*s encompasses a comprehensive list of the stages through which Noble Beings may pass in their progress toward *nirvāṇa*. The comparative study of religion in human cultures has recognized such thinking with lists as *Listenwissenschaft* ("the systematic study of lists"). *Listenwissenschaft*, as Smith notes (1982: 47), is "the science which takes as prime intellectual activity the production and reflection on lists, catalogs, and classifications, which progresses by establishing precedent, by observing patterns, similarities, and conjunctions, by noting repetitions." As most students of Buddhism will immediately recognize, *Listenwissenschaft* in Buddhist cultures takes place through *Abhidharma*. For Buddhist scholars of *Abhidharma* lists are *mātṛkās* (Pali *mātika*; Tib. *ma mo*), summaries of comprehensive doctrinal concepts. The list incorporated into the first chapter of the *Abhisamayālaṃkāra* (AA 1.23–24) enumerates, like most lists found in Buddhist discourse, an "easily memorable systematization of the elements and principles of Buddhist doctrinal thinking" (Collins, 1982: 109).

In analyzing such lists, Buddhist scholars maintain the inherited traditional scholastic structure, but apply forms of analysis and exegesis to accommodate interests prevalent within the historical context of the given author. In terms of early South Asia Buddhist exegesis, the ideal *saṃgha* consisted of the eight Noble Persons (*āryapudgalas*) mentioned in the early *Nikāya* discourses and preserved in Pāli literature. Noble Persons were ideal figures considered worthy of veneration and worship. That set of ideal figures consisted of the four pairs of Noble Persons, the enterers to and abiders in the four results of progress in the Buddhist path: the Stream-enterer, Once-returner, Non-returner, and *Arhat*. In relating to these eight types of Noble Persons, *Abhidharma* scholars began to systematize and analyze the various subdivisions within the four main results of the path based on the subsequent and repeated examination of what the Buddha purportedly taught. The Buddha, as depicted in the *Nikāya* collections, taught various lists of Noble Persons classified based on acuity of faculties, karmic substrate, number of lives remaining till *nirvāṇa*, and so forth.

Buddhist scholars of *Abhidharma* subsequently had systematized and analyzed these classifications so much so that AA 1.23–24 embodies a mnemonic verse summary recalling the detailed analysis of the stages of progress to *nirvāṇa* as remembered in the statements attributed to the Buddha. This is to say that the literal content of the two stanzas of the AA that list the Twenty *Saṃghas* represent nothing new but are instead a continuity of a received tradition. However, what does become innovative and a point of contention is the interpretation of the content to reflect new trends in the exegetical environment.

The denaturalized terminology we charted in chapter 4 of the AA in comparison with other Indian Buddhist sources demonstrated that, from a terminological standpoint, the Twenty *Saṃghas* depicts a classification and listing of Noble Beings fairly well established by the sixth century in India. At this time in India a list of Noble Beings became canonical and formulaic, containing a brief summary of ideal figures. Chapter 4's comparison of nomenclature from Indian Buddhist sources revealed that the system of terminology employed by the *Abhisamayālaṃkāra* is closely related to the *Sarvāstivādin-Vaibhāṣika* school, as the technical terms resemble those in the *Abhidharmakośa.*

Our study therefore indicates that the Twenty Saṃghas in the AA delineates a taxonomic model of ideal figures derived from the *Abhidharma* tradition, just as Makransky (1997) has noted that the AA adapted the threefold *dharmakāya* schema from the *Yogācāra* one.

After the sixth-century canonization of this *Abhidharma* list in the AA, the problem for Indian commentators was how to interpret this *Abhidharmic* list of ideal figures and relate them to the ideal figure of the *bodhisattva* as presented in the *Prajñāpāramitā* literature. How was this list of *śrāvaka*s related to *bodhisattvas*? A number of Indian commentators were not explicitly clear on this relation; although, for all commentators, the list refers to irreversible *bodhisattvas*. However, the interpretative methods clarifying how the list of AA 1.23–24 relates to both *śrāvaka* ideal figures and *bodhisattva* ideal figures differed among Indian scholiasts, and as chapter 2 briefly illustrated, the Indian commentarial tradition is rather fragmented in this regard.

The Tibetan reception of the AA commentarial literature began in earnest in the eleventh century and this cycle of literature was fully assimilated and systematized over the next several centuries. The eleventh to fourteenth centuries was a historical period in Tibet in which all the major Indian commentaries of the AA had been translated and several generations of indigenous Tibetan AA commentaries had been composed. The cultural conditions at this time in Tibet allowed for important AA commentaries to be accessible and to be examined in a standardized religious language (*chos skad*). Beginning in the fourteenth century, Tibetan AA scholars defined the ideal figures of the *saṃgha* utilizing a distinction between the *allegorical saṃgha* (*mtshon par byed pa'i dpe'i dge 'dun*) and the *actual saṃgha* (*mtshon par bya ba'i don gyi dge 'dun*) for exegetical totalization. That division served as a heuristic technique to extend the domain of the closed canon embodied in the two stanzas of AA 1.23–24 to signify everything that can possibly be known about ideal figures in the textual resources available to Tibetan authors such as Tsong kha pa.

As discussed in chapter 2, Tsong kha pa occupied a pivotal period in the classical scholastic period of Tibetan Buddhism. The scholarship of Tsong kha pa represents a culmination of a long commentarial tradition of the AA. His works concerning the Twenty *Saṃgha*s mark the beginning of an innovative and new Tibetan systematization of Indian Buddhist doctrine. Here, rather than an already "worked-out" and unelaborated exegesis of the Twenty *Saṃgha*s, as found in commentaries of Ārya Vimuktisena and Haribhadra, the distinction between allegorical model of *śrāvaka*s and actual *saṃgha*s of *bodhisattva*s allows for Tibetan scholars to engage in hermeneutic feats of ingenuity. On the one hand, scholiasts were able to fully articulate the exegetical details and classificatory minutia of *śrāvaka Abhidharmic* categories previously not systematized or investigated. On the other, they were able to relate these *Abhidharma* categories to *bodhisattva* ideal figures without altering the canonical verses of the AA in the process. The allegorical and actual division and their interpretation gives the Tibetan hermeneute such as Tsong kha pa a totalizing heuristic technique to interpret the Twenty *Saṃgha*s. Tsong kha pa can classify the defining characteristics of ideal figures in the *śrāvaka, pratyekabuddha,* or *bodhisattva* vehicles, without altering the canonical verses of the AA. The exegetical method extends the value of the hierarchical status relation from one domain to the next, allowing for the listing of *bodhisattva*s to be based on a metaphorical model or mapping that does not involve relations of conceptual opposition but relations of encompassment.

In our analysis, Tsong kha pa appears to be engaged in two exegetical exercises while interpreting the Twenty *Saṃgha*s. First, Tsong kha pa sees himself as properly recovering and presenting the intentions (*dgongs pa*) of the two principal Indian *Abhisamayālaṃkāra* commentators, Ārya Vimuktisena and Haribhadra. Second, Tsong kha pa sees himself as establishing "his own system" (*rang lugs*) of interpreting the Twenty *Saṃgha*s by means of textual Buddhist hermeneutics. He engages in exegesis and analysis of "textual systems" (*gzhung lugs*) in order to arrive at the proper understanding of the defining characteristics (Skt. *lakṣaṇa;* Tib. *mtshan nyid*) of ideal figures.

Tsong kha pa seeks to establish a unified and coherent structure to the Twenty *Saṃgha*s, one that is able to create a homogenous system of ideal figure descriptions between the *Abhidharma* and *Prajñāpāramitā* materials available to him. This allows for Tsong kha pa's *Mahāyāna* system to be inclusive of *Abhidharmic* (i.e., *śrāvaka*) descriptions of ideal figures. At the same time, such exegesis allows Tsong kha pa to develop a system of interpreting the Twenty *Saṃgha*s that can be understood through multiple purviews. In other words, Tsong kha pa's exegesis is such that it produces an awareness of the Twenty *Saṃghas* that is coherent, at least for him and his followers, from the perspective of a *śrāvaka, pratyekabuddha,* or *bodhisattva* (*Stairway* 270).

This exposition involves presenting a description of the *śrāvaka saṃgha* as a model that serves as a metaphor to the *bodhisattva saṃgha,* the actual *saṃgha* that is represented in the *Abhisamayālaṃkāra* and PP *sūtra*s. This presentation and exegesis demonstrated how the Tibetan scholastic tradition and Tsong kha pa understood the *Abhisamayālaṃkāra* and its earliest commentators to be influenced by various *Abhidharma* traditions; namely, that the Indian commentator Ārya Vimuktisena was influenced by the *Abhidharmakośa* system and that Haribhadra followed the structure given in the *Abhidharmasamuccaya.*

Tsong kha pa, following in the footsteps of previous Indian and Tibetan commentators of the *Abhisamayālaṃkāra*, examined all the relevant Indian source material before him and combined various strands of *sūtra* and *śāstra* to provide a coherent explanation of the Twenty *Saṃghas*. His explanation presents the Twenty *Saṃgha*s based on a distinction between the *allegorical saṃgha* (*mtshon par byed pa'i dpe'i dge 'dun*) and the *actual saṃgha,* which indicates (*mtshon par bya ba'i don gyi dge 'dun*) the *Mahāyāna saṃgha* of irreversible *bodhisattva*s.

Tsong kha pa's exegesis of the *allegorical saṃgha* comprises an articulation of the Twenty *Saṃgha*s by means of the classic *Abhidharma* categories of the *śrāvakasaṃgha,* as enumerated in the sixth chapter of the *Abhidharmakośa* and the first part of the determination of attainments (*prāptiviniścaya)* section on the establishment of persons (*pudgalavyavasthāna*) in the *Abhidharmasamuccaya*. The most important organizing principle in Tsong kha pa's construction of the *allegorical saṃgha* model is the abandoning of defilements. This demonstrates that members of the *allegorical saṃgha,* those *śrāvaka*s who wish to escape *saṃsāra,* wander in the endless cycle of rebirth through the forces of karma and defilements. Tsong kha pa considers that *śrāvaka*s wish only to obtain a *nirvāṇa* that is the cessation of suffering and rebirth.

The *allegorical saṃgha* serves as an analogical template that exemplifies the *actual* (*don gyi*) *saṃgha* that is indicated in the *Prajñāpāramitā sūtra*s and found in the verses of the *Abhisamayālaṃkāra*. The *actual saṃgha* is composed of irreversible (*avaivartika*) *bodhisattva*s, those Noble Beings who are striving to be completely awakened into unsurpassable full enlightenment (*anuttarāṃ samyaksaṃbodhim abhisaṃbudhyante*) and achieve the state of *Mahāyāna arhat*—that is, Buddhahood. For Tsong kha pa, the *actual saṃgha* indicated (*mtshon bya don gyi*) signifies the "genuine" *saṃgha* that is presented as an object of refuge in the *Abhisamayālaṃkāra*. Tsong kha pa, along with the Indian commentators Ārya Vimuktisena and Haribhadra, correlated the relationship between these two distinctions of *saṃgha* with the analogies given in the *Avaivartikadharmacakrasūtra* (AAV 46; AAĀ 36). The enumeration of this *Mahāyāna saṃgha* depends upon imputing the names or designations of the *śrāvaka saṃgha* on to *bodhisattva*s. These *bodhisattva*s are nominally designated (*tsam po pa'i ming gis btags nas*) and exist in the sense of being merely named (*ming can*).

Tsong kha pa in both his *Stairway* and *Golden Garland* has made an effort to direct his interpretation of the *allegorical saṃgha* and *actual saṃgha* to be in agreement with statements from the *Abhidharmasamuccaya* and Haribhadra in his AAĀ and AASPh. In part, Tsong kha pa's concerns in following Haribhadra relate to the *Mahāyāna* soteriological theory of one ultimate vehicle (*ekayāna*). In following Haribhadra's interpretation of this theory, we demonstrated that Tsong kha pa was able to create a *Mahāyāna* scholastic exegesis that is all inclusive in its descriptions of ideal figures. The topic of the Twenty *Saṃgha*s becomes a tour de force of the narrative analysis of Noble Beings (*ārya*) that is catholic in scope and encyclopedic in proportion. Through this type of hermeneutic, Tsong kha pa correlated *Abhidharma* texts and Indian AA authors in order to articulate a homogeneous system of interpreting the Twenty *Saṃgha*s from the perspectives of both the *allegorical saṃgha* and the *actual saṃgha*. Yet, in spite of this style of exegesis that Tsong kha pa follows, Tsong kha pa rejected the correlation of the Twenty *Saṃgha*s to the stages of spiritual levels (*bhūmi*s) traversed by *Mahāyāna bodhisattva*s.

In this way, for Tibetan commentators such as Tsong kha pa, the Twenty *Saṃgha*s becomes an all-inclusive taxonomic *Abhidharma* scholastic model. The Twenty *Saṃgha*s, by presenting the defining characteristics of these individuals, is thought to provide a complete picture of all possible states on the path to enlightenment. Therefore, the heuristic distinction of *allegorical saṃgha* and *actual saṃgha* allows Tsong kha pa to articulate Noble Beings in all three vehicles—that is, *śrāvaka*s, *pratyekabuddha*s, and *bodhisattva*s—and to articulate Noble Beings from the perspective of either the *Hīnayāna* or the *Mahāyāna*. This skillful technique of exegesis also provides the background material necessary to understand the commentaries on the Twenty *Saṃgha*s by the two principal Indian Buddhist commentators, Ārya Vimuktisena and Haribhadra. Most importantly, this exegetical technique utilized by Tsong kha pa allows him to present a comprehensive scholastic discourse on the meaning of the Twenty *Saṃgha*s in the *Abhisamayālaṃkāra*.

The Twenty *Saṃgha*s can be interpreted as a descriptive structural analysis of a multilayered narrative of Buddhist soteriology. Viewed in this manner, the scholastic accounts of ideal figures are similar to a fictional character's soteriological narrative in progressing toward *nirvāṇa*. Drawing upon Indian Buddhist sources, Tsong kha pa himself provided a "structural metaphor" that illustrates such a soteriological narrative, the structure of a "stairway" (Skt. *sopāna*; Tib. *them skas*).

The stairway serves as a visual metaphor for the ascensional transformation that Noble Beings undergo in the journey through numerous lifetimes and various cosmological realms to reach *nirvāṇa*. Along these lines, the soteriological narrative of the Twenty *Saṃgha*s that we have documented is multilayered and tells two different stories, depending upon the understanding and perspective that one brings to it. On one level, the indices that we have described, the Stream-enterer, Once-returner, and so on, symbolize guidepoints in a narrative that relates to the journey of ideal characters (i.e., *śrāvaka*s) who wish to remove afflictional emotions, abandon the effects that arise from the karmic laws of cause and effect, and attain a state of peace, or *nirvāṇa*, that is the result of the cessation of suffering and rebirth.

The journey of the *śrāvaka* is mapped out through a taxonomic vertical hierarchy of ladder-like subordination and superordination based on the removal of mental afflictions and residual karmic substrate in relation to an established sequence of cosmic realms and meditative stages. The stairway of the *śrāvaka* therefore consists of a hierarchy of refined states of mental purity and cognitive insight. The gradience of mental purification and cognitive discernment is based on the acuity of faculties, the manner of rebirth, and the cosmological locus of transformation. The journey of a *śrāvaka* culminates in the figure of the *śrāvaka Arhat*.

A similar process of classification applies to the *pratyekabuddha*, whose attainment is superior to that of a *śrāvaka*. A *pratyekabuddha* has a greater level of realization than a *śrāvaka Arhat*, having removed part of the knowledge obstacles that prevent the Total Omniscience (*sarvākārajñatā*) that constitutes Buddhahood. The *pratyekabuddha* level is attained without the cosmological presence of a Buddha. Based on the *Mahāyāna* theory of one ultimate vehicle (*ekayāna*) followed by Tsong kha pa, the attainment of *śrāvaka Arhat* or *pratyekabuddha* is not terminal and leads into another level of the stairway, the *bodhisattva* journey to full Buddhahood. In comparative terms, the journey of a *śrāvaka* or *pratyekabuddha* is utopian (Smith, 1978: 147–51) in that they break the bonds (*bandhana*) and fetters (*saṃyojana*) of conditioned existence and escape the cosmic restraints of karma. This narrative description, according to Tsong kha pa, is related to the *allegorical saṃgha* or *saṃgha* illustration.

On another level, the indices within the soteriological narrative of the Twenty *Saṃgha*s signify the journey of ideal heroic characters, that is, *bodhisattvas*. *Bodhisattva*s aspire to achieve full Buddhahood for the welfare of all beings. They cultivate and engage the altruistic resolution, *bodhicitta*, to achieve this exalted state. The journey to full Buddhahood is long and arduous, taking three incalculable eons. In order to accomplish this journey, a *bodhisattva* will travel to many world realms by meditative stabilization and attainments to hear special instructions (*avavāda*) from innumerable Buddhas. *Bodhisattva*s will put on the armor (*saṃnāha*) of vows and resolutions and set out (*prasthāna*) to fulfill the altruistic goal of Buddhahood by accumulating the provisions (*saṃbhāra*) necessary to achieve the aim. *Bodhisattva*s cultivate special wisdom in conjugation with perfecting various virtues such as generosity, patience, and energy, all of which are practiced under the ethos of compassion. *Bodhisattva*s also master all types of concentrations, meditative stabilizations, attainments, and absorptions, not only within the desire realm, but also in the form and formless realms.

Within the narrative of the Twenty *Saṃghas*, *bodhisattvas* replicate the patterns of a *śrāvaka*'s birth, abandonment, and comprehension, but with a transvaluation of those patterns to the overarching goal to achieve Buddhahood rather than *śrāvaka Arhat*ship. There is also an amplification of the qualities of mental purity and cognitive discernment in that *bodhisattvas* attain Total Omniscience (*sarvākārajñatā*) in addition to the Empirical Omniscience (*sarvajñatā*) of *Arhat*ship. *Bodhisattvas* sustain the process of transvaluation and amplification of virtuous and cognitive qualities through the cultivated mastery of skill-in-means (*upāyakauśalya*). A *bodhisattva*, motivated by heroic and selfless aspirations and vows, utilizes skill-in-means to gain mastery over meditative concentrations and cognitive attainment without actualizing the correlative result of such attainments. *Bodhisattvas*, through implementing skill-in-means, avoid achieving rebirth in nonefficacious cosmological realms, such as the formless realm, or falling into inferior aims, such as *śrāvaka Arhat*ship or the state of *pratyekabuddha*, for the purpose of all livings beings' welfare and for deferring their accumulations of virtues and knowledge for the result of Buddhahood. A *bodhisattva*'s utilization of skill-in-means therefore fulfills a traditional double purpose (Lamotte, 1976: 19 citing *Bodhisattvabhūmi*): the welfare of others (*svaparārthasādhana*) and the *bodhisattva*'s own attainment of Buddha qualities (*buddhadharmasamudāgama*). On the one hand, *bodhisattvas* master and learn all the *śrāvaka* or *pratyekabuddha* attainments in order to establish living beings in those attainments according to the inclinations, aspirations, and capacities of those beings. On the other, *bodhisattvas* voluntarily take on innumerable rebirths to accumulate the virtues and knowledge necessary to attain an inconceivable type of *nirvāṇa* that results in supreme and perfect enlightenment (*anuttarasamyaksaṃbodhi*).

In the context of the Twenty *Saṃghas*, *bodhisattvas* are therefore liminal figures (Turner, 1967) that parallel the utopian hierarchical order of *śrāvaka* or *pratyekabuddha* attainment. That is, *bodhisattvas* are "'betwixt and between' all the recognized fixed points in the space-time of structural classification" (Turner, 1967: 97). Throughout their heroic journey to Buddhahood, *bodhisattvas* are at the "threshold" (*limen*) performing a balancing act between actualizing a *śrāvaka* attainment and deferring that attainment through countering tactics (Nattier, 2003: 155, 171–72) to transform virtue and knowledge. *Bodhisattvas* resemble all degrees of *śrāvaka* attainment through mere nominal designation but are not fully categorized into that domain. *Bodhisattvas* take on the gestures, guises, and appearances of various types of Noble Beings in order to help living beings mature in their progress toward *nirvāṇa*. This *bodhisattva* purview or narrative interpretation of the Twenty *Saṃgha*s is related to the actual *saṃgha* found in the *Prajñāpāramitā sūtra*s through a hermeneutical technique derived from the *Avaivartikadharmacakrasūtra*.

I believe that there is enough textual evidence to support Tsong kha pa's presentation as being reasonable but not necessarily *the* one and only interpretation of the twenty-third and twenty-fourth verses of the *Abhisamayālaṃkāra*'s first chapter. I am not stipulating that Tsong kha pa's reading of AA 1.23–24 may be *the correct* one or even that it represents *the original* intentions of the author of the AA. On the other hand, I am advocating that Tsong kha pa's interpretation is a viable one that is well informed and has utility in coming to terms with how indigenous authors articulate elliptical cryptical texts like the AA. Tsong kha pa's interpretation of the Twenty *Saṃgha*s makes intelligible how *Mahāyāna*-based systems of Buddhist soteriology envision and map the process to Buddhahood. My analysis has demonstrated the doctrinal breadth of Tsong kha pa's approach to the Twenty *Saṃgha*s and their soteriological significance for the Tibetan Buddhists who came to follow him. For Tsong kha pa and his followers, the Twenty *Saṃgha*s provides the structure and worldview in which soteriological results of the path can take place; it reveals the cosmographic framework that makes a narrative of spiritual progress possible, and most importantly, it generates an awareness for the definitive meaning of the *Mahāyāna Saṃgha* Jewel in Tibetan Buddhist thought.

Notes

Chapter One. The Topic of the Twenty *Saṃghas*

1. *Nirvāṇa* is polysemous term in Buddhist cultures with multiple connotations and multiple types. In general, *nirvāṇa* signifies an event in which all forms of misery and suffering have been brought to cessation. A basic sense of the term is the cessation of all psychophysical turbulence propelled by mental afflictions such as hatred, lust, and anger, along with their residual habituations. In this sense, *nirvāṇa* signifies the culmination of a process and is a state of "liberation" or "emancipation" from the conditioned existence of repeated death and rebirth. *Nirvāṇa* may also be interchangeable with *bodhi*, a psychological and cognitive term signifying "awakening," "understanding," or "enlightenment." There are multiple levels of enlightenment—the perfect, full enlightenment (*samyaksaṃbodhi*) of a Buddha, the enlightenment of a Listener (*śrāvaka*), and the solitary or self-made enlightenment of a Solitary Buddha (*pratyekabuddha*). The multivalence of *nirvāṇa*, along with the associated degrees of attainment and knowledge in reaching this event, will become apparent in the course of our study. For a brief overview of *nirvāṇa* in Buddhist culture see Gomez (2004). Collins (1998) examines *nirvāṇa* in Pāli-based forms of Buddhism. Obermiller (1934a) provides a detailed study of categories of *nirvāṇa* in Tibetan forms of Buddhism, while Welbon (1968) examines the Euro-North American scholarly reception of the term.

2. We follow Ruegg (2000: vi) concerning the epithet "Indo-Tibetan" as referring to cultural and intellectual developments marked by continuities and what he describes as "family resemblances."

3. Although the Twenty *Saṃgha*s always consists of a list of twenty, various interpretations can lead to various lists of twenty, as is detailed in our fourth chapter. While one can point to other scholastic lists with fixed numbers but varying contents, the Twenty *Saṃgha*s differs from many of these lists, inasmuch as one cannot provide any easy formula to compute its possible contents. As we shall see, this lack of regularity indicates the complexity of the topic.

4. Our usage of "soteriology" is in a Buddhist sense and conforms to that found in Buswell and Gimello (1992: 2–3): "the theory according to which certain methods of practice, certain prescribed patterns of religious behavior, have transformative power and will lead, somehow necessarily, to specific religious goals." The term *soteriology* is a theological term brought into early Christianity from the Greek medical tradition. The etymology is derived from the Greek *sōtērion*, "salvation," which as Buswell and Gimello (1992: 310) note,

the root *sōtēr* can mean "to heal"—a point that can be compared to the Buddha's traditional role as doctor and his teachings of the Dharma as medicine.

5. For the rendering of this term, see BHSD: 615. I have here followed the rendering in the extant editions of AKBh, where the hiatus between the final initial vowels is preserved.

6. Authorial intent is a problematic notion in determining any given author's intentions. As we will discuss below, this is particularly true with regard to the topic of the Twenty *Saṃghas*.

7. We should note that our utilization of the Tibetan sources to approach the AA is in a manner *similar* to the method employed by Gethin in approaching the *Nikāyas*, but not the *same* exact procedure. In the following citation, the Tibetans did not compile the AA commentaries in the same manner that the Pāli commentators compiled their literature.

8. See Ruegg (1995: 156–57). For similar viewpoints, cf. Griffiths (1994: 19); Cabezón (1994: 3ff).

9. See for instance Manné, "Case Histories from the Pāli Canon II: Sotāpanna, Sakadāgāmin, Anāgāmin, Arahat—The Four Stages Case History or Spiritual Materialism and the Need for Tangible Results." *Journal of the Pali Text Society* 21 (1995): 35–128.

10. See Apple (2001: 20–27) for an understanding of the Twenty *Saṃghas* through Barthe's structural analysis of narratives.

11. These are set forth in the *Sūtra on the Four Reliances* (*catuḥpratisaraṇa-sūtra*). For more detail and a full discussion of these see AK, ix; LVP, 246; Traité, 1949: 536n1; Thurman, 1978: 19–39; Napper, 1989: 658, 733–34.

12. See Scherrer-Schaub, 1981: 193–97.

13. See, for example, Lamotte, 1988a: 12; MN I.265: *nanu bhikkhave yad eva tumhākaṃ sāmaṃ ñātaṃ sāmaṃ diṭṭhaṃ sāmaṃ viditaṃ tad eva tumhe vadethā ti.*

14. See Ruegg (1985, 1988) for more on Tibetan hermeneuticians' own interpretation regarding "thought/intention" (Skt. *abhiprāya*; Tib. *dgongs pa*).

15. "Exegesis" (Gr. *exēgēsis*, f. *exēgeisthai*, "interpret") stems from a tradition of biblical study involving a range of techniques to elucidate the implications of textual meaning. In some usages, exegesis is interchangeable with "interpretation." In our work, exegesis refers to an expository interpretation based on a close reading of the relevant texts. See, for example, Hayes (1994: 362) for a brief description of the approach of exegesis.

16. For more on constructive postmodern thought and what it entails see Griffin (2000: xxi–xxvi). According to Griffin (xxiii), constructive postmodernism can also be called "revisionary, constructive, or—perhaps best—reconstructive. . . . It seeks to overcome the modern worldview not by eliminating the possibility of worldviews . . . but by constructing a postmodern worldview through a revision of modern premises and traditional concepts in the light of inescapable presuppositions."

17. Tsong kha pa undoubtedly draws the analogy of a stairway (*them skas*; Skt./Pāli, *sopāna* [sa + upāyana]) from Yaśomitra's AKV (Śāstrī, pp. 927–28) citation of three *sadṛṣṭāntāni sūtrāni* found in the *Saṃyuktāgama* (T 99, ch. 16, p. 113a–b) on the Buddha's assertion that the comprehension of the four Noble Truths are progessive and not simultaneous (*caturṇām*

āryasatyānām anupūrvābhisamayo na tv ekābhisamayaḥ). These three comparisons are of a storied mansion (*kūṭāgāra*), a stairway with four flights (*catuṣkadevara sopāna*), and a ladder with four rungs (*catuṣpadikā niḥśreṇī*). Cf. *Saṃyuttanikāya* (5). See also *Dīgha Nikāya* 2.178; *Dhammapada* v.239, *Aṅguttaranikāya* 4, pp. 200–201. In Tibetan Buddhist artwork this is depicted as a four-runged ladder.

18. We will be documenting in the notes to chapter 4 citations from the *Puggala-paññatti*, edited by Richard Morris (1972), and a critical edition of the *Sgra sbyor bam po gnyis pa* (GBBN), edited by Mie Ishikawa (1990).

19. A listing of these twenty-one Indian commentaries may be found in Obermiller (1932: 9–11); Conze (1978b: 111–17); and Makransky (1997: 395–96).

20. We should note here that although the Twenty *Saṃgha*s tradition that we are presenting is Indian and Tibetan, we will employ Sanskrit terminology throughout this work to express the denaturalized technical jargon that describes ideal figures. In brief, our reasoning for utilizing Sanskrit throughout our work is that Sanskrit serves as a lingua franca of *Mahāyāna* Buddhist scholasticism and therefore can be utilized as a unitary medium of communication in the transposition between Tibetan, Chinese, Japanese, and even non-*Mahāyāna* Buddhist traditions.

21. The full title of this text is *Zhugs pa dang gnas pa'i skyes bu chen po rnams kyi rnam par bzhag pa blo gsal bgrod pa'i them skas zhes bya ba*. Tohoku Catalogue 5413, volume Tsha 1–42. The edition I will be using is in volume 27, folios 265–309 of the collected works of Tsong kha pa, the *Khams gsum chos kyi rgyal po tsong kha pa chen po'i gsung bum*. Delhi: dGe ldan gsung rab mi nyams rgyun phel series 79–105, published by Nga dbang dge legs bde mo, 1975–79. This text is also referred to as the *Dge 'dun nyi shu chen mo* by Ngag dbang bkra shis in his *Dge 'dun nyi shu'i mtha' dpyod*, folio side 215, an instuctional manual (*yig cha*) of Sgo-mang college.

22. This is Tsong kha pa's first major work and grand detailed exegesis of the *Abhisamayālaṃkāra*, along with its *Sphuṭārthā* subcommentary by Haribhadra. The full title of the edition I will be using is *Bstan bcos mngon rtogs rgyan 'grel pa dang bcas pa'i rgya cher bsad pa legs bsad gser phreng zhes bya ba bzhugs so*. Sarnath: Lama Thuptan Jungnes, 1970, volume 1. There is also an edition in the *The Collected Works*, volumes 26 and 27 called *Shes rab kyi pha rol tu phin pa'i man ngag gi bstan bcos mngon par rtogs pa'i rgyan 'grel pa dang bcas pa'i rgya cher bshad pa'i legs bshad gser gyi phreng ba*, which is the title used by Tsong kha pa (*Golden Garland* 1970: 13).

23. The Tibetan title: *Dge 'dun nyi shu bsdus pa rjes gnang ba dang zhugs gnas bshugs so*, Tohoku Catalogue 5420, volume Tsha 1–7. Collected Works, volume 27, fols. 593–606, 1977. The title refers to the work as an "oral permission or bestowal" (*rjes gnang*). Conze in his *Prajñāpāramitā Literature* (1978b: 114) cites this text as *Bzhugs gnas skyes bu chen po' dka 'gnad*, being an "oral (discourse on the) essential points of the individual enterers and abiders (of the *Blo gsal grod pa'i them skas*)." Therefore, this text may be considered to be an oral discourse given by Tsong kha pa and written down by one of his disciples.

CHAPTER 2. TSONG KHA PA AND THE *ABHISAMAYĀLAṂKĀRA* COMMENTARIAL TRADITION

1. *Prasphuṭapadā*, Pk 5194, vol. 91, 65.2.8–66.3.2.

2. The major transmissional lineage to be followed here will be based on that given in Se ra rje btsun chos kyi rgyal mtshan's commentary *Klu dbang rol mtsho*, folio 3a–4a. This lineage list, up to the time of Bo dong brtson 'grus rdo rje, is indentical to that given in the record of teachings received (*gsan yig*) of the Fifth Dalai Lama, Klong rdol bla ma and Jaya *paṇḍita* within the *Dge lugs pa* tradition. See Samten, 1997: 834ff. Se ra rje btsun's lineage list of Indian predecessors also mirrors that given by Bu ston rin chen grub in his *Gsan yig*, *The Collected Works of Bu ston*, Part 21 (La), ed. Lokesh Chandra. New Delhi, 1971. Surprisingly, Tsong kha pa does not give an AA (i.e., *phar phyin*) lineage list in his record of teachings recieved, *Rje rin po che blo bzang grags pa'i dpal gyi gsan yig*. Khams gsum chos gyi rgyal po tsong kha pa chen po'i gsum 'bum. Vol. Ka, PP, 233–93.

3. The following legendary accounts of the Indian and Tibetan scholars who preceded Tsong kha pa in the AA lineage are based on these principal sources unless otherwise noted: Khetsun Sangpo, *Biographical Dictionary of Tibet and Tibetan Buddhism*, 12 volumes (Dharamsala: Library of Tibetan Works and Archives, 1973–1981); N. Roerich, trans., *The Blue Annals* (Delhi: Motilal Banarsidas, 1976); Tshe mchog gling yongs 'dzin yes shes rgyal mtshan (1713–1793), *Byang chub lam gyi rim pa'i bla ma brgyud pa'i rnam par thar pa rgyal bstan mdzes pa'i rgyan mchog phul byung nor bu'i phreng ba* [Garland of Perfect Jewels, Supreme Ornament which beautifies the Spiritual Biographies of the Successive Gurus of the Stages of the Path to Enlightenment Teachings] (vol. 1, Ngawang Gelek Demo, 1970); Bu ston, *History of Buddhism*, translated by E. Obermiller (Heidelberg, 1931–1932); A. Chattopadhyaya and L. Chimpa, *Tārānātha's History of Buddhism in India* (Simla: Indian Institute of Advanced Study, 1970).

4. The question of Maitreyanātha's historicity is too long and complex for our present study. See Stcherbatsky (1905: 141–55), Tucci (1930), and Noriaki Hakamaya (1986: 235–68) for a discussion on this topic. As Conze (1978b: 101) and Griffiths (1990: 43) note, the earliest reference to Maitreya and Asaṅga in an Indian text is Sthiramati's *ṭīkā* to the *Madhyāntavibhāgabhāṣya* where Maitreya is called the "promulgator" (*praṇetṛ*). Griffiths (1994: 36) also notes the term *praṇetṛ* is explained in the subcommentary to mean "creator" or "maker" (*kartṛ*) and that it would not be misleading to think of Maitreya as the author of *Madhyāntavibhāga*. The same principles may be applied to the AA. Interestingly, this subcommentary of Sthiramati repeats an aspect of the story we will see below of how Asaṅga received the AA from Maitreya (ibid. 36): "This treatise has been made manifest and declared to him [i.e., to Asaṅga] through the grace of the noble Maitreya by the [concentration called] 'stream of doctrine' " (*tasya hīdaṃ śāstram abhivyaktam ākhyātaṃ cāryamaitreyādhiṣṭhānād dharmasrotasā* /).

5. On Asaṅga's life and times see Willis (1979: 3–12), Keenan (1980: 181–242), Griffiths (1983: 13–49), and remarks in Thurman (1984: 28–33).

6. The "Five texts of Maitreya" are the AA, *Mahāyānasūtrālaṃkāra, Madhyāntavibhaṅga, Dharmadharmatā-vibhaṅga,* and the *Uttaratantra*. The tradition of the "five texts" is late to Tibet as the *Ldan dkar* catalogue (Lalou, 1953: 313–53) does not know of it, and there is no clear evidence to it in Tibet until the twelfth or thirteenth century CE. Davidson (1985) suggests that the tradition of the "five texts" was carried into Tibet by Ngog blo ldan shes rab (1059–1109). Also of note is the lack of mention of any such "five texts" tradition or even the AA by the great seventh-century Chinese pilgrim and devotee of Maitreya, Hsüan Tsang (596–664 CE), who traveled throughout India and Central Asia.

7. Note that in the Euro-North American academic tradition there are some scholars who posit the existence of two Vasubandhus, a theory that has been subject to debate and is not at all acknowledged in the Indo-Tibetan tradition that influenced Tsong kha pa. See E. Frauwallner (1951, 1961).

8. Ye shes rgyal mtshan, 1990: 79.

9. Sources for Vasubandhu's life may be found in Frauwallner (1951), Jaini (1958: 48–53), Griffiths (1983: 175–93), Hall (1983: 13–21), Thurman (1984: 41–44), and Anacker (1970: 9–34, 1984).

10. The *Śatasāhasrikāpañcaviṃśatisāhasrikāṣṭādaśasāhasrikāprajñāpāramitā-bṛhaṭṭīka* is known in Tibetan as the *Yum gsum gnod 'joms.*

11. The Sanskrit manuscript was acquired by G. Tucci from Nepal and is well known through the critical edition of the first section prepared by C. Pensa in Serie Orientale Roma 37, *L'Abhisamayālaṃkāravṛtti di Ārya-Vimuktisena* (Rome, 1967). The Tibetan translation, by Go mi 'chi med and Rngog blo ldan shes rab, is in the Bstan 'gyur with the Sanskrit title *Āryapañcaviṃśatisāhasrikāprajñāpārmitopadeśaśāstrābhisamayālaṃkāravṛttiḥ*. It is also called *Pañcālokā* (Obermiller, 1932–1933), as reflected in the Tibetan abbreviation *Nyi khri snang ba.*

12. This is a praise given in the lineage lists. Haribhadra, in his *Abhisamayālaṃkārasphuṭārthā,* describes Ārya Vimuktisena as one "who delineated [the AA] with an awareness of abiding in the middle way." Amano (2000: 3): *'phags pa'i khongs su gtogs pa yi / rnam par grol ba shes byas kyang / des byas byas pa min mthong nas / dbu mar gnas pa'i blos rnam phye //* Tripāṭhī (1977: 3) reconstructs as *āryāntargaṇitaḥ khyāto vimuktir iti tatkṛt / akṛtām iva tāṃ draṣṭavā cakre'nyāṃ madhyayā dhiyā* / See also Naughton (1991: 16).

13. Ruegg, 1968: 305. On the *Kaurukullakas* branch of the *Sammatīya* school see A. Bareau, 1955: 25–26.

14. I would like to acknowledge and thank E. Gene Smith who provided me with this information.

15. We should note here that in providing the chronology of Tsong kha pa's life, we have documented his age from birth according to Western count. In Tibet and Japan, the custom of counting the years of one's life begins at conception such that a person is already one year old when he or she is born. Also, if a person is born before the New Year, then when the New Year comes, the person would be two years old. This may account for some numeric discrepancies between Tsong kha pa's age and the date when documenting his life's activities.

16. The main source of the life of Tsong kha pa is the biographical account given by his disciple, Mkhas grub dpal bzang po (1385–1438), in his

Rje btsun bla ma tsong kha pa chen po'i ngo mtshar rma du byung ba'i rnam par thar pa dam pa'i 'jug ngog (New Delhi, 1977). Another source is the account given by 'Jam dpal rgya mtsho (1356–1428) in his *Rje btsun tsong kha pa'i rnam thar chen mo'i zur 'debs rnam thar legs bshad kun 'dus* (Varanasi, 1970). These two biographies seem to be the sources for all subsequent accounts of Tsong kha pa's life. Van der Kuijp (1985: 52) mentions a biography given by Gnas rnying pa kun dga' bde legs (1446–1496), but this is not available to me. A number of later versions of Tsong kha pa's life exist in Tibetan that expand upon the earlier sources and are mixed with oral tradition. These include a biography given in the *Lam rim bla ma brgyud pa'i rnam thar* of Tshe mchog gling ye shes rgyal mtshan (1713–1793), material from Blo bzang tshul khrims cha har dge bshes (1740–1810), and the *Rnam thar chen mo* (Varanasi, 1967) by Blo bzang 'phrin las gnam rgyal (fl. 1840–1860). A chronology of the works and important dates of Tsong kha pa is found in the *Bod rgya tshig mdzod chen mo* (1995) and *Bstan rtsus kun las btus pa* (1982).

Euro-North American sources on the life of Tsong kha pa are for the most part based on the above material. This includes an article by Obermiller (1934–1935), material by Kaschewsky (1971), and books by Ngawang Dhargyey (1975) and Thurman (1982). Additional bibliographical remarks are found in review articles by van der Kuijp (1985, 1999) and in works by Sparham (1993, 1999).

17. *Dam pa'i 'jug ngog* (1966: 18): *yum chen rgyas 'bring bsdus gsum gyi / rgyun du gyur pa'i mngon rtogs rgyan / thog mar bslab cing nan tan bya. . . .* / The advice continues for a couple of pages. A paraphrase of the statement is in Obermiller (1935: 323). These statements are also found in the *Rnam thar chem mo* (1967: 112–13) and *Lam rim bla ma brgyud pa'i rnam thar* (1990: 321–22).

18. Mkhas grub, 1966: 30; Rnam rgyal, 1967: 126–27; Kaschewsky, 1971: 3.10v–III,11r. Thurman (1984: 72) provides a translation of the experience from Mkhas grub.

19. Tsong kha pa's combination of verse sections of the *Pramāṇavārttika* occurs at *Stairway* (1977: 332). This is a combination of *pramāṇasiddhi* chapter, verses 139–42a, as listed in Vetter (Vienna, 1990).

CHAPTER 3. CONTEXTUAL AND DOCTRINAL PRESUMPTIONS

1. Obermiller (1932: 7, 341). See also P. Arènes (1998: 201–209). Here, within a Tibetan context, one should make a distinction between "hidden meaning" (*sbas don*) and "implicit meaning" (*shugs bstan*). "Hidden meaning" is that which is possible to comprehend through the force of reasoning that analyzes the explicit or direct sense (*dngos bstan*). "Implicit meaning" is that in which it is not possible at all to comprehend through analysis without the explanation from the instructions of a master (Arènes, 205–206). The application of the term *hidden meaning* (*sbas don*) in reference to the AA is mentioned by Rgyal tshabs Dar ma rin chen in his *Rnam shad rnying po rgyan*, while Tsong kha himself uses "implicit meaning" (*shugs don*) in the *Golden Garland* (1970: 9.16–17), a usage that is articulated by Dharmamitra in his *Prasphuṭapadā* (Pk 5194, 3b4–7). Modern *Dge lugs pa* scholars seem to use the terms *sbas don* and

shugs don interchangeably. An example of the application of "implicit meaning" is demonstrated with the *Heart Sūtra* (*Prajñāpāramitāhṛdayasūtra*): where the *sūtra* says, "no form, no feeling, no impulse, etc. . . ." (*na rūpaṃ, na vedanā, na saṃjñā, . . .*), the explicit sense (*dngos bstan*) is that these bases lack inherent nature (*svabhāvaśūnyān*), while implicitly the bases that are negated exist, but not inherently (Geshe Sopa oral communication).

2. Tsong kha pa cites a *śloka*, attributed to Asaṅga and Vasubandhu, for this meaning in *Golden Garland* 24.5–10: "When [a text has] the quality of curing or protecting, curing all the enemies of the afflictions or protecting from the existences of lower rebirth, then it is a *śāstra*; these two are not found in other systems" (*nyon mongs dgra rnams ma lus 'chos pa dang / ngan 'gro srid las skyob pa gang yin pa / 'chos skyob yon tan phyir na bstan bcos te / gnyis po 'di dag gzhan gyi lugs la med*). The Sanskrit is in the *Madhyāntavibhāgaṭīkā* (ed. Lévi, 1934: 3): *yac chāsti ca kleśaripūn aśeṣān saṃtrāyate durgatito bhavāc ca / tac chāsanāt trāṇa guṇāc ca śāstram etad dvayaṃ cānyamateṣu nāsti //* Cf. *Prasannapadā* (La Vallèe Poussin, 1900): 3. Also at *Golden Garland*: 1970: 89.23–90.1. See also Griffiths, 1994: 44ff. We should note that Buddhist etymological constructs given here are not "etymologies" in the linguistic sense, but rather are what is referred to in the Indian scholastic tradition as *nirukti*, hermeneutical devices employed to give contextual doctrinal meaning.

3. MW 199, *Tshig mdzod chen mo*: 2056: *thabs kyi snying po 'am thabs zab mo /* Cabezón, 1994: 82, cites Bu ston rin chen grub's definition: "It is that which makes one quickly understand the object to be understood and which teaches either the hidden meaning or a condensed and brief method for understanding the [otherwise] extensive meaning of the *sūtras*" *Lung gi snye ma*, 5: *shes par bya ba'i yul myur du khong du chud pas byed pa ste / mdo don rgya chen rtog par byed pa'i thabs nyung 'dus sam sbas pa'i don ston pa'o /*.

4. These three understandings of the term *prajñāpāramitā* can be traced back to Dignāga in his *Prajnāpāramitārthasaṃgraha* (Tucci, 1947: 54 (v.1): "Consummation of wisdom is non-dual wisdom. It is the *Tathāgata*, and is to be accomplished. Because the treatise[s] and the path have that as the goal, that name also applies [to them]" (*prajñāpāramitā jñānam advayaṃ sa tathāgataḥ / sādhyatādarthyayogenatācchābyaṃ granthamārgayoḥ //*). Haribhadra in his AAĀ cites this verse and adds (23.8): "The principal [meaning of PP] is the Lord Buddha, the non-dual wisdom which is like an illusion. Also harmonious in obtaining that [meaning] are the texts of accumulated words and sentences and the paths characterized as seeing and so forth which are metaphorically *prajñāpāramitā*" (*mukhyā buddho bhagavān māyopamaṃ jñānam advayaṃ / tatprāptyanukūlatvena tu padavākyasamūho grantho darśanādilakṣaṇo mārgaś ca gauṇī prajñāpāramitā /*). Tsong kha pa at first mentions that "*sher phyin*" has the meaning of the root *sūtra* (*rtsa ba'i mdo*) (*Golden Garland* 1970: 13), but then later on gives a long discussion of PP and its meanings (*Golden Garland* 1970: 101ff). Haribhadra provides an explanation of the term *prajñāpāramitā* in his AAĀ (23.3–6) for which, see Kajiyama (1970: 136–42). See also Obermiller (1932: 7).

5. Dharmamitra, in his PSPh (discussion from 5a.6–6b3), is possibly the first of our Indian written sources to introduce this additional understanding of PP. He states that this nature is the suchness of things such that it is

inexpressable as either the same or different from things. Then he relates this suchness to something that is very dear (*rab tu gces pa*) to all beings (5b.1ff: *ngo bo nyid . . . / ji ltar zhe na / chos rnams kyi de bzhin nyid chos rnams las de nyid dang gzhan nyid du brjod par bya ba ma yin pa ni rang bzhin gyi shes rab kyis pha rol tu phyin pa ste../*).

6. *Golden Garland*: 21.3–8. Tsong kha cites (*Golden Garland* 21.8–12) the MSA (1.3) for his source of this sense of "ornament": "In the manner that form, possessing the qualities of a nature and adornment, reflected in a mirror produces special joy through the force of its view, likewise the dharma, possessing the qualities of a nature and that which is well spoken, here also produces continual enjoyment for the wise people who investigate various meanings." Dharmamitra, in his *Prasphuṭapadā* (7b.3ff), also cites this verse for the analogy of "ornament." A second meaning is mentioned by Tsong kha pa in *Golden Garland* 22.8–10, quoting from *Madhyamakālaṃkāra* (Ichigō, 1985), 21: *klan ka ngan pa'i dri ma bsal bas 'di dbu ma'i rgyan zhes bya 'o /*. Most Tibetan Dge lugs pa scholars cite this usage of "ornament" from the abbreviated explanation of rGyal tshab's *rnam bshad snying po rgyan* (1994). Cf. Gonda, 1939: 97–114. Gonda compares *aram* and *alam* ("being fit, good, sufficient," etc., p. 98) to the latin *ornare* ("to fit out, to prepare, to supply with everything needed," etc., p. 113). Conze (1954a, 192–97) following Stcherbatsky, notes that *alaṃkāra* is used to denote a "short summary of the salient points of [a doctrinal] system."

7. These two meanings are drawn from MW 60 and 1152 respectively. It should be noted that MW is not reliable in all instances.

8. The Tibetan tradition draws out the meaning *abhi* of *abhisamaya* from among four meanings presented in the MSA and *Bhāṣya* (11.3cd): "Abhidharma is overpowering because of directly facing and repetition (*abhimukhato 'thābhīkṣṇyād abhibhavagatito 'bhidharmaś ca*). PSPh (65a.5–8) gives the following meaning: "*abhi* means directly facing; *sama* means certainty; *iya* means to understand; and therefore, this path that reaches wisdom by directly understanding with certainty the nature of things is *abhisamaya*."

9. This paragraph relies on Kyosho Hayashima's article on "*Abhisamaya*" from the *Encylopedia of Buddhism*, vol. 1, A Aoki, pp. 104–14, 1961, and the AKBh on AK vi.2 (1975: 328): *abhisamaya iti ko 'rthaḥ / abhisaṃbodha iṇo bodhanārthatvāt* / Varied meanings of *abhisamaya* are discussed in AKBh on AK vi.27.

10. By the time of Tsong kha, the AA was understood to be representative of all the Mother PP *sūtras* (*Golden Garland* 1970: 27). This was a tradition started by Haribhadra (based on a stanza from Dignāga's *Prajñāpāramitāpiṇḍārtha*: vs. 7), who while awkwardly fitting the AA on to the *Aṣṭasāhasrikā*, mentioned in his AAĀ (p. 11.26–12.8), that the AA is an ornament that gives clear realization to all (PP) *sūtras*. Ārya Vimuktisena relates the AA to each section of the *Pañcaviṃśati*. This has been extensively analyzed in Makransky *Buddhahood Embodied*, 1997.

11. Indeed, this is said to be the very reason that Maitreyanātha imparted the AA to Asaṅga, according to Haribhadra in AAĀ (75.17–22): "Even though the Noble Asaṅga had attained to the realization and knew the discourse's entire meaning, he did not realize the precise signification of the

individual words, because of the profundity and because of the repetition. He was unable to unpack the *Prajñāpāramita*'s meaning and became depressed. With him in view, the Bhagavat Maitreya explained the PP *sūtra*s and composed the AA."

12. The translation of this *śloka* is based on David Reigle's interpretation from his "The 'Virtually Unknown' Benedictive Middle in Classical Sanskrit: Two Occcurences in the Buddhist *Abhisamayālaṅkāra*," *Indo-Iranian Journal* 40: 119–23, 1997. The Tibetan is: *rnam pa thams cad mkhyen pa nyid lam / ston pas 'di las bshad pa gang / gzhan gyis myong ba ma yin te / chos spyod bcu yi bdag nyid kyi // mdo don dran pa la bzhag nas / blo dang ldan pas mthong 'gyur phyir / bde blag du ni rtogs pa zhes / bya ba brtsom pa'i dgos pa yin //* According to Reigle, the Tibetan verb forms *mthong 'gyur phyir* for *vīkṣiṣīran* and *rtogs pa* for *pratipatīran* do not help in rendering the benedictive forms of the Sanskrit. In regard to "tenfold practice," Tsong kha pa in his *Golden Garland* mentions ten kinds of activities in relation to *sūtra*s based on the *Madhyāntavibhāgabhāṣya* (Nagao, 1964: 63): (1) copying (*lekhanā*), (2) worship (*pūjanā*), (3) giving to others (*dāna*), (4) listening (*śravaṇa*), (5) reading (*vācana*), (6) accepting (*ud-grahaṇa*), (7) teaching (*prakāśanā*), (8) chanting (*svādhyāya*), (9) reflecting (*cintanā*), and (10) cultivation (*bhāvanā*). However, he also mentions that the tenfold activities could refer to either the ten perfections or to the ten topics to Total Omniscience, beginning with *bodhicittodpāda*, set out in AA I.4–5. PSPh (Pk 28b3–5) mentions that since the ten activities mentioned in the *Madhyāntavibhāgabhāṣya* are carried out in the path of accumulation, the ten activities mentioned here must be perfections that are performed throughout the five paths.

13. AA, homage, W 1. I have translated this passage in accordance with the commentaries that interpret PP to be the Mother of Buddhas and also of *śrāvaka*s and *bodhisattva*s. AASPh, Amano (2000: 5). Haribhadra is the only early Indian writer to give a detailed exposition of the homage. He does this in the AASPh and not the AAĀ.

14. See Conze, 1978b: 13. There is not much evidence for this *Abhidharmic* layered meaning of *mātṛkā*, but a thirteenth-century commentary by *Kassapa* of *Cola* on the *mātikā*s of the *Abhidhamma* explains as follows:

> In what sense is (*Abhidhamma*) like a *mātikā*? In the sense of being like a mother. For a *mātikā* is like a mother as a face is like a lotus. For as a mother gives birth to various different sons, and then looks after them and brings them up, so a *mātikā* gives birth to various dhammas and meanings, and then looks after them and brings them up so that they do not perish. Therefore, the word *mātikā* is used. For independence on the *mātikā*, and by way of the seven treatises beginning with the *Dhammasaṅgaṇi*, dhammas and meanings without end or limit are found as they are spread out, begotten, looked after and brought up, as it were, by the mātikā.

See Rupert Gethin, 1992: 161. This is the same sense in which the AA is looked upon as a "mother."

15. Here Tsong kha pa, drawing from the *Śuddhamatī* (Pk 5199) of Śāntipa, states in the *Golden Garland* (62–63): "Just as it is said in the world that the only person who gives great benefit is one's mother, likewise the clear

realizations (*abhisamaya*) of the three individuals, through fully accomplishing the three essential final purposes of each individual, is the mother of these individuals." Cf. Obermiller, 1932: 65.

16. For an essay on these two terms see Ah-yueh Yeh, "A Study of the Theories of *yāvadbhāvikatā* and *yathāvadbhāvikatā* in the *Abhidharmasamuccaya*," JIABS (7.2) 1984: 185–207.

17. For a more extensive analysis and presentation of the AA's remaining chapters see the works of Obermiller, 1932, 1933, and Alexander Naughton, 1991.

18. The following abbreviated account of these ten topics is based on Haribhadra's AAĀ 16–17. See also Ruegg, 1969: 127–28.

19. These four practices are also called "aids to penetration" (Conze, 1957, Buswell, 1997). MW (558) gives *nirvedha* as "penetration, insight." The AKBh (246; on vi.20a–b) provides the following contextual etymology (*nirukti*): *nirvedhabhāgīyānīti ko 'rthaḥ / vidha vibhāge / niścito vedho nirvedhāḥ āryamārgas tena vicikitsā prahāṇāt satyānāṃ ca vibhajanād idaṃ duḥkhamayaṃ yāvat mārga iti / tasya bhāgo darśanamārgaikadeśaḥ / tasyāvāhakatvena hitatvān nirvedhabhāgīyāni /* (What is the meaning of *nirvedhabhāgīyas*? Piercing in portions. *Nirvedha* signifies "definitely known" because of abandoning doubt through the Noble Path and the Truths are distinguished: "This is suffering" up to "This is the path." One part of that is the path of seeing. Useful to one part of the path because they lead to it are the *nirvedhabhāgīyāni*.) Because these factors lead up to and provide stability for the analysis that takes place on the path of seeing, we will refer to these as "preparatory analytical factors."

20. AS 104; ASBh 150.

21. MSA 14.17; *Golden Garland* (1970: 177–178).

22. MSA 14.3; *Golden Garland* (1970: 178).

23. AAĀ 32.12–14; AASPh (Amano, 2000: 13). *yathokta-*[emended from *yahtokta-*] *prabhedabodhicittapratipattau saṃvṛtiparamārthasatyānatikrameṇa śrāvakādyasādhāraṇānupalambhayogena varttanam iti śikṣaṇaṃ pratipattyavavādaḥ* /.

24. The following section is based on AAĀ 32.14–33.22; AASPh (Amano, 2000: 13–14).

25. This correlation of the ten special instructions with the altruistic mind generation is mentioned by Ārya Vimuktisena (AAV 52–53), Haribhadra (AAĀ 35.1–7), and Tsong kha pa (*Golden Garland* 181).

26. *Saṃgha* = *sam* + *han* meaning "struck or hammered together, a combination or collection" (MW: 1129).

27. *"diṭṭhisīlasāmaññasaṃghātabhāvena saṅgho,"* Dutt (1971: 73–76) citing *Vimānavatthuaṭṭhakathā*.

28. AKBh *ad* vi.75b, Śāstrī, 1026: "The Bhagavat is a perfect buddha. Well-taught is his discipline of dharma, well-cultivated is his community of śrāvakas, thus because they have [this] nature [they are in this order] like doctor, medicine, and attendants" (*samyaksaṃbuddho bata bhagavān svākhyāto 'sya dharmavinayaḥ supratipanno 'sya srāvakasaṃgha iti vaidyabhaiṣajyopasthāyakabhūtatvāt*). Like attendants or nurses (BHSD, *upasthāyaka*—"attendant," p. 144) because they mutually attend to obtaining the well-being of *nirvāṇa* (*upasthāyakabhūtaḥ saṅgho nirvāṇārogyaprāptaye parasparopasthānāt*), AKV, Śāstrī, 1026.

29. This is according to Sera rje mtsun pa chos kyi rgyal mtshan's *Klu dbang gi rol tshol*. Rgyal tshab, in his commentary on the *Uttaratantra*, the *Theg chen po rgyud bla ma'i ṭīkka* (Collected works, New Delhi, 1972: 13) states: "The *Saṃgha* in the ultimate sense are the knowledges and liberations in the mental continuum of the *Mahāyāna* Noble Being and in the conventional sense the assembly of *Mahāyāna* Noble Beings."

30. The sense of *saṃgha* as being "unbreakable" is expressed by Haribhadra in his AAĀ (8.27–9.2) following Candrakīrti's *Triśaraṇagamanasaptati* (Sorenson, 1986: 34–35): *buddhadharmau tathā saṃgho mārakoṭiśatair api / bhettuṃ na śakyate yasmāt tasmāt saṃgho 'bhidhīyate //* (Since even one hundred ten million Māra-devils are incapable of breaking apart the Buddha, his Dharma, and the Community, therefore it is called "Community.") Asaṅga, in his *Saṃghānusmṛtivyākhyā* (Pk 5484: 19.5), notes that *saṃgha* means to be firm in faith that is unbreakable (*mi phyed pa'i dad pa brtan po dang ldan pa'i phyir dge 'dun*).

31. *Ratnagotravibhāga* 1.14: Tib. *ji bshin ji snyed nang gi ni / ye shes gzigs pa dag pa'i phir / blo ldan phyir mi ldog pa'i tshogs / bla med yon tan dang ldan nyid* / Quoted in *Golden Garland* (1970: 204.5) and *Rgyal tshab dar ma rin chen* in his *rNams bshad snying po'i rgyan*, see Bastian, 1980: 218. The Sanskrit: *yathāvadyāvadadhyātma-jñānadarśanaśuddhitaḥ / dhīmatām avivartyānām anuttaraguṇair gaṇaḥ* / For Obermiller's translation, see *The Sublime Science*, page 268, in *The Uttaratantra of Maitreya*, ed. H. S. Prasad, 1991. The *Uttaratantravyākhyā*, atrributed to Asaṅga, comments that: "with this [verse] it is explained, in brief, [that] the pure visionary supermundane pristine cognition of the irreversible *bodhisattva* assembly jewel is endowed with unsurpassable qualities through its twofold aspect of [seeing] existence as it is and the extent of existence" (*anena samāsato 'vaivartikabodhisattvagaṇaratnasya dvābhyam ākārabhyāṃ yathāvadbhāvikatayā yāvadbhāvikatayā ca lokottarajñānadarśanaviśuddhito 'nuttaraguṇānvitatvam udbhāvitam*). The later *Dge lugs pa* tradition (*Se ra rje mtsun pa* onward) attributed eight qualities of the *Saṃgha* Jewel from this verse. The first three define the knowledge of the *Mahāyāna saṃgha*. The second three enumerate three purifications of the *Mahāyāna saṃgha* that free them from the three primary obstacles to emancipation. These three obstacles are: (1) passion obstacles (Skt. *kleśāvaraṇa*; Tib. *nyon sgrib*), (2) knowledge obstacles (Skt. *jñeyāvaraṇa*; Tib. *shes sgrib*), (3) obstacles of inferior purpose (Tib. *dman sgrib*). See Bastian, 1980: 218. The seventh and eighth qualities respectively categorize the first and second three characteristics in terms of their knowledge and their becoming free from the three obstacles. Nevertheless, Tsong kha pa (*Golden Garland*: 204.7–11), citing reference to the root text and commentary, discards this system of interpretation.

32. AAV, Pensa, 44: *arhaṃs tu samyaksambuddha evaṃ sa buddharatnāvavāde nirdiṣṭatvān na punar ihocyate /*.

33. AASPh, Amano, 2000: 13. Cf. Obermiller, 1933: 40; and Naughton, 1991: 33. Haribhadra repeats this same statement in his AAĀ (1932: 32.26–29).

34. See remarks by Lamotte in *Śgs* 1998: 185–86.

35. Outside of the indigenous Tibetan and Indian commentaries on the subject, the works of Ruegg (1969) discuss these various factors.

36. See AKBh on AK vi. 65b–d (Pradhan, 382); AKV (Śāstri, 1013).

37. See Obermiller (1932: 15). Obermiller draws out this definition from Mkhas grub dge legs dpal's *Sa lam gyi mkhas pa'i yid 'phrog*. The synonyms are taken from Dkon mchog 'jigs med dbang po's *Sa lam gyi rnam gzhag theg pa gsum gyi mdzes rgyan* in *The Collected Works of dkon mchog 'jigs med dbang po* (New Delhi: Nga wang Gelek Demo, 1972), 428.3–4. For a detailed explanation of the Tibetan definitions of the "path" see Hopkins, "A Tibetan Perspective on the Nature of Spiritual Experience" in *Paths to Liberation* (ed. Buswell and Gimello, Kuroda Institute, 1992: 225–68).

38. *Lam rim chen mo*, D, folio 3a: *gdams ngag 'di spyir rje btzun byams pas mdzad pa'i mngon par rtogs pa'i rgyan gyi gdams ngag yin la . . . /*

39. These six texts are attributed to Nāgārjuna: *Mūlamadhyamakakārikā (rtsa ba shes rab), Vigrahavyāvartanīkārikā (rtson ldog), Ratnāvalī (rin chen phreng ba), Śūnyatāsaptatikārikā (rtong nyid bdun cu pa), Yuktiṣaṣṭikākārikā (rigs pa drug cu pa),* and *Vaidalyaprakaraṇa (zhib mo rnam 'thag).*

40. The AA employs a slightly different terminology but there is a correspondence with the following five-path system mentioned in AS 65.12–14: "Moreover, the path is fivefold: the path of accumulating provisions, the path of preparation, the path of seeing, the path of cultivation, and the path of termination." Compare with AK vi.65b–d, 381.19–22: "Many divisions of the path have been named: the mundane path, the supramundane path, the path of seeing, the path of cultivation, the path of no more learning, the path of preparation, the uninterrupted path, the path of liberation, and the distinctive path. In brief, how many types of path are there? In brief, the path is fourfold: the distinctive path, of liberation, uninterrupted, and of preparation."

41. The lineages (*gotra*) of *śrāvaka*s, *pratyekabuddha*s, and *bodhisattva*s in the AA are provisional (*ma nges pa*) and not definitive (*nges pa*), as in the strictly *Yogācāra* system. The AA states this at 1.39 (Amano, 2000: 22): "The distinctions among the lineages are not correct because the dharmadhātu has no distinctions. However, the distinctions are declared by distinguishing the qualities which they rely upon." Haribhadra comments (AASPh, Amano, 2000: 22) that just as jars baked from the same clay differ as containers of honey, sugar, etc., likewise the qualities that support Noble Beings, the paths to be realized, are described as different within the three vehicles. These provisional lineages will be connected with the special theory of *ekayāna*, "one ultimate vehicle," which Haribhadra and Tsong kha pa both accept. See Ruegg, 1969: 123–55. Tibetan doxographers such as Mkhas grub dge legs dpal cites this verse of the AA as proof that it is a *Prāsaṅgika-Madhyamaka* text.

42. These points concerning three vehicles to train individuals in the PP is brought out by Dharmamitra in his *Prasphuṭapadā* (Pk nya 16a.1–6). See also ACIP 4, *Pañcaviṃśati*-PP, book 2, for numerous citations of three vehicles in the PP. Dharmamitra (Pk nya 16a–16b) equates these three vehicles with three types of realization: that of *śrāvaka*s and *pratyekabuddha*s realizing a selflessness that is directed toward the person (*gang zag la bdag med*) and *bodhisattvas* and *buddha*s having a realization of the selflessness of person and things (*gang zag dang chos bdag med pa nyid*). He cites the *Āryasaddharmasmṛti sūtra* and *Ārya Gaṇḍhavyūha* as sources of these realizations. Tsong kha pa, beginning in his *Golden Garland* (vol. 27, 1977, major argument at 159.5) and his followers will

insist that both *śrāvakas* and pratyekabuddhas realize the selflessness of things (*chos kyi bdag med*).

43. Haribhadra explicitly demonstrates this from *sūtra*, specifically the *Pañcaviṃśati* (*madhyamāyāṃ jinajananyāṃ*), in his *Sphuṭārthā* (Amano, 2000: 6.9–14): "Subhūti, all paths should be generated by *bodhisattvas*, all paths should be known: the paths of the *śrāvakas*, the paths of the *pratyekabuddhas*, and the paths of the *Buddhas*. Those [paths] should be fully completed and the actions of the paths performed by them. Until they have fully accomplished their aspirations, fully developed beings, and completely purified their buddha-field, they should not fully perceive the reality limit."

44. In this section we will be following primarily the outline of the *Vaibhāṣika* path structure based on the *Abhidharmakośa* vi.17–25ff, its related commentaries, and Obermiller, 1932: 18–26. Similar outlines may be found in Lamotte, 1988b: 678–86; Guenther, 1976: 215–32, Conze, 1967a: 175–77; Sopa and Hopkins, 1989: 203–20; Frauwallner, 1995: 149–84.

45. AS; Rahula (1971: 14; Pradhan, 87).

46. This knowledge of the *śrāvaka*'s path is mentioned explicitly at AA 2.2 (Amano, 2000: 36), with the understanding that *bodhisattvas* should not perceive any inherent natures (*svabhāvānupalambhataḥ*): "This path of the *śrāvakas* should be known in the manner of path-omniscience without perceiving the aspects of the Nobles' Four Truths."

47. AAĀ 138.17–139.9. Compare with the *Sphuṭārthā* (AASPh, Amano, 2000: 37.1–13). Several enumerations of the sixteen aspects are also found in the AKBh on AK vii.13a (Pradhan), 400–401. See also Hopkins, 1983: 292–96.

48. *Sa lam mdzes rgyan* f.428.6.

49. AS, Rahula, 104–105, Pradhan, 65. Listening to the doctrine is a prime characteristic of the *śrāvakas* path of accumulation, *Sa lam mdzes rgyan*, 429.3. For a discussion of the twelve constituent parts (*dvādaśāṅga*) of the law, see Lamotte, 1988b: 145–47.

50. AK vi. 9a–b (Pradhan), 337.

51. AK vi. 14, 341.

52. *Sa lam mdzes rgyan* 429.4, 430.1. AK vi.16, 343.

53. AASPh *Sphuṭārthā* (Amano, 2000: 16) commenting on AA 1.25–26.

54. AKBh 343.

55. AKBh vi. 18 (344). AKV 908.

56. AKBh 346.

57. Note here the meaning of *kṣānti* (forbearance). Śāntideva notes in both his *Bodhicaryāvatāra* (Vaidya, 1960: 83) and *Śikṣāsamuccaya* (Vaidya, 1961: 100), based on the *Dharmasaṅgīti Sūtra*, that *kṣānti* has three aspects: forbearance in the acceptance of unhappiness; forbearance in discerning the Dharma; and forbearance in eschewing others' evil acts. (*kṣāntis trividhā dharmsaṅgītisūtre'bhihitā duḥkhādhivāsanakṣāntiḥ dharmanidhyānakṣāntiḥ parāpakāramarṣaṇakṣāntiś ceti /*). As noted by J. May (*Prasannapadā*, 212n717): *Kṣānti* is firstly a *nirvedhabhāgīya*; secondly, eight moments of the *darśanamārga*; thirdly, the third *pāramitā*. We are concerned with *kṣānti*, generally translated as "forbearance," in the sense of discerning the Dharma within the path system. In the first sense, connected with the *nirvedhabhāgīya*, we shall translate *kṣānti* as

"certainty" because of attaining a level of stability in the path of preparation. In connection with the path of seeing, we shall translate *kṣānti* as "intellectual receptivity." Here *kṣānti* is a process in the path of "being ready in advance to accept knowledge." For others meanings of *kṣānti* see Lamotte, 1998: 143, n119.

58. AK 346, vi.20.

59. AKBh vi. 1c–d: 327.

60. AK vi.28c–d: 352.

61. Tsong kha pa uses the term *rtag gcig rang dbang can gyi gang zag* in the *Golden Garland* (ACIP 5412 page 196a). Nevertheless, the exact terminology used above to characterize a *śrāvakas* knowledge in the path of seeing is not found in Tsong kha pa's *Golden Garland* or other Indian AA works. Tsong kha pa only utilizes the above terminology in his later works, the *Legs bshad snying po* and *Dbu ma dgongs pa rab gsal*. See Jinpa (1997: 82–87). The first occurrence in AA-related works I have found is from mKhas grub rje dge legs dpal bzang po's *Sa lam gyi rnam gzhag mkhas pa'i yid 'phrog* (Collected Works, volume 9, New Delhi, 1982): 312–13.

62. The Tibetan terminology of "learned defilements" (*nyon sgrib kun brtags*) and "instinctual defilements" (*nyon sgrib lhan skyes*) seems to have developed from ideas and terminology found in the AKBh and ASBh. Particularly when commenting on the AS (26.1–7) sections on the *darśanaprahātavya* and *bhāvanāprahātavya*, the ASBh (30.8) mentions the terms *parikalpitagrahaṇaṃ* and *sahajasatkāyāntagrāhadṛṣṭi*.

63. AKBh commenting on vi.66a, 382.

64. *Sa lam mdzes rgyan* 434.1–2.

65. *Sa lam mdzes rgyan* 434.3–4.

66. AKBh vi. 66a.

67. *Sa lam mdzes rgyan* 434.1–2.

68. AK vi.25c–d, 26a; AKBh 350.

69. This discussion is found in AKBh 352 and AKV (Śāstrī) 929. Haribhadra applies this image of closing the door on the thief for the *Mahāyāna* path of seeing in AAĀ 76.25.

70. AK vi. 28c–d.

71. *Golden Garland* (ACIP, page 4 346a.21–22). Haribhadra rejects the fifteen moments of the AK and accepts sixteen moments for the *Mahāyāna* path of seeing at AAĀ 170.

72. *Stairway* (1977: 270.3–4).

73. AA 3.11; *Sphuṭārthā* (Amano, 2000: 52).

74. AAĀ 35.15. Compare also *Sphuṭārthā* (Amano, 2000: 15).

75. La Vallèe Poussin (1971: vi) and Lamotte (1988b: 616).

76. AKBh 327.8.

77. *Golden Garland* (ACIP 4 page 223a–23b).

78. AKV 168. Tibetan *zhi rags* = *zhi sogs rags sogs rnam pa can* = *śāntādyudārādyākāraḥ* = *śantaudārika*.

79. AK vi.49; AKBh 368.

80. AKBh 366.

81. AA 4.53 (Amano, 2000: 74).

82. AK vi.33; AKBh *ad* vi.33c–d (355).

83. AKBh 355. Also, *Sphuṭārthā* (Amano, 2000: 47) on AA 2.30.
84. AK vi.44, 364; AKBh 364.
85. AK vi.45a; AKBh 365.
86. AKBh 383.1.
87. AK vi.67a.
88. See section *Mahāyāna Soteriological Theory and the One Ultimate Vehicle* for this aspect of *Mahāyāna* soteriology.
89. *Golden Garland* (1970: 48.11–20; ACIP 4 page 030a–030b).
90. A brief summary of the five paths for the *pratyekabuddha* vehicle is given in Obermiller, 1932: 26–28. In each of the paths the *pratyekabuddha* is said to focus on the unreality of the external world.
91. *Golden Garland* (1970: 532.9–15). Cf. *Pratyekabuddhabhūmiḥ*, Wayman, 1960: 376. See also Kloppenborg, 1974: 126–29.
92. This nonverbal conduct is known as the physical conduct of a *pratyekajina*. See the story in the *Stairway* (1977: 351) concerning the legend of a monkey who, through instructing non-Buddhist yogis in the physical conduct of a *pratyekabuddha*, causes them to achieve the *pratyekabuddha* state. This is a condensed and slightly different account of a legendary story that occurs in the *Divyāvadāna* (Vaidya, 1959: 216–17), specifically the *Pāṃśupradānāvadāna*. A similar account is found in AKBh on iii, 94a–b. It should be noted that *bodhisattvas* will also at times manifest the "bodily attitudes" (*īryāpatha*) of *pratyekabuddhas*, see *Śgs* (Lamotte, 1998: 111, 215).
93. AA 2.6ab, 7 (Amano, 2000: 38); *Sphuṭārthā* (Amano, 2000: 38).
94. *Golden Garland* (1970: 533.1–4).
95. AA 2.8 (Amano, 2000: 39). Tsong kha pa notes (*Golden Garland* 1970: 544.12) that a *pratyekabuddha* possesses two distinctions of the "supported," that being abandonment (*spangs ba*) and realization (*rtogs pa*), and a distinction (546.11 to 552.3) of the "support" (*ādhārata*), that being the individual life support of the practitioner (*sgrub pa po'i rten gyi gang zag*) and the object of practice, the support of the very nature of things (*chos nyid kyi rten*). In our summarization of this path, we will discuss only the distinctions of abandonment and realization.
96. *Golden Garland* (1970: 544–45).
97. Tsong kha pa provides a discussion of the *pratyekabuddha*'s manner of realization in the *Golden Garland* (1970: 545–46). Cf. AAĀ 1932: 158.
98. Our remarks in this section will be brief. They aim to show the continuity of the AA path system. The one ultimate vehicle theory (*ekayāna*), which is maintained by *Mādhyamikans* such as Candrakīrti and Haribhadra, involves a conglomeration of *Mahāyāna* soteriological concepts combined with various interpretative measures to account for a harmonious overall schema. The theory takes in particular understandings of *gotra*, the *dharmadhātu*, *tathāgatagarbha*, *śūnyatā*, etc., and the fundamental standpoints of the natural luminosity of the mind (*prabhāsvaracitta*) and the adventitiousness of the defilements (*āgantukakleśa*) in order to have coherence. See Gonta, 1992: 59–66; Ruegg, 1969: 89–217.
99. This section is based on Haribhadra's AAĀ on AA ii.1 (133). Haribhadra cites the *Saddharmapuṇḍarīka sūtra*, *Laṅkāvatāra sūtra* and *śāstra* citation (see next note) in connection with this theory. Tsong kha pa in his *Golden Garland* (1970: 501ff) compares, in addition to the above *sūtras*, the scriptural testimony of the *Śrīmālādevīsūtra*, *Ratnagotravibhāga*, and PP literature to

demonstrate the differences between the one-final-vehicle theory and three-final-vehicle theory.

100. This is cited by Haribhadra in the AAĀ (134: we follow Sorensen here). The stanzas appear in the *Triśaraṇasaptati* as verses 45–47, see Sorensen, 1986: 42–44. Tsong kha pa's version differs slightly from above editions, see *Golden Garland* (1970: 508). The Tibetan tradition, including Tsong kha pa (*Golden Garland* 1977: 163) (Tsong kha pa utilizes this passage as part of his early argument for *śrāvakas* and *pratyekabuddhas* realizing the essencelessness of things), attributes this passage to Nāgārjuna's *Bodhicittavivaraṇa*; for discussion, see *La Théorie du Tathāgatagarbha et du Gotra* (Ruegg, 1969: 194–211). *Bodhicittavivaraṇa* vv. 95–96 does express a similar idea; for which see Lindtner, 1986: 64–65. On the unafflicted ignorance of the *arhat* consult P. Jaini, "On the Ignorance of the *Arhat*," *Paths to Liberation* (Buswell and Gimello, eds., Kuroda Institute, 1992: 135–46). Tsong kha pa notes (*Golden Garland*, ACIP 318b) that after an *Arhat* obtains *bodhicitta* and enters the *Mahāyāna* path, it may take one (according to Abhayākaragupta) or four incalculable aeons to achieve full Buddhahood.

101. Obermiller (1932: 33) notes that the fundamental element that exists at the outset of the path, the *prakṛtisthagotra*, must be activated into the *paripuṣṭagotra* in order to undergo the process of spiritual development.

102. AA 1.18 (Amano, 2000: 10).

103. AA 4.32–34.

104. AA 1.46–47. Seventeen is accounted for by counting in the six *pāramitās* beginning with generosity and so forth (*dānādikaṃ*). This section is missing in the manuscript (ASPh, Amano, 2000: 26) and is supplemented based on AAĀ.

105. AAĀ 36.25–37.5.

106. AAĀ 63.23–64.6.

107. AASPh (2000: 74).

108. AASPh (2000: 47).

109. AASPh (2000: 91).

110. We give below a brief outline of *Vaibhāṣika* cosmology of which the most substantial work is that of La Vallèe Poussin: 1919. See also Gethin: 1997; Gombrich: 1975; Hastings (1908–27) 2: 129–39; Masefield: 1983; Sadakata: 1997; and Zahler: 1997.

CHAPTER 4. ANALYSIS OF THE TWENTY *SAṂGHAS*

1. The Sanskrit is from Amano (2000: 15). See also Dutt, 1934, xxvii; Conze, 1957: 31. The Tibetan (Hyodō 2000: 378) for these verses reads: *dbang po rtul dang rnon po dag / dad dang mthong thob rigs nas rigs // bar chad gcig par skyes nas dang / byed dang byed min 'og min 'gro* // (AA 1.23). // *'phar gsum srid rtse'i mthar thug 'gro / gzugs kyi chags bcom mthong ba yi // chos la zhi lus mngon sum byed / bse ru dang ni nyi shu'o* // (AA. 1.24).

2. Literal translation according to Conze (1957), Naughton (1991: 35). The literal translation falls outside the scope of the traditional enumerations

given by the Indo-Tibetan commentaries, particularly the traditions that follow either Ārya Vimuktisena or Haribhadra. There are several Indians who do follow a literal interpretation and the resulting translation. According to Tsong kha pa (*Golden Garland* 247.14): "*Buddhaśrījñāna* and *Śāntipa* draw out twenty [*Saṃghas*] literally from the root text [*Abhisamayālaṃkāra*]" (*bud dha shr'i dang sh'anti pa ste rtza ba'i sgra ji bzhin du nyi shu 'dren pas so*).

3. *Prasannapada,* May, 1959, 281, fn740. La Vallèe Poussin 486.8. We will not discuss the definition of the Noble Beings according to Candrakīrti in the *Prasannapadā* as well as Tsong kha pa's *Rtsa shes ṭik chen* (1973: 395–99), since this represents a different system of interpretation.

4. AKBh 369; AK vi.51a.

5. *Dhammapada* #265: *yo cha sameti pāpāni aṇuṃ thūlāni sabbaso samitattā hi pāpānaṃ samaṇo 'ti pavuchchati* / "One who totally subdues pollutions, both great and small, is known as a *samaṇa,* because he is the conqueror of all pollutions."

6. AKBh 369. La Vallèe Poussin (241) identifies the sūtra from the *Madhyama,* 48.

7. AKV 979.

8. AK vi.51; AKBh 369–70; AKV 980.

9. AK v.45a–c (Pradhan, 311).

10. AK vi.52c–53b (Pradhan, 370).

11. See section on the Stream-enterer and section on those who skip fruitions.

12. AKBh 72.10, 444.2, 445.15. See also Ruegg 1989: 164–67. It is interesting to note that the term *thod rgal* is well known in the Rdzogs chen tradition, yet carries a different meaning than the one Tsong kha pa appropriates to the term.

13. See Angdu (1973: 80): *anāgamyam = nāsyagamyaṃ / bsam gtan dang po la snyoms par 'jug pa'i sems kyis khams gsum gyi nyon mongs pa thams cad spongs mi nus pa med pas na ni lcogs pa med pa zhes bya* / Cf. MVP #1483. Also see AK iv.18, vi.20,47, vii.22; LVP 235n3; Traité, 1036ff.

14. AK vi.47c–d.

15. AK vi.55; Pruden, 998–99; Śāstrī, 987–88.

16. AKBh 356.

17. ASBH, Tatia, 119.

18. AKBh 353. Also AKBh, 380.

19. *Stairway* 271. AS, Pradhan, 88. Compare with Pugg #36, 15: "The faculty of faith of one entering to the stage of stream-entry develops to a large extent. One cultivates the Noble Path carrying with it faith, preceded by faith, this one is said to be an individual who follows through faith. A person striving for the fruition stage of stream-enterer like this is one who follows through faith." MVP #1021, GBBN (1990: 48): "A *śraddhānusārin* is called such since '*śraddhā*' means faith and *anusārin* means to follow. When an individual does not realize through insight but rather engages in the Noble path through faith, as in the case of listening to scripture, one is called 'a follower through faith.' "

20. AKBh 353.

21. *Stairway* 271. AS, Pradhan, 88. Compare with Pugg #35, 15. "The faculty of insight of a individual entering to the result of stream-entry develops to a great extent. One cultivates the Noble Path carrying with it insight,

preceded by insight, this one is said to be an individual who follows through the doctrine. A person striving for the fruition stage of stream-enterer like this is one who follows through doctrine." MVP #1022, GBBN (1990: 49): "*dharmmānusāri* means *dharmma anusartuṃ śīlanayasya;* that is, one with sharp faculties, who does not engage through the confidence of another and applies reasoning which is congruent with the nature of the doctrine is one who is a follower of doctrine."

22. AKBh, Pruden, 953, Śāstrī, 933.

23. *Stairway* 272; *Rje snang*, 606. Pugg #47, p. 17 is much different: "A person who enters into abandoning the three fetters is one who enters into striving for the result of Stream-enterer."

24. *Stairway* 272; Pugg #47, 17: "The individual who abandons the three fetters, this one is called an stream-enterer individual." MVP #1009, GBBN (1990: 45–46): "A *srota-āpanna* is called such since *'srota'* is like a stream of water and *'āpanna'* means to enter into and therefore a 'Stream-enterer' is one who enters into the stream of the Noble Path that flows into *nirvāṇa*."

25. AKBh, Pruden, 955; Śāstrī, 935–36; AKV, Śāstrī, 936.

26. *Stairway* 274. MVP #1010, GBBN (1990: 46): "One called *saptakṛbhava parama* is a Stream-enterer who does not exhaust the afflictions to be abandoned by cultivation and who, having attained the result, takes seven rebirths among humans, seven rebirths among gods, and included within this takes seven human intermediate state rebirths and seven god intermediate state rebirths such that one takes rebirth up to twenty-eight times and is called one who 'takes seven rebirths at the most.' " As we will see this is consonant with Tsong kha pa's definition. The Pugg #37, pp. 15–16, offers a different interpretation: "Here a certain person abandons the three fetters and becomes an enterer, one does not backslide to a lower rebirth and is certain to achieve enlightenment, one runs on and transmigrates up to seven times among gods and men and achieves the end of suffering, this one is called an individual who 'does not take rebirth more than seven times.' "

27. AKBh, Pk nyu 26b.7–8; Pruden, 969; Śāstrī, 953; AKV, Pk chu 223b.8–224a.2; Śāstrī, 953.

28. *Stairway* 275.

29. AK vi.34c–d; Pk nyu 24b3; Pruden, 962; Pradhan, 357; Śāstrī, 944.

30. AKBh, Pruden, 962; Śāstrī, 944; Pradhan, 357: *(janmato)dvitrijanmāvaśeṣatvāt* /; Pk nyu 24b4 mistakenly says "one or two rebirths remaining." Tsong kha pa's text agrees here with the Sanskrit readings.

31. AKBh, Pk 024b.6; Pruden, 963; Śāstrī, 945.

32. *Stairway* 291. This definition corresponds to MVP #1011, GBBN (1990: 46): "A *'kulaṃ kula'* is a Stream-enterer who is liberated from either three or four desire realm afflictions and when transmigrating up to two or three rebirths is born in a good family among gods and men and is called 'one born from family to family.' " Pugg #38, p. 16, is similar: "Here a person having abandoned the three fetters becomes a Stream-enterer, no longer falls into low rebirth and is certain to achieve enlightenment; one who runs and transmigrates among two or three families and puts an end to suffering, this one is called a person who transmigrates family to family."

33. AK, vi.35a–b, Pk nyu 025a1, Pruden, 963, Pradhan, 357: "One who has conquered up to five categories is an enterer to the second [result]."

34. AS, Rahula, 153, Pradhan, 89: "Who is one that enters to the fruit of Once-returner? This is the person who, in the path of cultivation, abides in the path of abandoning the five aspects of the afflictions pertaining to the desire [realm]."

35. *Stairway* 293. MVP #1012, GBBN (1990: 46) gives an etymological definition: "*Sakṛdāgami* is called such that *sakṛt* means 'one time' and *āgami* means 'to come'; since one does not achieve emancipation in this very life but takes rebirth in this world one more time, one is called a 'Once-returner.' " Pugg #40, p. 16: "Here a certain person, having completely abandoned the three fetters—lust, hatred, and delusion—becomes a Once-returner; one comes back to this world only once, putting an end to suffering. Such a person is called a Once-returner."

36. *Stairway* 293–94; MVP #1013; GBBN (1990: 47): "A Once-returner that is called '*eka vīcika*' abandons the seventh and eighth desire realm affliction and is called 'One with a single interval' since being separated from the result of *nirvāṇa* by one birth or an interval from attaining the state on Non returner." In Pugg #39, p. 16, an *Ekabīja* is a type of Stream-enterer: "Here a certain person, having abandoned the three fetters, does not degenerate but is certain to reach enlightenment; one who returns to this human existence and makes an end of suffering, this is a person called 'One with a single seed.' " Pugg-A (1972: 196) clarifies what "single-seed" means: "What is called seed of the aggregates indicates the seed. A Stream-enterer who has a single seed of the aggregates to remove and who takes one existence is called one who is single-seeded."

37. ASBh, Tatia, 120.

38. AS, Rahula, 155, Pradhan, 90.8.

39. *Stairway* 296. MVP #105, GBBN (1990: 47): "One called 'anāgāmi' because of abandoning the five dharmas of the lower destinies and thereby no longer born in the desire realm is called a 'Non-returner.' " Pugg #41, p. 16: "Here a certain person abandons the five fetters related to rebirth in the lower worlds, becomes 'a being of apparitional rebirth' (*opapātiko*), and then attains *nibbāna*; because of the quality of not returning from that world, this person is called a 'Non-returner.' "

40. *Stairway* 297. MVP #1015, GBBN (1990: 47):"A Non-returner called *antarā parinirvvāyī* [is one who], having passed from a single existence is no longer born in another and in the life of the intermediate state manifests the result of Arhant, thereby achieving emancipation; this one is called 'One who is emancipated in the intermediate state.' " The Pāli tradition in the Pugg #42, p. 16, has a totally different interpretation.

41. AKV commenting on AK, vi.38. See *Stairway* 298.

42. AS, Rahula, 155, Pradhan, 90: "Who is the person that attains *nirvāṇa* in the intermediate existence? This is a person who, abandoning the fetters of birth but not abandoning the fetters of coming into existence, when progressing toward the intermediate existence, having made manifest the path, obtains the end of suffering; or one who, progressing in the intermediate existence,

while thinking to transmigrate in the existence of rebirth, manifests the path and obtains the end of suffering; or one who, having reflected (*abhisaṃcetayitva*), does not yet arrive at the existence of rebirth, manifests the path and obtains the end of suffering."

43. *Stairway* 299. MVP #1016, GBBN (1990: 47):"A Non-returner called *upapadya parinirvvāyī* is one who, when dying makes effort and enters into the path, immediately upon rebirth abandons all the afflictions and manifests *nirvāṇa* with remnant; [on account of this] one is called 'One who achieves *nirvāṇa* through birth.' " Pugg #43, pp. 16–17, has *upahaccaparinibbāyī*, which is different from the above definitions.

44. MVP #1018, GBBN (1990: 48): "A Non-returner called *anabhisaṃskāraparinirvvāyī* does not enter into the path with effort but rather, at the time of ripening the mental contiuum obtains the result of Arhat and achieves *nirvāṇa*; one is called 'one who achieves *nirvāṇa* without effort.' " Pugg #44, p. 17: "Here, a person having abandoned the five lower fetters causing rebirth, takes an apparitional rebirth, then attains *nibbāna*, not returning from that realm; one brings forth the path without effort abandoning the fetters of the upper realms; this one is called a person who achieves *nibbāna* without effort."

45. MVP #1017, GBBN (1990: 47): "A Non-returner called *sābhisaṃskāraparinirvāyī* is one who makes effort through rebirth but does not cut off the transmigrating continuum; by training in the path with effort one is called 'one who achieves *nirvāṇa* with effort.' " Pugg #45, p. 17: "Here, a person having abandoned the five lower fetters causing rebirth, takes an apparitional rebirth, then attains *nibbāṇa*, not returning from that realm; one brings forth the path with effort, abandoning the fetters of the upper realms; this one is called a person who achieves *nibbāna* with effort."

46. For this discussion Tsong kha pa is relying on Yaśomitra's comments on AKBh vi.37a–c, AKV, Śāstrī, 949.

47. *Stairway* 303. MVP #1019, GBBN (1990: 48): "A Non-returner called *ūrdhvaṃsrotaḥ* is one who does not achieve *nirvāṇa* in that very rebirth in an upper abode and, in addition, taking birth in the deva realms achieves *nirvāṇa*, [that one] is called 'One who goes higher.' "

48. *Stairway* 304. MVP or GBBN does not provide a definition that divides the *Ūrdhvaṃsrotas*. Pugg #46, p. 17, subsumes the *Ūrdhvaṃsrotas* and *Akaniṣṭhagaḥ* under one definition: "Here a certain person, having abandoned the five inferior fetters that cause rebirth in the lower regions, takes an apparitional rebirth, then attains *parinirvāṇa* not returning from that world; one who having deceased from the *Aviha* heaven (Skt. *Abṛha*), goes to *Atappa* heaven (Skt. *Atapa*), having deceased from *Atappa*, one goes to *Sudassa* (Skt. *Sudṛśa*) having deceased from *Sudassa*, one goes to *Sudassi* (Skt. *Sudarśana*), having deceased from Sudassi one goes to *Akaniṭṭha* (Skt. *Akaniṣṭha*), in *Akaniṭṭha* one brings forth the Noble Path such that one can abandon the higher fetters. This one is a person called 'One who goes upward to *Akaniṭṭha* heaven.' "

49. All of the preceding discussion has been based on AKBH, Pk nyu 026a8-026bb3, Pruden, 968, Śāstrī, 951–52.

50. AK, vi.42b, Pruden, 975, Pradhan, 362.

51. AKBh, Pk nyu 029a.2, Poussin, 222, Pruden, 976, Śāstrī, 961.

52. *Lineage* (Skt. *gotra*, Tib. *rigs*), as Ruegg (1976, 1969) explains, is a term that connotes in Indian and Tibetan Buddhism either "an *extensionally* designated (soteriological) category or class; or *intentionally* designated spiritual factor or capacity that determines classification in such a category or class. In these meanings, the term *gotra* is evidently related to the concept of a lineage, clan, or family, or of a genus; and its meanings are then associated with a sociobiological metaphor (*gotra* = *kula*, *vaṃśa* 'family,' etc.) and a biological or botanical metaphor (*gotra* = *bīja*, 'seed, germ')" (Ruegg, 1976: 341–42).

53. Tsong kha pa adapts this method of counting from AKBh on AK vi.43c–d with categorical details from AKV (Śāstrī, 964–65). Canonical Tibetan is Pk nyu 029b8–030a4.

54. AS, Rahula, 150, Pradhan, 88. MVP #1020, GBBN (1990: 48): "A Non-returner called *kāyasākṣin* is one who directly witnesses with the body the attainment of cessation which is like *nirvāṇa*, one who cultivates the attainment of cessation bringing to cessation the mind and mental factors in a way similar to *nirvāṇa*, one is called a 'bodily witness.' " Pugg #32, p. 14: "Here, when a certain person experiences and dwells in the eight liberations with the body, and having seen with insight, completely abandons the defilements; this is a person who is called 'bodily witness.' "

55. Briefly, the eight liberations (*aṣṭavimokṣa*) is a meditation exercise that progresses through the eight levels of concentration and aids in overcoming all bodily and nonbodily factors. It consists of (1) cognitions of internal and external forms; (2) cognition of external forms but not internal; (3) cognition of the beautiful; (4) attainment of the state of limitless of space; (5) attainment of the state of limitless consciousness; (6) attainment of the state of nothingness; (7) attainment of the state of neither perception nor nonperception; (8) cessation of perception and feeling (*nirodha samāpatti*). See AKV viii.32–34; DN, II: 71.

56. Tsong kha pa quotes this section of his comments from the AKBH on AK vi.43c–d. Pradhan, 363.

57. AKBh, Pruden, 973, Śāstrī, 958 *ad* AK vi.41a–b.

58. AKV, Śāstrī, 958.

59. AS, Rahula, 154, #13, Pradhan, 89–90: "Who is the *Arhat*? The person who abides in the path of abandoning the nine aspects of afflictions of the Peak of Existence."

60. The AKBh, Pradhan, 373–74 glosses these six as follows: "Here a Parihāṇadharman is one who may fall away and is not a Cetanādharman, etc. . . . A Cetanādharman is one who puts an end to his existence; an Anurakṣaṇādharman is one who protects himself; a Sthitākampya is one who when powerful conditions of falling away are absent, even without protecting himself, remains stable, does not fall away, yet without effort, does not progress; a Prativedhanādharman is one who enters into the immovable; an Akopyadharman is one who does not fall away."

61. MVP #1027, GBBN (1990: 50): "An *Arhat* called *prajñāvimukta* is *prajñayā vimukta prajñāvimukta*, that is, one who is liberated from the subtle defilements by wisdom who does not achieve the attainment of cessation; that one is called 'liberated through wisdom.' " Pugg #31, p. 14: "Here a certain

individual does not experience the eight liberations with the body but through perceiving with insight, abandons the defilements; this one is an individual called liberated by means of insight."

62. MVP #1028, GBBN (1990: 50): "Concerning *ubhayato bhāga vimukta*, '*ubhaya*' means both; *bhāga* means 'factor'; *vimukta* means liberated. If an Arhat is liberated from both the obscurations of afflictions and the obscurations of attainment (*samāpatti*), it is called 'liberated from both factors.' " Pugg #30, p. 14: "Here a certain individual experiences the eight liberations with the body and through perceiving with insight abandons the defilements; this one is an individual called liberated in both ways."

63. AS, Rahula, 158, Pradhan, 91.

64. AKV, Śāstrī, 996.

65. AKBh, Pk 038b.4, Pruden, 1006, LVP Śāstrī, 996. Cf. SN ii.50 (Kalārasutta). The first and last result can only be obtained by the pure path (= *āryaprajñā*), AK vi.45c.

66. AKBh, Pk 038b.4, Pruden, 1006, Śāstrī, 997. Cf. SN, iv.25.

67. AKBh, Pk 039b.2–3, Pruden, 1008–1009, LVP, 262, Śāstrī, 1000–1001. See also AK 5.34.

68. Tsong kha pa has paraphrased this section from AKBh, Pk 039b.3–4, Pruden, 1009, Śāstrī, 1001.

69. Tsong kha pa draws remarks from AKBh (Pruden, p. 1009, p. 1076, fn #380) and AKV, Śāstrī, 1002.

70. MVP #1025, GBBN (1990: 49–50): "A dull faculty *Arhat* who is a follower through faith is called a *samayavimukta*, one is liberated from the afflictions and obtains the result when possessing the necessities with respect to an occasion; since one is unable to achieve liberation without them, one is 'liberated on occasion.'" Pugg #1, p. 11: "Here a certain person experiences the eight liberations with the body from time to time and having seen through insight, some of the defilements are abandoned; this person is called 'liberated on occasion.' "

71. MVP #1026, GBBN (1990: 50): "A sharp faculty Arhat follower of doctrine is called *asamayavimukta*, because one is able to abandon the afflictions without having to rely on an occasion or provisions is called 'liberated without occasion.' " Pugg #2, p. 11: "Here a certain person experiences the eight liberations with the body and not from time to time, having perceived through insight, abandons the defilements; this one is called a person liberated not on occasion. Indeed, all Noble Beings are not occasionally delivered with respect to the Noble liberation."

72. AKBh, Pruden, 1006–1007.

73. Sanskrit found in the AKV, Śāstrī, 998.

74. AKBh, Pk 031b.5–6, Pruden, 985, Śāstrī, 973.

75. AKBh, Pk 031b.6–7, Pruden, 985, Śāstrī, 973.

76. AK vi.31a, c–d, Pk nyu 022a2, 022a5, Pruden, 934, Pradhan, 354.

77. AK vi.32, Pk nyu 022a8, Pruden, 935, Pradhan, 354.

78. AS, Pk sems-tsam, Li, 130b.4–8, Rahula, p. 160, Pradhan, p. 92. Pradhan reads *aprāptasamāpatti*, while Tsong kha pa reads *anāgamya*. The four form *dhyānas* and the four formless *dhyānas* each have a liminal threshold

called *sāmantaka* (*nyer bsdogs*). The one before the first *dhyāna* is specifically known as *anāgamya*.

79. AS, Rahula, 146–47, Pradhan, 87. Tsong kha pa's quote follows the options given by Pradhan, 87 in footnotes 5 and 6.

80. MVP #1005, GBBN (1990: 44): "One called *pratyekabuddha* is *ekam ādtmānaṃ pratibuddhavan iti pratyekabuddha*, that is, when one does not act for the purpose of many beings but achieves bodhi and liberation for oneself, one is called a *pratyekabuddha*." Pugg #29, 14: "Here a certain person thoroughly understands in regard to doctrines unheard before, and does not achieve omniscience nor mastery over its results; this one is called a person who is a *paccekasambuddha*."

81. MVP #1006, GBBN (1990: 44): "*khaḍgaviṣāṇakalpa* means '*khaḍga viṣāṇa tulyatvāt*'; '*khaḍga viṣāṇa kalpa*' means a *Pratyekabuddha* who is not like one of sharp faculties who accumulates provisions for up to a hundred aeons but since one dwells in solitude similar to a rhinoceros, one is called '*Pratyekabuddha* who is similar to a rhinoceros.' "

82. MVP #1007, GBBN (1990: 45): "*Vargga cāri* refers to *vargga,* a clan, group, many people gathered together; *cāri* is *cāra gatyartha;* that is, the *pratyekabuddha* goes [together] by coming and going, and performing as a single troop; one is called 'practicing with a group.'"

CHAPTER 5. AN ASSEMBLY OF IRREVERSIBLE *BODHISATTVAS*

1. AAV 44: *arhaṃs tu samyaksambuddha evaṃ ca buddharatnāvavāde nirdiṣṭatvān . . . /*

2. *Śatasāhasrikā* 266. Different wording in *Pañcaviṃśati* 60.

3. *Āryaśatasāhasrikāpañcaviṃśatisāhasrikāṣṭadaśasāhasrikāprajñāpāramitābṛhaṭṭīkā,* Pk 5206. This is a commentary to the 100,000, 25,000, and 18,000 verse PP *sūtra* known in Tibetan as "*yum gsum gnod 'joms*." Tsong kha attributes to Daṃṣṭasena the text that previous Tibetan scholars have attributed to Vasubandhu.

4. Tibetan from *Golden Garland,* 1970.

5. The following citations from the *Pañcaviṃśati* present the reading that Tsong kha pa gives in this *Golden Garland* (1970: 250–60). I have noted the citation from either the AAV (Pensa, 1967) or the *Pañcaviṃśati* (Dutt, 1934: 60–72) depending on which text correlates the best with Tsong kha pa's citations. An English translation based on the Sanskrit of his own recension may be found in Conze (1975: 66–74).

6. AAV 39. Dutt, 1934: 60. Conze, 67.

7. AAV 39: *avaivartikabodhisattva vacanaṃ tu tīkṣṇendriyamārgeṇa tatbhūmiprapter /*

8. *Pañcaviṃśati,* Dutt, 1934: 61; AAV 39.

9. AAV 39; *Pañcaviṃśati,* Dutt, 1934: 60.

10. AAV 39: *tatro yo mārgajñatāyaṃ darśanamārgaḥ ṣoḍaśakṣaṇiko vakṣyamāṇas teṣu ṣoḍaśasu kṣaṇeṣu mṛdvindriyo . . . /*

11. AAV 40.6: *yato dvitīyatṛtīyaphalapratipannakaṃ śraddhādhimuktam adhikṛtyāha . . . /*

12. AAV 40.12: *dvitīyatṛtīyaphalapratipannakadṛṣṭiprāptam adhikṛtyāha . . .* /
13. AK vi.29a–b, 353: *mṛdutīkṣendriyau teṣu śraddhādharmanusāriṇau* /
14. AAV 40; Dutt, 1934: 61; Conze, 1979; 68.
15. AAV 40; Dutt, 1934: 62; Conze, 1979: 68.
16. *Pañcaviṃśati* 62–63; AAV 40; Conze, 1979: 69.
17. AAV 40: *sakṛd imaṃ lokam āgatya teṣām anyatra parinirvāṇāt* /
18. *Pañcaviṃśati* 63; AAV 40; Conze, 69.
19. AAV 41: *ya eṣa srota-āpanna ity uktaḥ sa eva dvividhaḥ kulaṃkulo veditavyaḥ* /
20. *Pañcaviṃśati* 64; AAV 41; Conze, 69.
21. *Pañcaviṃśati* 64–65; AAV 41: Conze, 70.
22. AAV 41: *sa hi tṛtīyacaturthakleśaprakāraprahāṇena tatpratipakṣānāsravendriyalābhena dvitrijanmāvaśeṣatayā ca srota-āpannād viśiṣyata iti kṛtvā* /
23. AAV 41: *ya eṣa sakṛdāgamīty uktaḥ sa evaikavīcikaḥ* /
24. *Pañcaviṃśati* 65; AAV 41; Conze, 70.
25. AAV 41: *sa hi saptāṣṭakleśaprakāraprahāṇena tatpratipakṣānāsravendriyalābhena ekajanmāvaśeṣatvāc ca sakṛdāgāmino viśiṣyata iti kṛtvā* /
26. ASBH, Tatia, 120: "The Ekavīcika Once-returner is only an enterer to the result of Non-returner who, having transmigrated a single existence among the gods, is emancipated. For one who has 'one interval' [MW, p. 1004, 'wave, ripple'] means the intermediate state, the intermediate time between birth (*janmāvakāśaḥ*), that is the Ekavīcika."
27. AAV 41: *ya eṣa navamakleśaprakāraprahāṇād anāgāmīty uktaḥ sa pañcadhā veditavyaḥ* /
28. AK vi.37a–c, 358; AKBh 358; AKV 948.
29. *Pañcaviṃśati* 65–66; AAV 41; Conze, 70.
30. *Pañcaviṃśati* 66; AAV 41; Conze, 70–71.
31. *Pañcaviṃśati* 66; AAV 41–42; Conze, 71.
32. Nya dbon kun dga' dpal (1978: f193a): *byang se[ms] phyir mi ong 'du byed pa dang bcas 'da' ba'i ming can ni / . . . / 'phags pa spyan ras gzigs sgrol ma 'jam pa'i dbyangs lta bu'o thub dgongs so* /
33. *Pañcaviṃśati* 66–67; AAV 42; Conze, 71.
34. The Vks describes *bodhisattvas* as roaring the great lions's roar (*mahāsiṃhanādanādin*). See Lamotte (1994: 2n4).
35. Dharmamitra (PSPh 51a.6): *mngon par 'du byed pa med par yongs su mya ngan las 'das pa ni . . . / 'di ltar dge slong mi 'khrugs pa dang bram ze rgya mtsho'i rdul . . .* / Rong ston shes bya kun rig (1988; 35b.5): *mngon par 'du byed med par mya ngan las 'da' ba ni / . . . bram ze rgya mtsho'i rdul dang / dge slong mi 'khrug pa lta bu'o* / Nya dbon kun dga' dpal (1978: f193b). See Lamotte (1994: 243, fn 9) concerning the story of the bhikṣu who became the Buddha of the Eastern Universe Akṣobhya.
36. AAV 41 on *bodhisattva* with effort: *sa hy abhiprayuktamārgavāhīti kṛtvā / sābhisaṃskāraparinirvāyī . . .* / Page 42 on *bodhisattva* without effort: *sa hy abhiyogāvāhimārga iti kṛtvā* /
37. AAV 42: *ūrdhvaṃsrotaś ca pañcamaḥ / yasyordhvaṃ gatir na tatraiva parinirvāṇaṃ yatropapannaḥ / sroto gatir ity arthaḥ / sa dvividhaḥ / akaniṣṭhaparamo bhavāgraparamaś ca* /
38. AAV 42: *so 'yam akaniṣṭhaparama ūrdhvaṃsrotas trividho bhavati* /

39. *Pañcaviṃśati* 67; AAV 42; Conze, 71.

40. AAV 42: *tatra pluto nāma yo dhyānatrayāt parihīṇaḥ / prathamaṃ dhyānam āsādya brahmakāyikeṣūpapannaḥ / pūrvābhyāsavaśāc caturthadhyānaṃ vyavakīrya tasmāt pracyuto 'kaniṣṭheṣu deveṣūpapadyate / sa hi madhye nimajjanāt pluta ity ucyate /*

41. *Pañcaviṃśati* 67; AAV 42; Conze, 71.

42. AAV 42–43: *ardhapluto nāma yo brahmakāyikebhyaś cyutvā śuddhāvāseṣūpapadya madhyād ekam adhiṣṭhānāntaraṃ vilaṃdhyākaniṣṭhān praviśati /*

43. *Pañcaviṃśati* 68; AAV 43; Conze, 72.

44. AAV 43: *sarvasthānacyuto nāma yaḥ sarvāṇi sthānāntarāṇi saṃcaryākaniṣṭhān praviśati /*

45. *Pañcaviṃśati* 68. AAV 43; Conze, 72.

46. AAV 43: *bhavāgraparamo yaḥ samāpattyantarāṇy āsādayan sarvasthānāntareṣūpapadyāpraviśyaiva śuddhāvāsān ārūpyakramopapattito bhavāgraṃ gatvā nānābuddhakṣetreṣv abhisambudhyate /*

47. *Pañcaviṃśati* 69; AAV 43; Conze, 72.

48. AAV 43: *sarvasthānāntareṣūpapadyāpraviśyaiva śuddhāvāsān ārūpyakramopapattito*

49. *Pañcaviṃśati* 69; AAV 43; Conze, 72.

50. AAV 43: *rūpavītarāgo 'nāgāmī sa itaś cyutvā ārūpyeṣūpapadyate /*

51. AAV 43: *dṛṣṭdharmaparinirvāyī tu saptamo yad āha . . . /*

52. AAV 43; *Pañcaviṃśati* 69; Conze, 72–73.

53. *Pañcaviṃśati* 70; AAV 44; Conze 73.

54. AAV 44: *yas tu nirodhasamāpattilābhy anāgāmī sa kāyasākṣīty ucyate nirvāṇasadṛśasya dharmasya kāyena sākṣātkaraṇāt / kathaṃ punaḥ kāyena sākṣātkaroti / cittābhāvāt kāyāśrayeṇa tadutpatteḥ /*

55. Tsong kha pa quotes this section of his comments from the AKBH on AK vi.43c–d. Pradhan, 363: "When the [Noble Being] emerges from the absorption of cessation, from the moment when thinking, 'This cessation is calm like *nirvāṇa*,' a calmness of the afflicted body which has consciousness is obtained that was never previously acquired. In this way he directly witnesses by the body [the calmness of extinction]."

56. AAV 44: *ya eṣo 'nāgāmīty uktaḥ / tasya yadi bhāvāgrikāṇāṃ kleśānām aṣṭamaḥ prakāraḥ prahīṇo bhavati tato 'sāv arhatvaphalapratipannaka ity ucyate /*

57. AAV 44; *Pañcaviṃśati* 71; Conze, 73–74.

58. Rong ston shes bya kun rig (1988: 36a.2) makes note of this as well: *dpa' bar 'gro ba'i mdor / bskal pa rnam par snang pa la / 'jam dpal gyis rang rgyal du sprul nas sems can gyi don byed par gsungs so /*

59. Cf. AAĀ 35: *saṃgha ratne mṛdvindriyādibodhisattvānāṃ ayaṃ prabhedo grāhyaḥ / vakṣyamāṇamārgajñatā-saṃgṛhītaṣoḍaśakṣaṇadarśanamārgaṃ āśritya pañcadaśasu darśanamārgacittakṣaṇeṣu śraddhādharmānusāri-bhedena prathamaphalapratipannako dvividhaḥ /*

60. Cf. AAĀ 35: *tato yaḥ kāmāvītarāgaḥ sa ṣoḍaśe darśanamārgacittakṣaṇe srota-āpannaḥ /*

61. AAĀ 35: *tato bhāvanāmārge yāvac caturthakleśaprakāraprahāṇād devamanuṣyakulaṃkulatvena sa evānyo dvividhaḥ/*

62. AAĀ 35: *tataḥ kāmāvacarapañcaprakārakleśaprahāṇena dvitīyaphalapratipannako mṛdutīkṣṇendriya evaikaḥ śraddhādṛṣṭiprāptaḥ/*

63. AAĀ 35: *tataḥ kāmāvacaraṣaṭprakārakleśaprahāṇāt sakṛdāgāmī /*

64. AAĀ 35: *tataḥ sa evaikajanmāvaśeṣatvād deveṣv ekavīciko'paraḥ /*

65. AAĀ 35: *tataḥ kāmāvacarasaptāṣṭakleśaprakāraprahāṇāt tṛtīyaphala-pratipannakaḥ pūrvavac chraddhādṛṣṭiprāptaḥ /*

66. AAĀ 35: *tato yaḥ kāmāvacaranavamakleśaprakāraprahāṇād anāgām'īty ucyate sa pañcadhā veditavyaḥ /*

67. AAĀ 35: *tatropapattisaṃyojanaprahāṇād abhinirvṛttisaṃyojanāprahāṇād antarābhavaṃ abhinirvartayann evābhinirvṛtte vāntarābhave mārgasaṃmukhībhāvena duḥkhāntaprāptāv antarāparinirvāyī /*

68. AAĀ 35: *ubhayasaṃyojanāprahāṇād rūpadhātāv upapadya duḥkhānta-prāptāv upapadyaparinirvāyī /*

69. AAĀ 35: *tatraivopapanno'bhisaṃskāreṇa mārgasaṃmukhībhāvād duḥkhāntaprāptāv abhisaṃskāraparinirvāyī / tadviparyayād anabhisaṃskāraparinirvāyī /*

70. AASPh 15: *tato'nāgāmy antaropapadyasābhisaṃskārānabhisaṃskāra-parinirvāyīti caturvidhaḥ /*

71. AAĀ 36: *ūrdhvaṃsrotaś ca pañcamaḥ / sa punar akaniṣṭhaparamo bha-vāgraparamaś ca /*

72. AAĀ 36: *tatrākaniṣṭhaparamaḥ plutārdhaplutasarvasthānacyutvenākaniṣṭha-praveśas trividhaḥ/*

73. AAĀ 36.3–4: *bhavāgraparamaś ca rūpavītarāgo dṛṣṭadharmaśamaḥ kāyasākṣīti dvividhaḥ/* Peking edition and Tsong kha pa has "*ni*" for "*ca,*" construing *rūpavītarāga* as an epithet of *bhavāgraparam.*

74."*rgyal srid sna bdun,*" *Tshig mdzod* 558, the seven valuables: precious disk, precious jewel, precious consort, precious minister, precious elephant, precious horse, and precious army.

75. AAĀ 36: *tato bhāvāgrikāṣṭamakleśaprakārāṇāṃ prahāṇād arhattva-phalapratipannakaḥ /*

76. AAĀ 36: *tataḥ śrāvakapiṭakam ev'ālambya svamārgasaṃmukhīkaraṇād abuddhotpāde pratyekabuddha . . . /*

77. *Prasphuṭapadā*, Pk 5194, nya 52a.3: *de ltar tha mar bstan pa 'di gsum ni rang dang gzhan gnyi ga'i don las byang chub sems dpa' mchog tu bstan to /*

78. AAĀ 36.12: *(tathā ca) prathmadvitīyaphalasthaṃ caturthaphalprati-pannakaṃ ca pudgalaṃ sugamatvenāsaṃgṛhyoktaṃ . . . /*

79. Cf. *Bod rgya tshig mdzod chen mo* 449: *dge 'dun nyi shu / dge 'dun dkon mchog mtshon byed dpe' dge 'dun nyi shu ste / rgyun zhugs lnga dang / phyir 'ong gsum / phyir mi 'ong bcu / dgra bcom zhugs pa / bse ru lta bu'i rang sangs rgyas bcas nyi shu tham pa'o /*

80. *Golden Garland* 1970: 262.

81. *Golden Garland* 1970: 262.

82. Close to *Ratnaguṇasaṃcayagāthā* 29.6cd.

83. AS, Rahula, 158, Pradhan, 91.

84. ASBh, Tatia, 121.

85. Cf. Rngog blo ldan shes rab (1993: 41–42): *de nas sa bcu la gnas pa yin par 'dod do / de yang bzhi ste 'jig rten las 'das pa'i sems dang po bskyed pa dang / spyod pa la zhugs pa* (42) *dang / phyir mi ldog pa dang / skye ba gcig gis thogs pa'o / dang po la lnga ste / dad pa'i rjes su 'brang ba dang / chos kyi rjes su 'brang ba dang / rgyun du zhugs pa'i 'bras bu'i dngos gzhi la gnas pa dang / de'i khyad par la gnas pa gnyis te lnga'o / spyod pa la zhugs pa ni bzhi ste / dad pas mos pa dang*

/ mthong pas thob pa dang / lan gcig phyir 'ong ba'i dngos gzhi la gnas pa dang / de'i khyad par bar chad gcig pa'o / phyir mi ldog pa ni dgu ste / phyir mi 'ong ba'i dngos gzhi la gnas pa gcig dang / de'i khyad par la gnas pa brgyad do / dgra bcom pa'i rgyu la zhugs pa ni skye ba gcig gis thogs pa yin no / rang sangs rgyas kyang ji ltar rigs par de bzhir 'du ba nyid do /

86. *Golden Garland* 1970: 265.

87. See Handurukande (1973) for an overview of this *sūtra*. As a side note, I have visited a temple in Hōren-chō, Nara city, Nara prefecture, Japan called "Futai-ji" = Futaiten bōrin ji = *Avinivartanīya-dharmacakra* temple. Named after this *sūtra*, the temple was established in 847 of the Common Era.

88. Tsong kha pa paraphrases in the *Golden Garland* 265. I have not located an exact passage in the *sūtra* that corresponds to this, but there are many that are similar. See for instance, Taipei #240, 493.

89. *Golden Garland* 1970: 265.

90. *Avaivartikadharmacakra sūtra*, T, fol. 499.3. The following citations are from Taipei edition of Bka'i 'gyur, vol. 13: 416–33.

91. Ibid., 502.7.

92. Ibid., 506.6.

93. Ibid., 510.7.

94. Ibid., 514.6.

95. Ibid., 518.6.

96. Ibid., 524.6–525.1.

97. Ibid., 531.3.

98. Ibid., 539.7–540.1.

99. An example from the *Pañcaviṃśati* (38.19–21) refers to *bodhisattva* and *bodhi* as only a name, but this extends to all things, including stages of Noble Beings: *bodhisattvaḥ prajñāpāramitāyāṃ carann evam upaparīkṣate nāmamātram idaṃ yad idaṃ bodhisattva iti nāmamātram idaṃ yad uta bodhir iti nāmamātra idaṃ yad uta buddha iti /*

100. *Aṣṭa*, Conze, 1975b: 98–99.

101. This intention occurs for the stages of Once-returner, Non-returner, and *Arhat* as well. *Vajracchedikā*, Conze, 1957: 33ff, section 9a: *tat kiṃ manyase Subhūte api nu srota-āpannasyaivaṃ bhavati mayā srota-āpattiphalaṃ prāptaṃ iti / Subhūtir āha no hīdaṃ Bhagavan na srota-āpannasyaivaṃ bhavati mayā srota-āpattiphalaṃ prāptaṃ iti . . . /*

102. AAV 45: *yāni tu śrāvakamārgalabhyāni srotaāpattiphalādīni yac ca pratyekabuddhamārgalabhyaṃ pratyekabuddhatvaṃ tāni bodhisattvo na ca tāvat tena tena mārgeṇa prāpnoty atha ca sattvān srotaāpattiphale yāvat pratyekabudhau pratiṣṭhāpayati /*

103. From the *Golden Garland* 1970: 267: *zla 'od du nyan thos kyi gang zag dang ming 'dra ba ni dge 'dun nyid du yid ches ba'i don du'o /*

104. Here we follow Tsong kha pa's Tibetan reading of AS (1971), Rahula, 174, which corresponds to Pradhan, 101. However, as de Jong (1973) notes, *bodhim anavadyām avakrāntaḥ* "who has entered immaculate *bodhi*" should read *bodhisattvaniyāmāvakrānta* "entered into the certainty of the *bodhisattva*," i.e., the certainty of achieving supreme perfect enlightenment. See Boin-Webb, 2001: 237n134.

GLOSSARY

abhijñā (Tib. *mngon par shes pa*): "supernatural knowledge," extrasensory perception gained by *Arhats* as well as *bodhisattvas* who train for Buddhahood, such as magical apparition (*ṛddhijñāna*), divine vision (*divyacakṣu*), divine hearing (*divyaśrota*), reading others' minds (*paracittajñāna*), recollection of previous lives (*pūrvanivāsānusmṛtijñāna*), and realization of the extinction of contamination (*āsravakṣayajñāna*).

abhinirvṛttikarma (Tib. *mngon par 'grub pa'i las*): "karma of coming into being," a type of karmic connection (*mtshoms sbyor*) that propels an individual into an intermediate state existence among the form realm heavens.

abhinirvṛttisaṃyojana (Tib. *mngon par 'grub pa'i kun tu sbyor ba*): "fetter of coming into existence," a defilement held by Non-returners that propels them to achieve *nirvāṇa* in the intermediate state (*antāraparinirvāyī*).

abhisamaya (Tib. *ngon par rtogs pa*): "clear realization," the wisdom that directly understands with certainty the nature of things.

akaniṣṭhagaḥ (Tib. *'og min gyi mthar thug 'gro ba*): literally, "One who transmigrates to *Akaniṣṭha* heaven," a type of *ūrdhvaṃsrotas* Non-returner who transmigrates through form realm heavens in the process of achieving *nirvāṇa* in *Akaniṣṭha*. There are three types: *Pluta* (Jumper), *Ardhapluta* (Half-jumper), *Sarvasthānacyuta* (One who dies in all form realm heavens).

anabhisaṃskāraparinirvāyīn (Tib. *mngon par 'du byed pa med pa yongs su mya ngan las 'da' ba*): "One who achieves *nirvāṇa* without effort," a type of Non-returner who achieves *nirvāṇa* with remnant (*sopadhiśeṣa*) through birth in the form realm (*upapyaparinirvāyī*).

anāgāmin (Tib. *phyir mi 'ong ba*): Non-returner, a type of Noble Being who will never be reborn in the desire realm (*kāmadhātu*) but attains *nirvāṇa* in one of the form realm heavens (*rūpadhātu*) based upon the removal of seventy-two path-of-cultivation defilements. A Non-returner has removed all five inferior fetters (*pañca avarabhāgīya*) but none of the five superior fetters (*pañca ūrdhvabhāgīya*).

anāgamyasāmantaka (Tib. *mi lcogs med pa nyer sdogs*): the "not-incapable preparatory threshold" located between desire realm mental awareness and the first level of meditative concentration (*dhyāna*) in which conditions are suitable for the removal of defilements.

ānantaryamārga (Tib. *bar chad med lam*): "uninterrupted path," moments of receptivity during the paths of seeing and cultivation that cannot be hindered in its elimination of afflictions.

anāsrava (Tib. *zag med*): "uncontaminated," something that is not amenable to the increase of contaminations from being either a cognitive object (*ālambana*) or associated with a mental affliction (*kleśa*).

anāsravamārga (Tib. *zag pa med pa'i lam*): "uncontaminated path," moments of path consciousness that are not contaminated with impure cognitive objects or mental afflictions such as the Noble paths of seeing (*darśana*), cultivation (*bhāvanā*), and no more learning (*aśaiksa*).

anātman (Tib. *bdag med*): "selflessness," in general, a person's lack of a permanent, unique, independent self.

antarābhava (Tib. *bar srid*): "intermediate state," the intermediate state existence between a life and an ensuing rebirth. Intermediate states may occur for individuals reborn in the desire realm (*kāmadhātu*), reborn in the form realm (*rūpadhātu*), or who are leaving the formless realm (*arūpyadhātu*).

antarāparinirvāyīn (Tib. *bar do 'da' ba*): "One who achieves *nirvāṇa* in an intermediate state," a type of Non-returner who attains *nirvāṇa* in the intermediate state among the sixteen form realm heavens excluding *Mahābrahma*.

ānupūrvika (Tib. *rim gyis pa*): "gradual progressor," individuals who progress in a sequential and gradual manner through the results of Stream-enterer, Once-returner, Non-returner, and *Arhat*.

anuśaya (Tib. *phra rgyas*): "latent defilement" or "outflows," mental impurities that lie dormant in the mental continuum. In Tibetan exegesis, "defilements" are mutually inclusive with fetters (*saṃyojana*), bonds (*bandhana*), and afflictions (*kleśa*) and are differentiated based on the manner of enumeration. See **kleśa**.

anuttarasamyaksaṃbodhi (Tib. *bla na med pa yang dag par rdzogs pa'i byang chub*): "unsurpassable and perfectly complete enlightenment," the awakened insight of Omniscient Buddhahood.

aparaparyāyavedanīyakarma (Tib. *lan grangs gzhan la myong 'gyur gyi las*): "karma that will be experienced for another time," a type of karmic connection (*mtshoms sbyor*) that propels a Non-returner to take more than one rebirth in the form realms before attaining *nirvāṇa*.

ardhapluta (Tib. *phyed du 'phar ba*): "One who Half-jumps," a type of *ūrdhvaṃsrotas* form realm Non-returner who attains *nirvāṇa* in *Akaniṣṭha* after initially jumping over the first form realm of *Brahmakāyika* and taking rebirth among the interval form realm heavens up to *Sudṛśa*.

arhat (Tib. *dgra bcom pa*): *Arhat*, "one who is worthy" (of offerings) or "one who has destroyed the (inner) enemy (of the defilements)," a Noble Being who has attained *nirvāṇa* having completely eradicated all karmic and mental defilements and fetters. An *Arhat* is considered *aśaikṣa*, no longer in training. In mainstream Buddhist traditions and *Mahāyāna* formations, *Arhat* is also an epithet for a Buddha. Tsong kha pa will distinguish *Mahāyāna Arhat*s (*theg chen gyi dgra bcom pa*), fully awakened Buddhas, from Inferior Vehicle *Arhat*s (*theg dman dgra bcom pa*), that is, *Arhat*s of the *śrāvaka* (*nyan thos*) and *pratyekabuddha* (*rang sang rgyas*) vehicles.

ārūpyadhātu (Tib. *gzugs med khams*): formless realm, the subtle immaterial levels of existence among the three worlds (*triloka*) or realms (*tridhātu*) in Buddhist cosmology. There are four cosmological levels of increasing immaterial subtlety that correspond to four kinds of increasingly refined meditative absorption: *Ākāśānantya* ("limitless space"), *Vijñānāntya* ("limitless consciousness"), *Akiṃcanya* ("nothingness"), and *Naivasamjñānāsamjñāyatana* ("neither perception nor nonperception"), also known as *Bhavāgra* ("Peak of Existence").

ārūpyagaḥ (Tib. *gzugs med du nye bar 'gro*): "formless realm transmigrator," a class of Non-returners who achieve liberation in the formless realm.

ārya (Tib. *'phags pa*): "Noble Being," one who has developed a cognitive and meditative understanding of reality (*tattva*) through following the practices of the Buddhist path.

āryadharma (Tib. *'phags pa'i chos*): "Noble quality," factors that develop or are cultivated on a Noble path.

āryamārga (Tib. *'phags lam*): "Noble path," a supermundane path such as the paths of seeing (*darśana*) and cultivation (*bhāvanā*), where one begins to remove defilements from the mental continuum.

āryasaṃgha (Tib. *'phags pa'i dge 'dun*): the community of Noble Beings.

aśaikṣamārga (Tib. *mi slob lam*): "path of no more training," the clear realization (*abhisamaya*) pertaining to a particle vehicle (*yāna*) that occurs at the end of a Noble Being's course of training marking a level of achieved knowledge and cognitive purification.

asaṃskṛta (Tib. *'dus ma byas*): "unconditioned," that which is not constructed through aggregation of causes and conditions. *Abhidharma* traditions will differ as to what is included in this classification and Buddhist philosophers will differ as to what qualifies it. A common list is three: the cessation arising from insight (*pratisaṃkhyānirodha*), the cessation not arising through insight (*apratisaṃkhyānirodha*), and space (*ākāśa*).

āśraya (Tib. *rten pa*): "life support," the basis for an individual's embodiment in a given cosmological realm.

aṣṭamaka (Tib. *brgyad pa;* Pāli *aṭṭhamaka*): "Eighth individual," traditionally the lowest among the eight *āryapudgalas* in mainstream Buddhist scholasticism. For some commentators of the Twenty *Saṃghas*, the Eighth individual is the enterer to the result of Stream-enterer who is separated from attachment previous to the path of seeing (*vītarāgapūrvin*).

aṣṭavimokṣa (Tib. *rnam par thar pa brgyad*): "eight liberations," a meditation exercise that progresses through the eight levels of concentration and aids in overcoming all bodily and nonbodily factors. It consists of (1) cognitions of internal and external forms; 2) cognition of external forms but not internal; (3) cognition of the beautiful; (4) attainment of the state of limitless of space; (5) attainment of the state of limitless consciousness; (6) attainment of the state of nothingness; (7) attainment of the state of neither perception nor nonperception; (8) cessation of perception and feeling (*nirodha samāpatti).*

aṣṭāvakṣanāḥ (Tib. *mi lom pa brgyad*): "eight inopportune states of rebirth," eight conditions that lack the leisure and freedom to learn from Buddhist teachings, such as rebirth as (1) an animal (*naraka*), (2) a hungry ghost (*preta*), (3) a hell-being (*tiryañca*), (4) an uncultured person in a border region (*mlecchā*), (5) a mute and stupid person (*mūkatā*), (6) a person with wrong views (*mithyādṛṣṭi*), (7) at a time when a Buddha does not exist (*buddhakāntāra),* (8) or among deities with a long life (*dīrghāyuṣo devāḥ*).

ātmadarśana (Tib. *bdag lta*): "false view of the self," see **satkāyadṛṣṭi.**

avaivartika (Tib. *phyir mi ldog pa*): "Irreversible," a class of *bodhisattvas* who have at least reached the *Mahāyāna* path of preparation and are irrevocability destined for supreme and complete Buddhahood.

avaivartikaṣamgha (Tib. *phyir mi ldog gi dge 'dun*): "Irreversible Spiritual Community," *bodhisattvas* who are Noble Beings and have reached the *Mahāyāna* path of preparation.

āvaraṇa (Tib. *sgribs ba*): "obstructions," that which impedes or prevents attaining liberation, such as the afflictive obstructions (*kleśāvaraṇa, nyon sgrib*), or that which impedes or prevents full cognitive awareness of objects, particularly omniscient Buddha knowledge (*thams cad mkhyen pa*), such as the obstructions to knowledge (*jñeyāvaraṇa, shes sgrib*). Obstructions may be intellectually acquired (*kun btags*) or instinctual (*lhan skyes*). Buddhist scholars will differ as to how obscurations are enumerated and will differ as to what qualifies the enumeration.

avavāda (Tib. *gdams ngags*): "instructions," advice that councils meditative equipoise to beings who lack meditative stability and teaches liberation to those whose minds have reached meditative equipoise.

avidyā (Tib. *ma rig pa*): "ignorance" or "misknowledge," an active or dormant mental state of misknowing that is confused about and misperceives the true mode of being of all things, suchness (*tathatā*). Misknowledge is the root of *saṃsāra* that leads one throughout the three realms (*traidhātuka*) and is taught as the first of the twelve members of dependent origination since it is the basis for all karma and afflictions (*kleśa*).

avinirvartanīya bhūmi (Tib. *phyir mi ldog pa'i sa*): "Irreversible Stage," the stage at which a *bodhisattva* becomes irreversible from attaining full Buddhahood.

bhava (Tib. *srid pa*): "conditioned existence," states of being and rebirth among the three realms (*traidhātuka*) propelled by karmic propensities and mental afflictions (*kleśa*).

bhavāgra (Tib. *srid pa'i rtse mo*): "Peak of Existence," the highest realm in conditioned existence and the most subtle of formless realms (*ārūpyadhātu*), also known as *Naivasaṃjñānāsaṃjñāyatana*, the sphere of neither perception nor nonperception.

bhavāgraparamagaḥ (Tib. *srid pa'i rtse mo'i mthar thug gro*): "One who transmigrates up to the Peak of Existence," a type of *Ūrdhvaṃsrotas* Non-returner who takes rebirth in the form realms and then gradually takes rebirth among the four formless realms, attaining *nirvāṇa* at the Peak of Existence (*bhavāgra*).

bhāvanāheyakleśa (Tib. *bsgom pas spang bya nyon mongs*): "affliction removed by path of cultivation," a class of defilement that is removed by a path of cultivation.

bhāvanāmārga (Tib. *bsgom lam*): "path of cultivation," the practice of developed mental absorption that repeatedly considers, assesses, and contemplates what has been previously understood in an intellectual manner. There are two types: the mundane (*laukika*) and the supermundane (*lokottara*). The mundane path of cultivation (*laukikabhāvanāmārga*) includes those meditative practices, Buddhist or non-Buddhist, which are not related to cultivating a repeated analysis of the sixteen aspects of the Nobles' Four Truths. The supermundane (*lokottara*) path of cultivation consists of familiarization (*abhyāsa*) and uncontaminated concentrated awareness (*samāhitajñāna*) on meditative objects related to the Nobles' Four Truths that vary according to the *śrāvaka*, *pratyekabuddha*, or *bodhisattva* cognitive perspective.

bhūyovītarāga (Tib. *phal cher chags dang bral ba*): "one who is separated from attachment for the most part," one who enters the path of seeing having partially removed attachment to the desire realm and then becomes an enterer to the result of Once-returner.

bodhicittotpāda (Tib. *byang chub tu sems bskyed*): the production of an altruistic mind set on achieving perfect awakening in Omniscient Buddhahood for the sake of all beings.

bodhipakṣyā dharmāḥ (Tib. *byang chub phyogs kyi chos rnams*): "factors conducive to awakening," there are usually thirty-seven factors (*saptatriṃśad, sum cu rtsa bdun*) in seven sets: (i) the four foundations of mindfulness, (ii) the four right efforts, (iii) four bases of magical powers, (iv) five faculties, (v) five powers, (vi) seven factors of awakening, and (viii) the eightfold noble path.

bodhisattva (Tib. *byang chub sems dpa'*): a "Buddha-to-be," one who is intent to achieve full Buddhahood for the welfare of beings. In order to achieve this aim, a *bodhisattva* undertakes a long and arduous journey through innumerable lifetimes, accumulating provisions of wisdom (*jñāna*) and merit (*puṇya*), while employing tactical skill (*upāya*) in the course of perfecting such practices as generosity (*dāna*), ethics (*śīla*), patience (*kṣānti*), diligence (*vīrya*), concentration (*dhyāna*), and discernment (*prajñā*).

brahmakāyika (Tib. *tshang ris*): "Brahma form heaven," the first of the seventeen abodes of the form realm, and one of the three form realm abodes that correspond to the first concentration.

bṛhatphala (Tib. *'bras bu che*): "Great fruit heaven," one of the eight abodes of the form realm that corresponds to the domain of the fourth concentration.

Buddha (Tib. *sangs rgyas*): "Awakened One," one who has completely removed (*sangs*) the afflictive and knowledge obscurations (Tib. *sgrib*; Skt. *āvaraṇa*) and has expansively (*rgyas pa*) awakened to seeing reality just as it is (Tib. *ji lta ba*; Skt. *yathāvat*) and to its utmost extent (Tib. *ji snyed*; Skt. *yāvat*).

buddhakṣetra (Tib. *sangs rgyas kyi zhing*): "Buddha-field," a domain where a particular Buddha has activity and influence.

catvāry apramānāṇi (Tib. *tshad med bzhi*): "four immeasurables," also known as the four "abodes of Brahma" (*brahmavihāra*), the contemplations of immeasurable compassion, love, joy, and equanimity.

catvāri āryasatyāni (Tib. *'phags pa'i bden pa bzhi*): "Nobles' Four Truths," the four propositions taught by the Noble One, the Buddha—the truth of suffering (*duḥkha*), the origin of suffering (*samudaya*), the cessation of suffering (*nirodha*), and the path (*mārga*) leading to the cessation of suffering. These are realized in sixteen aspects by Noble Beings (*ārya*) from various cognitive perspectives.

cittakṣaṇa (Tib. *sems kyi skad chig*): "thought-moment," moments of consciousness that comprise the path of seeing (*darśanamārga*).

darśanamārga (Tib. *mthong lam*): "path of seeing," the direct cognition of the Nobles' Four Truths in sixteen thought-moments where one begins the Noble Path (*āryamārga*).

devakulaṃakula (Tib. *lha'i rigs nas rigs*): "One who goes from family to family among gods," a distinctive Stream-enterer who gradually takes two rebirths among the six heavens of desire realm gods before achieving *nirvāṇa*.

dharmānusārin (Tib. *chos kyi rjes su 'brang ba*): "One who follows by way of Doctrine," an enterer to the result of Stream-enterer who has sharp faculties (*tīkṣṇendriya*) and does not rely on another to pursue cognition of the Nobles' Four Truths.

dharmaśrotasamādhi (Tib. *chos kyi rgyun gyi ting nge 'dzin*): "stream of doctrine meditative stabilization," a technique utilized by *bodhisattvas* to receive doctrinal instructions (*avavāda*) from Buddhas in other cosmological realms.

dhyāna (Tib. *bsam gtan*): "concentration," single-pointed undivided attention on a meditative object that cultivates refined states of awareness. Levels of concentration are cosmological as well as psychological states. There are four lower levels equivalent to the form realm (*rūpadhātu*) and four upper levels equivalent to the formless realm (*ārūpyadhātu*).

dhyānānāsrava (Tib. *bsam gtan zag med*): "uncontaminated concentration," a concentration free of impurity and mental afflictions.

dṛṣṭadharmaśramaḥ (Tib. *mthong ba'i chos la zhi ba*): "One who is pacified in the present life," a distinctive Non-returner who attains *nirvāṇa* in the life support that first attained the state of Non-returner.

dṛṣṭadharmasukhavihāra (Tib. *mthong ba'i chos la bde bar gnas pa*): "abiding in bliss during the present life," the bliss of body and mind that arises from a mundane concentration's meditative stabilization (Tib. *'jig rten pa'i bsam btan gyi ting nge 'dzin*).

dṛṣṭiheyakleśa (Tib. *mthong bas spang bya nyon mongs*): the mental afflictions that are removed by the path of seeing; namely, the defilements learned or imputed through incorrect philosophical views and intellectual predispositions (*nyon sgrib kun brtags*). There are also three fetters removed by the path of seeing (*mthong spang kun sbyor gsum*)—belief in the perishable aggregates (*satkāyadṛṣṭi*), doubt (*vicitsā*), belief that ethics and rituals are supreme (*śilavrataparāmarśa*).

dṛṣṭiprāpta (Tib. *dad pas mos pa*): "One who obtains by seeing," a sharp-faculty follower of doctrine (*dharmānusārin*) who passes through the sixteenth moment of the path of seeing and abides in either the result of Stream-enterer, Once-returner, or Non-returner dependent upon defilements previously removed through the path of cultivation.

ekajātipratibaddha (Tib. *skyes ba gcig gis thogs pa*): "separated from Awakening by one birth," a type of *bodhisattva* one lifetime away from achieving full Buddhahood.

ekāsanika (Tib. *stan gcig pa*): "single-session meditative equipoise," the ability to generate in one sitting uninterruptedly both the path of preparation and the path of seeing.

ekavīcika (Tib. *bar chad gcig pa*): "One who possesses a single interval," a distinctive abider in the result of Once-returner who is obstructed by a single affliction and obstructed by a single life for obtaining *nirvāṇa*.

ekayāna (Tib. *theg pa gcig pa*): "single vehicle" or "one ultimate vehicle," seeing all vehicles as leading to Buddhahood, or the *Mahāyāna* theory that the end results of other paths are provisional (*ma nges pa*) and that the result of complete Buddhahood is the final, essential, culmination of the definitive *bodhisattva* vehicle (*mthar thug nges don snying po'i theg pa*).

jñeyāvaraṇa (Tib. *shes sgrib*): "obscuration to knowledge," that which impedes or prevents full cognitive awareness of objects, particularly seeing reality just as it is (*yathāvat*) and to its utmost extent (*yāvat*), omniscient Buddha knowledge (*thams cad mkhyen pa*).

kāmadeva (Tib. *'dod pa'i lha*): "desire realm deity," a deity who lives among the six heavens of the desire realm (*kāmadhātu*).

kāmadhātośraya* (Tib. *'dod pa'i rten*): "desire realm life support," an embodiment or support that lives in the desire realm.

kāmadhātu (Tib. *'dod khams*): "desire realm," the realm of sentient beings who are influenced by the five objects of sensory desire—form (*rūpa*), sound (*śabda*), smell (*gandha*), taste (*rasa*), and touch (*spraṣṭavya*).

kāmarāga (Tib. *'dod pa'i 'dod chags*): "desire realm attachment," mental affliction that arises due to perceiving the five sense pleasures such as form and sound in the desire realm.

kāmavītarāga (Tib. *'dod pa'i 'dod chags dang bral ba*): "separation from desire realm attachment," one who enters the path of seeing having completely removed attachment to the desire realm and then becomes an enterer to the result of Non-returner.

karma (Tib. *las*): "action," the law of cause and effect pertaining to activities of body, speech, and mind that condition a life support over innumerable lifetimes. Virtuous actions lead to happiness and nonvirtuous actions lead to suffering. Actions accrue over multiple lifetimes forming imprints, latencies, or residues that predispose an individual toward virtuous or nonvirtuous courses of rebirth, environmental conditions, or experiences.

kāśyapīya (Tib. *'od srungs pa*): *Kāśyapīya*, an *Abhidharma* tradition that traces its beginnings to the *Arhat* Kāśyapa and which flourished in north-west India four hundred years after the life of the Buddha.

kāyaśakṣin (Tib. *lus mngon byed*): "bodily witness," the Non-returner who is able to enter into absorption on the eight liberations (*aṣṭavimokṣa*) and witnesses with the body the calmness of cessation.

kleśa (Tib. *nyon mongs*): "affliction" or "defilement," a mental factor that disturbs the mental continuum based on nonvirtuous actions of body, speech, mind, and their imprints. The six fundamental afflictions are: attachment (*'dod chags, rāga*), anger (*khong khro, pratigha*), pride (*nga rgyal, māna*), ignorance (*ma rig pa, avidyā*), doubt (*the tshom, vicikitsā*), and false views (*lta ba, dṛṣṭi*). Fetters (*saṃyojana*), bonds (*bandhana*), and latent defilements (*anuśaya*) are mutually inclusive with afflictions. These categories are differentiated according to the manner of enumeration.

kleśāvaraṇa (Tib. *nyon mongs pa'i sgrib pa*): "afflictive obstruction," the principal conceptualizations that block or prevent liberation from cyclic existence (*saṃsāra*) based upon the cognitive grasping at a substantially existent, independently real, autonomous person.

kramanairyāṇika (Tib. *mthar gyis pa*): "One who is liberated gradually," one who attains a result of the path in a sequentially and progressive manner.

kṣānti (Tib. *bzod pa*): "forbearance," a term that has multiple meanings connoting fortitude, perseverance, composure, or receptivity dependent upon the context in which it occurs; the third level of "certainty" among the preparatory analytical factors (*nirvedhabhāgīya*); the eight moments of "intellectual receptivity" in the path of seeing (*darśanamārga*); a perfection (*pāramitā*) in *bodhisattva* path systems.

kulaṃkula (Tib. *rigs nas rigs*): "One who goes from family to family," a distinctive abider in the result of Stream-enterer who has abandoned three desire realm afflictions and will gradually take rebirth among gods (*deva*) or humans (*manuṣya*) before attaining *nirvāṇa*.

kuśalamūla (Tib. *dge ba'i rtsa ba*): "roots of virtue," mundane virtuous qualities acquired during the path of preparation.

lakṣyalakṣaṇāsaṃgha* (Tib. *mtshon bye dpe'i dge 'dun*): "Allegorical *Saṃgha*," "the *Saṃgha* that is indicated as an allegory," the articulation of the Noble Beings that constitute the Twenty *Saṃgha*s by means of the classic *Abhidharma* categories of *śrāvaka* ideal figures.

lakṣyārthasaṃgha* (Tib. *mtshon bya don gyi dge dun*): "Actual *Saṃgha*," "the *Saṃgha* whose actual meaning is indicated," the *Mahāyāna* community of Noble Irreversible *bodhisattva*s (*avaivartika, phyir mi ldog pa*) who are destined for the state of Buddhahood through attaining *anuttarasaṃyak-saṃbodhi*.

laukikamārga (Tib. *'jig rten pa'i lam*): "mundane path," practices and cultivations that lead to higher rebirth in conditioned existence.

lokottaramārga (Tib. *'jig rten las 'das pa'i lam*): "supermundane path," practices and cultivations that lead to *nirvāṇa* or awakening (*bodhi*).

mahābrahma (Tib. *tshangs chen*): "Great Brahma heaven," the third abode among the seventeen divisions of the form realm, corresponding to the first concentration. Noble Beings are not reborn in this heaven since it is a place of wrong view.

Mahāyāna (Tib. *theg pa chen po*): "Great Vehicle," the way of the *bodhisattva*, the practices and knowledge that lead to the achievement of full Buddhahood.

māna (Tib. *nga rgyal*): pride, inflated attitude in reliance upon the false view of the perishable aggregates (*satkāyadṛṣṭi*) that functions to provide a basis for disrespect and suffering.

manuṣyakulaṃkula (Tib. *mi'i rigs nas rigs*): "One who goes from family to family among humans," a distinctive Stream-enterer who gradually takes two rebirths among humans before achieving *nirvāṇa*.

mārgajñatā (Tib. *lam shes*): "path omniscience," the beneficial knowledge realized by buddhas and *bodhisattva*s that thoroughly understands the paths of *śrāvaka*s, *pratyekabuddha*s, and *bodhisattva*s.

mokṣamārga (Tib. *thar pa'i lam*): "path of deliverance," a path that liberates from *saṃsāra*.

mṛdvindriya (Tib. *dbang po brtul po*): "dull faculty," dense, obtuse, and sluggish sense faculties and intellect.

nirodhasatya (Tib. *'gog pa'i bden pa*): truth of cessation or "true cessation," an unconditioned result of the path of seeing or path of cultivation where a certain level of mental affliction is permanently removed from the mental continuum.

nirupadhiśeṣanirvāṇa (Tib. *lhag med kyi mya ngan las 'da'*): "*nirvāṇa* without remnant," the attainment of *nirvāṇa* without the residue or remnant of the appropriated aggregates (*skandha*).

nirvāṇa (Tib. *mya ngan las 'das pa*): literally, "extinguish," the extinguishment, or unbinding, of the fires of attachment, delusion, and hatred. The Tibetan translates as "passing beyond misery." The term has multiple connotations and there are multiple types of *nirvāṇa*. For *śrāvaka*s and *pratyekabuddha*s, it is the state of having completely eradicated the suffering of conditioned existence and repeated rebirth along with the blissful liberation of being unaffected by mental afflictions. *Bodhisattva*s aim for a nonlocalized *nirvāṇa* (*apratiṣṭhita*) that does not dwell in peace, because of compassion, and does not dwell in *saṃsāra*, because of insight (*prajñā*), in actualizing Buddhahood.

nirvedhabhāgīya (Tib. *nges par 'byed cha mthun pa*): "preparatory analytical factors," factors that comprise the path of preparation (*prayogamārga*) that are conducive to a penetrative, yet mundane, understanding of the Nobles' Four

Truths (*catvāri āryasatyāni*). There are four divisions: heat (*uṣmagata*), summit (*mūrdhagata*), forbearance (*kṣānti*) and the stage that constitutes the peak of the mundane path, the highest worldly dharma (*laukikāgradharma*).

pañca avarabhāgīyāḥ (Tib. *tha ma'i cha dang mthun pa lnga*): "five inferior fetters," that which bind beings in the desire realm (*kāmadhātu*) including belief in the perishable aggregates (*satkāyadṛṣṭi*), doubt (*vicitsā*), belief that ethics and rituals are supreme (*śilavrataparāmarśa*), sensual pleasure (*kāmarāga*), and hostility (*vyāpāda*). These are abandoned in part by a Stream-enterer (*srota-āpanna*) and a Once-returner (*sakṛdāgāmi*) and totally by a Non-returner (*anāgāmin*).

pañca ūrdhvabhāgīyāḥ (Tib. *gong ma'i cha dang mthun lnga*): "five superior fetters," desire for existence in the form realm (*rūparāga*), desire for existence in the formless realm (*ārūpyarāga*), pride (*māna*), delusion (*moha*), and excitability (*auddhatya*).

parinirvāṇa (Tib. *yongs su nya ngan las 'da' ba*): "completed emancipation," "full *nirvāṇa*," to fully complete a process of attainment or degree of realization. For instance, Ārya Vimuktisena (AAV 34.25–35.6) states: "Those who have attained the summit (*mūrdhagata*) of the preparatory analytical factors (*nirvedhabhāgīya*) have a full *nirvāṇa* from the roots of virtue (*kuśalamūla*) being severed; those who have attained forbearance (*kṣānti*) of the preparatory analytical factors have a full *nirvāṇa* from lower states of rebirth (*apāya*) . . . a Stream-enterer has a full *nirvāṇa* from an eighth rebirth; a Once-returner has a full *nirvāṇa* from a second existence in the desire realm (*kāmadhātu*); a Non-returner has a full *nirvāṇa* from the desire realm; the *Arhat* has a *nirvāṇa* with remnant (*sopadhiśeṣanirvāṇa*) and *nirvāṇa* without remnant (*nirupadhiśeṣanirvāṇa*)."

phala (Tib. *'bras bu*): "result," states produced as a result of a path.

phalastha (Tib. *'bras bu la gnas pa*): "Abider in a result," a Noble Being who stays or resides in a certain state of progress on the way to *nirvāṇa*.

phalaviśeṣa (Tib. *'bras bu khyad par can*): "distinctive fruition," superior or distinctive status within the results of Stream-enterer, Once-returner, and Non-returner.

pluta (Tib. *'phar ba*): "One who Jumps," a type of Non-returner who attains *nirvāṇa* in *Akaniṣṭha* heaven after having taken rebirth in *Brahmakāyika* heaven and jumping over all other form realm heavens in between the first heaven of *Brahmakāyika* up to the last form realm heaven of *Akaniṣṭha*.

prahāṇa (Tib. *spong ba*): "abandonment," processes that eliminate mental afflictions and karmic propensities.

prajñā (Tib. *shes rab*): "wisdom" "insight," or "discernment," a mental state that arises based on the investigation of something under analysis and whose function is to exclude doubt (*vicikitsā*).

prajñāpāramitā (Tib. *shes rab kyi pha rol tu phyin pa*): "perfection of wisdom," the highest nondual wisdom (*advayajñāna*) exemplified through the *dharmakāya* aspect of Buddhahood, the path leading to this wisdom, and the texts outlining this path and that nondual wisdom.

prajñāvimukti (Tib. *shes rab rnam par grol ba*): "One who is liberated through wisdom," *Arhat*s who are not able to enter the meditative absorption on the eight liberations and are liberated from afflictive obscurations by the wisdom that cognizes selflessness.

pratipakṣa (Tib. *gnyen po*): "antidote," counteragents that have the potency to eradicate mental afflictions.

pratipannaka (Tib. *zhugs pa*): "enterer to a result," individuals who are approaching or entering into a state of progress on the way to *nirvāṇa*.

pratyekabuddha (Tib. *rang sang gyas*): "Solitary Buddha," an "individually awakened one" who cognizes the emptiness of external objects through realizing dependent arising but does not thereby attain the full omniscience of a Buddha. *Pratyekabuddha*s do not have much compassion and attain their awakening in solitude.

pratyekajina (Tib. *rang rgyal*): "solitary conqueror," a synonym of *pratyekabuddha*.

prayogamārga (Tib. *sbyor lam*): "path of preparation," a mundane path (*laukikamārga*) constituted by four preparatory analytical factors (*nirvedhabhāgīya*) that "joins" (*prayoga*) the practitioner to the process of directly perceiving the Nobles' Four Truths.

pṛthagjana (Tib. *so so skyes bo*): "ordinary individual," a person who has not attained the Noble Path (*āryamārga*).

pudgala (Tib. *gang zag*): "person" or "individual," a being designated in dependence upon any among the five aggregates (*skandha*).

rāga (Tib. *'dod chags*): "attachment," the craving after external or internal miserable objects of the three realms having perceived them as pleasing and delightful.

ratnasaṃgha (Tib. *dge 'dun dkon mchog*): "Jewel of the *Saṃgha*," one of the three jewels (*triratna*) of refuge along with the Buddha and Dharma.

rūpadhātu (Tib. *gzugs khams*): "form realm," a realm consisting of seventeen divisions that are classified into four main areas correlated in ascending order with levels of concentration (*dhyāna*). The first concentration marks the beginning of the form realm and is composed of three abodes. The first is the *Brahmakāyika*; the second, *Brahmapurohita*; and the third, *Mahābrahma*. The second concentration has three abodes. They are, in ascending order, called *Parīttābhā*, *Apramāṇābhā*, and *Ābhāsvara*. The third concentration also has three abodes, which are, in ascending order, *Parīttaśubha, Apramāṇaśubha,* and *Śubhakṛtsna.* The last main area of the form realm is the domain of the fourth concentration. It consists of eight abodes with the first three being called, in ascending order, *Anabhraka, Puṇyaprasava,* and *Bṛhatphala.* The remaining five abodes of the fourth concentration are known as the *Śuddhāvāsakāyika* ("the pure places"), the abodes of *Abṛha, Atapas, Sudṛśa, Sudarśana,* and *Akaniṣṭha.*

rūpadhātudeva (Tib. *gzugs khams kyi lha*): "form realm deity," a being or embodiment that lives among the seventeen divisions of the form realm.

rūpagaḥ (Tib. *gzugs su nye bar 'gro ba*): "form realm transmigrator," ten general types of Non-returners who achieve *nirvāṇa* in various form realm heavens differentiated according to previous desire realm embodiments and the meditation technique of alternating cultivations (*vyavakīrṇabhāvanā*).

rūparagaḥ (Tib. *gzugs kyi 'dod chags*): "form realm desire," the attachment for existence that occurs when form realm meditative attainments (*samāpatti*) within the form realms are misperceived as paths of liberation.

sābhisaṃskāraparinirvāyīn (Tib. *mngon par 'du byed pa yongs su mya ngan las 'da' ba*): "One who achieves *nirvāṇa* with effort," a type of Non-returner who achieves *nirvāṇa* with effort in the form realm.

sakalabandana (Tib. *'ching ba mtha' dag dang ldan pa*): literally, "One who is bound by all the bonds," an individual who is entering toward the result of Stream-enterer (*srota-āpanna*) who has not removed any defilements.

sakṛdāgāmi (Tib. *lan cig phyir 'ong ba*): "Once-returner," a Noble Being who will be reborn once more in the desire realm, who abandons the sixth desire realm affliction but does not abandon the ninth affliction on obtaining the sixteenth moment of the path of seeing.

sakṛnnairyāṇika (Tib. *cig car nges par 'byin pa*): "One who abandons simultaneously," individuals who abandon instantaneously the nine most subtle of the subtle afflictions of the desire, form, and formless realms to be removed by the path of cultivation. The classification applies only to Stream-enterers or *Arhat*s.

samādhi (Tib. *ting nge 'dzin*): "meditative stabilization," a mental factor (*caitta*) that one-pointedly directs the mind continuously and completely in the perception of a designated entity or object of cultivation.

sāmantaka (Tib. *nyer sdogs*): "preparatory threshold," thresholds at each of the four concentrations and four formless absorptions that enhance the attainment of meditative stabilization.

samāpatti (Tib. *snyoms 'jug*): "absorption," one-pointedness of mind that is established equally upon a meditative object such as the mind and mental factors or the bodily elements at a given level of concentration.

śamatha (Tib. *zhi gnas*): "calm abiding" or "quiescence," the maintenance of one-pointedness of mind and concentration on a given object without distraction; serves as the general basis for all meditative stabilizations.

saṃbhāramārga (Tib. *tshogs lam*): "path of acquiring the provisions," various types of preliminary practices that accumulates the virtuous qualities and cognitive tools necessary to achieve awakening within a particular vehicle.

saṃgha (Tib. *dge 'dun*): "community," the Buddhist community in two general categories: the conventional and institutional *saṃgha* of five or more monks or nuns who perform rituals and recite the *Pratimokṣa* vows together and the *saṃgha* in the ultimate sense, the knowledges and liberations of Noble Beings who have achieved the Path of Seeing (*darśanamārga*) and are actualizing the Truth of Cessation (*nirodhasatya*) and the Truth of the Path.

saṃsāra (Tib. *'khor ba*): "cyclic existence," literally "wandering," has two connotations in Indo-Tibetan Buddhist formations: (i) the beginningless cycle of repeated birth and death among realms of gods, demigods, humans, animals, hungry ghosts, and hell-beings, and (ii) the influx of impure constitutive elements of a being's life stream.

saṃyojana (Tib. *kun tu sbyor ba*): "fetter" or bond, something that binds one to conditioned existence. In general, there are ten: belief in the perishable aggregates (*satkāyadṛṣṭi*), doubt (*vicitsā*), belief that ethics and rituals are supreme (*śilavrataparāmarśa*), sensual pleasure (*kāmarāga*), hostility (*vyāpāda*), desire for existence in the form realm (*rūparāga*), desire for existence in the formless realm (*ārūpyarāga*), pride (*māna*), delusion (*moha*), and excitability (*auddhatya*). Noble Beings will become free of different fetters in the path to *nirvāṇa*. The first five are called the "five inferior fetters" (*pañca avarabhāgīya*) and the second five are known as the "five superior fetters" (*pañca ūrdhvabhāgīya*).

santāna (Tib. *rgyun*): "mental continuum," the temporal succession of preceding and succeeding moments of cognitive awareness.

śāntaudārika (Tib. *zhi rags*): "rough calm abiding," the mundane path of cultivation that progresses through cosmological stages and corresponding states of consciousness by means of meditative absorption (*dhyāna*). This is achieved by a cultivation of developing distaste and detachment for one's current state of existence in comparison with the apparent peacefulness of upper realms. This cultivation is mundane in that one cannot progress beyond the first eight of the nine levels of meditative absorption because there is no higher stage to which the ninth can be compared. This cultivation only temporarily removes defilements.

saptakṛtparama (Tib. *re ltar thogs na lan bdun pa*): "One who takes up to seven existences," an abider in the result of Stream-enterer who has the accrued karma to experience rebirth in sets of seven in the desire realm at the time of rebirth.

saptasthānakuśala (Tib. *gnas bdun la mkhas pa*): "One who is wise in seven objects," one who cognizes seven modes of analysis for a given object, such as with form: (i) the purity of form, (ii) the arising of form, (iii) the cessation of form, (iv) the path of going to the cessation of form, (v) the taste of form, (vi) the punishing fault of form, and (vii) the definite arising of form. An *Abhidharma* analogy utilized for classifying a Stream-enterer who takes up to seven rebirths.

sarvacyuta (Tib. *gnas thams cad cu 'chi 'pho ba*): "One who dies in all abodes," a type of Non-returner who attains *nirvāṇa* in *Akaniṣṭha* heaven after having taken rebirth in all other form realm heavens.

sāsrava (Tib. *zag bcas*): "contaminated," something that is amenable to the increase of impure karma from being either an cognitive object (*ālambana*) or associated with a mental affliction (*kleśa*).

satkāyadṛṣṭi (Tib. *'jig tshogs la lta ba*): "false view of the perishable aggregates," apprehending the notions of "I" and "mine" through any idea, inclination, or point of view which considers as true the idea of 'self' or 'belonging to a self' with regard to the five appropriated aggregates.

śilavrataparāmarśa (Tib. *tshul khrims brtul shugs mchog dzin pa*): "holding ethics and ritual as supreme," a point of view that considers ethics and rituals, where the basis for those ethics and rituals are the five persishable aggregates, as true, pure, and conducive to *nirvāṇa*.

skandha (Tib. *phung po*): "aggregate," the five components that constitute an individual: form (*rūpa*), feeling (*vedanā*), recognition (*saṃjñā*), mental formations (*saṃskāra*), and consciousness (*vijñāna*).

sopāna (Tib. *them skas*): "stairway," the central analogy that the path of the Buddha and the Nobles' Four Truths are comprehended in a progressive and gradual manner and not simultaneously.

sopadhiśeṣanirvāṇa (Tib. *lhag bcas kyi mya ngan las 'da'*): "*nirvāṇa* with remnant," the attainment of *nirvāṇa* with the residue or remnant of the appropriated aggregates (*skandha*).

śraddhā (Tib. *dad pa*): "faith," confidence, trust, or affection for the Buddha's teachings and the qualities they embody.

śraddhādhimukta (Tib. *dad pas lhag par mos pa*): "One who aspires by faith," a follower of doctrine (*śraddhānusārīn*) with dull faculties who passes through the sixteenth moment of the path of seeing and abides in either the result of Stream-enterer, Once-returner, or Non-returner dependent upon defilements previously removed through the path of cultivation.

śraddhānusārīn (Tib. *dad pas rjes su 'brang ba*): "One who follows by way of Faith," an enterer to the result of Stream-enterer with weak faculties who acquires path provisions and realizes truths based on teachings given by others.

śrāmaṇya (Tib. *dge sbyong gi tshul*): stainless and uncontaminated, wholesome meditative practices that pacify mental afflictions.

śrāvaka (Tib. *nyan thos pa*): "listener," one who has heard or studied the Buddha's teachings and who seeks the peace of *nirvāṇa* through cultivating a direct realization of the Nobles' Four Truths.

srota-āpanna (Tib. *rgyun du zhugs pa*): "Stream-enterer," the first degree of Noble Being who has entered the stream leading to *nirvāṇa.* A Stream-enterer will never be reborn as a hell-being, hungry ghost, or animal. A Stream-enterer has abandoned the false view toward the perishable aggregates (*satkāyadṛṣṭi*), doubt (*vicitsā*), and holding that ethics and rituals are supreme (*śilavrataparāmarśa*).

śuddhāvāsakāyika (Tib. *gnas gtsang ma*); "the pure places," the upper form realm heavens of *Abṛha, Atapas, Sudṛśa, Sudarśana,* and *Akaniṣṭha* where Noble Beings are born as a result of the technique of "alternating cultivations" (*vyavakīrṇabhāvanā*).

tīkṣṇendriya (Tib. *dbang po rnon po*): "sharp faculty," keen, acute, and perceptive sense faculties and intellect.

traidhātuka (Tib. *khams gsum*): "three realms," the desire realm (*kāmadhātu*), form realm (*rūpadhātu*), and formless realm (*ārūpyadhātu*) that constitute cyclic existence (*saṃsāra*).

ubhayatobhāgavimuktaḥ (Tib. *gnyis ka'i cha las rnam grol ba*): "One who is liberated by both ways," a type of *Arhat* who is liberated from both the obscuration of entering absorption (*snyoms 'jug gi sgrib pa*) and the obscurations of the afflictions (*nyon sgrib*).

upapadyaparinivāyīn (Tib. *skyes nas 'da' ba mngon par 'du byed pa*): "One who achieves *nirvāṇa* through birth," a type of Non-returner who transmigrates to the form realm and attains *nirvāṇa* in the initial form realm embodiment among the sixteen form realm heavens.

upapadyavedanīyakarma (Tib. *skyes nas myong las*): "karma that causes the experience of rebirth," subtle karmic propensities that are removed by Non-returners who transmigrate among the form realm heavens.

upapattisaṃyojana (Tib. *skyes ba'i kun sbyor ba*): "fetter of rebirth," a karmic propensity that binds one to further rebirth in conditioned existence.

upāyakauśalya (Tib. *thabs la mkas pa*): "skill-in-means," (i) the tactical skills and methods utilized by a *bodhisattva* in mastering attainments and realizations (such as giving, ethics, meditative absorption, etc.) for accumulating the provisions of merit and knowledge required to achieve Buddhahood. Such methods require a *bodhisattva* to perform a balancing act between *realizing* a cognitive attainment and *actualizing* the correlative result of such an attainment so as to avoid achieving an inferior aim such as *śrāvaka* or *pratyekabuddha arhat*ship; (ii) the expedient means employed by a Buddha to lead beings to awakening by imparting provisional teachings until they have the capacity for ultimate teachings.

ūrdhvadhātu (Tib. *khams gong ma*): "upper realms," the form realm (*rūpadhātu*) and formless realm (*ārūpyadhātu*).

ūrdhvaṃsrotas (Tib. *gong du 'pho ba*): "One who goes higher," a type of form realm Non-returner who transmigrates in the form realm that, while not attaining *nirvāṇa* in the embodiment of first birth in the form realm, goes higher among the upper form realms to attain *nirvāṇa*.

ūṣmagata (Tib. *drod pa*): "heat," the first of the four phases of the preparatory analytical factors (*nirvedhabhāgīya*) where a state of complete mental quiescence that is connected with analytical insight (*vipaśyanā*) discerns for the first time the essential nature of the Nobles' Four Truths.

vaibhāṣika (Tib. *bye brag tu smra ba*): "*Vaibhāṣika*," a mainstream Buddhist exegetical tradition that flourished in north-west India and derives its name from the *Mahāvibhāṣa*, an encyclopedic treatise of *Abhidharma* compiled in the third century.

vedanā (Tib. *tshor ba*): "feeling," one of the five aggregates, the pleasant, unpleasant, and indifferent experiences arising from karma and mental afflictions.

vicikitsā (Tib. *the tshom*): "doubt," afflicted incertitude with regard to the Nobles' Four Truths that provides a basis for not engaging with that which is virtuous. One of the three fetters removed through the path of seeing.

viṃśatiprabhedasaṃgha (Tib. *dge 'dun nyi shu*): "Twenty Varieties of the *Saṃgha*," an enumerated list consisting of systematically classified Noble Beings who have achieved the sixteenth moment of the Path of Seeing (*darśanamārga*) and who are actualizing the Truth of Cessation (*satyanirodha, 'gogs bden*) and the Truth of the Path (*mārgasatya, lam bden pa*).

vimuktimārga (Tib. *rnam par grol ba lam*): path of liberation, moments of path consciousness that arise after a defilement is abandoned.

visaṃyoga (Tib. *'bral ba*): the disconnection of afflictions from the mental continuum.

viśeṣaṇa (Tib. *khyad par can*): "distinguished," a special status while residing in a given result that signifies continued progress toward a higher degree of attainment.

vītarāgapūrvin (Tib. *chags bral sngon song*): "separation from attachment previous to path of seeing," individuals who separate from the attachment produced by desire realm *kleśas* in the period previous to the path of seeing.

vyavakīrṇabhāvanā (Tib. *spel mar bsgom pa*): "alternating cultivation," meditative technique that consists of mixing contaminated and uncontaminated moments of concentration to cause rebirth in the *śuddhāvāsa* form realm heavens.

vyutkrāntakaphalīn (Tib. *'bras bu thod rgal ba*): "fruition skipper," an individual who removes defilements to be abandoned by the path of cultivation by a mundane path before reaching the path of seeing. There are two types: a *bhūyovītarāga* ("One who is separated from attachment for the most part" [*phal cher chags dang bral ba*]) and a *kāmavītarāga* ("One who is separated from attachment in the desire realm" [*'dod chags dang bral ba*]).

yāna (Tib. *theg pa*): "vehicle" or "way," that which leads or carries one toward a goal of realization. A set of teachings and practices that enable one to journey toward higher rebirth in the upper realms, liberation from *saṃsāra*, or complete Buddhahood. The AA mentions three vehicles: the inferior vehicles (*theg dman*) of the *śrāvaka* (*nyan thos kyi theg pa*) and *pratyekabuddha* (*rang rgyal gyi theg pa*) and the great vehicle (*Mahāyāna, theg pa chen po*) of the *bodhisattva* (*byang chub sems dpa'i theg pa*). See **ekayāna.**

References

Principle Indian Sources

Abhidharmakośabhāṣya (AKBh) by Vasubandhu. Translated and annotated by Louis de La Vallèe Poussin (1971). *L'Abhidharmakośa de Vasubandhu.* Nouvelle éd. anastatique présentée par Étienne Lamotte. Bruxelles: Institut belge des Hautes êtudes chinoises, 6 tomes. (MCB, 16). English translation by Leo M. Pruden (1989), Volumes 1 to 4, Asian Humanities Press, Berkeley. Translated by Jinamitra, Dpal brtsegs. *Chos mgnon pa'i mdzod kyi bshad pa.* Pk 5591, Volume 115. Edited by P. Pradhan (1967, Reprint 1975). *Abhidharmakośabhāṣya of Vasubandhu.* Patna: K. P. Jayaswal Research Institute (Tibetan Sanskrit Works Series, Volume 8). Compiled by A. Hirakawa (1973–1978). *Index to the Abhidharmakośabhāṣya.* Part I: Sanskrit-Tibetan-Chinese. Part II: Chinese-Sanskrit. Part III: Tibetan-Sanskrit. Tokyo: Daizo Shuppan, 3 volumes.

Abhidharmakośabhāṣyavyākhyā (AKV) by Yaśomitra. Edited by Swami Dwarikadas Śāstrī (1971). *Abhidharmakośa and Bhāṣya of Ācārya Vasubandhu with Sphuṭārthā Commentary of Ācārya Yaśomitra.* Bauddha Bhāratī Series, No. 5 Vārāṇasī: Bauddha Bhāratī, 4 volumes. Translated by Viśuddhisiṃha, Dpal brtsegs. *Chos mngon pa'i mdzod kyi 'grel bshad.* Pk. 5593, Volume 116.

Abhidharmakośakārikā (AK) by Vasubandhu. Edited by V. V. Gokhale (1946). "The Text of the *Abhidharmakośakārikā* of Vasubandhu." *Journal of the Bombay Branch, Royal Asiatic Society* 22: 73–102; (1947) 23: 12. Translated by Jinamitra, Dpal brtsegs. *Chos mngon pa'i mdzod kyi tshig le'ur byas pa.* Pk 5590, Volume 115.

Abhidharmāmṛtarasaśāstra by Ghosaka. Translated and annotated by José van den Broeck (1977). *La Saveur de L'Immortel = A-p'it-t'an Kan Lu Wei Lun: la version chinoise de l'Amṛtarasa de Ghosaka.* (T 1553). Broeck. Louvain-la-Neuve: Université catholique de Louvain, Institut orientaliste; Louvain: commandes.

Abhidharmasamuccaya (AS) of Asanga. Fragments edited by V. V. Gokhale (1947). "Fragments from the *Abhidharmasamuccaya* of Asanga." *Journal of the Bombay Branch, Royal Asiatic Society* 23: 13–38. Edited by Pralhad Pradhan (1950). *Abhidharmasamuccaya.* Santiniketan: Visvabharati. Translated by Jinamitra, Śīlendrabodhi, Ye she sde. *Chos mngon pa kun las btus pa.* Pk 5550, Volume 112. Translated by Rahula (1971). *Le Compendium de la superdoctrine (Philosophie) (Abhidharmasamuccaya) d'Asaṅga.* Publications de l'École franṛaise d'Extrême-Orient, Volume 78. Paris: École franṛaise d'Extrême-Orient. Translation of Rahula (1971) by Boin-Webb (2001). *Abhidharmasamuccaya: The Compendium of the Higher Teaching (Philosophy) by Asaṅga.* Fremont: Asian Humanities Press.

Abhidharmasamuccayabhāṣya (ASBh) by Jinaputra. Edited by Nathmial Tatia (1976). *Abhidharmasamuccayabhāṣya*. Patna: K. P. Jayaswal Research Institute. Translated by Jinamitra, Śīlendrabodhi, Ye she sde. *Chos mngon pa kun las btus pa'i bshad pa*. Pk 5554, Volume 113.

Abhisamayālaṃkāra (AA). Edited by Th. Stcherbatsky and E. Obermiller (1929). *Abhisamayālaṃkāraprajñāpāramitopadeśaśāstrakārikā*. Leningrad. (Bibliotheca Buddhica, 23, fasc. 1.) Delhi: Sri Satguru Publications, 2nd edition, 1992. Translated by Go mi 'chi med, Blo ldan shes rab. *Shes rab kyi pha rol tu phyin pa'i man ngag gi bstan bcos mngon par rtogs pa'i rgyan zhes bya ba'i tshig le'ur bya pa*. Pk 5184, Volume 88. Translated by E. Conze (1954). *Abhisamayālaṅkāra. Introduction and Translation from Original Text with Sanskrit-Tibetan Index*. Roma: Istituto Italiano per il Medio ed Estremo Oriente.

Abhisamayālaṃkāradurbodhālokā by Dharmakīrtiśrī. Translated by Dīpaṃkaraśrījñāna, Rin chen bzang po. *Mngon par rtogs pa'i rgyan ces bya ba'i 'grel pa rtogs par dka' ba'i snang ba shes bya ba'i 'grel bshad*. Pk 5192, Volume 91.

Abhisamayālaṃkārakārikāvṛttiśuddhamatī by Śāntipa. Tib. *Shes rab kyi pha rol tu phyin pa'i man ngag gi bstan bcos mngon par rtogs pa'i rgyan gyi tshig le'ur byas pa'i 'grel pa dag par ldan pa*. Pk 5199, Volume 91.

Abhisamayālaṃkārālokā Prajñāpāramitāvyākhyā (AAĀ) by Haribhadra. Edited by U. Wogihara (1932–1935). *The Work of Haribhadra*. Tokyo: Toyo Bunko. Edited by Giuseppe Tucci (1932). Baroda: Oriental Institute. Compiled by Ryusei Keira and Noboru Ueda (1998). *Sanskrit Word Index to the Abhisamayālaṃkārālokā Prajñāpāramitāvyākhyā (U. Wogihara Edition)*. Tokyo: Sankibo Press.

Abhisamayālaṃkāraprasphuṭapadā (PSPh) by Dharmamitra. Translated by Abhiyuktaka Tāraśrīmitra, Chos kyi shes rab. *Mngon par rtogs pa'i rgyan gi tshig le'ur byas pa'i 'gral bshad tshig rab tu gsal ba shes bya ba*. Pk 5194, Volume 91.

Abhisamayālaṃkārasphuṭārthā (AASPh) by Haribhadra. Edited Sanskrit Manuscript by Hirofusa Amano (2000). *Abhisamayālaṃkāra-kārikā-śāstra-vivṛti: Haribhadra's Commentary on the Abhisamayālaṃkāra-kārikā-śāstra Edited for the First Time from a Sanskrit Manuscript*. Kyoto, Heirakuji-shoten, 2000. Translated by Vidyākaraprabha, Dpal brtsegs. *Shes rab kyi pha rol tu phyin pa'i man ngag gi bstan bcos mngon par togs pa'i rgyan ces bya ba'i 'grel pa*. Pk 5191, Volume 90. Edited by Rāmaśaṅkara Tripāṭhī. *Prajñāpāramitopadeśaśāstra Abhisamayālaṅkāravṛttiḥ Sphuṭārthā Ācāryaharibhadraviracitā*; Saṃskṛtarūpāntarakāraḥ sampādakaś ca Sāranāthah: Kendriya-Tibbati-ucca-Siksha-Samsthanam, 1977.

Abhisamayālaṃkāraśuddhamatī by Ratnākaraśānti. Translated by Śrī Subhūtiśānti, Śākya blo gros, Dge ba'i blo gros. Revised by Śāntibhadra, Lha btsas. *Mngon par rtogs pa'i rgyan gyi tshig le'ur byas pa'i 'grel pa dag ldan shes bya ba*. Pk 5199, Volume 91.

Abhisamayālaṃkāravārttika by Bhadanta Vimuktisena. Translated by Śāntibhadra, Śākya 'od. *Mngon par rtogs pa'i rgyan gyi tshig le'ur byas pa'i rnam par 'grel pa*. Pk 5186, Volume 88.

Abhisamayālaṃkāravṛtti (AAV) by Ārya Vimuktisena. Edited by Corrado Pensa (1967). *L'Abhisamayālaṃkāravṛtti di Ārya-Vimuktisena. Primo Abhisamaya. Testo e note critiche*. Roma: Istituto Italiano per il Medio ed Estremo

Oriente. Translated by Śāntibhadra, Śākya 'od. *Mngon par rtogs pa'i rgyan gyi 'grel pa*. Pk 5185, Volume 88.

Aṅguttaranikāya (AN). Edited by R. Morris, R. Hardy, and E. Hardy (1885–1900). Pali Text Society, London, 5 volumes. Translated by F. L. Woodward and M. Hare (1932–1936), *Gradual Sayings*. London: Pali Text Society, 3 volumes.

Āryaśatasāhasrikāpañcaviṃśatisāhasrikāṣṭādaśasāhasrikāprajñāpāramitābṛhaṭṭīkā by Daṃṣṭrasena. Translated by Surendrabodhi, Ye shes sde. *Yum gsum gnod 'joms. 'Phags pa shes rab kyi pha rol tu phyin pa 'bum pa dang nyi khri lnga stong pa dang khri brgyad stong pa'i rgya cher bshad pa*. Pk 5206, Volume 93.

Aṣṭādaśasāhasrikāprajñāpāramitāsūtra. Edited and translated by E. Conze (1974). In The Gilgit Manuscript of the *Aṣṭādaśasāhasrikāprajñāpāramitā*: Chapters 70 to 82, Corresponding to the Sixth, Seventh, and Eighth *Abhisamayas*. Roma: Istituto Italiano per il Medio ed Estremo Oriente.

Aṣṭasāhasrikāprajñāpāramitāpañjikāsāratamā by Ratnākaraśānti. Translated by Subhūtiśānti, Śākya blo groa. Pk 5200, Volume 92. Edited by P. S. Jaini (1979). *Sāratamā: A Pañjikā on the Aṣṭasāhasrikā by Ācārya Ratnākaraśānti*. Tibetan Sanskrit Works Series, 18. Patna: Kashi Prasad Jayaswal Research Institute.

Aṣṭasāhasrikāprajñāpāramitāsūtra (Aṣṭa). Edited by U. Wogihara; included in *Abhisamayālaṃkārālokā*. Edited by P. L. Vaidya (1960). *Aṣṭasāhasrikā Prajñāpāramitā, with Haribhadra's Commentary Called Āloka*. Buddhist Sanskrit Texts, #4. Darbhanga, India.

Aṣṭasāhasrikāprajñāpāramitāvṛttimarmakaudmudī by Abhayākaragupta. Translated by Abhayākaragupta, Shes rab dpal. *'Phags pa shes rab kyi pha rol tu phyin pa brgyad stong pa'i 'grel pa gnad kyi zla ba'i 'od ces bya ba*. Pk 5202, Volume 92.

Avaivartacakranāmamahāyānasūtra. Translated by Jinamitra, Dānaśīla, Munivarma, Ye shes sde. *'Phags pa phyir mi ldog pa'i 'khor lo zhes bya ba theg pa chen po'i mdo*. Pk 906, Volume 36.

Dhammapada. Pāli text with English translation in John Ross Carter and M. Palihawadana (trans.) (1992) *Sacred Writings, Buddhism: The Dhammapada*. New York: Quality Paperback Book Club.

Dīghanikāya (DN). Edited by T.W. Rhys-Davids and J. Estlin Carpenter. 3 vols. 1890. Reprint. London: Pali Text Society, 1960–1967. English translation by Maurice Walshe, *The Long Discourses of the Buddha*. Boston: Wisdom Publications, 1995.

Madhyāntavibhāgaṭīkā by Sthiramati. Edited by Sylvain Lévi. Nagoya: Librairie Hajinkaku, 1934.

Mahāyānasūtrālaṃkāra (MSA) by Asaṅga. Edited and translated by Sylvain Lévi. *Paris: Champion, 1907–11*. English translation by L. Jamspal, et al., *The Universal Vehicle Discourse Literature*. New York: American Institute of Buddhist Studies, 2004.

Mahāvyutpatti (MVP). Hon'yaku myōgi taishū: Bon-zō-kan-wa yon'yaku taikō. Chosakusha Sakaki Ryōzaburō. Kyōto: Shingonshū Kyōto Daigaku, Taishō 5–14, 1916–1925.

Mahāyānottaratantraśāstra. Edited by E. H. Johnston and T. Chowdhury. *The Ratnagotravibhāga Mahāyānottaratantraśāstra*, Patna: Bihar Research Society

(1950). Translation by E. Obermiller. "Sublime Science of the Great Vehicle to Salvation, *Acta Orientalia*, 9 (1931): 81–306. Translation by J. Takasaki. *A Study on the Ratnagotravibhāga*. Rome: Istituto Italiano per il Medio ed Estremo Oriente (1966).

Majjhimanikāya (MN). Edited by V. Trenckner and R. Chalmers. 3 volumes. 1888–1902. Reprint, London: Pali Text Society, 1960–1964.

Pañcaviṃśatisāhasrikāprajñāpāramitāsūtra (Pañcaviṃśati). Edited by N. Dutt (1934). Calcutta: Calcutta Oriental Series No. 28. Translated by E. Conze (1975). *The Large Sutra on Perfect Wisdom, with the Divisions of the Abhisamayālaṅkāra*. Berkeley: University of California Press.

Prajñāpāramitāvajracchedikāṭīkā by Kamalaśila. Translated by Mañjuśrī, Jinamitra, Ye shes sde. *'Phags pa shes rab kyi pha rol tu phyin pa rdo rje gcod pa'i rgya cher 'grel pa*. Toh. 3817, Shes phyin, vol. ka. Critically edited Tibetan and restored Sanskrit by Pema Tenzin (1994). *Prajñāpāramitāvajracchedikāsūtra with Prajñāpāramitāvajracchedikāṭīkā of Kamalaśila*. Sarnath: Central Institute of Higher Tibetan Studies.

Puggala-paññatti (Pugg). Edited by Richard Morris (1972). London: Luzac for the Pali Text Society. Translation by Bimala Charan Law. *Designation of Human Types (Puggalapaññatti)*. London: Luzac (for the Pali Text Society), 1969 [c1924].

Puggala-paññatti-atthakathā (Pugg-A). Edited by Georg Landsberg and Mrs. Rhys Davids (1972). London: Luzac (for the Pali Text Society).

Ratnaguṇasamcayagāthā. Sanskrit and Tibetan text edited by E. Obermiller (1960). *Prajñāpāramitā-ratnaguṇasamcayagāthā: photomechanic reprint with a Sanskrit-Tibetan-English index by Edward Conze*. 's-Gravenhage: Mouton. Translation by Edward Conze (1962). *The Accumulation of Precious Qualities: New Delhi*, International Academy of Indian Culture. Edited with an introduction, bibliographical notes, and a Tibetan version from Tunhuang by Akira Yuyama (1976). *Prajñāpāramitāratnaguṇasamcayagāthā*. New York: Cambridge University Press.

Saṃyuttanikāya (SN). Edited by L. Feer. 5 volumes. 1884–1898. Reprint. London: Pali Text Society, 1973–1990. English translation by Bhikkhu Bodhi, *The Connected Discourses of the Buddha*. Boston: Wisdom Publications, 2000.

Śatasāhasrikāprajñāpāmitāsūtra. Edited by P. Ghosha (1902–1914). Bibli. Ind. 1, Nos. 146–48. Calcutta: Asiatic Society of Bengal. Contains only chapters 1–12. Pk 730, Volumes 12–18 (complete).

Śatasāhasrikāprajñāpāramitāvivaraṇa by Dharmaśrī. Tib. *'Phags pa shes rab kyi pha rol tu phyin pa stong phrag brgya pa'i rnam par 'grel pa*. Pk 5203, Volume 92.

Śūraṃgamasamādhisūtra (Śgs). Translated by Lamotte (1965) and Webb (1998). *The Concentration of Heroic Progress. An Early Mahāyāna Buddhist Scripture*. Richmond, Surrey: Curzon Press in association with the Buddhist Society.

Tibetan Tripiṭaka, Peking Edition (Pk). Edited by D. T. Suzuki. 168 volumes. Tokyo-Kyoto: Tibetan Tripiṭaka Research Institute, 1956–1961.

Tibetan Tripiṭaka, Taipei Edition (Taipei). Edited by A. W. Barber. 72 volumes. Taipei: SMC, 1991.

Triśaraṇasaptati by Candrakīrti. Edited, translated, and annotated by Per K. Sorenson. *The Septuagint on the Three Refuges.* Wien: Arbeitskreis für Tibetische und Buddhistische Studien, Universität Wien, 1986.

Vajracchedikāprajñāpāramitāsūtra. Edited and translated with introduction and glossary by Edward Conze (1957). *Vajracchedikāprajñāpāramitāsūtra.* Rome. Translated and explained by Edward Conze (1958). *Buddhist Wisdom Books, Containing The Diamond Sutra and The Heart Sutra.* London: G. Allen and Unwin.

Vimalakīrtinirdeśasūtra (Vks). Translated by Étienne Lamotte. English translation by Sara Boin-Webb. *Vimalakīrtinirdeśasūtra. The Teaching of Vimalakīrti.* London: Pali Text Society, (1976, reprint 1994).

Principle Indigenous Tibetan Sources

A mchog Rinpoche Blo bzan mkhyen rab rgya mtsho. "Introduction." *Lotsaba chen po'i bsdus don bzhugs so = Commentary on the Abhisamayālaṃkāra by Rnog Lotsaba Blo-ldan-'ses-rab; with an Introduction by the Eighty-first Abbot of Shar-rtse Grva-tshan, Fourth A-mchog Rinpoche Blo-bzan-mkhyen-rab-rgya-mtsho and David P. Jackson.* Dharamsala, H.P.: Library of Tibetan Works and Archives, 1993.

Blo bzang 'phrin las rnam rgyal, Rgyal dbang chos rje dar han mkhan po (fl. 1840–1860) (Rnam rgyal). *'Jam mgon chos kyi rgyal po Tsong-kha-pa-chen-po'i rnam thar thub bstan mdzes pa'i rgyan gcig ngo mtshar nor bu'i 'phreng ba zhes bya ba bzhugs so.* Sarnath: Mongolian Lama Guru Deva, 1967.

Bod rgya tshig mdzod chen mo (The Extensive Tibetan-Chinese Dictionary). Beijing: National Minorities Press, Mi rigs dpe skrun khang (one volume), 1998.

Bstan pa dar rgyas, Ser Smad Mkhas grub (1493–1568). *Dge 'dun ni shu'i mtha' dpyod bzhugs so.* Dge-'dun-bstan-dar-ba chen po'i gsung. Ser Smad Grwa-tshan, 1969.

Bu ston rin chen grub (1290–1364). *Bde bar gshegs pa'i bstan pa'i gsal byed chos kyi 'byun gnas gsun rab rin po che'i mdzod ces bya ba.* Translated from Tibetan by E. Obermiller. *History of Buddhism (Chos 'byung),* Heidelberg, 1931–1932.

———. *Gsan yig. The Collected Works of Bu-ston,* part 21 (La), New Delhi, 1971.

———. *Shes rab kyi pha rol tu phyin pa'i man ngag gi bstan bcos mngon par rtogs pa'i rgyan ces bya ba'i 'grel pa'i rgya cher bshad pa lung gi sne ma* (Lung gi sne ma). *The Collected Works of Bu-ston,* part 18 (Tsha), New Delhi, 1971.

Dkon mchog 'jigs med dbang po (1728–1791). *Sa lam gyi rnam gzhag theg pa gsum gyi mdzes rgyan.* In *The Collected Works of dkon mchog 'jigs med dbang po.* New Delhi: Nga wang Gelek Demo, 1972.

Go ram pa bsod nams seng ge (1429–1489). *Zhugs gnas kyi rnam gzhag skyes bu mchog gi gsal byed.* Sa skya'i 'kah 'bum, Volume 14. Tokyo: Toyo bunkyo, 1969.

'Jam dpal rgya mtsho, Rtogs ldan, 1356–1428. *Rje btsun tsong kha pa'i rnam thar chen mo'i zur 'debs rnam thar legs bshad kun 'dus bzhugs so.* Varanasa: Legs bshad gter mdzod par khan, 1970.

mKhas grub dge legs dpal bzang po (1385–1438). *Rje btsun bla ma tsong kha pa chen po'i no mtshar rmad du byung ba'i rnam par thar pa dad pa'i 'jug ngogs zhes bya ba'i bzhugs so*. Vārānasī: K. Lhundup and Lama Samdup, 1966.

Ngag dbang bkra bshis (1678–1738). *Zhugs pa dang gnas pa'i 'phags pa'i dge 'dun gyi rnam gzhag gi mtha' dpyod skal bzang 'jug ngogs* in *dge 'dun nyi shu'i mtha' dpyod; with Other Minor Texts from the Yig-cha of Sgo-mang College*. Delhi: Kesang Thabkhes, 1980.

Nya dbon kun dga' dpal (fourteenth century). *Bstan bcos mngon par rtogs pa'i rgyan 'grel pa dang bcas pa'i rgyas 'grel bshad sbyar yid kyi mun sel*. bKra shis 'khil ba'i chos grva edition. New Delhi, 1978.

rGyal tshab dar ma rin chen (1364–1432). *Shes rab kyi pha rol tu phyin pa'i man ngag gi bstan bcos mngon par rtogs pa'i rgyan gyi rtsa ba 'grel pa dang bcas pa'i rnam bshad snying po'i rgyan* (= *rnam bshad nying po'i rgyan*). (Sung 'bum, t. kha).

rNam gyal dbang chen (contemporary). *Dbu sems kyi lta ba dang tshad mar sgrub pa'i le'u'i snying don, mngon rtogs rgyan gyi tshig don bcas gsal bar bstan pa'i legs bshad utpala'i gru char*. Bras spung blo gsal gling dpe mdzod khan, Karanataka, 1996.

rNgog blo ldan shes rab, "rNgog lo tsā ba" (1059–1109). *Lo tsa ba chen po'i bsdus don: A Commentary on the Abhisamayālaṃkāra. Introduction by Blo bzang mkhyen rab rgya mtsho and Dr. David P. Jackson*. Library of Tibetan Works and Archives, 1993.

Rong ston shes bya kun rig (1367–1449). *Mngon par rtogs pa'i rgyan 'grel pa dang bcas pa'i dka' ba'i gnas rnam par 'byed pa zab don gnad kyi zla 'od: A Detailed Exegesis of the Abhisamayālaṃkāra and Its Commentary by Haribhadra*. Gangtok: Sherab Gyaltsen, 1979.

———. *Rong-ston on the Prajñāpāramitā Philosophy of the Abhisamayālaṃkāra: His Subcommentary on Haribhadra's "Sphuṭārthā."* Edited by David P. Jackson in collaboration with Shunzo Onoda. Kyoto: 1988.

Śākya mchog ldan, Gser mdog Pan chen, (1428–1507). *Dge 'dun nyi shu'i mtha'rnam par dpyad pa'i thal 'gyur ngag gi dbang po'i mdzes rgyan zhes bya ba bzhugs so. Complete Works of Gser mdog paṇchen śākya mchog ldan*, Thimphu Bhutan, Volume 13, 1–111, 1975.

———. *Mngon par rtogs pa'i rgyan 'grel pa don gsal ba dang bcas pa'i rnam par bshad pa shing rta'i srol gnis gcig tu bsdus pa'i lam po che zhes bya ba bzhugs so*. Lhun-grub-rtse'i-rdzon, 1969.

Se ra rje btsun Chos kyi rgyal mtshan (1469–1546). *Bstan bcos mngon par rtogs pa'i rgyan 'grel pa dang bcas pa'i rnam bshad rnam pa gnis kyi dka' ba'i gnas gsal bar byed pa legs bshad skal bzang klu dbang gi rol mtsho zhes bya ba*. Bylakuppe: Se-ra Byes Grwa-tshan, 1980.

———. *Dge 'dun nyi shu'i mtha' gcod: Rje-btsun Chos-kyi-rgyal-mtshan-dpal-bzan-po'i gsung rtsom dri ma med pa mkhas pa'i mgul rgyan zhes bya ba bzhugs so*. Sbag-sa: Se-ra Byes Grwa-tshan, 1968.

Sgra sbyor bam po gnyis pa (GBBN). Ishikawa, Mie, editor. *A Critical Edition of the sGra sbyor bam po gnyis pa. An Old and Basic Commentary on the Mahāvyutpatti*. Studia Tibetica, 18, Materials for Tibetan-Mongolian Dictionaries, Volume 2, Tokyo: Toyo Bunko, 1990.

Shes rab rgya mtshan, Dol po pa, 1292–1361. *Rnam bshad mdo'i don bde blag tu rtog pa,* Volume 6, 323–882, in *The 'Dzam-thang Edition of the Collected Works (gsung-'bum) of Kun-mkhyen Dol-po-pa Shes-rab-rgyal-mtshan.* Collected and presented by Matthew Kapstein. Delhi, India: Shedrup, 1992.

Tāranātha, Jo nang pa, b. 1575. Translated from the Tibetan by Lama Chimpa and A. Chattopadhyaya. Edited by D. Chattopadhyaya. *Rgya gar chos 'byung. Tāranātha's History of Buddhism in India.* Simla: Indian Institute of Advanced Study, 1970.

Tshe mchog gling yongs 'dzin Ye shes rgyal mtshan, 1713–1793. *Byang chub lam gyi rim pa'i bla ma brgyud pa'i rnam thar.* Biographies of the Eminent Gurus in the Transmission Lineages of the Teachings of the Graduated Path: Being the Text of *Byang chub lam gyi rim pa'i bla ma brgyud pa'i rnam par thar pa rgyal bstan mdzes pa'i rgyan mchog phul byung nor bu'i phreng ba.* New Delhi: Ngawang Gelek Demo, 1970–1972.

Tsong kha pa blo bzang grags pa (1357–1419). *Dbu ma la 'jug pa'i rnam bshad dgongs pa rab gsal.* Sarnath: Gelupa Students Union, 1973.

———. *Dbu ma rtsa ba'i tshig le'ur byas pa shes rab ces bya ba'i rnam bshad rigs pa'i rgya mtsho.* Va na mtho slob dge ldan spyi las khang nas, 1975.

———. *Dge 'dun nyi shu bsdus pa rjes gnang ba dang zhugs gnas bzhugs so* (Rjes gnang); fols. 593–606. Collected Works, 1977, Volume 27.

———. *Drang nges legs bshad snying po = The Essence of Eloquent Speech on the Definitive and Interpretable.* Mundgod, District North Kanara, Karnataka, India: SOKU, 1991.

———. *Khams gsum chos kyi rgyal po tsong kha pa chen po'i gsung 'bum. Collected Works.* Dge ldan gsung rab mi nyams rgyun phel series 79–105, published by Ngag dbang dge legs bde mo, 1975–1979.

———. *Rje rin po che blo bzang grags pa'i dpal gyi gsan yig. Khams gsum chos kyi rgyal po tsong kha pa chen po'i gsum 'bum.* Volume Ka, pp. 233–93.

———. *Shes rab kyi pha rol tu phyin pa'i man ngag gi bstan bcos mngon par rtogs pa'i rgyan 'grel pa dang bcas pa'i rgya cher bshad pa legs bshad gser phreng zhes bya ba bzhugs so (= Golden Garland).* Volume 1. Sarnath: Lama Thuptan Jungnes, 1970. Also Collected Works, 1977, Volumes 26 and 27, gSung 'bum lHa sa edition, v. tsa and tsha.

———. *Yid dang kun gzhi'i dka' ba'i gnad rgya cher 'grel ba legs bshad rgya mtsho,* New Delhi, Volume 27, 1977. Introduced and translated by Gareth Sparham in collaboration with Shotaro Iida. *Ocean of Eloquence: Tsong Kha Pa's Commentary on the Yogācāra Doctrine of Mind.* Albany: State University of New York Press, 1993.

———. *Zhugs pa dang gnas pa'i skyes bu chen bo rnams kyi rnam par bzhag pa blo gsal bgrod pa'i them skad zhes bya ba bzhugs so* (Stairway) in *The Collected Works (gsung 'bum) of Rje Tsong-kha-pa Blo-bzang-grags-pa.* Reproduced from an example of the old Bkra-sis-lhun-po redaction from the library of Klu 'khyil Monastery of Ladhakh by Ngawang Gelek Demo. New Delhi: 1977, Volume 27.

Zhang zhung chos sbang grags pa (1404–1469). *Shes rab kyi pha rol tu phyin pa'i man ngag gi bstan bcos mngon par rtogs pa'i rgyan gyi 'grel pa don gsal ba'i rnam bshad rtogs par dka' ba'i sngang ba* (= *rtogs dka'i snang ba*). In *Collected Works of mKhas grub rje* (gSung 'bum, vol. ka).

Secondary Sources

Amano, Koei H. 1961. "A Fragment from the *Abhisamayālaṃkāra-nāma-prajñāpāramitopadeśa-śāstravṛtti*, alias 'Sphuṭārthā' of Haribhadra." *Annual Report of the Tohoku Research Institute of Buddhist Culture* 3: 1–25. [In Japanese]

———. 1969. "On the Composite Purpose of the *Abhisamayālaṃkāra-kārikā-śāstra*—Haribhadra's Way of Explaining." *Journal of Indian and Buddhist Studies* 17.2: 59–69. [In Japanese]

———. 1975. *A Study of the Abhisamaya-alaṃkāra-kārika-śāstra-vṛtti*. Tokyo: Japan Science Press.

Amano, Hirofusa. 2000. *Abhisamayālaṃkāra-kārikā-śāstra-vivṛti: Haribhadra's Commentary on the Abhisamayālaṃkāra-kārikā-śāstra edited for the first time from a Sanskrit Manuscript*. Kyoto: Heirakuji-shoten.

Anacker, Stefan. 1970. "Vasubandhu: three aspects; a study of a Buddhist philosopher." PhD dissertation, University of Wisconsin.

Angdu, Sonam, editor. 1973. *Tibetan-Sanskrit Lexicographical Materials, the sGra ryor bam po gnyis, the Dag yiz za ma tog, and the Dag yig li shi'i gur khang*. Leh: Basgo Thongspon Publication.

Apple, James. 2001. "Twenty Varieties of the *Saṃgha*: Tsong kha pa's Soteriological Exegesis." PhD dissertation, University of Wisconsin–Madison. University Microfilms International, Ann Arbor, Michigan.

———. 2003. "Twenty Varieties of the *Saṃgha*: A Typology of Noble Beings (*Ārya*) in Indo-Tibetan Scholasticism (Part I)." JIP 31, no. 5–6, pp. 503–92.

———. 2004. "An Assembly of Irreversible *Bodhisattva*s. Twenty Varieties of the *Saṃgha*: A Typology of Noble Beings (*Ārya*) in Indo-Tibetan Scholasticism (Part 2)." JIP 32: 211–79, 2004.

Arènes, Pierre. 1998. "Herméneutic des tantra: Étude de quelquels usages du sens caché." JIABS 21.2: 173–225.

Bareau, André. 1947. "Les Sectes Bouddhiques du Petit Vehicule et Leurs Abhidhamma Piṭaka." *Bulletin de l'Ecole Française d'Extrême-Orient* 44 (1947): 1–11.

———. 1954. "Trois Traités sur les Sectes Bouddhiques Attribues á Vasumitra." *Journal Asiatique* 229–66 (1956): 167–299.

———. 1955. *Les Sectes Bouddhiques du Petit Véhicule*. Saïgon: École Francaise d'Extrême-Orient.

———. 1957. "Les Controverses Relative á la Nature de L'Arhant dans le Bouddhisme Ancien." *Indo-Iranian Journal* 1: 241–50.

Barthes, Roland. 1966. "Introduction à l'analyse structurale des récits." *Communications* 8.

———. 1967. *Elements of Semiology*. Jonathan Cape, London.

Bastian, Edward Winslow. 1980. "Mahāyāna Buddhist religious practice and the perfection of wisdom according to the *Abhisamayālaṃkāra* and the

Pañcaviṃśatisāhasrika-prajñāpāramitā (the interpretation of the first two topics by Haribhadra, rGyal-tshab dar-ma-rin-chen, and rJe-btsun chos-kyi rgyal-mtshan)." PhD dissertation, University of Wisconsin–Madison.

Buswell, Robert E. 1997. "The Aids to Penetration (*Nirvedabhāgīya*) According to the *Vaibhāṣika* School." JIP 25: 589–611.

Buswell, Robert E., and Robert M. Gimello, eds. 1992. *Paths to liberation: The Mārga and Its Transformations in Buddhist Thought*. Honolulu: University of Hawaii Press.

Cabezón, José. 1992. Buddhism, Sexuality, and Gender. Albany: State University of New York Press.

———. 1994. *Buddhism and Language: A Study of Indo-Tibetan Scholasticism*. Albany: State University of New York Press.

———. 1998. "Introduction." In *Scholasticism: Cross-cultural and Comparative Perspectives*. Edited by José Cabezón. Albany: State University of New York Press, pp. 1–18.

Chandra, Lokesh, ed. 1985. *Materials for a History of Tibetan Literature*. New Delhi: Sharada Rani.

Chattopadhyaya, D. (ed.). 1970. *Rgya gar chos 'byung. Tāranātha's History of Buddhism in India*. Simla: Indian Institute of Advanced Study.

Collins, Steven. 1982. *Selfless Persons: Imagery and Thought in Theravāda Buddhism*. Cambridge: Cambridge University Press.

———. 1998. *Nirvāṇa and Other Buddhist Felicities: Utopias of the Pali Imaginaire*. New York and Cambridge, UK: Cambridge University Press.

Conze, Edward. 1947. "On Omniscience and the Goal." *The Middle Way* 22.3: 62–63.

———. 1952. "The Composition of the *Aṣṭasāhasrikā Prajñāpāramitā*." BSOAS (London) 14: 251–62.

———. 1953. "The Ontology of the *Prajñāpāramitā*." *Philosophy East and West* 3.2: 117–29.

———. 1954a. *Abhisamayālaṃkāra*. Roma: Istituto Italiano per il Medio ed Estremo Oriente.

———. 1954b. "Maitreya's *Abhisamayālaṃkāra*." *East and West* 5.3: 192–97.

———. 1957. "Marginal Notes to the *Abhisamayālaṃkāra*." *Sino-Indian Studies* 5: 21–36.

———. 1958. "The Oldest *Prajñāpāramitā*." *The Middle Way* 32: 136–41.

———. 1961. "*Abhisamayālaṃkāra* (1)." *Encylopedia of Buddhism*. Fascicule I. Colombo: Government of Ceylon: 114–16.

———. 1967a. *Buddhist Thought in India*. Ann Arbor: University of Michigan Press.

———. 1967b. *Materials for a Dictionary of the Prajñāpāramitā Literature*. Tokyo: Suzuki Research Foundation.

———. 1975a. *The Large Sutra on Perfect Wisdom, with the Divisions of the Abhisamayālaṅkāra*. Berkeley: University of California Press.

———. 1975b. *The Perfection of Wisdom in Eight Thousand Lines*. Bolinas, CA: Four Seasons.

———. 1978a. "Notes on the Text of the *Aṣṭasahāsrikā*." *Journal of the Royal Asiatic Society* 1: 14–20.

———. 1978b. *The Prajñāpāramitā Literature*. 2nd ed. Tokyo: Reiyukai.

Cox, Collet. 1992. "Attainment through Abandonment: The *Sarvāstivādin* Path of Removing Defilements." In Buswell and Gimmello eds., 63–106.

Dantinne, Jean. 1983. *La splendeur de l'inébranlable (Akṣobhyavyūha)*. Université catholique de Louvain, Institut orientaliste.

Davidson, Ronald Mark. 1985. "Buddhist Systems of Transformation: *āśraya-parivṛtti / parāvṛtti* among the *Yogācāra*." PhD dissertation, University of California, Berkeley.

De Jong, J. W. 1971. Review of Étienne Lamotte, *Traité de la Grande Vertu de Sagesse de Nāgārjuna*. III. *Asia Minor* 17: 105–12.

———. 1973. Review of Rahula's *Abhidharmasamuccaya*. *T'oung Pao* 59: 339–46.

———. 1979. *Buddhist Studies*, Berkeley: Asian Humanities Press.

———. 1986. Review of J. Hopkins's *Meditation on Emptiness*. JIABS 9.1: 124–28.

———. 1999. Review of J. Makransky, *Buddhahood Embodied*. *Indo-Iranian Journal* 42: 70–75.

De Silva, Lily. 1978. "Cetovimutti Paññavimutti and Ubhatobhagavimutti." *Pali Buddhist Review* 3.3: 118–45.

Dreyfus, Georges. 1997. "Tibetan Scholastic Education and the Role of Soteriology." JIABS 20.1: 31–62.

Dutt, Nalinaksha. 1930. *Aspects of Mahāyāna Buddhism and Its Relation to Hīnayāna*. London: Luzac.

———. 1971. *Early Monastic Buddhism*. Calcutta: Firma K. L. Mukhopadhyay.

Edgerton, Franklin. 1953 (Reprint 1977). *Buddhist Hybrid Sanskrit Grammar and Dictionary* (BHSD). Volume 1: Grammar. Volume 2: Dictionary. New Haven. Motilal Banarsidass.

Frauwallner, Erich. 1951. *On the Date of the Buddhist Master of the Law Vasubandhu*. Roma: Serie Orientale.

———. 1961. "Landmarks in the History of Indian Logic." In *Wiener Zeitschrift für die Kunde Süd-Ostasiens*, Volume 5, 131.

———. 1995. *Studies in Abhidharma Literature and the Origins of Buddhist Philosophical Systems*. Albany: State University of New York Press.

Gethin, Rupert. 1992. "The *Mātikās*." *In the Mirror of Memory*. See Janet Gyatso, ed., 1992.

———. 1997. "Cosmology and Meditation: From the *Aggaṭṭa-Sutta* to the Mahāyāna." *History of Religions* 36.3: 183–217.

———. 2001. *The Buddhist Path to Awakening: A Study of the Bodhi-Pakkhiyā Dhammā*. Oxford: Oneworld.

Gombrich, Richard F. 1975. "Ancient Indian Cosmology." In *Ancient Cosmologies*. Edited by Carmen Blacker and Michael Loewe, 110–42. London: Allen and Unwin.

———. 1990. "Recovering the Buddha's Message." *Buddhist Forum*, Volume 1, Seminar Papers 187–88, ed. T. Skorupski, London: 5–20.

Gómez, Luis O. 2004. "*Nirvāṇa*." *Encyclopedia of Buddhism*. Edited by Robert E. Buswell, Volume 2: 600–605. New York: Macmillan.

Gonda, Jan. 1939. "The Meaning of the Word *Alaṃkāra*." *A Volume of Eastern and Indian Studies*. Bombay: Karnatak, 97–114.

Gonta, Sonam Gyaltsen. 1992. "Tsong kha pa's View on the Theory of *Ekayāna*." *Tibetan Studies, Narita 1989*. Edited by Ihara Shōten et al., Narita: 59–66.

Griffin, David Ray. 2000. "Introduction to SUNY Series in Constructive Postmodern Thought." *Spiritual Titanism* by Nicholas F. Gier, xxi–xxvi. Albany: State University of New York Press (2000).

Griffiths, Paul J. 1983. "Indian Buddhist meditation-theory: history, development and systematization." PhD dissertation, University of Wisconsin-Madison, 1983.

———. 1990. "Omniscience in the Mahāyānasūtrālaṅkāra." IIJ 33: 85–120, 1990.

———. 1994. *On Being Buddha: The Classical Doctrine of Buddhahood*. Albany: State University of New York Press.

Guenther, Herbert V. 1976. *Philosophy and Psychology in the Abhidharma*. Berkeley: Shambhala.

Gyatso, Janet, ed. 1992. *In the Mirror of Memory: Reflections on Mindfulness and Remembrance in Indian and Tibetan Buddhism*. Albany: State University of New York Press.

Hall, Bruce. 1983. "Vasubandhu on aggregates, spheres, and components: being chapter one of the *Abhidharmakośa*." PhD dissertation, Harvard University, 1983.

Handurukande, Ratna. 1973. "*Avaivartacakra-Nāma-Mahāyāna-Sūtra*." EOB 2.3: 400–402.

Harrison, Paul. 1989. "Buddhism: A Religion of Revelation after All?" *Numen* 36 (1989): 256–64.

Hastings, James, ed. 1955–1958. *Encyclopaedia of Religion and Ethics*. New York: Scribner's.

Hayes, Richard P. 1994. "Nāgārjuna's Appeal." JIP 22: 299–378.

Hayashima, Kyosho. 1961. "*Abhisamaya*." EOB 1: 104–14.

Hopkins, Paul Jeffrey. 1980. *Compassion in Tibetan Buddhism: With Kensur Lekden's Meditations of a Tantric Abbot*. New York: Snow Lion.

———. 1983. *Meditation on Emptiness*. London: Wisdom.

———. 1992. "A Tibetan Perspective on the Nature of Spiritual Experience." In Buswell and Gimello, *Paths to Liberation*. Honolulu: University of Hawaii Press, 225–68.

———. 1999. *Emptiness in the Mind-Only School of Buddhism*. Berkeley: University of California Press.

Horner, I. B. 1934. "The Four Ways and the Four Fruits in Pāli Buddhism." *Indian Historical Quarterly* 10: 785–96.

———. 1979. *The Early Buddhist Theory of Man Perfected*. New Delhi: Oriental Books Reprint.

Hurvitz, Leon. 1967. "The Road to Buddhist Salvation as Described by Vasubhadra." JAOS 87: 434–86.

———. 1977. "Path to Salvation in the *Jñāna-prasthāna*." *Studies in Indo-Asian Art and Culture* 5: 77–102.

———. 1979. "Dharmaśrī on the Sixteen Degrees of Comprehension." JIABS 2.2: 7–30.

Hyodō, Kazuo. 2000. *Hannyakyoshaku genkansōgonron no kenkyu* (Study of the *Abhisamayālaṃkāra*, commentary on the *Prajñā sūtras*). Kyoto: Bun'eidō shoten.

Ichigō, M. 1985. *Madhyamakālaṃkāra of Śāntarakṣita with His Own Commentary or Vṛtti and the Subcommentary or Pañjikā of Kamalaśīla*. Kyoto: Buneido.

Ishikawa, Mie, ed. 1990. *A Critical Edition of the sGra sbyor bam po gnyis pa: An Old and Basic Commentary on the Mahāvyutpatti.* Studia Tibetica, 18, Materials for Tibetan-Mongolian Dictionaries, Volume 2, Tokyo: Toyo Bunko.

Isoda, Hirofumi. 1970. "A Study of *Cittotpāda* in the *Abhisamayālaṃkāra.*" JIBS 19.1: 71–76.

———. 1972. "A Study on the *Nirvedha-bhāgīya* in the *Abhisamayālaṃkāra.*" JIBS 20.2: 541–46.

Jackson, Roger R., and John J. Makransky, eds. 2000. *Buddhist Theology: Critical Reflections by Contemporary Buddhist Scholars.* London: Curzon.

Jaini, Padmanabh S. 1958. "On the Theory of Two Vasubandhus." BSOAS 21: 48–53.

———. 1972. "The *Āloka* of Haribhadra and the *Sāratamā* of Ratnākaraśānti: A Comparative Study of the Two Commentaries of the *Aṣṭasāhasrikā.*" *Bulletin of the School of Oriental and African Studies* Volume 35: 271–94.

———. 1992. "On the Ignorance of the *Arhat.*" In *Paths to Liberation.* Ed. Buswell and Gimello. Honolulu: Kuroda Institute, pp. 135–46.

Jinpa, Thupten. 1997. " 'Self', Persons and *Madhyamaka* Dialectics: A Study of Tsongkhapa's Middle Way Philosophy." PhD dissertation, University of Cambridge, U.K.

———. 1998. "Delineating Reason's Scope for Negation, Tsongkhapa's Contribution to Madhyamaka's Dialectical Method." JIP 26: 275–308.

———. 1999. "Tsongkhapa's Qualms about Early Tibetan Interpretations of *Madhyamaka* Philosophy." *Tibet Journal* 24.2: 3–28.

———. 2000. "The Question of 'Development' in Tsongkhapa's *Madhaymaka* Philosophy." *Études Asiatiques* 54.1: 5–44.

Joshi, Lal Mani. 1991. "A Survey of the Conception of *Bodhicitta.*" *Journal of Religious Studies* 3.1: 70–79.

Kajiyama, Yuichi. 1982. "On the Meanings of the Words *Bodhisattva* and *Mahāsattva* in *Prajñāpāramitā* Literature." In *Indological and Buddhist Studies: Volume in Honor of Prof. J. W. de Jong on His Sixtieth Birthday.* Canberra: Faculty of Asian Studies.

Karunatilleke, W. S. 1967. "Aṣṭa-Prajñā-pāramitā-vyākhyābhisamayālaṃkāra-ālokaḥ." EOB 2.2: 252–55.

Kaschewsky, Rudolf. 1971. *Das Leben des lamaistischen Heiligen Tsongkhapa Blo-Bzaṅ-Grags-Pa* (1357–1419), *dargestellt und erläutert anhand seiner Biographie "Quellenort allen Glücks."* 2 vol. Asiatische Forschungen, Volume 32. Wiesbaden: Harrassowitz.

Katz, Nathan. 1982. *Buddhist Images of Human Perfection.* Delhi: Motilal Banarsidass.

Keenan, John K. 1980. "A study of the Buddhabhūmyupadeśa: the doctrinal development of the notion of wisdom in Yogācāra thought." PhD dissertation, University of Wisconsin.

Kloppenborg, Ria. 1974. *The Paccekabuddha: A Buddhist Ascetic. A Study of the Concept of the Paccekabuddha in Pāli Canonical and Commentarial Literature.* Leiden: Brill.

Kobayashi, Mamoru. 1981. "On Ratnākara-śānti's Commentaries on the *Abhisamayālaṃkāra.*" JIBS 30.1: 132–33.

Kritzer, Robert. 2000. "Rūpa and the *Antarābhava.*" JIP 28: 235–72.

Kuijp, Leonard W. J. van der. 1983. *Contributions to the Development of Tibetan Buddhist Epistemology: From The Eleventh to the Thirteenth Century*. Wiesbaden: Steiner.

———. 1985. "Apropos of a Recent Contribution to the History of Central Way Philosophy in Tibet: Tsong Khapa's Speech of Gold." *Berliner Indologische Studien* 1: 47–74.

———. 1999. "Remarks on the 'Person of Authority' in the Dga' ldan pa/ Dge lugs pa School of Tibetan Buddhism." JAOS 119.4: 646–72.

Lakatos, I. 1978. "History of Science and Its Rational Reconstructions." In J. Worral and G. Currie (eds.), *Imre Lakatos: The Methodology of Scientific Research Programmes*. Philosophical Papers Volume 1, Cambridge: Cambridge University Press, pp. 102–38.

Lalou, Marcelle. 1953. "Les textes bouddhiques au temps du roi Khri-sro'-ldebcan." *Journal Asiatique* 361: 313–53.

Lamotte, Étienne. 1944. *Le Traité de la Grande Vertu de Sagesse de Nāgārjuna*. Volume 1 (3–620), Louvain, 1944; Volume 2 (621–1118), Louvain, 1949; Volume 3 (1119–1733), Louvain, 1970; Volume 4 (1735–2162), Louvain, 1976; Volume 5 (2163–2451), Louvain-la-Neuve, 1980. Louvain: Institut Orientaliste Louvain-la-Neuve.

———. 1965. *La Concentration de la Marche Héroique* (*Śūraṃgamasamādhisūtra*), traduit et annoté, Mélanges Chinois et Bouddhiques, Bruxelles. English translation by Sara Boin-Webb. 1998. *Śūraṃgamasamādhisūtra: The Concentration of Heroic Progress. An Early Mahāyāna Buddhist Scripture*. Richmond, Surrey: Curzon (in association with the Buddhist Society).

———. 1976. *Vimalakīrtinirdeśasūtra. The Teaching of Vimalakīrti*. English translation by Sara Boin-Webb. London: The Pali Text Society.

———. 1988a. "Assessment of Textual Interpretation in Buddhism." Trans. Sara Boin-Webb. In Lopez (1988): 11–25.

———. 1988b. *History of Indian Buddhism from the Origins to the Śaka Era*. Trans. Sara Boin-Webb. Louvain: Institut Orientaliste Louvain-la-Neuve.

La Vallèe Poussin, Louis de. 1906. "Pali and Sanskrit." *Journal of the Royal Asiatic Society* 446–51.

———. 1910a. "Bodhisattva." *Encyclopaedia of Religion and Ethics*. Ed. J. Hastings, 2: 739a–753b.

———. 1910b. "Mahāyāna." *Encyclopaedia of Religion and Ethics*. Ed. J. Hastings, 8: 330a–336b.

———. 1910c. "Pratyekabuddha." *Encylopaedia of Religion and Ethics*. Ed. J. Hastings, 10: 153b.

———. 1919. *Vasubandhu et Yaçomitra. Troisième chapitre de l'Abhidharmakoça Kārikā, Bhāsya et Vyākyā, avec une analyse de Lokaprajñāpti et de la Kāranaprajñāpti de Maudgelyāyana. Versions et textes établis d'après les sources sanscrites et tibétaines*. Bruxelles, Hayez, impr. de l'Académie royale.

———. 1923. *L'Abhidharmakośa de Vasubandhu* (LVP). Paris: Geuthner.

———. 1925. *Nirvāṇa*. Etudes sur L'Histoire des Religions, 4. Paris: Gabriel Beauchesne.

———. 1930. "Documents d'Abhidharma 1. Textes Relatifs au *Nirvāṇa* et aux *Asaṃskṛtas* en General." *Bulletin de l'Ecole Francaise d'Extrême-Orient* 30 (1930): 1–28.

———. 1931–1932. "Documents d'Abhidharma 2. La Doctrine des Refuges." *Mélanges Chinois et bouddhiques* 1 (1931–1932): 65–109.

———. 1970. *Mūlamadhyamakakārikās (Mādhyamikasūtras) de Nāgārjuna, avec la Prasannapadā commentarie de Candrakīrti.* St. Petersburg: Bibliotheca Buddhica 4. Reprint Osnabrück: Biblio Verlag.

Lethcoe, Nancey R. 1976. "Some Notes on the Relationship between the *Abhisamayālaṃkāra*, the Revised *Pañcaviṃśatisāhasrikā* and the Chinese Translation of the Unrevised *Pañcaviṃśatisāhasrikā*." JAOS 96: 499–511.

Lévi-Strauss, C. 1966. *The Savage Mind.* Translated from the French, *La Pensée sauvage.* Chicago: University of Chicago Press.

Lindtner, Christian. 1986. *Master of Wisdom.* Berkeley: Dharma.

Lopez, Donald S. (ed). 1988. *Buddhist Hermeneutics.* Honolulu: University of Hawaii Press.

Macy, Joanna. 1976. "Perfection of Wisdom: Mother of All Buddhas." *Anima* 3.1: 74–80.

Makransky, John J. 1997. *Buddhahood Embodied: Sources of Controversy in India and Tibet.* Albany: State University of New York Press.

Malalasekera, G. P. 1973. *Encyclopaedia of Buddhism.* Sri Lanka: Government of Sri Lanka.

Manné, Joy. 1995. "Case Histories from the Pāli Canon II: *Sotāpanna, Sakadāgāmin, Anāgāmin, Arahat*—The Four Stages Case History or Spiritual Materialism and the Need for Tangible Results." *Journal of the Pali Text Society* 21: 35–128.

Mano, Ryūkai. 1967. "Gotra in Haribhadra's Theory." JIBS 40.2: 22–28.

———. 1970. "On the Three *Jñatās.*" JIBS 43.2: 21–26.

———. 1972. *A Study of the Abhisamayālaṃkāra* (In Japanese). Tokyo: Saniko Buddhist Book Store.

Margolis, John. 1998. "Structuralism in Literary Theory." *Routledge Encyclopedia of Philosophy.* Ed. Edward Craig, 9: 181–84.

Masefield, Peter. 1983. "Mind/Cosmos Maps in the Pāli Nikāyas." In *Buddhist and Western Psychology,* edited by N. Katz, 69–93. Boulder: Prajñā.

———. 1986. *Divine Revelation in Pali Buddhism.* London: Allen & Unwin.

Masuda, Jiryo. 1925. "Origin and Doctrines of Early Indian Buddhist Schools." *Asia Major* 2: 1–78.

May, Jacques. 1959. *Candrakīrti Prasannapadā Madhyamakavṛtti.* Douze chapitres traduits du sanscrit et du tibétaine, accompagnés d'une introduction, de notes et d'une édition critique de la version tibétaine. Paris: Adrien-Maissonneuve.

Monier-Williams, Monier. 1899. *A Sanskrit-English Dictionary.* Oxford: The Clarendon Press.

Moriyama, Seitetsu. 1984. "The *Yogācāra-mādhyamika* Refutation of the Position of the *Satyākāra* and *Alīkāra-vādins* of the *Yogācāra* School. Part 1: A Translation of Portions of Haribhadra's *Abhisamayālaṃkārālokā Prajñāpāramitā-vyākhyā.*" *Bukkyo Daigaku Daigakuin Kenkyu Kiyo* 12: 1–58.

Mullin, Glenn H., trans. 1985. *Essence of Refined Gold: Selected Works of the Dalai Lama III, Commentary by H.H. the Dalai Lama XIV.* Ithaca: Snow Lion.

Nagao, Gadjin M. (ed.). 1964. *Madhyāntavibhāga-bhāṣya: A Buddhist Philosophical Treatise.* Tokyo: Suzuki Research Foundation.

Napper, Elizabeth. 1989. *Dependent-arising and Emptiness: A Tibetan Buddhist Interpretation of Madhyamika Philosophy Emphasizing the Compatibility of Emptiness and Conventional Phenomena*. London: Wisdom.

Nattier, Jan. 2003. *A Few Good Men: The Bodhisattva Path According To the Inquiry of Ugra (Ugraparipṛcchā)*. Honolulu: University of Hawaii Press.

Naughton, Alexander T. 1989. "The Buddhist Path to Omniscience." PhD dissertation, University of Wisconsin–Madison.

———. 1991. *Classic Mahāyāna Soteriology—An Annotated Translation of Chapters 1–7 of Haribhadra's Short Commentary on the Abhisamayālaṃkāra known as Sphuṭārtha* (sic), Annual Memoirs of the Otani University, Volume 9 Kyotō: Shin Buddhist Comprehensive Research Institute.

Nishi, Yoshio. 1953. *Genshi bukkyo ni okerru hannya* (*Prajñā* in Early Buddhism) Yokohama: Okurayama bunka kagaku kenkyusho, 299–318.

Noriaki, Hakamaya. 1986. "Chibetto ni okeru Maitreya no gohō no kiseki." *Chibetto no Bukkyō to Shakai*. Ed. Yamaguchi Zuihō. Tokyo: Shunjusha, 235–68.

Norman, Kenneth Roy. 1997. *A Philological Approach to Buddhism*. London: School of Oriental and African Studies.

Obermiller, Eugene. 1931. *The Sublime Science*. Budapest: Acta Orientalia IX.

———. 1932. *The Doctrine of the Prajñāpāramitā as Exposed in the Abhisamayālaṃkāra of Maitreya*. Budapest: Acta Orientalia XI.

———. 1933. *Analysis of the Abhisamayālaṃkāra*. London: Luzac.

———. 1934a. "*Nirvāṇa* According To the Tibetan Tradition." *Indian Historical Quarterly* 10.2: 211–57.

———. 1934b. "A Study of the Twenty Aspects of *Śūnyatā* based on Haribhadra's *Abhisamayālaṃkārāloka* and the *Pañcaviṃśatikasāhasrikā*." *Indian Historical Quarterly* 9.1: 170–87.

———. 1935. "Tsoṅ-kha-pa le Pandit." *Mélanges Chinois et Bouddhiques*. Bruxelles 3: 319–38.

———. 1986. *The Jewelry of Scripture by Bu-ston*. Delhi: Sri Satguru.

Peri, N. 1911. "A propos de la date de Vasubandhu." *Bulletin de l'Ecole francaise d'Extrême-Orient* 11: 339–90.

Pettit, Philip. 1977. *The Concept of Structuralism: A Critical Analysis*. Berkeley: University of California Press.

Pezzali, Amalia. 1981. "*Bodhisattva* et *Prajñāpāramitā*, L'essence du *Madhyamaka*." *Indologica Taurinensia* 8–9: 307–12.

Prasda, H. S. (ed.). 1991. *The Uttaratantra of Maitreya: Containing Introduction, E. H. Johnston's Sanskrit Text, and E. Obermiller's English Translation*. Delhi: Sri Satguru.

Rahula, Walpola. 1962. "A Comparative Study of *Dhyānas* According to *Theravāda, Sarvāstivāda* and *Mahāyāna*." *Maha Bodhi* 190–99.

———. 1971. *Le Compendium de la super-doctrine (Philosophie) (Abhidharmasamuccaya) d'Asaṅga*. Publications de l'École française d'Extrême-Orient, Volume 78. Paris: École française d'Extrême-Orient. English translation by Boin-Webb (2001). *Abhidharmasamuccaya. The Compendium of the Higher Teaching (Philosophy) by Asaṅga*. Fremont: Asian Humanities Press.

———. 1978. "The Problem of the Prospect of the *Saṅgha* in the West." *Zen and the Taming of the Bull: Towards the Definition of Buddhist Thought*. London: Gordon Fraser, pp. 55–67.

Raja, K. Kunjunni. 1969. *Indian Theories of Meaning*. 2nd ed. Madras: Adyar Library and Research Centre; Wheaton, Ill.: agents, Theosophical Publishing House.

Reigle, David. 1997. "The 'Virtually Unknown' Benedictive Middle in Classical Sanskrit: Two Occurrences in the Buddhist *Abhisamayālaṅkāra*." *Indo-Iranian Journal* 40: 119–23.

Roerich, George (trans.). 1976. *The Blue Annals*. Delhi: Motilal Banarsidass.

Ruegg, David Seyfort. 1966. *The Life of Bu ston Rin po che, with the Tibetan Text of the Bu ston rNam thar*. Roma: Istituto italiano per il Medio ed Estremo Oriente.

———. 1967. *The Study of Indian and Tibetan Thought: Some Problems and Perspectives*. Inaugural Lecture, Chair of Indian Philosophy, Buddhist Studies and Tibetan, University of Leiden. Leiden: Brill.

———. 1968. "The dGe-lugs-pa Theory of the *Tathāgatagarbha*." *Pratidānam, Studies Presented to F.B.J. Kuiper*, Janua Linguarum Series Maior, The Hague 34: 500–509.

———. 1968–1969. "Ārya and Bhadanta Vimuktisena on the Gotra-Theory of the *Prajñāpāramitā*." WZKSO, 12–13: 303–17.

———. 1969. *La Théorie du tathāgatagarbha et du gotra*. Publications de l'êcole Francaise d'Extrême-Orient. Paris: Maisonneuve.

———. 1973. *Le Traité du tathāgatagarbha de Bu ston rin chen grub*. Publications de l'êcole Francaise d'Extrême-Orient, Volume 88. Paris: Maisonneuve.

———. 1976. "The Meaning of the Term *Gotra* and the Textual History of the *Ratnagotravibhāga*." *Bulletin of the School of Oriental and African Studies* 39: 341–63.

———. 1977. "The *Gotra, Ekayāna* and *Tathāgatagarbha* Theories of the *Prajñāpāramitā* According to Dharmamitra and Abhayākaragupta." In *The Prajñāpāramitā and Related Systems: Studies in Honor of Edward Conze*. Ed. L. Lancaster et al., Berkeley Buddhist Studies, I, Berkeley, CA, pp. 283–312.

———. 1980. "On the Reception and Early History of the dbu ma (Madhyamaka) in Tibet." In *Tibetan Studies in Honor of Hugh Richardson*, M. Aris and A. Suu Kyi, eds., 277–79. New Delhi: Vikas.

———. 1981. *The Literature of the Madhyamaka School of Philosophy in India*. Wiesbaden: Harrassowitz.

———. 1985. "Purport, Implicature and Presupposition: Sanskrit *abhiprāya* and Tibetan *dgoṅ pa / dgoṅ gzi* as Hermeneutical Concepts." JIP 13: 309–25.

———. 1988. "An Indian Source for the Tibetan Hermeneutical Term *dgoṅ gzi* 'intentional ground.' " JIP 16: 1–4.

———. 1989. *Buddha-nature, Mind and the Problem of Gradualism in a Comparative Perspective: On the Transmission and Reception of Buddhism in India and Tibet*. London: School of Oriental and African Studies, University of London.

———. 1995. "Some Reflections of the Place of Philosophy in the Study of Buddhism." JIABS, 18.2: 145–81.

———. 2000. *Studies in Indian and Tibetan Madhyamaka Thought*. Part 1. Wien: Arbeitskreis für Tibetische und Buddhistische Studien, Universität Wien.

———. 2002. *Studies in Indian and Tibetan Madhyamaka Thought*. Part 2. Wien: Arbeitskreis für Tibetische und Buddhistische Studien, Universität Wien.

Sadakata, Akira. 1997. *Buddhist Cosmology: Philosophy and Origins*. Tokyo: Kōsei.

Samten, Jampa. 1997. "Notes on the Late Twelfth- or Early Thirteenth-Century Commentary on the *Abhisamayālaṃkāra*: A Preliminary Report of a Critical Edition." Proceedings of the Seventh IATS, Volume 1, *Tibetan Studies*, Wien: 831–41.

Sangpo, Khetsun. 1973–1981. *Biographical Dictionary of Tibet and Tibetan Buddhism*. 9 volumes. Dharamsala, H. P.: Library of Tibetan Works and Archives.

Scherrer-Schaub, Cristina Anna. 1981. "Le terme yukti: primière étude." *Études Asiatiques* 35.2: 185–200.

Sharf, Robert H. 1995. "Buddhist Modernism and the Rhetoric of Meditative Experience." *Numen* 42.3: 228–83.

Smith, Jonathan Z. 1978. *Map Is Not Territory: Studies in the History of Religions*. Chicago: University of Chicago Press.

———. 1982. *Imagining Religion*. Chicago: University of Chicago Press.

———. 2004. *Relating Religion: Essays in the Study of Religion*. Chicago: University of Chicago Press.

Sopa, Geshe Lhundup et al. 1985. *The Wheel of Time: The Kalachakra in Context*. Madison: Deer Park.

Sopa, Geshe Lhundup, and Jeffrey Hopkins. 1989. *Cutting through Appearances: Practice and Theory of Tibetan Buddhism*. Ithaca: Snow Lion.

Sorenson, Per K. 1986. *The Septuagint on the Three Refuges*. Wien: Arbeitskreis für Tibetische und Buddhistische Studien, Universität Wien.

Sparham, Gareth. 1987. "Background Material for the First of the Seventy Topics in Maitreyanātha's *Abhisamayālaṃkāra*." JIABS 10.2: 139–58.

———. 1989. "A Study of Haribhadra's *Abhisamayālaṃkārālokā Prajñāpāmitāvyākhyā*." PhD dissertation, University of British Columbia.

———. 1993. *Ocean of Eloquence: Tsong kha pa's Commentary on the Yogācāra Doctrine of Mind*. Albany: State University of New York Press.

———. 1996. "A Note on Gnyal zhig 'Jam pa'i rdo rje, the Author of a Handwritten Sher phyin Commentary from about 1200." *Tibet Journal* 21.1: 19–29.

———. 1999. *The Fulfillment of All Hopes: Guru Devotion in Tibetan Buddhism*. Boston: Wisdom.

Stcherbatsky, Theodore. 1905. "Notes de Littérature Bouddhique: la Littérature *Yogācāra* d'après Bouston." *Le Muséon*: 141–55.

Steinkellner, Ernst, and Helmut Tauscher, eds. 1983. *Contributions on Tibetan and Buddhist Religion and Philosophy*. Wiener Studien zur Tibetologie und Buddhismuskunde Heft 11. Wien: Arbeitskreis für Tibetische und Buddhistische Studien, Universität Wien.

Thurman, Robert A.F. 1978. "Buddhist Hermeneutics." *Journal of the American Academy of Religion* 46.1: 19–39.

———. 1982. *The Life and Teachings of Tsong Khapa*. Dharmsala, India: Library of Tibetan Works and Archives.

———. 1984. *Tsong Khapa's Speech of Gold in the Essence of True Eloquence*. Princeton, N.J.: Princeton University Press.

Tillemans, Tom J. F. 1983. "The 'Neither One Nor Many' Argument for *Śūnyatā* and Its Tibetan Interpretations." In E. Steinkellner and H. Tauscher (eds.), 305–20.

———. 1990. *Materials for the Study of Āryadeva, Dharmapāla and Candrakīrti: The Catuḥśataka of Āryadeva, Chapters 12 and 13, with the Commentaries of Dharmapāla and Candrakīrti.* Wien: Arbeitskreis für Tibetische und Buddhistische Studien, Universität Wien.

Tucci, Giuseppe. 1930. *On Some Aspects of the Doctrines of Maitreyanātha and Asanga.* Calcutta University Readership Lectures, Calcutta.

———. 1932. *The Commentaries on the Prajñāpāramitās, Volume 1: The Abhisamayālaṃkārāloka of Haribhadra.* Gaekwad's Oriental Series, #62 Baroda: Oriental Institute.

———. 1947. "Minor Sanskrit Texts on the *Prajñāpāramitā*: 1. The *Prajñāpāramitā-piṇḍārtha* of Diṅnāga." *Journal of the Royal Asiatic Society* 1 & 2: 53–75.

Turner, Victor W. 1967. *The Forest of Symbols: Aspects of Ndembu Ritual.* Ithaca: Cornell University Press.

Vetter, Tilmann. 1990. *Der Buddha und seine Lehre in Dharmakīrtis Pramāṇavārttika.* Arbeitskreis für Tibetische und Buddhistische Studien, Wien: Arbeitskreis für Tibetische und Buddhistische Studien, Universität Wien.

Wayman, Alex. 1960. "The Sacittikā and Acittikā Bhūmi and the Pratyekabuddhabhūmi." JIBS 8.1: 375–79.

———. 1974. "The Intermediate-State Dispute in Buddhism." *Buddhist Studies in Honour of I.B. Horner.* Reidel, Dordrecht.

Welbon, Guy Richard. 1968. *The Buddhist Nirvāṇa and Its Western Interpreters.* Chicago: University of Chicago Press.

Werner, Karel. 1983. "*Bodhi* and *Arhataphala*: From Early Buddhism to Early *Mahāyāna*." *Buddhist Studies Ancient and Modern*: 167–81.

Willemen, Charles, Bart Desein, and Collet Cox. 1998. *Sarvāstivāda Buddhist Scholasticism.* Handbuch der Orientalistik: Abt. 2, Indien; Bd. 11. Leiden: Brill.

Williams, Paul. 1989. *Mahāyāna Buddhism: The Doctrinal Foundations.* London; New York: Routledge.

Willis, Janice Dean. 1979. *On Knowing Reality: The Tattvārtha Chapter of Asaṅga's Bodhisattvabhūmi.* New York: Columbia University Press.

Wylie, Turrell. 1959. "A Standard System of Tibetan Transcription." *Harvard Journal of Asiatic Studies* 22: 261–67.

Yeh, Ah-yueh. 1984. "A Study of the Theories of *yāvad-bhāvikatā* and *yathāvad-bhāvikatā* in the *Abhidharmasamuccaya*." JIABS 7.2: 185–207.

Yü-chia, Che'n. 1987. "The Explanation of the Twentyfold *Mahāyāna Saṃgha* in Tsong kha pa's mNgon par rtogs pa'i rgyan legs bshad ser gyi phreng ba." [in Chinese] *Chung-Hwa Buddhist Journal: Chung-Hwa Institute of Buddhist Studies* 1: 181–228.

Zahler, Leah. 1997. *Meditative States in Tibetan Buddhism.* Boston: Wisdom Publications.

INDEX

A

AA. See *Abhisamayālaṃkāra*

AAĀ. See *Abhisamayālaṃkārālokā*

AASPh. See *Sphuṭārthā*

AAV. See *Abhisamayālaṃkāravṛtti*

"Abbreviated Bestowal" (*dge 'dun nyi shu bsdus pa rjes gnang*), 19, 36, 193n23

Ābhāsvara (*'od gsal*) heaven, 90, 91, 130

Abhayākaragupta (*'Jigs med 'byung gnas sbas pa*), 31, 35, 150, 152, 159, 164, 173, 175

Abhidhamma Piṭaka, 95

Abhidharma (*chos mngon pa*), 6, 25, 26, 30, 34, 41, 43, 44, 45, 46, 47, 50, 68, 98, 99, 101, 102, 114, 122, 133, 140, 144, 155, 182, 183, 184, 186, 199n14

  Path structure, 47

Abhidharmakośa (*Chos mngon pa mdzod*), 22, 28, 34, 35, 41, 43, 46, 63, 67, 69, 72, 73, 76, 95, 98, 104, 105, 107, 108, 114, 116, 120, 121, 122, 132, 134, 137, 141, 145, 146, 153, 154, 155, 159, 173, 182, 184, 185, 192n11, 203n44

Abhidharmakośabhāṣya (*Chos mngon pa mdzod 'grel*), 28, 35, 41, 46, 101, 114, 116, 119, 120, 121, 122, 131, 132, 137, 139, 141, 142, 143, 192n5, 215n55

Abhidharmakośabhāṣyavyākhyā (*Chos mngon pa'i mdzod kyi 'grel bshad*), 101, 114, 137, 139, 140, 142, 143

Abhidharmasamuccaya (*Chos mngon pa kun las btus pa*), 27, 35, 43, 69, 76, 86, 95, 98, 101, 105, 114, 115, 116, 122, 124, 127, 134, 136, 137, 138, 146, 147, 148, 173, 175, 180, 184, 185

Abhidharmasamuccayabhāṣya (*Chos mngon pa kun las btus pa'i bshad pa*), 35, 101, 114, 123, 147, 159, 175

Abhijñā, 157

Abhinirvṛttikarma (karma of coming into being), 127

Abhiprāya. See Authorial intention

Abhisamaya (*ngon par rtogs pa*, "clear realization"), 49, 52, 53, 73, 74, 76, 100, 116, 198n8, 198n9, 200n15

Abhisamayālaṃkāra (*mngon rtogs rgyan*), 3, 4, 5, 10, 14, 17, 18, 19, 35, 47, 48, 49, 50, 52, 53, 55, 56, 58, 59, 63, 64, 65, 66, 67, 68, 69, 70, 76, 77, 79, 81, 83, 86, 94, 98, 101, 104, 116, 133, 146, 149, 150, 151, 152, 153, 155, 160, 163, 166, 167, 170, 171, 176, 180, 182, 183, 184, 185, 186, 189, 197n4, 198nn10–11, 199n11–14, 192n7, 194nn2–4, 195n6, 198n11, 202nn40–41

  and *Bodhisattva* path, 83–88

  Body of, 50

  Chapter on Empirical Omniscience, 76

  Commentaries on, 16, 17

  Four difficult topics within, 4

  Homage verses of, 50

  Indian commentators of, 11

  Intention of, 12

  Lineage tradition of, 21, 23–31

  as *Mātṛkā* of *Prajñāpāramitā sūtras*, 51

  Meaning of title, 48–49

  173 topics of, 4

  Origins of, 26–27

  and Path of cultivation, 77–78

  Path and yoga systems of, 47, 66–69

  Relation to *Yogācāra*, 26

  Seventeen types of provisions in, 85, 206n104

  Śrāvaka path in, 79–81

  as Summary of all *Prajñāpāramitā sūtras*, 49

  and Ten types of practice, 49, 199n12

  Title of, 48–49

  and Topic of Twenty *Saṃghas*, 10, 93–94

  Translation of verses I.23–24, 94, 171

  and Twenty-one Indian commentaries, 16, 193n19

Abhisamayālaṃkārālokā (Haribhadra), 16, 24, 27, 28, 29, 30, 32, 34, 65, 70–71, 76, 165, 167, 170, 171, 173, 177, 185, 197n4
Abhisamayālaṃkārasphuṭārthā. See *Sphuṭārthā*
Abhisamayālaṃkāravṛtti (Ārya Vimuktisena), 16, 29, 65, 87, 139, 154, 155, 158, 159, 161, 162, 163, 165, 167, 177, 195n11
Abhisamayālaṃkāravṛttipiṇḍārtha (Prajñākaramati), 31, 173
Abhisaṃskāraparinirvāyin (*mngon par 'du byed pa yongs su mya ngan las 'da' ba*), 112, 126, 128, 135, 159, 161, 166, 169, 172
Abhyāsa. See Familiarization
Abiding in bliss for the present life, 139, 140
Abiding with a group. See *Vargacāri*
Abṛha (*mi che ba*) heaven, 90, 91, 130
Absorption, 131, 138, 163, 185. See also *Dhyāna*
Absorption of cessation, 164
Acalā, 66
Achievement of the sixteen aspects, 71
Achieving *nirvāṇa* with effort. See *Abhisaṃskāraparinirvāyin*
Achieving *nirvāṇa* without effort. See *Anabhisaṃskāraparinirvāyin*
Activity of emergence (*niryāṇapratipatti, nges 'byung sgrub pa*), 55, 56
Activity of procuring equipment (*saṃbhārapratipatti, tshogs kyi sgrub pa*), 55, 56
Activity of putting on armor (*saṃnāhapratipatti, go cha'i sgrub pa*), 55, 56
Activity of setting out (*prasthānapratipatti, 'jug pa'i sgrub pa*), 55, 56
Actual Saṃgha (*mtshon par bya ba'i don gyi dge 'dun*), 33, 34, 45, 98, 101, 102, 104, 125, 146, 149–180, 183, 185, 186, 189
  Three qualities of resemblance with *Allegorical Saṃgha*, 173–180
Adhimātra, 78
Adhyātmajñāna, 63
Afflictional obscurations. See *Kleśāvaraṇa*
Afflictions (*kleśa, nyon mongs*). See Defilements
aggregates (*skandha, phung po*), 82
AK. See *Abhidharmakośa*
AKBh. See *Abhidharmakośabhāṣya*
Akaniṣṭha heaven (*'og min*), 90, 112, 118, 130, 131, 133, 160, 161, 162, 163, 169, 170, 171, 172
Akaniṣṭhaga (*'og min gyi mthar thug 'gro ba*), 112, 126, 130, 135, 155, 161, 166
  Tsong kha pa's definition of, 130
Ākāśānantyāyatana formless realm, 78, 91, 163
Ākiṃcanya formless realm, 78, 91
Akopyadharman (*mi 'khrugs pa'i chos can*), 134, 138, 139, 142
Akṣobhya, 161
Ālambana, 60
Alaṃkāra (*rgyan*), 48, 198n6
Allegorical Saṃgha (*mtshon par byed pa'i dpe'i dge 'dun*), 33, 34, 44, 93, 98–148, 149, 150, 152, 154, 155, 159, 162, 164, 165, 167, 171, 173, 183, 185, 186, 187
All-knowledge. See *Sarvajñatā*
Ālokalabdha (attaining illumination), 85
Alternating concentrations (*vyavakīrṇabhāvanā, spel mar bsgom pa*), 112, 130, 131, 132
Amano, Hirofusa, 50, 195n12, 199n13, 202n41
Anabhisaṃskāraparinirvāyin (*mngon par 'du byed pa med pa yongs su mya ngan las 'da' ba*), 112, 126, 128, 135, 159, 161, 166, 169, 172
Anabhraka (*sprin med*) heaven, 91, 92, 130
Anacker, Stefan, 195n9
Anāgāmin. See Non-returner
Anāgāmiphalasthā. See Non-returner abider
Anāgāmipratipannaka. See Non-returner enterer
Anāgamya (*mi lcogs med pa*, "not-incapable preparatory threshold"), 72, 106, 107, 146, 147, 212–213n78
Anāgamyasāmantaka, 106
Analogy of light dispelling darkness, 78
Analogy of washing cloth, 78, 102
Analogy of waterless *Jetavana* grove, 177
Analytical knowledge, 160
Ānanda, 178
Ānantaryamārga. See Uninterrupted path
Ananyayānagamanahetu, 60
Ānāpānasmṛti. See Mindfulness of breathing
Anāsrava (*zag med*), 76, 77, 92

Anāsravadhātu (*zag med kyi dbyings*, uncontaminated realm), 83
Anāśuparinirvāyin (*myur ba ma yin pa yongs su mya ngan las 'da' ba*), 126, 127, 135
Anāthapiṇḍada, 177
Anātma, 70
Aṅgārakarṣūpama Sūtra (*sol ba'phung po lta bu'i mdo*), 139, 141
Anger, 88, 139
Aṅguttaranikāya, 95, 127, 193n17
Animals (*tiryañc*), 90, 100, 163
Anitya, 70
Antagrāhadṛṣṭi (extreme view), 87
Antarāparinirvāyin (*bar do 'da' ba*), 112, 125, 126, 127, 128, 129, 134, 135, 159, 166, 169, 172, 175
 Tsong kha pa's definition of, 127
Antidote (*pratipakṣa*), 86
Anupalambhākāra, 60
Anupārvābhisamaya (*mthar gyis pa'i mngon rtogs*, gradual full understanding), 53, 54, 56
Ānupārvaka (*rim gyis pa, mthar gyis pa*), 143, 144, 153, 154, 157–165. See also Gradual progressors
Anuśaya. See Defilement, latent
Anutpādajñāna, 79
Anurakṣaṇadharman (*rjes su bsrungs pa'i chos can*), 134, 137, 138
Anutpattidharmakṣānti (receptivity toward understanding that dharmas are unproduced), 87
Anuttarasamyaksaṃbodhi (*bla na med pa yang dag par rdzogs pa'i byang chub*),15, 47, 84, 88, 98, 149, 165, 176, 180, 185, 188. See also Buddhahood
Anvayajñāna, 60, 74, 75
Anvayajñānakṣānti, 73, 74, 75
Aparagodānīya, 91
Aparaparyāyavedanīyakarma (*lan grangs gzhan la myong 'gyur gyi las*, "karma that will be experienced for another time"), 127
Aparapratyayāgāmanahetu, 60
Aparihāṇadharman (*yongs su nyams par mi 'gyur ba'i chos can*), 142
Apariśrānti. See Indefatigability
Apple, James, 192n10
Application (one the ten topics), 85. See also *Pratipatti*
Apramāṇaśubha (*tshad med bde*) heaven, 90, 91, 130
Ardhapluta. See Half-jumper
Arénes, Pierre, 196n1
Arhat (*dgra bcom pa*), 3, 4, 7, 9, 64, 79, 80, 101, 103, 104, 109, 112, 132, 134, 136, 137–142, 143, 144, 146, 147, 153, 157, 167, 177, 178, 179, 182, 187, 188, 211n59, 211n60
 Akopyadharman (*mi 'khrugs pa'i chos can*), 134, 138, 139, 142
 Anurakṣaṇadharman (*rjes su bsrungs pa'i chos can*), 134, 137, 138
 Aparihāṇadharman (*yongs su nyams par mi 'gyur ba'i chos can*), 142
 Asamayavimukta (*dus dang mi sbyor bar rnam par grol ba*), 138, 141, 212n71
 Cetanādharman (*bdag gsod pa'i chos can*), 134, 137, 138, 142
 Degeneration from fourth concentration, 141
 Degeneration from the state of, 139–141
 Kṣīṇāsrava (*gang zag pa zad pa*), 141
 Parihāṇadharman (*yongs su nyams pa'i chos can*), 134, 137, 138
 Prajñāvimukta (*shes rab kyis rnam par grol ba*), 137, 138, 142, 211–212n61
 Prativedhanādharman (*rab tu rtogs pa'i 'os su gyur pa*), 134, 137
 Samayavimukta (*dus dang sbyor bar rnam par grol ba*), 138, 141, 212n70
 Śrāvaka arhat as analogous to BA degree, 6–7
 Sthitākampya (*gnas pa las mi bskyod pa*), 134, 137, 138
 Ubhayatogbhāgavimutka (*gnyis ka'i cha las rnam par grol ba*), 132, 137, 138, 142, 212n62
 Vaibhāṣika understanding of, 139–140
Arhat-enterer (*arhat pratipannaka, dgra bcom pa zhugs pa*), 80, 94, 143, 155, 164, 165, 166, 167, 170, 171, 172, 175, 176
 Tsong kha pa's definition of, 137
Armor. See Activity of putting on armor
Ārūpya concentration, 107
Ārūpyadhātu. See Formless realm
Ārūpyarāga (desire for existence in the formless realm), 99

Arūpyopaga (*gzugs med du nye bar 'gro,* formless realm transmigrator), 112, 125, 126, 163
Ārya. See Noble Being
Āryamārga. See Noble Path
Āryapudgala, 93, 94. See also Noble Being
Āryaśaikṣa, 140
Āryavaṃśa. See Noble attitudes
Āryāvaivartikabodhisattva, 59, 64. See also *Avaivartika*
Ārya Vimuktisena ('Phags pa rnam grol sde), 10, 11, 12, 16, 23, 27, 28, 34, 35, 47, 65, 67, 87, 95, 98, 115, 150, 152, 153, 155, 157, 158, 159, 161, 162, 163, 164, 165, 167, 171, 172, 173, 179, 183, 184, 185, 186, 195n12, 200n25
  interpretation of AA I.23d–24ab, 163
  and *Kaurakulla-Āryasammatīya* school, 28, 195n13
  and *Pañcaviṃśatisāhasrikāprajñāpāramitā*, 29
  system of Twenty *Saṃghas*, 152–165
Ārya wisdom, 140
Aśaikṣa (*mi slob pa*), 63, 80, 95, 140, 142
Aśaikṣamārga. See Path of no more training
Asakta. See Non-attachment
Asamayavimukta (*dus dang mi sbyor bar rnam par grol ba*), 138, 141, 212n71
Asaṃskṛta (*'dus ma byas,* unconditioned), 102
Asaṃskṛtanirodhasatya (unconditioned true cessations), 103
Asaṃskṛtaprabhāvita, 65
Asaṅga (Thogs med), 12, 14, 23, 26, 27, 58, 114, 127, 129, 134, 150, 194nn4–5, 197n2, 198n11, 201n30
  and *Tattvaviniścaya*, 27
Aspires by faith. See *Śrāddhādhimukta*
Asrava (vices), 141
Āśraya (*rten,* foundation), 60, 62
Aṣṭādaśasāhasrikā (18,000 verse) *prajñāpāramitā*, 151
Aṣṭamaka (*brgyad pa*), 153–156, 166, 177, 178, 179
Aṣṭāryapudgala. See Noble Eight Individuals
Aṣṭasāhasrikāprajñāpāramitā, 24, 25, 29, 151, 167, 198n10
Aśubhābhāvanā, 80
Āśuparinirvāyin (*myur ba yongs su mya ngan las 'da' ba*), 126, 127, 135
Asuras, 90
Atapas (*mi gdung ba*) heaven, 90, 91, 130
Atiśa, 27, 171
Ātmadarśana, 139
Attaining illumination (*ālokalabdha*), 85
Auddhatya (excitability), 99, 104
Authorial intention (*dgongs pa, abhiprāya*), 10, 165, 184, 189, 192n6, 192n14
Avaivartika (*phyir mi ldog pa,* irreversible) *bodhisattva*, 20, 31, 59, 63, 64, 65–66, 93, 98, 149, 150, 151, 153, 171, 172, 173, 175, 176, 180, 185
Avaivartika Saṃgha, 65, 153, 180
Avaivartikadharmacakrasūtra, 29, 98, 177–179, 180, 185, 189, 217n87
Avalokiteśvara (Spyan ras gzigs kyi dbang phyug), 161
Avarabhāgīya, 103
Avavāda (*gdams ngags,* "special instruction"), 2, 27, 55–56, 58–62, 85, 93, 149, 187
Avavartikadharmaksāntilabdha, 66
Avekṣyātikrāmati, 87
Avivartacaryā bhūmi (*phyir mi ldog pa'i sa*), 153
Avyāvṛttigamanahetu, 60
Āyatana, 82

B

Bandhana (bonds), 99
Bareau, André, 195n13
Barthes, Roland, 5
Bastian, Edward, 201n31
Bhadrakalpa, 156
Bhagavatī, 51
Bhavāgra (*srid pa'i rtse mo,* peak of existence), 78, 79, 92, 108, 112, 130, 133, 136, 137, 142, 163, 164, 165, 169, 174
Bhavāgraparamaga (*srid pa'i rtse mo'i mthar thug gro*), 112, 125, 126, 130, 133, 135, 161, 166, 169, 170, 172, 174
  Tsong kha pa's definition of, 133
Bhāvanā (cultivation), 80, 111, 112, 113
Bhāvanāmārga. See Path of cultivation
Bhāvanāprahātavya (*sgom spang bya ba*), 78. See also Defilements, Abandoned by path of cultivation
Bhikṣu, 62
Bhikṣuṇī, 62

Bhūmi (*sa*), 66, 84, 88, 150, 159, 161, 173, 175–176, 186
Bhūyovītarāga (*phal cher chags dang bral ba*), 106, 142, 143, 144
Bodhicitta (*byang chub sems*), 28, 40, 55, 84, 149, 187, 206n100
Bodhicittotpāda (*byang chub tu sems bskyed*), 84
Bodhisattva (*byang chub sems dpa'*), 7, 12, 14, 15, 20, 50, 51, 52, 53, 55, 56, 58, 59, 63–66, 68, 69, 71, 81, 82, 83, 84, 85, 86, 87, 88, 89, 90, 94, 98, 101, 102, 115, 125, 149, 150, 151, 152, 153, 155, 156, 157, 158, 159, 160, 161, 162, 163, 164, 167, 168, 170, 174, 175, 176, 177, 178, 179, 180, 183, 184, 186, 187, 188, 189, 202nn41–42
  as Analogous to medical student, 7
  Arhat-enterer, 170
  Forty-eight types of, 151–152
  and Four activities (*pratipatti*), 56
  Heroic journey of, 187–189
  Irreversible. See *Avaivartika bodhisattva*
  Lists in the *Prajñāpāramitā sūtras*, 25
  and Nominal designation, 167, 179, 185, 188, 217n99
  Non-returner, 159–165, 168, 174, 175
  Once-returners, 158–159, 168
  Path of, 83–88
  and Practices for Total Omniscience, 55–56
  Pratyekabuddha, 165, 170
  and Skill-in-means, 188
  Stream-enterers, 158
Bodhisattvāṣṭamakaḥ (Candidate to the First Fruit), 94
Bodhisattvayāna, 102, 180, 198
Bodhisattva saṃgha (byang chub sems dpa'i dge 'dun), 45, 136, 146, 157, 177, 184
Bodily attitudes (*īryāpatha*), 165
Bodily witness. See *kāyasākṣī*
Bod rgya tshig mdzod chen mo, 216n79
Bonds. See *bandhana*
Bound by all the bonds. See *Sakalabandhana*
Brahmakāyika heaven (*tshang ris*), 90, 128, 130, 131, 133, 161, 162, 163, 169
Brahmapurohita heaven (*tshang mdun*), 90, 130
Brahma world, 169
Brahmin rgya mtsho'i rdul, 161
Bṛhatphala heaven (*'bras bu che*), 90, 91, 130, 131, 163
Buddha (*Sangs rgyas*), 23, 52, 56, 58, 59, 62, 63, 82, 83, 132, 146, 147, 148, 150, 156, 157, 161, 165, 170, 177, 178, 179, 181, 182, 191n1, 192n17, 202n42
Buddhadharmasamudāgama, 188
Buddha-field (*sang rgyas kyi zhing*), 7, 149, 151, 153, 157, 160, 161, 162, 163, 164
Buddhahood, 6, 7, 20, 23, 49, 53, 55, 56, 66, 69, 84, 89, 98, 102, 149, 176, 177, 179, 180, 185, 187, 188, 189, 206n100
Buddha-less world systems, 165
Buddhaśrījñāna, 150, 152
Buddha Akṣobhya, 161
Buddha Bhagavat, 48
Buddha eye, 59
Buddha Jewel, 58–59, 60, 64
Buddhist cosmology, 88. See also Cosmology
Buddhist hermeneutics, 11
Buddhist soteriology, 14, 66, 186, 189
Buddhist theology, 11
Bu ston rin chen grub, 26, 33, 45, 46, 98
Buswell, Robert E., 3, 200n19
Byang chub ye shes, 168, 176

C

Cabezón, José, 16, 17, 18, 51, 192n8, 197n3
Cakravartin, 161
Calm abiding. See *Śamatha*
Calmness and coarseness cultivation. See Rough calm abiding
Candrakīrti (Zla ba rags pa), 23, 83, 201n30, 205n98, 207n3
Caryāpratipanna (spyod pa la zhugs pa, bodhisattva stage of entering into activity), 175–176
Catvāri āryasatyāni. See Nobles' Four Truths
Caturāryasatya. See Nobles' Four Truths
Caturmahārājakāyika. See Four Great Kings Heaven
Cause. See *Hetu*
Certainty. See *Kṣānti*
Cetanādharman (*bdag gsod pa'i chos can*), 134, 137, 138, 142
Chattopadhyaya, A., 26, 194n3
Chimpa, L., 194n3

Ciraparinirvāyin (*yun ring mo mya ngan las 'da' ba*), 126, 127, 135
Cittakṣaṇa. See Sixteen thought-moments of the path of seeing
Clear realization. See *Abhisamaya*
Collins, Steven, 182, 191n1
Community of disciples. See *Śrāvaka saṃgha*
Concealed meaning. See Hidden meaning
Concentrated awareness (*samāhitajñāna*), 78
Concentration. See *Dhyāna*
Conceptualization of objects (*grāhya*), 86
Conceptualization of subjects (*grāhaka*), 86
Conceptualizing entities, 60, 61
Conquering Harm to the Three Mothers (*yum gsum gnod 'joms*), 151, 152, 174, 213n3
Constructive postmodernism, 14, 19, 192n16
Continuance of knowledge. See *Anvayajñāna*
Controlling Others' Emanations heaven (*paranirmitavaśavartin, gzhan 'phrul dbang byed*), 90, 91, 158
Conze, Edward, 4, 25, 66–67, 94, 152, 193n19, 193n23, 194n4, 198n6, 199n14, 200n19, 203n44, 206n2
  on Four phases of *Prajñāpāramitā sūtra* development, 24
Cosmology, 47, 88–92
  of the Form realm, 130
Culminating insight. See *Mūrdhābhisamaya*
Cultivation of the loathsome. See *Aśubhābhāvanā*
Cyclic existence. See *Saṃsāra*

D

Dalai Lama, 2, 194n2
Daṃṣṭrasena, 28, 195n10, 213n3
Darśana (vision), 87, 111, 112, 113
Darśanamārga. See Path of seeing
Darśanaprahātavya. See Defilements, Abandoned by the path of seeing
Daśabhūmi. See Ten stages (*daśabhūmi*)
Davidson, Ronald, 195n6
Defilements, 51, 63, 68, 70, 71, 72, 73, 74, 76, 77, 78, 79, 87, 88, 99, 100, 101, 103, 107, 109, 117, 119, 120, 121, 122, 123, 124, 125, 137, 139, 140, 142, 144, 145, 147, 153, 154, 157, 158, 159, 165, 167, 170, 185, 205n98, 208n26
  Abandoned by the path of cultivation (*bhāvanāheya, sgom spang*), 78, 82, 100, 103, 120, 134, 137, 140, 145, 146, 147, 154, 167, 168, 170, 175
  Abandoned by the path of seeing (*dṛṣṭiheya, mthong spang*), 73, 87, 99, 103, 147, 170, 175
  Acquired, 60
  Artificial, 87
  Eighty-one, 78, 82
  Gradual or simultaneous abandonment of, 79, 142
  Innate, 78
  Instinctual (*nyon sgrib lhan skyes*), 90, 204n66
  Latent (*anuśaya, phra rgyas*), 99, 140, 141
  Learned (*nyon sgrib kun brtags*), 73, 75, 204n62
  Mental, 47
  Six fundamental, 87
  Ten basic, 99
Definitive meaning (*nītārtha*), 11, 13
Deity. See Gods
Deliverance, sixteenth aspect of. See *Nairyāṇika*
Denaturalized discourse, 17–18, 176–177, 180, 182, 193n20
Dependent co-arising. See *Pratītyasamutpāda*
Desire, 88, 139, 140
Desire realm (*kāmadhātu, 'dod khams*), 74, 75, 77, 78, 88, 90, 91, 99, 100, 108, 110, 111, 112, 113, 124, 125, 128, 132, 135, 136, 137, 140, 144, 145, 147, 148, 154, 157, 158, 160, 167, 168, 175, 180, 188
Desire realm defilements, 109, 117, 120, 122, 139, 148, 168
Desire realm deity, 112, 124, 158
Desire realm embodiment, 131, 132, 136, 170
Desire realm transmigrator, 120
Devakulaṃkula (*lha'i rigs nas rigs*), 121, 158, 166
Dge 'dun nyi shu bsdus pa rjes gnang. See "Abbreviated Bestowal"
Dge 'dun nyi shu'i mtshan nyid 'phreng ba, 36

Dge lugs pa school, 13
Dhammapada, 193n17, 207n5
Dhāraṇī, 153, 154
Dharma, 176, 181
Dharmābhisamaya (*chos ngon par rtog pa*), 71
Dharmacakṣu, 59
Dharmadhātu (*chos kyi dbyings*), 55, 56, 87
Dharmajñāna, 74, 75, 87
Dharmajñānakṣānti, 73, 74, 87
Dharmakāya (*chos kyi sku*), 26, 30, 48, 52, 53, 54, 183
Dharmakāyābhisamaya, 53
Dharmakīrti (Chos kyi grags pa), 30, 31, 140
Dharmakīrtiśrī (Chos kyi grags pa dpal), 31, 35, 171
Dharmamitra (Chos kyi bshes gnyen), 23, 27, 30–31, 161, 173, 196n1, 197–198nn5–6, 202n42, 214n35
Dharmanairātmya, 52, 63, 82, 84, 202n42
Dharmānusārin (*chos kyi rjes su 'brang ba*, follower through doctrine), 110, 116, 145, 153, 154, 176, 177, 178, 208n21
Dharmaśrotas-samādhi (*chos kyi rgyun gyi ting nge 'dzin*), 27, 58, 85
Dharmas, 178
Dharmatā, 63
Dharma eye. See *Dharmacakṣu*
Dharma Jewel, 58, 59, 149
Dhātu, 82
Dhyāna (*bsam gtan*, concentration), 72, 78, 90, 91, 130, 131, 132, 134, 137, 141, 145, 149, 156, 157, 158, 160, 162, 163, 164, 174, 175, 188
Dhyānāntara, 72
Diamond-like concentration (*vajropamasamādhi*), 78, 79
Dīgha Nikāya, 193n17
Dignāga (Phyogs glang), 30, 197n4, 198n10
Distinctive Non-returner, 125, 137
Distinctive Once-returner, 123. See *Ekavīcika*
Distinctive path. See *Viśeṣamārga*
Distinctive Stream-enterer, 117, 120, 167
Divine eyes. See *Divyacakṣu*
Divyacakṣu, 59
Dīvyāvadāna, 9
Dol po pa shes rab rgyal mtshan, 34
Don mgnon rtogs, 72
Doubt. See *Vicikitsā*
Dreyfus, Georges, 3, 14
Dṛṣṭadharmaparinirvāyin (*mthong ba'i chos la zhi ba 'thob pa*), 135, 136, 137, 163
Dṛṣṭadharmaśrama (*mthong ba'i chos la zhi ba*), 125, 126, 166, 170, 172
Dṛṣṭadharmasukhavihāra (*mthong ba'i chos la bde bar gnas pa*, abiding in bliss for the present life), 139, 140
Dṛṣṭiprāpta (*dad pas mos pa*, one who obtains by seeing), 145, 154, 156, 157, 166, 168, 173
Dṛṣṭiparāmarśa (holding a [wrong] view as supreme), 87
Duḥkha, 70, 74
Duḥkhe dharmajñāna, 75
Duḥkhe dharmajñānakṣānti, 75
Dull faculties (*mṛdvindriya*). See Faculties, Dull
Durbodhāloka (Dharmakīrtiśrī), 31, 173
Dutt, N., 94, 200n27
Dvādaśāṅga, 203n49

E

Eight afflictions, 103
Eight knowledges, 103
Eight liberations (*aṣṭavimokṣa*, *rnam pa thar pa brgyad*), 103, 136, 138, 211n55, 212n62
Eight moments of intellectual receptivity (*kṣānti*), 60, 65
Eight moments of knowledge (*jñāna*), 60, 65
Eight noble individuals. See Noble Eight Individuals
Eight powers, 140
Eight subjects (*padārtha*, *dngos po*), 52–55
Eighteen special qualities of a Buddha, 159, 160
Eighty-one defilements, 78, 82
Ekajātipratibaddha (*skye bag cig gis thogs pa*, *bodhisattva* obstructed by one life), 157, 159, 175, 176
Ekakṣaṇābhisamaya (*skad cig gcig mngon rtogs*, instantaneous realization), 53, 54, 88
Ekakṣaṇābhisaṃbodha (*skad cig cig pa'i mngon par rdzogs par byang chub pa*, simultaneous illumination), 88

Ekavīcika (*bar chad gcig pa*), 112, 123–124, 155, 159, 166, 168, 172, 175, 176, 214n26
Etymology for, 159, 214n26
Tsong kha pa's definition of, 123
Ekayāna (*theg pa gcig*), 66, 79, 149, 185, 187, 202n41, 205n98
Emergence. See Activity of emergence
Emic analysis, 5–6, 181
Empirical Omniscience. See *Sarvajñatā*
Emptiness (*śūnyatā*, *stong pa nyid*), 41, 48, 55, 58, 64, 68, 70, 84, 86, 179
Engagement (*prasthāna*), 84
Enjoying Emanation (*nirmāṇarati*, *'phrul dga'*) heaven, 90
Erroneous judgment, 141
Essencelessness of the person, 52, 63, 84
Essencelessness of things, 52, 63, 82, 84, 85, 202n42
Etic analysis, 5–6
Etymology (*nirukti*), 114, 116, 197n2
Exegesis, 12, 47, 181, 182, 183, 184, 186, 192n15
Expanded illumination (*vṛddhāloka*), 86
Extreme view (*antagrāhadṛṣṭi*), 88

F

Factors conducive to liberation (*mokṣabhāgīya*), 84
Faculties (*indriya*, *dbang po*), 116, 134, 138, 139, 156, 164, 166, 172, 182
Change of, 168
Classification of *bodhisattva*, 156–157
Dull (*mṛdu*, *brtul po*), 116, 132, 134, 138, 139, 145, 151, 153, 155, 156, 167, 168, 171, 172, 174, 175
Moderate (*madhya*), 134
Pure, 164
Sharp (*tīkṣṇa*, *rnon*), 116, 132, 134, 138, 139, 145, 151, 153, 154, 155, 156, 167, 168, 171, 172
Weak, 132, 141, 142, 175
Faith (*śraddhā*), 85
False view (*mithyādṛṣṭi*), 87
False view of the imaginary self (*ātmadarśana*), 139
False view of the perishable aggregates (*satkāyadṛṣṭi*), 88
Familiarization (*abhyāsa*), 78
Fetters (*saṃyojana*, *kun tu sbyor ba*), 95, 99, 103, 135, 187
of Becoming, 169
Five "inferior" fetters (*avarabhāgīya*, *tha ma'i cha dang mthun pa lnga*), 103
Five "superior" fetters (*ūrdhvabhāgīya*, *gong ma'i cha dang mthun pa lnga*), 103, 104
of Taking rebirth, 169
Three abandoned by path of seeing (*mthong spang kun sbyor gsum*), 103
Five aggregates (*pañcaskandha*), 53
Five aspects of Non-returners, 159
Five causes of four results, 104
Five eyes (*pañcacakṣu*, *spyan lnga*), 58, 59, 60, 61
Five objects of sensory desire, 90
Five paths system, 68, 71
Five Pure Heavens (*Śuddhāvāsakāyika*), 91
Five texts of Maitreya (*byams gzhung sde lnga*), 26, 32, 195n6
Fleshly matured eyes (*māṃsavaipākika*), 59
Follower through doctrine. See *Dharmānusārin*
Follower through faith. See *Śraddhānusārin*
Forbearance. See *Kṣānti*
Form and formless realm meditative absorption (*bsam gzugs*), 4, 40
Form realm (*rūpadhātu*, *gzugs khams*), 73, 74, 75, 77, 78, 79, 88, 90, 91, 99, 100, 110, 111, 112, 113, 120, 124, 125, 127, 128, 130, 131, 132–135, 137, 138, 157, 160, 162, 169, 170, 171, 175, 188
Form realm cosmology, 130
Form realm deity, 158
Form realm transmigrator. See *Rūpopaga*
Formless attainment. See Four formless attainments
Formless realm (*ārūpyadhātu*, *gzug med khams*), 73, 74, 75, 77, 78, 88, 90, 91, 92, 99, 110, 111, 112, 113, 120, 124, 125, 128, 133, 135, 138, 157, 160, 163, 170, 174, 175, 188
Formless realm absorption, 174
Formless realm embodiment, 133
Formless realm transmigrator. See *Arūpyopaga*

Formless sphere mind, 91
Forty artificial defilements, 87
Four clear realizations, 56
Four concentrations (*caturdhyāna, bsam gtan bzhi*), 107, 158, 159, 162, 164
Four-day fever, 118
Four formless attainments (*caturārūpyasamāpatti, gzugs med pa'i snyoms par 'jugs pa bzhi*), 72–73, 157, 158, 164, 170
Four Great Kings (*Cāturmahārājakāyika, rgyal chen rigs bzhi*) heaven, 90, 91 158
Four immeasurables (*caturapramāṇa, tshad med bzhi*), 157, 158, 164
Four limbs of insight. See *Nirvedhabhāgīya*
Four mindfulnesses (*smṛtyupasthāna*), 71, 72, 80
Four Noble Truths. See Nobles' Four Truths
Four paths, 56
Four periods of Buddhist development in Tibet, 22
Four practices, 54
Four Reliances (*catvāri pratisaraṇāni, rton pa bzhi*), 11, 192n11
Four roots of virtue, 72, 80. See also *Kuśalamūla*
Four stations of mindfulness. See *Smṛtyupasthāna*
Fourth concentration, 131, 132, 141
Frauwallner, E., 14
Fruition skipper (*thod rgal, vyutkrāntika*), 105, 109, 139, 142–146, 172, 173, 207n12
  Who enters the state of Non-returner, 144
  Who enters the state of Once-returner, 144

G

Gauṇī, 67
Gautika (Pali, Godhika), 139, 141
Generation of the thought for enlightenment (*bodhicittotpāda, byang chub tu sems bskyed*), 84
Gethin, Rupert, 5, 192n7, 199n14
Gimello, Robert M., 3, 191n4
Gods (*deva*), 90, 158, 160, 163, 168, 171, 172, 174, 208n26
Golden Garland of Eloquent Sayings (*legs bshad gser phreng*), 11, 19, 28, 31, 32, 36, 43, 44, 47, 48, 63, 68, 76, 81, 98, 101, 104, 105, 106, 115, 119, 122, 123, 130, 131, 133, 135, 136, 137, 142, 144, 145, 146, 148, 150, 151, 152, 155, 157, 158, 159, 160, 164, 167, 168, 169, 170, 171, 173, 175, 176, 178, 180, 185, 193n22, 196n1, 197n2, 198n6, 199–200n15, 205n99
Gombrich, Richard, 5
Gomez, Luis, 191n1
Go mi 'chi med (Amaragomin), 32
Gonda, Jan, 198n6
Gonta, Sonam Gyaltsen, 205n98
Gotra, 66, 68, 134. See also Lineage
Gnoseological constitution, 65
Gnyal zhig pa 'jam dpal rdo rje, 32, 45
Gradual abandonment, 79, 117
Gradual full understanding. See *Anupūrvābhisamaya*
Gradual progressors, 109, 112, 114–142, 143, 159 172
Grāhaka (conceptualization of subjects), 82, 86, 89
Grāhya (conceptualization of objects), 82, 86, 89
Great Compassion (*mahākaruṇā, snying rje chen po*), 84, 149, 165
Great Stages of the Path. See *Lam rim chen mo*
Griffin, David Ray, 192n16
Griffiths, Paul, 17, 192n8, 194nn4–5, 195n9, 197n2
Grounds (*bodhisattva* stages). See *Bhūmi*
Guenther, Herbert V., 203n44

H

Hakamaya, Noriaki, 194n4
Half-jumper (*ardhapluta, phyed du 'phar ba*), 112, 126, 130, 131, 133, 135, 162, 166, 169, 172
Hall, Bruce, 195n9
Haribhadra (Seng ge bzang po), 10, 11, 12, 16, 25, 27, 31, 34, 35, 47, 64, 65, 67, 70, 72, 76, 79, 83, 85, 86, 94, 95, 98, 115, 150, 152, 165, 167, 168, 170,

Haribhadra *(continued)*
171, 172, 173, 183, 184, 185, 186, 193n22, 195n12, 197n4, 198n11, 199n12, 200n18, 200n25, 201n30, 202n41, 203n43, 205n98, 205n99
and Dharmapāla, 30
on Different forms of *Prajñāpāramitā sūtras*, 24
on Sixteen aspects of the Nobles' Four Truths, 70–71
System of Twenty *Saṃghas*, 165–171
Textual works on *Prajñāpāramitā* and *Abhisamayālaṃkāra*, 29
Hayes, Richard P., 192n15
Heart Sūtra (*shes rab snying po*), 24, 41, 197n1
Heat. See *ūṣmagata*
Heavens of the Desire Realm, 158
Hell denizens (*nāraka, dmyal ba*), 90, 100, 163
Hetu (cause), 70
Hidden meaning (*sbas don*), 26, 48, 55, 196–197n1
Highest worldly dharma. See Path of preparation, highest wordly dharma
Hīnayāna (*theg dman*), 69, 87, 164, 186
Hīnayāna arhats (*theg dman dgra bcom pa*), 83, 85
Holding a [wrong] view as supreme (*dṛṣṭiparāmarśa*), 87
Holding [wrong] ethics and rituals as supreme (*śīlavrataparāmarśa*), 87
Hopkins, Jeffrey P., 203n44, 203n47
Hsüan Tsang, 25
Human beings (*manuṣya, mi*), 90, 91, 150, 160, 171, 172, 174, 208n26
Hungry ghosts (*preta, yi dvags*), 90, 100

I

Ichigō, Masamichi, 198n6
Ideal figures, 3, 6, 11, 13, 14, 16, 18, 47, 182, 183, 184, 186, 187
as Analogous to degrees in secondary education, 6
and Buddhist cultural values, 7–8
as Indexical reference points in Buddhist literature, 9
as Indices of attainment, 15
Relevance in Buddhist cultures, 6–9
as Sociological reference points, 9
Ignorance, 88
Illumination of wisdom (*jñānāloka*), 85
Immeasurable. See Four immeasurables
Impermanence. See *Anitya*
Impure. See *Sasrava*
Imputed knowledge obstacle, 87
Indefatigability (*apariśrānti, yongs su ngal ba med pa*), 58, 59, 60, 61
Indo-Tibetan, 20, 94, 181, 191n1
Buddhist culture, 15
Cosmological factors, 47
as Trans-Himalayan lineage tradition, 22
Indriya. See Faculties
Instantaneous realization. See *Ekakṣaṇābhisamaya*
Intellectual receptivity. See *Kṣānti*
Intellectual receptivity to the doctrine. See *Dharmajñānakṣānti*
Intermediate state (*antarābhava, bar srid*), 112, 127, 128, 129, 135, 159, 160, 169, 171, 175
Intermediate of the three realms, 160
Interpretable meaning (*neyārtha*), 13
Intertextualist documentation, 15–16
Irreversible *bodhisattvas*. See *Avaivartika bodhisattva*
Īryāpatha (bodily attitudes), 165
Ishikawa, Mie, 193n18

J

Jackson, David, 31, 32
Jaini, Padmanabh S., 195n9, 206n100
Jambudvīpa (*'dzam bu gling*), 90, 91, 121
Janmāvakāśaḥ, 123
Jeta Grove of Anāthapiṇḍada, 177
Jinpa, Thupten, 13, 204n61
Jñāna. See Knowledge
Jñānāloka, 85
Jñānavistarasūtra. See *Sūtra of Expanded Gnosis*
Jñeyāvaraṇa, 84
Jumper (*pluta, 'phar ba*), 112, 126, 130, 131, 133, 134, 135, 155, 162, 166, 169, 172
Jumper who dies in all abodes (*sarvasthānacyuta, gnas thams cad cu 'chi 'pho ba*), 112, 126, 130, 131, 135, 162, 166, 169, 172

K

Kāmacchanda (sensual desire), 103
Kāmadhātu. See Desire realm
Kāmarāga (sensual pleasure), 99
Kāmāvacara, 91

Kāmavītarāga (*'dod pa'i 'dod chags dang bral ba*), 106, 142, 143, 144
Kāyasākṣī (*lus mgnon byed*), 125, 126, 135, 136, 137, 164, 166, 170, 171, 172, 175, 211n54
Tsong kha pa's definition of, 136
Keenan, John K., 194n5
Khaḍgaviṣāṇakalpa, 148
Khri srong lde btsan, 31
Kleśa (*nyon mongs*). See Defilement
Kleśāvaraṇa, 84. See also Obscurations
Knowledge (*jñāna, shes pa*), 60, 73, 75
of All things. See *Sarvajñatā*
Continuance of (*anvayajñāna, rjes shes*), 74, 75, 87
that Defilements have been destroyed (*kṣayajñāna*), 79, 80
that Defilements will not arise again (*anutpādajñāna*), 79
of the Doctrine (*dharmajñāna, chos shes*), 7, 74, 75, 87
of the Paths. See *Mārgajñatā*
Knowledge obstacles, 82, 87
Kṣānti (*bzod pa*), 60, 72, 73, 80, 85, 86, 203–204n57
as Intellectual receptivity, 75
Receptivity to the doctrine (*dharmajñānakṣānti, chos shes pa'i bzod pa*), 75
Receptivity that understands dharmas are unproduced (*anutpattidharmakṣānti*), 87
Kṣayajñāna, 79, 80
Kṣīṇāsrava, 141
Kulaṃkula (*rigs nas rigs*, born from family to family), 110, 117, 120–122, 123, 155, 158, 167, 171, 172, 175, 208n32
Devakulaṃkula (*lha'i rigs nas rigs*), 121, 158, 166, 167
Manuṣyakulaṃkula (*mi'i rigs nas rigs*), 121, 158, 166, 167
Three distinctive qualities of, 120
Tsong kha pa's definition of, 121
Kulandatta, 150, 173
Kumārajīva, 25
Kuru, 90
Kuśalamūla (*dge ba'i rtsa ba*, roots of virtue), 55, 72, 85

L

La Vallée Poussin, Louis de, 127, 175, 204n75, 206n110
Lalou, Marcelle, 195n6
Lam rim chen mo (*Great Stages of the Path*), 38, 68, 202n38
Lamotte, Étienne, 188, 192n13, 201n33, 203n44, 203n49, 204n57, 204n75
Land without combat (*yāma*), 90
Large Sūtra on Perfect Wisdom, 24, 49
Laukika (mundane), 68, 72, 76, 77, 80, 100, 116, 142, 145, 147
Laukikabhāvanāmārga. See Path of cultivation, mundane
Laukikabhāvanāmaya (mundane meditative realization), 85
Laukikāgradharma. See Path of preparation, highest worldly dharma
Lethcoe, Nancy, 25
Levels of *bodhisattva*. See *Bhūmi*
Lévi-Strauss, Claude, 181
Liberation. See Path of liberation
Liminal figures, 188
Limitless space (realm), 163
Lineage, 134, 139, 141, 155, 161, 202n41
of Extensive deeds (*udārācāraparamparā, rgya chen spyod pa'i brgyud*), 23
as Heuristic device, 21
of Profound tradition, 23
Spiritual (*gotra, rigs*), 202n41, 211n52
of Tibetan *Abhisamayālaṃkāra* tradition, 31–36
Listenwissenschaft, 181–182
Lokottara (supermundane), 68, 73, 77–79, 80, 89, 100, 108, 147
Lokottaramārga, 73, 80
Long-lived deities heaven, 151, 156, 174
Lung gyi ye ma (Bu ston rin chen grub), 33, 34, 35, 98

M

Madhyamāgama, 95
Madhyamaka (*dbu ma*), 4, 30, 38, 65
Mahābrahma heaven (*tshangs chen*), 90, 127, 130, 131, 133
Mahākaruṇa, 84, 149
Mahākaruṇācitta, 165
Mahāsattva, 153, 157, 158, 159, 160, 161, 163, 164, 165
Mahāvyutpatti, 25, 95, 114
Mahāyāna (*theg pa chen po*), 6, 7, 8, 9, 11, 13, 20, 30, 33, 47, 55, 56, 58, 59, 63, 64, 65, 66, 68–69, 79, 83, 115, 149, 151, 152, 174, 177, 180, 184, 185, 186, 189, 193n20

Mahāyāna Arhat (*theg chen gyi dgra bcom pa*), 6, 64, 89, 149, 170, 185
Mahāyāna Buddhist soteriology, 47, 66, 152
Mahāyāna lineage, 84
Mahāyāna path of seeing, 76, 86, 87
Mahāyāna path systems, 66, 83. See also Path
Mahāyāna śaikṣa, 64
Mahāyāna saṃgha (*theg chen gyi dge 'dun*), 20, 63, 64, 102, 150, 180, 185, 189, 201n31
Mahāyānasūtrālaṃkāra (*theg pa chen po'i mdo sde'i rgyan*), 48, 69, 198n8
Mainstream Buddhism, 19–20
Maitreyanātha (Byams pa dgon po), 14, 23, 26, 35, 58, 63, 176, 177, 180, 194n4, 195n6, 198n11
Makransky, John, 11, 25, 26, 30, 183, 193n19, 198n10
Māṃsavaipākika cakṣu. See Fleshly matured eyes
Māna (*nga rgyal*), 99, 104
Manné, Joy, 192n9
Mañjuśrī ('jam dpal byangs), 23, 161, 165
Manuṣya. See Human beings
Manuṣyakulaṃkula (*mi'i rigs nas rigs*), 121, 158, 166, 167
Mārga (*lam*). See Path
Mārgajñatā (*lam shes nyid*, knowledge of the paths), 50, 51, 52, 53, 68, 69, 89, 167, 203n46
Marmakaumudī (Abhayākaragupta), 31, 152, 173, 180
Masefield, Peter, 127
Mātṛkā (*ma mo*), 50, 51, 182, 199n14
Meaning of the doctrine, 80
Meditative absorption, 77, 83, 108, 138
Meditative absorption of the stream of the doctrine (*srotānugatasamādhi*), 85
Meditative stabilization (*samādhi, ting nge 'dzin*), 88, 132, 138, 141, 142, 145, 153, 154, 158, 164, 185
Mental body, 83
Mindfulness of breathing (*ānāpānasmṛti*), 71, 80
Mithyādṛṣṭi, 87
Moha (*gti mug*, delusion), 99, 104
Mokṣabhāgīya (*thar pa'i cha dang mthun pa*), 55, 84, 85
Morris, Richard, 193n18
Mother of the Buddhas. See *Prajñāpāramitā* as Mother
Mount Meru, 90
Mṛdutīkṣṇendriyau ("those with dull and sharp faculties"), 116
Mundane concentration, 138, 145
Mundane meditative realization (*laukikabhāvanāmaya*), 85
Mundane path. See Path, mundane
Mundane path of cultivation. See Path of cultivation, mundane
Munimatālaṃkāra (Abhayākaragupta), 31, 152, 161, 164, 165, 173, 175
Mūrdhābhisamaya (*rtse mo'i mngon rtogs*, summit of full understanding), 53
Mūrdhagata (summit), 72, 80, 85, 86

N

Nāgārjuna (Klu sgrub), 23, 202n39
Nairyāṇika, 71
Naivasamjñānāsamjñāyatana ("neither perception nor non-perception"), 91. See *Bhavāgra*
Napper, Elizabeth, 192n11
Nattier, Jan, 7, 9, 188
Naughton, Alexander, 195n12, 200n17
Never-returner. See Non-returner
Nikāya, 5, 62, 95, 182, 192n7
Nikāya/Agama tradition, 95
Nine realms of existence, 78
Nirmāṇarati (*'phrul dga'*) heaven, 90, 91
Nirodhasamāpatti (*'gog pa'i snyoms par 'jug pa*), 136, 164, 211n55, 215n55
Nirodhasatya, 63, 102
Nirukti (etymology), 102, 197n2
Nirupadhiśeṣa. See *Nirvāṇa* without remnant
Nirvāṇa (*mya ngan las 'das pa*), 1, 3, 14, 15, 18, 19, 51, 63, 67, 69, 77, 79, 83, 89, 90, 99, 101, 118, 123, 124, 125, 127, 128, 129, 130, 131, 135, 136, 141, 160, 161, 164, 169, 174, 175, 176, 181, 182, 185, 186, 187, 189, 191n1, 215n55
Nirvāṇa resembling an extinguished light. See *Pradīpanirvāṇaprakhyanirvāṇa*
Nirvāṇa with remnant (*sopadhiśeṣa, lhag bcas kyi mya ngan las 'da'*), 83, 129, 160
Nirvāṇa without remnant (*nirupadhiśeṣa, lhag med kyi mya ngan las 'da'*), 83, 129

Nirvedhabhāgīya (*nges par 'byed cha mthun pa*, preparatory analytical factors), 55, 65, 72, 85, 80, 88, 114, 115, 150, 200n19
Attaining illumination (*ālokalabdha*), 85
Five factors of *bodhisattva*, 85
Illumination of wisdom (*jñānāloka*), 85
Niryāṇapratipatti. See Activity of emergence
Niṣyandaphala (outflowing results), 102
Noble attitudes (*āryavaṃśa, 'phags pa'i rigs*), 71
Noble Beings (*ārya,'phags pa*), 1, 2, 7, 15, 65, 68, 80, 85, 90, 92, 94, 100, 102, 109, 114, 118, 121, 131, 132, 136, 137, 139, 140, 142, 143, 148, 149, 150, 174, 179, 180, 181, 182, 185, 186, 188, 202n41, 207n3, 212n71, 217n99
Essentially seven types of, 143–144
Not born in *Mahābrahma* heaven, 131
Noble Eight Individuals (*aṣṭāryapudgala*), 63, 64, 80, 94, 95, 101, 105, 143, 182
Noble Eightfold Path (*ārya-aṣṭāṅga-mārga, 'phags pa'i lam yan lag brgyad pa*), 4
Noble Path (*āryamārga, 'phags lam*), 2, 71, 73, 164, 174
Nobles' Four Truths, 56, 60, 70, 72, 73, 75, 76, 77, 78, 80, 82, 85, 87, 89, 99, 100, 103, 104, 137, 147, 159, 197n17, 203n46
Sixteen aspects of, 70–71, 77, 80, 89, 100, 104, 137, 143, 149, 203n47
Nominally existing beings (*prajñapti-puruṣa*), 86
Non-attachment (*asakta, ma zhen pa*), 58, 59, 60
Non-Buddhist, 73, 76, 77, 145, 205n92
Non-dual wisdom (*advayajñāna*), 48
Non-perception, 87
Non-retreating advance. See *Avyāvṛttiga-manahetu*
Non-returner (*anāgāmin, phyir mi 'ong ba*), 3, 4, 7, 18, 64, 80, 94, 95 101, 103, 105, 107, 108, 109, 112, 120, 122, 124–137, 139, 140, 143, 144, 145, 146, 148, 153, 155, 156, 157, 159, 160, 165, 166, 167, 168, 169, 171, 175, 177, 178, 179, 180, 182, 209n39, 214n26
Distinctive, 125
in the Form realm, 125–134
Three illustrations of the form realm, 127
12,960 types of, 9, 134
Non-returner abider (*anāgāmiphalasthā, phyir mi 'ong ba gnas pa*), 112, 124, 144, 148, 168. See also Non-returner
Non-returner enterer (*anāgāmipratipannaka, phyir mi 'ong ba zhugs pa*), 80, 112, 123, 124, 143, 145, 154, 166, 171, 172, 175, 176
Tsong kha pa's definition of, 124
Nothingness formless realm. See *Akiṃcanya*
Not-incapable preparatory threshold. See *Anāgamya*
Nu mgo rgyal ba rin chen, 36, 45
Nya dbon kun dga' dpal, 34–35, 45, 46, 161, 214n35

O

Obermiller, Eugene, 24, 26, 39, 72, 85, 191n1, 193n19, 194n3, 195n11, 196n1, 196n17, 197n4, 200n15, 200n17, 201n31, 201n33, 202n37, 203n44, 205n90 206n101
Obscurations (*āvaraṇa, sgribs ba*), 116, 117, 118, 120, 121, 134, 138, 201n31
Coarse knowledge, 82
Innate afflictional, 78, 84, 88
Knowledge (*jñeyāvaraṇa, shes sgribs*), 82, 84, 87, 88, 89
Three types of, 201n3
Obstacles. See Obscurations
Omniscience,
Three types of, 51, 52, 53, 68
See also *Mārgajñatā, Sarvajñatā* (Empirical Omniscience), *Sarvākārajñatā* (Total Omniscience)
Once-returner (*sakṛdāgāmi, lan cig phyir 'ong ba*), 3, 4, 7, 15, 64, 80, 81, 94, 99, 100, 101, 103, 105, 107, 108, 109, 111, 120, 122, 123, 124, 128, 132, 136, 137, 139, 140, 143, 144, 146, 148, 153, 154, 155, 156, 157, 158, 159, 165, 166, 167, 168, 171, 172, 175, 177, 178, 179, 180, 182, 186, 214n26
Tsong kha pa's definition of, 122
Once-returner abider (*sakṛdāgāmiphalasthā, phyir 'ong ba gnas pa*), 122, 144, 171, 172

Once-returner enterer (*sakṛdāgāmipratipannaka, phyir 'ong ba zhugs pa*), 80, 122, 143, 144, 166, 168, 171, 172, 175
Tsong kha pa's definition of, 122
One Ultimate Vehicle. See *Ekayāna*
Ordinary individual (*pṛthagjana, so so skyes bo*), 64, 71, 80, 85, 100, 116, 118, 148
Ornament. See *Alaṃkāra*
Ornament for Clear Realization. See *Abhisamayālaṃkāra*
Outflowing results (*niṣyandaphala*), 102

P
Pacification, 70
Pāli literature, 182, 191n1, 192n7
Pāli tradition, 114
Pañcacakṣu. See Five eyes
Pañcaviṃśatisāhasrikāprajñāpāramitāsūtra, 4, 24, 25, 69, 93, 94, 98, 151, 152, 153, 154, 156, 157, 158, 159, 160, 162, 164, 165, 167, 176, 179, 203n43, 213n5, 217n99
Pañcaviṃśatisāhasrikāprajñāpāramitāsūtra (revised edition), 25
Paranirmitavaśavartin heaven. See Controlling others' emanations
Parihāṇadharman (*yongs su nyams pa'i chos can*), 134, 137, 138, 142
Parinirvāṇa (*yongs su nya ngan las 'da' ba*), 121, 128, 137, 210n48
Parīttābhā (*'od chung*) heaven, 90, 130
Parīttaśubha (*bde chung*) heaven, 90, 91, 130
Parivṛttajanma, 137
Path (*mārga, lam*), 47, 67, 70, 74, 202n40
Fivefold system of, 202n40
General definition of, 67–68, 202n37
Mahāyāna, 83–88
Mundane (*laukika,'jig rten pa*), 68, 72, 76, 80, 100, 107, 139, 140, 142, 144, 145
Supermundane (*lokottara, 'jig rten las 'das pa*), 68, 73, 76, 139 140, 146
Path of abandoning, 77
Path of accumulation 84
Path of acquiring the provisions (*sambhāramārga, tshogs lam*), 68, 80, 187
Bodhisattva, 71
Śrāvaka, 71
Path of cultivation (*bhāvanāmārga, sgom lam*), 53, 58, 60, 65, 68, 76, 77, 78, 80, 90, 99, 100, 105, 107, 109, 110, 118, 119, 120, 125, 133, 134, 139, 142, 144, 145, 150, 167, 168, 170
Defilements of, 147, 154, 175
Hīnayāna, 88
Mahāyāna, 88
Mundane (*laukika, 'jig rten pa*), 77, 100, 116, 117, 142, 144, 145, 147, 171
Śrāvaka, 76–79
Supermundane (*lokottara, 'jig rten las 'das pa*), 77–79, 100, 108, 147
Path of liberation (*vimuktimārga, rnam grol lam*), 67, 70, 73, 74, 75, 78, 102, 103, 122, 133, 141, 142, 148, 168
Conditioned (*saṃskṛtavimuktimārga*), 103
Path of no more training (*aśaikṣamārga, mi slob lam*), 68, 79, 80
Mahāyāna, 88
Śrāvaka, 79
Path of preparation (*prayogamārga, sbyor lam*), 55, 68, 69, 75, 80, 88, 105, 114, 148, 150
Forbearance (*kṣānti, bzod pa*), 72, 86
Heat (*uṣmagata, dro bar gyur pa*), 72, 85
Highest worldly dharma (*laukikāgradharma, 'jig rten pa'i chos kyi mchog*), 72, 75, 80, 85 86
Mahāyāna, 86
Śrāvaka, 71, 72–73
Summit (*mūrdhagata, rtse mor gyur pa*), 86
Path of seeing (*darśanamārga, mthong lam*), 56, 58, 60, 61 63, 66, 68, 69, 73, 74, 75, 76, 77, 78, 80, 99, 100, 105, 107, 108, 109, 110, 114, 116, 140, 142, 143, 144, 145, 146, 147, 150, 153, 154, 155, 156, 157, 166, 167, 168, 170
Fifteenth moment of, 144, 154
Mahāyāna, 76, 86, 87
Sixteen moments of, 76, 88, 144, 203n47, 204n71
Sixteenth moment of, 76, 109, 117, 122, 145, 147, 154, 167
Śrāvaka, 73–76, 81, 84, 107
Tsong kha pa's definition of, 76
Path Omniscience. See *Mārgajñatā*

Peak of Existence. See *Bhavāgra*
Pensa, Corrado, 50, 125n11
Phalastha (*gnas pa*, abider), 101, 110, 111, 112, 113
Pluta. See Jumper
PP. See *Prajñāpāramitā sūtras*
Practices. See *Pratipatti*
Pradīpanirvāṇaprakhyanirvāṇa, 83
Prahāṇamārga, 68, 73
Prajñā, 51
Prajñācakṣu, 59
Prajñākaramati, 31, 35, 150, 171, 173
Prajñāpāramitā (*shes rab kyi pha rol tu phyin pa*), 48, 49, 51, 54, 58, 60, 65, 66, 67, 69, 152, 171, 179, 183, 184
  as Mother (*mātṛ*, *yum*), 50, 51, 52, 68, 198n10, 199n13, 199–200n15
  the Nature of, 48
  Three meanings of, 48, 52, 197n4
Prajñāpāramitā sūtras, 4, 23, 35, 47, 48, 49, 53, 55, 64, 65, 66, 68, 94, 149, 150, 151, 152, 174, 176, 179, 184, 185, 189, 198n10, 199n11
Prajnāpāramitārthasaṃgraha, 197n4, 198n10
Prajñaptipuruṣa (nominally existing beings), 86
Prajñāvimukta (*shes rab kyis rnam par grol ba*), 137, 138, 142, 211–212n61
Prakarṣa, 141
Pramāṇapuruṣa (*tshad ma'i skyes bu*), 30, 31
Pramāṇavārttika (*tshad ma rnam 'grel*), 22, 42, 43, 67, 140
Pramuditā, 88
Praṇidhi, 84
Prāntakoṭicaturthadhyāna, 129
Prāptiviniścaya (determination of attainment), 98, 185
Prasannapadā, 207n3
Prasphuṭapadā (Dharmamitra), 27, 30, 169, 170, 173, 196n1, 197n5
Prasthāna, 84, 187
Prasthānapratipatti. See Activity of setting out
Prathamacittotpādika (*sems dang po bskyed pa*, *bodhisattva* stage of arising first supermundane thought), 175
Pratipannakāḥ (*zhugs pa*, enterers), 110, 111, 112, 113
Pratipatti, 58, 71
Pratītyasamutpāda, 82
Prativedhanādharman (*rab tu rtogs pa'i 'os su gyur pa*), 134, 137
Pratyekabuddha (*rang sangs rgyas*), 12, 20, 51, 52, 53, 64, 68, 69, 76, 81, 83, 84, 87, 89, 98, 101, 115, 146, 147–148, 153, 165, 166, 167, 170, 171, 172, 175, 176, 177, 178, 179, 180, 184, 186, 187, 188, 191n1, 202n41–42, 205n95, 206n100, 213n80
  Abiding within a group (*vargacāri*), 148, 213n82
  *Arhat*ship of, 82, 83, 89
  as Analogous to MA degree, 7
  like the Horn of a rhinoceros (*khaḍgaviṣāṇakalpaḥ*), 148, 165, 213n81
  Non-verbal conduct, 82, 205n92
  Path of, 81–82
  Six objects of cultivation, 82
  Three main characteristics of, 81
Pratyekajina (*rang rgyal ba*). See *Pratyekabuddha*
Prayogamārga. See Path of preparation
Preparatory analytical factors. See *Nirvedhabhāgīya*
Pṛthagjana. See Ordinary individual
Pudgaladravya (substantially existing persons), 86
Pudgalavyavasthāna (section of AS), 116, 185
Puggalapaññatti, 95, 114, 193n18, 207n19, 207–208n21, 208n23, 208n26, 208n32, 209nn35–36, 209n39, 210nn44–45, 210n48, 211n54, 211–212nn61–62, 212nn70–71, 213n80
Puṇyaprasava (*bsod names skyes*) heaven, 91, 92, 130
Pūrvavideha, 91

R

Rahula, Walpola, 2, 203n45, 203n49
Ratnagotravibhāga, 63–64, 201n31
Ratnaguṇasaṃcayagāthā, 174
Ratnākaraśānti, 31, 150, 152
Realm of infinite space. See *Ākāśānantyāyatana* formless realm
Receptivity. See *Kṣānti*
Receptivity of the doctrine. See *Dharmajñānakṣānti*

Receptivity of subsequent knowledge. See *Anvayajñānakṣānti*
Red mda' ba gzhon nu blos gros, 35, 41, 42, 44, 46
Reigle, David, 199n12
Resolution (*praṇidhi*), 84, 177, 187
Rhinoceros, like the horn of a, 148, 165, 171
Rigs tshogs drug. See "Six Collections of Reasoning"
Rngog lo tsā ba Blo ldan shes rab, 31, 175–176, 216–217n85
Rong ston shes bya kun rig, 30, 161, 214n35, 215n58
Root of virtue (*kuśalamūla*), 85
Rough calm abiding (*śāntaudārika, zhi rags*), 77, 108, 204n78
rP. See *Pañcaviṃśatisāhasrikāprajñāpāramitāsūtra* (revised edition)
Ruegg, David Seyfort, 5, 11, 21, 22, 33, 65, 191n2, 192n8, 192n14, 195n13, 200n18, 201n35, 202n41, 205n98, 206n100, 211n52
Rūpadhātu. See Form realm
Rūparāgahan, 166, 172, 174
Rūpavītarāga (*gzugs kyi 'dod chags dang bral ba*), 170, 174
Rūpopaga (*gzugs su nye bar 'gro ba*), 125, 126

S

Sabhāgahetu (homogeneous cause), 102
Sābhisaṃskāraparinirvāyin, 161, 169. See also *Abhisaṃskāraparinirvāyin*
Ṣaḍabhijñā. See Six supernatural knowledges
Saddharmapuṇḍarīka sūtra, 66, 205n99
Sahajakleśāvaraṇa, 78
Śaikṣa (*slob pa*), 63, 95, 140, 141
Śaikṣasaṃgha, 64
Sakalabandhana (*'ching ba mtha' dag dang ldan pa*, "bound by all the bonds"), 116, 134
Sakṛdāgāmī. See Once-returner
Sakṛdāgāmiphalasthā. See Once-returner abider
Sakṛdāgāmipratipannaka. See Once-returner enterer
Sakṛnnairyāṇika (*cig car nges par 'byin pa*, "One who abandons simultaneously"), 142
Śākyamuni Buddha, 23, 62
Samādhi (*ting nge 'dzin*), 83
Samāhitajñāna, 78
Śamatha (*zhi gnas*), 56, 71, 85, 107, 108
Śamathavipaśyanāyuganaddha, 85
Sāmantaka, 107
Samayavimukta (*dus dang sbyor bar rnam par grol ba*), 138, 141, 212n70
Saṃbhāra, 187
Sambhāramārga. See Path of acquiring the provisions
Saṃbhārapratipatti. See Activity of procuring equipment
Saṃgha (*dge 'dun*), 62–66, 98, 173, 176, 181, 200n26
  Comparison to medical assistants, 62, 200n28
  Conventional and in the highest sense, 63, 201n29
  Etymology of, 200n26
  Institutional, 2
  Irreversible, 153, 180
  Jewel of the, 24, 58, 59, 62, 63, 64, 65, 93, 150
  Spiritual, 2
  See also *Actual Saṃgha, Allegorical Saṃgha, bodhisattva saṃgha, śrāvaka saṃgha*
Saṃgha illustration. See *Allegorical Saṃgha*
Saṃnāha (armor), 187
Saṃnāhapratipatti. See Activity of putting on armor
Saṃsāra (*'khor ba*), 71, 77, 84, 90, 101, 149, 176, 185
Samten, Jampa, 194n2
Saṃyojana. See Fetters
Saṃyuktāgama, 192n17
Saṃyuttanikāya, 193n17
Saṃskṛta (*'dus byas*, conditioned), 102
Saṃskṛtavimuktimārga (*'dus byas rnam grol lam*, conditioned paths of liberation), 103
Sanskrit as unitary medium of *Mahāyāna* Buddhist scholasticism, 193n20
Śāntaiṣiṇaḥ, 69
Śāntarakṣita (Zhi ba 'tsho), 27
Śāntaudārika, 77
Śāntideva (Zhi ba ha), 23
Śāntipa, 150, 152, 199n15
Saptakṛtvaparama (*re ltar thogs na lan bdun pa*), 110, 117, 118–119, 130
  Tsong kha pa's definition of, 118

Saptaparṇa (*'dab ma bdun pa*, "seven-petaled" tree), 119
Saptasatpuruṣagatī sūtra (*skyes bu dam pa'i 'gro pa bdun pa'i mdo*), 127, 128, 129, 134
Saptasthānakuśala (*gnas bdun la mkhas pa*, "wise in seven objects"), 119
Śāriputra, 150, 159, 164, 165, 179
Sarvadharmālambanapūrvakaṃ, 56
Sarvajñatā (*thams cad shes pa nyid*, Empirical Omniscience), 50, 51, 53, 54, 56, 60, 68, 69, 76, 81, 89, 188
Sarvākārābhisaṃbodha (*rnam rdzogs sbyor ba*, realization of all aspects), 53, 54, 56
Sarvākārajñatā (*rnam pa thams cad mkhyen pa nyid*, Total Omniscience), 2, 50, 51, 52, 54, 55, 56, 60, 66, 68, 69, 81, 84, 89, 187, 188
Sarvākārajñatāparipūrihetu, 60
Sarvasthānacyuta. See Jumper who dies in all abodes
Sarvāstivādin-Vaibhāṣika school. See *Vaibhāṣika*
Sasrava, 92
Śāstra, 48, 197n2
Śatasāhasrikā (100,000 verse) *Prajñāpāramitā*, 24, 151, 152, 170
Śatasāhasrikāvivaraṇa, 158
Satkāyadṛṣṭi, 87, 103
Satya (*bden pa*, truth[s]), 58
Sautrāntikas, 139
Scholastic language. See Denaturalized discourse
Scholasticism, 13–20
  Intra-Buddhist, 13
Selflessness of the person, 82, 84, 139, 202n42, 204n61
Sense sphere mind, 91
Sensory sphere. See *Āyatana*
Sensual desire, 141
Se ra rje mtsun pa chos kyi rgyal mtshan, 30, 194n2
Serial progression. See *Ānupūrvaka*
Seven-footed serpent, 118
Seven treasures of a *bodhisattva*, 170
Seventeen types of provisions in AA, 85, 206n104
Seventy topics (*don bdun cu*), 48, 53, 55
Sgra sbyor bam po gnyis pa, 107, 207n19, 208n21, 208n24, 208n26, 208n32, 209nn35–36, 209nn39–40, 210nn43–45, 210nn47–48, 211n54, 211n61, 212n62, 212nn70–71
Śīlavrataparāmarśa (holding [wrong] ethics and rituals as supreme) 87, 99, 103
Simultaneous abandoners, 146, 147
Simultaneous abandonment, 79, 117, 142, 146–147
Single session of meditative equipoise (*ekāsanika*, *sbyor lam stan gcig*), 115
"Six Collections of Reasoning" (*rigs tshogs drug*), 23, 68
Six fundamental afflictions, 87, 88
Six heavens of desire realm, 91
Six perfections (*ṣaṭpāramitā*, *phar phyin drug*), 56, 149, 160, 161, 163, 174
Six supernatural knowledges (*ṣaḍabhijñā*, *mngon par shes pa drug*), 58, 59, 60, 61, 157
Sixteen aspects of the Nobles' Four Truths. See Nobles' Four Truths
Sixteen thought-moments of the path of seeing, 60, 73, 75, 76, 80, 85, 100, 146, 154, 167, 175, 203n47, 204n71
Sixteenth moment of the path of seeing, 76, 142, 145, 147, 154, 167
Skill-in-means (*upāyakauśalya*, *thabs la mkhas pa*), 51, 149, 150, 151, 152, 156, 157, 158, 160, 162, 163, 164, 165, 174, 175, 176, 177, 179, 188
Skipping fruitions. See Fruition skipper
Smith, E. Gene, 195n14
Smith, Jonathan Z., 8, 181, 187
Smṛtyupasthāna, 71, 72
Sopa, Geshe, 2, 3, 9, 197n1, 203n44
Sopadhiśeṣa. See *Nirvāṇa* with remnant
Sopāna. See Stairway, metaphor of
Soteriology, 2, 145, 186, 189, 191–192n4. See also Buddhist soteriology
Sparham, Gareth, 32, 33, 196n16
Special insight. See *Vipaśyanā*
Special instructions (*gdams ngag*). See *Avavāda*
Sphuṭārthā (Haribhadra), 27, 29, 30, 32, 35, 64, 65, 72, 167, 173, 185, 193n22, 195n12, 199n13
Śrāddhādhimukta (*dad pas lhag par mos pa*, one who aspires by faith), 145, 154–155, 156, 157, 168, 172
Śraddhā (*dad pa*, faith) 85

Śraddhānusārin (*dad pas rjes su 'brang ba*, follower through faith), 110, 116, 145, 153, 154, 176, 177, 178, 207n19
Śraddhāprāpta, 166
Śrāmaṇera, 62
Śrāmaṇya (*dge sbyong gi tshul*), 102–104, 105, 108, 124, 137, 143
Classifications of, 105–106
Path parameters of, 106–109
Śrāvaka (*nyan thos pa*), 15, 19, 58, 63, 68, 69, 70, 71, 72, 73, 76, 78, 79, 81, 82, 83, 84, 87, 89, 90, 98, 99, 115, 128, 131, 135, 136, 137, 142, 147, 148, 149, 152, 164, 165, 170, 171, 173, 176, 177, 178, 179, 180, 183, 184, 185, 186, 187, 188, 191n1, 202nn41–42, 203n49, 206n100
Śrāvakabhūmi, 127
Śrāvakapudgalakramāḥ, 95
Śrāvakayāna, 102
Śrāvaka arhat (*nyan thos dgra bcom pa*), 83, 89, 108, 149, 170, 187, 188
Śrāvaka saṃgha (*nyan thos pa'i dge 'dun*), 33, 64, 95, 98, 99, 102, 106, 114, 174, 176, 184, 185
Śrāvastī, 177
Srota-āpanna. See Stream-enterer
Srota-āpannaphalasthā. See Stream-enterer abider
Srota-āpannapratipannaka. See Stream-enterer enterer
Srotānugatasamādhi (meditative absorption of the stream of the doctrine), 85. See also *Dharmaśrotas-samādhi*
Stages (of *bodhisattvas*). See *Bhūmi*
Stairway (*sopāna*, *them skas*), metaphor of, 15, 20, 186, 192–193n17
Stairway Taken by Those of Lucid Intelligence (*blo gsal bgrod pa'i them skas*), 11, 12, 19, 36, 42–46, 76, 98, 101, 104, 105, 114, 116, 117, 119, 121, 122, 123, 124, 125, 127, 128, 129, 130, 131, 133, 135, 136, 137, 138, 139, 140, 141, 142, 144, 145, 146, 147, 148, 173, 184, 185, 186, 193n21
Stcherbatsky, Theodore, 194n4, 198n6
Sthiramati, 194n4
Sthitākampya (*gnas pa las mi bskyod pa*), 134, 137, 138
Stream-enterer (*srota-āpanna*, *rgyun du zhugs pa*), 4, 8, 14, 15, 64, 80, 89, 100, 101, 103, 104, 105, 107, 108, 109, 110, 114–122, 128, 132, 136, 137, 139, 142, 143, 144, 145, 146, 148, 153, 155, 157, 158, 165, 166, 167, 168, 171, 175, 176, 177, 178, 179, 180, 182, 186
Stream-enterer abider (*srota-āpannaphalasthā*, *rgyun du zhugs pa gnas pa*), 117–122, 144, 166, 167, 168, 171, 172
Tsong kha pa's definition of, 117
Stream-enterer enterer (*srota-āpannapratipannaka*, *rgyun du zhugs zhugs pa*), 80,114, 115–116, 144, 166, 167, 172
Stream of doctrine meditative stabilization. See *Dharmaśrotas-samādhi*
Structural analysis, 5
Śubhakṛtsna (*bde rgyas*) heaven, 90, 91, 130, 163
Subhūti, 179
Subsequent intellectual receptivity. See *Anvayajñānakṣānti*
Subsequent knowledge. See *Anvayajñāna*
Substantially existing persons (*pudgaladravya*), 86
Suchness. See *tathatā*
Sudarśana (*shin tu mthong ba*) heaven, 90, 91, 130
Śuddhamatī (Ratnākaraśānti), 31, 150, 152, 160, 161, 165, 169, 199–200n15
Śuddhāvāsakāyika heavens (*gnas gtsang ma*, "the pure places"), 91, 92, 130, 131, 132, 133, 134, 162, 163, 169
Sudṛśa (*gya nom snang ba*) heaven, 90, 91, 130
Sukhopapatti ("realms generating delight), 92
Summit. See *Mūrdhagata*
Śūnyatā. See Emptiness
Supermundane path. See *Lokottara*; Path, supermundane
Supermundane path of cultivation, 77–79, 100, 108, 147
Śūraṃgamasamādhi sūtra, 66, 165
Sūtra of Expanded Gnosis (*jñānavistarasūtra*), 174
Sūtra Showing the Seven Transmigrations of Holy Individuals. See *Saptasatpuruṣagatī*
Svaparārthasādhana (welfare of others), 188
Synchronic analysis, 14

T
Tārā, 161
Tārānātha, 26
Tathāgata, 157, 158, 162
Tathāgatagarbha (*de gzhin gshegs pa'i snying po*), 66, 84
Tathatā, 65
Ten *bhūmis*. See Ten stages
Ten powers of a *Tathāgata*, 160
Ten special instructions for *bodhisattvas*, 58–62
Ten stages, 57, 66, 84, 88
Ten virtuous actions (of *bodhisattvas*), 161
Theg pa chen po la 'jug pa (Gnyal zhig pa 'jam dpal rdo rje), 32
Thirty-seven auxiliaries to enlightenment, 81, 156, 157, 160
Thirty-three gods (*trāyatriṃśa*), 90
Thirty-two marks of a Buddha, 163
Three fetters, 103
Three forms of Omniscience, 50, 51, 52, 54, 56, 68
Three Jewels (*triratna, dkon mchog gsum*), 2, 58, 60, 62, 150, 181
Three Jumpers, 161, 162
Three Knowledges, 52, 54
Three qualities of *bodhisattvas*, 158, 159
Three Realms (*traidhātuka, khams gsum*), 77, 83, 90, 146, 147, 160
Three Refuges, 60. See also Three Jewels
Three worlds. See *triloka*
Thurman, Robert A. F., 13, 192n11, 194n5, 195n9, 196n16
Tibetan monastic coursework related to *Abhisamayālaṃkāra*, 40, 46
Tibetan religious language (*chos skad*), 22, 183
Tibetan scholarship
and Indology, 11, 17
and Internal history, 11
Tibetan scholastic tradition, 18
Tillemans, Tom F., 11
Total Omniscience. See *Sarvākārajñatā*
Traidhātuka, 83. See also Three Realms
Traité, 192n11
Transmigration, 120, 124, 125, 164
Transmigrator, 127, 128, 130, 131, 133, 163, 174
Triloka, 77, 79, 90
Triśaraṇasaptati, 83, 206n100
trāyatriṃśa (*sum cu rtsa gsum*, Thirty-three gods), 90, 91
Truth of suffering, 70, 75
Truth of the arising of suffering, 70
Truth of the cessation of suffering, 70
Truth of the path, 71
Tsong kha pa blo bzang grag pa
and *Abhisamayālaṃkāra*, 39
and Bde-ba-can monastery, 40, 43, 44
Buddhist scholarship of, 11, 12
Commentaries of, 9
Definition of Twenty *Saṃghas*, 171
and Don grub rin chen, 39
Exegetical approach of, 11–12
Founder of the Dga' ldan pa school, 38
Four great deeds of, 38
Four major treatises of, 38
and Gradualist interpretation of Twenty *Saṃghas*, 13
and Hermeneutics, 10–13, 184
Importance in Tibetan Buddhist culture, 38
and Internal history, 11
Life of, 36–39, 195–196n16
Location in Tibetan history, 21
and Relationship between *Golden Garland* and *Stairway Taken by Those of Lucid Intelligence*, 45
and Study of *Abhidharma*, 41–42, 43, 46
and Study of *Prajñāpāramitā*, 39–42, 45
and Study of *Pramāṇavārttika*, 42, 43
System of Twenty *Saṃghas*, 65, 165–171
Use of reasoning in textual analysis, 12
and Writing of *Golden Garland*, 44
and Writing of *Stairway Taken by Those of Lucid Intelligence*, 42–46
Tube, The (London Underground), 8
Tucci, Giuseppe, 194n4, 195n11, 197n4
Turner, Victor, 188
Tuṣita heaven (*dga' ldan*), 26, 90, 91, 151, 153, 154, 157, 160, 162
Twenty *Saṃghas*, 65, 76, 81, 83, 94, 98, 106, 150, 163, 165, 167, 168, 170, 171, 173, 180, 181, 183, 186, 188, 189
and *Abhidharma*, 26

Twenty *Saṃghas (continued)*
and Academic program guidelines, 8
as Archetypal worldview of Buddhist soteriology, 3, 19–20
as Categorical list, 18, 191n3
as Conceptual map, 8, 189
Contextualization of, 55
Exegetical approached to, 19
and Great Prayer Festival (*mon lam chen mo*), 9
as Indexical reference, 9
and Indian Buddhist scholasticism, 16–17
Indo-Tibetan exegesis of, 17
Location in the *Abhisamayālaṃkāra*, 47–62, 66, 93–94
and Monastic study, 1, 9, 40, 46
and Multiple levels of coherence, 12
as Narrative of Buddhist soteriology, 5, 14–16
as One of Three Jewels, 2, 59, 62, 67
and Psychological case histories, 5, 192n9
as Special topic in the *Abhisamayālaṃkāra*, 4
Terminological comparison of, 95–98
Textual sources for the study of, 19
and Tibetan Buddhist culture, 9
and Tibetan scholarly tradition, 17
Topic of, 1, 3, 8, 9, 18
Topic in monastic curriculum, 1
Tsong kha pa's writings on, 12, 13, 14, 15, 19, 44–45

U

Ubhayatogbhāgavimutka (*gnyis ka'i cha las rnam par grol ba*), 132, 137, 138, 142, 212n62
Ultimate Reality. See *Dharmadhātu*
Unconditioned (*asaṃskṛta, 'dus ma byas*), 102
Unconditioned true cessations (*asaṃskṛtanirodhasatya, 'dus ma byas 'gog bden)*, 103
Uncontaminated. See *Anāsrava*
Uncontaminated awareness, 80
Uncontaminated faculties, 158
Uncontaminated karma (*zag med kyi las*), 83
Uncontaminated path, 121
Uncontaminated realm. See *Anāsravadhātu*
Unified path of calm abiding and special insight (*śamathavipaśyanāyuganaddha*), 85
Uninterrupted path (*ānantaryamārga, bar chad med lam*), 73, 74,75, 77, 78, 107, 108
Upadeśa (*man ngag*), 48, 50, 197n3
Upapadyaparinirvāyin (*skyes nas 'da' ba mngon par 'du byed pa*), 112, 125,126, 127, 128, 129, 134, 135, 155, 159, 160, 161, 165, 166, 169, 172
Upāya. See Skill-in-means
Ūrdhvaṃsrotas (*gong du 'pho ba*), 94, 112, 118, 125, 126, 127, 128, 129, 130, 133–135, 159, 161, 162, 166, 169, 171, 175
Tsong kha pa's definition of, 129
Ūṣmagata (*dro bar gyur pa*, heat), 72, 85, 115
Uttarakuru, 91
Uttaratantra. See *Ratnagotravibhāga*

V

Vaibhāṣika (*bye brag tu smra ba*), 95, 99, 114, 128, 132, 133, 134, 138, 139, 140, 141, 164, 182, 203n44, 206n110
Vairāgya, 107, 134
Vajracchedikāprajñāpāramitāsūtra, 217n101
Vajropamasamādhi. See Diamond-like concentration
Van der Kuijp, Leonard, 13, 38, 44, 196n16
Vargacāri, 148
Vastujñāna (*gzhi shes*). See *sarvajñatā* (Empirical Omniscience)
Vasubandhu (Dbyig gnyen), 23, 27–28, 129, 134, 140, 141, 164, 195n7, 197n2
Vetter, Tilmann, 196n16
Vicikitsā (*the tshom nyon mongs can*, doubt), 103
Vijñānānantyāyatana (realm of infinite consciousness), 78
Vimalakīrtinirdeśa (*Dri med drags pas bstan pa*), 66
Vimuktimārga. See Path of liberation
Vinaya, 9, 38, 42, 44, 62
Vipaśyanā (*lhag mthong*, special insight), 56, 71, 72, 85, 107

Vīrya, 56
Visaṃyoga (*'bral ba*), 102
Viśeṣa (*khyad par can*), 123
Viśeṣagamanahetu, 60
Viśeṣamārga, 56
Vītarāgapūrvin (*chags bral sngon song*), 153, 156–157, 166, 173
Vṛddhāloka ("expanded illumination"), 86
Vyāpāda (hatred), 103

W
Wayman, Alex, 127
Welbon, Guy Richard, 191n1
Welfare of others. See *Svaparārthasādhana*
Willis, Janice Dean, 194n5
Wisdom eye. See *Prajñācakṣu*
Wisdom of study, 80
Wogihara, U., 167
Word of the doctrine, 80
Wrong view, 87

Y
Yāma (land without combat), 91
Yaśomitra, 35, 102, 127, 132, 143, 192n17
Yathāvadbhāvikatā (*ji lta ba yod pa*), 52, 63
Yāvadbhāvikatā (*ji snyed pa yod pa*), 52, 63
Yeh, Ah-yueh, 200n16
Yid kyi mun sel (Nya dbon kun dga' dpal), 34, 35
Yogācāra (*rnal 'byor spyod pa*), 4, 26, 30, 183, 202n41
Yogācāra-Svātantrika-Mādhyamika (*rnal 'byor spyod pa'i dbu ma rang rgyud pa*, Tibetan classification), 29, 32
Yoga, 153
Yogi, 77

www.ingramcontent.com/pod-product-compliance
Lightning Source LLC
Chambersburg PA
CBHW020642230426
43665CB00008B/275